About Island Press

Island Press is the only nonprofit organization in the United States whose principal purpose is the publication of books on environmental issues and natural resource management. We provide solutions-oriented information to professionals, public officials, business and community leaders, and concerned citizens who are shaping responses to environmental problems.

Since 1984, Island Press has been the leading provider of timely and practical books that take a multidisciplinary approach to critical environmental concerns. Our growing list of titles reflects our commitment to bringing the best of an expanding body of literature to the environmental community throughout North America and the world.

Support for Island Press is provided by the Agua Fund, The Geraldine R. Dodge Foundation, Doris Duke Charitable Foundation, The Ford Foundation, The William and Flora Hewlett Foundation, The Joyce Foundation, Kendeda Sustainability Fund of the Tides Foundation, The Forrest & Frances Lattner Foundation, The Henry Luce Foundation, The John D. and Catherine T. MacArthur Foundation, The Marisla Foundation, The Andrew W. Mellon Foundation, Gordon and Betty Moore Foundation, The Curtis and Edith Munson Foundation, National Fish and Wildlife Foundation, Oak Foundation, The Overbrook Foundation, The David and Lucile Packard Foundation, Wallace Global Fund, The Winslow Foundation, and other generous donors.

The opinions expressed in this book are those of the author(s) and do not necessarily reflect the views of these foundations.

MetroGreen

MetroGreen

Connecting Open Space in North American Cities

DONNA L. ERICKSON

Washington • Covelo • London

ISLAND PRESS is a trademark of the Center for Resource Economics.

Library of Congress Cataloging-in-Publication Data
Erickson, Donna L.
    Metrogreen : connecting open space in North American cities / Donna L.
Erickson.
        p. cm.
    Includes bibliographical references.
    ISBN 1-55963-843-5 (cloth : alk. paper) -- ISBN 1-55963-891-5
(pbk. : alk. paper)
    1. Open spaces—North America. 2. City planning—North America.
3. Regional planning—North America. 4. Metropolitan areas—North
America—Case studies. 5. Human ecology—North America. I. Title.
    HT169.N68E75 2006
    307.1'216097--dc22

                                           2006009618

Printed on recycled, acid-free paper ♻

Manufactured in the United States of America
10 9 8 7 6 5 4 3 2 1

To John, Reed, and Rye

Contents

Preface and Acknowledgments

The protection and design of open space is increasingly critical for human health, environmental integrity, and community cohesion. Across North America, metropolitan regions are planning and implementing connected open-space networks for the benefit of people and place. Open space has many forms and meanings and it is extremely difficult to piece together across the landscape. Different approaches are taken, based on varying political, cultural, natural, and economic contexts.

This volume focuses on connectivity, both as an ecological and social concept and as an outcome on the ground. It analyzes how metropolitan areas create open-space systems within a matrix of diverse land uses and complex environmental settings. It highlights strategies for success, using both Canadian and U.S. case studies, and focuses on interconnected networks, rather than on individual corridors. "Network" is used here to describe a meshed fabric of nodes and connecting corridors. It may include greenways, parkways, greenbelts, and other corridors, as well as the hubs of open land that anchor them.

Interest in landscape change, and in the many forms of planned open land, led me to the research on which this book is based. This work is largely based on research conducted over the last fifteen years that focused on cities doing innovative work toward open-space networks. It originated in a project done collaboratively with the National Park Service Rivers, Trails, and Conservation Assistance (RTCA) Program, which studied the implementation of metropolitan-wide greenway projects. The purpose of that study was to learn about the institutional structures used in various cities, aiming to apply that information to the fledgling southeast Michigan GreenWays Initiative in the Detroit region.

In the early 1990s, greenway advocates had completed plans and maps for a regional system in the seven-county Detroit region. Extensive citizen outreach was facilitated by RTCA. Following that, a model was needed on which to base institutional structure for greenway implementation in the area. That effort resulted in the publication, with Anneke Louisse Hagen, of *Greenway Implementation in Metropolitan Regions: A Comparative Case Study of North American Examples*, published jointly by RTCA and the Michigan chapter of the Rails-to-Trails Conservancy.[1] It summarized greenway network implementation in seven metropolitan regions. I am indebted to colleagues who worked with me on the original RTCA project, from whom I learned a great deal and enjoyed collaboration: Barbara Nelson-Jameson, Norm Cox, Larry Deck, and Anneke Louisse Hagen. Subsequently, the Southeast Michigan GreenWays Initiative was launched in the Detroit metropolitan area, led and funded by the Community Foundation for Southeastern Michigan.

By examining metropolitan-scale greenway programs around the continent, it became apparent that remarkable open-space networks were being built not only in the United States, but in Canadian cities as well. New questions formed as the greenway movement proliferated through the 1990s, not only about the perennial funding quests, but about leadership, organizational structure, objectives, collaborations, and spatial form. It also became apparent that focusing only on greenways left out a range of intriguing projects that dealt with open-space connectivity in other ways. A broader focus on green infrastructure, where greenways play one part, has been growing in recent years and coincides perfectly with a more robust examination of open-space networks.

Continued research added several Canadian and U.S. cities to the portfolio of case studies. This book synthesizes the stories of ten cities attempting to connect people to each other and to nature: Vancouver, Calgary, Toronto, and Ottawa in Canada, and Milwaukee, Chicago, Portland, Cleveland, Denver, and Minneapolis–St. Paul in the United States. The book took shape while I was a Fulbright Scholar at the University of British Columbia in Vancouver in 2003–04. I am deeply appreciative of the Fulbright fellowship, sponsored by the Canada–U.S. Fulbright program, which enabled focused attention on urban open-space issues, particularly in Canadian contexts. I thank my colleagues at UBC—Professors Doug Paterson, Moura Quayle, and the rest of the landscape architecture faculty, who so graciously hosted me in their department. The Canadian case studies were also funded by two research grants from the Canadian Embassy, for which I am quite grateful.

I am deeply indebted to a number of other people for their guidance, input, and feedback as this book went together. First, Julie Steiff made an imprint on this book through her superb editorial work. In addition to her keen eye for English usage, she helped guage the accessibility of the work to the non-planner–designer. Jane Spinner kept me on track and encouraged closure, quality, and accountability to the project. A number of people read parts of the manuscript and gave feedback. Particular thanks to Frederick Steiner and David Michener in this regard. Editor Jeff Hardwick at Island Press and his predecessor, Heather Boyer, gave invaluable advice. Heather helped frame the project initially; Jeff helped implement it and enhanced the final product. Thanks also to Shannon O'Neill at the press, for helping guide the process.

The following chapters synthesize ideas, conclusions, histories, and concepts that flow from the dozens of interviewees who shared their knowledge and expertise. While any shortcomings in this work are mine alone, I must share many of the ideas presented here with the informants who shaped the case studies. Some of them read draft chapters and commented on the written product. All of them provided resources, facts, and interpretations. I sincerely appreciate the valuable time they gave to discuss open-space planning in their cities. Without the data they provided the book could not have been written. In addition, it should be noted that this book is but a sampling of the exemplary open-space work being done across the continent. There are many places that are achieving outstanding open-space results. I would like to acknowledge the metropolitan open-space programs not summarized as case studies here, but from which I've learned a great deal in framing the book's conclusions.

I also appreciate the insights and inquisitiveness of many former students at the University of Michigan School of Natural Resources and Environment. More than any other influence, they have sharpened my thinking, kept me on my toes, and challenged my assumptions. I particularly appreciate the work by a number of former graduate students, who provided valuable support, particularly in preparing this book's illustrations. Thank you MetroGreen team! I couldn't have done it without you. Dorothy Buckley, Lisa DuRussel, Christopher Coutts, Vaike Haas, Karla Rogers, Richard Meader, and Marina Alvarez worked on various aspects of the project. They corresponded with a number of photographers and graphic experts in order to illustrate the case studies. I also appreciate the talents and cooperation of the professionals who provided illustrations, some of whom shared their materials free of charge. John Thompson's map-making expertise was invaluable.

In addition to funding from the Fulbright Foundation and Canadian Embassy, other support came from the George Gund Foundation, which funded the Cleveland case study, and the University of Michigan, which provided additional funding for the Fulbright fellowship. The UM School of Natural Resources and Environment enabled this work through a sabbatical leave and other support for the book's production. Dean Rosina Bierbaum was particularly encouraging about these intellectual pursuits.

A number of reviewers commented on peer-reviewed articles related to this project. Thank you to Julius Fabos, Robert Ryan, Rob Jongman, and anonymous reviewers for *Landscape and Urban Planning* and *Journal of Planning Literature.* They helped improve the clarity, purpose, and accuracy of this work. I have learned much from my professional interactions with landscape architects and other colleagues whose expertise in shaping the built environment is having profound effects on open lands: Daniel Smith, Paul Hellmund, Richard Forman, Robert Searns, Jack Ahern, Ted Cook, Paul Gobster, Cynthia Girling, Ewa Kaliszuk, and Sharon Pfeiffer. I would also like to thank mentors and colleagues whose knowledge and insights have helped shape my approach to natural resource problem-solving. Although the following people have been important influences on my thinking, they have no responsibility for this book's deficiencies: Hubert Van Lier, Kenny Helphand, Frederick Steiner, Robert Grese, Rachel Kaplan, Raymond De Young, and George Thompson.

Portions of this book were previously published in other forms (in addition to the RTCA monograph mentioned above). The Milwaukee and Ottawa case studies were synthesized in a special issue of *Landscape and Urban Planning.*[2] A chapter in *Ecological Networks and Greenways: New Paradigms for Ecological Planning* analyzed the greenway systems in five cities.[3] I am grateful to these publications for the new use of that material in book form.

Finally, and most importantly, my sincere gratitude to my spouse, John Koenig, for all he has done in support of this project, and to the rest of my family for their encouragement of my professional work.

Part 1

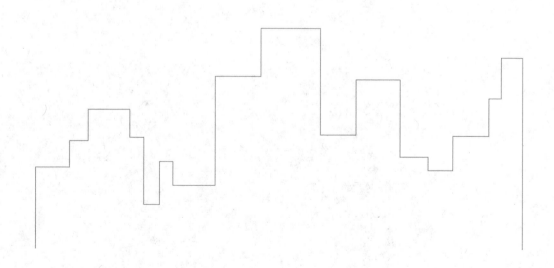

Connected Open Space

Connected Open Space:
The Metropolitan Scale

*There are a lot of open spaces around us and if they're all
gobbled up, we've lost something big. Once it's paved over,
it's gone forever.*

—*Mayor John Hieftje, Ann Arbor, Michigan*[1]

Mayor Hieftje expressed this lament for the potential loss of open space as he
promoted a protected greenbelt around his Michigan city. Ann Arbor is consistently rated
as one of the country's most livable small cities; easy access to open space is one of many
assets. In November 2003, voters approved an $84 million, thirty-year property tax levy to
preserve about 8,000 acres of open-space land around the city's edges. For the first time in
Michigan history, city residents voted to pay for land (and/or rights in land) outside the
city's borders. Two-thirds of the money will be spent in eight neighboring townships to
buy development rights for a greenbelt around the city.

Record numbers of voters turned out for the off-year election to weigh in on the highly
controversial proposal. Local and state homebuilders' groups were stunned. They had spent
a quarter of a million dollars to defeat the proposal, arguing that the greenbelt would raise

development costs, thereby further limiting affordable housing (in an environment where few affordable houses are being built to begin with). Since the election, developers have been scrambling to purchase land in the county for housing, retail complexes, and office parks. One executive for a national homebuilding corporation said, "Green space is like world peace: everyone is for it, but there can be bitter disputes on how to achieve it."[2]

One of this book's main themes is the tension between the widespread desire for open space and the complexity of and controversy over providing and protecting it. As often as not, the importance of urban open spaces is neglected in debates about land development, architectural design, and urban form. More theoretical and practical knowledge about creating greenspace is needed. Creating and protecting open-space networks across jurisdictional lines and with assorted land uses is a challenge. People have many different objectives for creating open-space networks—personal, community, and regionwide. However, using the criteria of landscape ecology and human ecology we can better understand both the motivations for and the benefits of greenspace. Landscape connectivity at a metropolitan scale can serve important human and natural functions; multiple objectives are often more effective and sustainable than one-dimensional solutions. A connected public realm is better than a fragmented one, and open-space connectivity can take many different shapes. Green infrastructure is explored as an approach that incorporates these multiple forms and functions.

Everyone Loves Open Space

Open-space protection is a topic of growing public dialog and concern. Where perhaps two decades ago planners, landscape architects, environmentalists, and park planners quietly pursued open-space planning and protection, today open space is on the front page, linked with issues of sprawl, health, lifestyle, and ecology. The smart-growth movement probably deserves the credit for this awareness. More and more people are fighting against sprawl and looking toward the promise that we can grow in more responsible, beautiful, and efficient ways. In fact, the protection of open space is a primary driver of efforts to curb sprawl.

Many people feel widespread remorse about the loss of open space in many land-use contexts and at many scales, which has generated significant funding for protecting open land.[3] According to the Natural Resources Inventory for the United States, 2.2 million acres are being converted to development each year. The backlash against sprawl has, among other things, created a blitz of programming, funding, and rhetoric for open space. In reviewing the environmental impacts of sprawl, Michael Johnson found twelve main factors, many of them connected to open-space destruction, such as the loss of environmentally fragile lands and the paving of farmland.[4] In particular, concern for the quality and quantity of open space at the local level has grown. Carys Swanwick and colleagues claim that worries about the declining condition of parks, growing emphasis on urban densities, priority for developing brownfield rather than greenfield land, and increased knowledge about the benefits of urban greenspace have helped fuel this concern.[5] These worries have been converted to votes. In 2002 three-quarters of local and state open-space conservation ballot proposals were passed. According to the Land Trust Alliance, these measures generated $10 billion, including about $5.7 billion specifically for land acquisition and restoration.[6]

The provision of green, open space in urban areas may lessen the desire for residents to move farther out of cities. A study of Leuven, Belgium, showed that 50 percent of families that moved out of the city core did so because of lack of greenspace.[7] "Improving the presence and quality of greenspace might help to deter commuting, so enhancing a city's sustainability," the study found.[8] These types of studies have proliferated, generally pointing toward the importance of open space in housing preference in the United States and Europe.[9] Claims from real estate research show that nearly 78 percent of all American homebuyers rated open space as essential or very important.[10] Another national survey in 1994 found that among people who shopped for or bought a home, of thirty-nine features critical to their choice, consumers ranked "lots of natural open space" and plenty of "walking and biking paths" as the second- and third-highest-rated aspects affecting their choices.[11] One conundrum lies in the fact that increasing development of urban areas through infill (a primary smart-growth solution) sometimes drives residents toward more roomy suburban areas. Trade-offs of one open-space type for other types seem inevitable as populations grow.

On the other hand, population growth has not been the main concern among smart-growth and open-space advocates. Alarming statistics about the ratio of developed land to population increase in various metropolitan regions demonstrate the extent of sprawl and consequent loss of open land. The amount of urbanized land in the United States increased by 47 percent from 1982 to 1997, with only a 17 percent population increase.[12]

In response, nearly every spatial plan for an American municipality or urban region (and in some cases, states) includes the protection of open space as a component of land-use plans or ordinances. Open-space planning and walkable neighborhoods are increasingly a part of large-scale plans for American cities. For example, Chicago's Metropolis 2020 plan, completed by the Commercial Club of Chicago, claims, "We can build a better region. We can spend less time in traffic. We can live nearer to our jobs. We can build communities that are friendlier to walking and biking—and therefore healthier for the people who live in them. We can make economic opportunity available to more of our region's residents."[13] Similarly, the new Envision Central Texas effort, like Metropolis 2020, developed alternative growth scenarios for the five-county Austin region, in the Texas Hill Country.[14] Through extensive public participation, a preferred scenario for future growth was developed.

The planning literature is filled with studies proposing open-space plans and planning processes for various metropolitan areas around the world—Nanjing City, Warsaw, London, Phoenix, and New York.[15] For example, D. A. Goode suggests five categories of open-space sites for Greater London that will encompass 20 percent of the total land area to produce a comprehensive nature-conservation strategy. These include sites of metropolitan importance, sites of borough importance, sites of local importance, wildlife corridors, and countryside conservation areas. For Warsaw, Poland, Barbara Szulczewska and Ewa Kaliszuk attempt to reconcile two main functions of open space—ecological and recreational. In addition, their greenspace plan tries to balance "green city" and "compact city" objectives through careful consideration of open-space types and objectives. Their work addresses an important tension between more dense human development (sacrificing certain types and quantities of open space in city centers in order to save it at the edges) and greening city centers (at the expense of density).

These plans are not only proliferating but taking on new characteristics. They incorporate new spatial territories, connect with new social and environmental initiatives, and involve new participants and constituents. Open-space planning has traditionally been linked to the design of new housing tracts. As subdivisions are laid out, so too are parks, nature reserves, and trails. Increasingly, though, open space is being thought of in new ways. For instance, natural areas can be incorporated into commercial landscapes, as brownfields are converted to new urban uses, and as farms, forests, prairies, and wetlands are embraced as amenities within the urban fabric. Rather than leaving open-space planning to the city parks department, other arms of municipal government are taking more active roles in open-space planning. In addition, the number of grassroots groups tackling these issues is impressive. Hundreds of citizens groups have organized across the continent in the last twenty-five years, dedicated to the protection and planning of open-space lands. They are concerned about the paving of open space, declining quality of remaining open space, diminished management budgets, universal access to open space, and lack of a strategic vision about open space in relation to new growth.

The Preliminary Blueprint for Renewal, a plan for Lower Manhattan following the September 11 tragedy, is a perfect example.[16] "Open spaces," it asserts, "are essential to the quality of life downtown, providing alternatives to steel and glass skyscrapers and, perhaps more importantly, a physical and psychological center around which the city can grow. Public open spaces stimulate and promote private and human development."[17] Although efforts are being made to preserve open space, agreeing on one definition of open space is often difficult.

What Is Open Space Anyway?

Just what is this open land that planners, designers, and citizens in hundreds of towns and cities are trying to designate and protect? Is it simply land without buildings? What is its spatial dimension? How does it function? At what scale is open space important for cultural and ecological values? Do connections between open-space sites matter? In order to protect open space, we need to know more about what we are trying to achieve. There is considerable ambiguity about the forms and functions of open space, as well as diverse approaches for incorporating these landscapes into larger land-use plans.

Each year I choreograph an exercise with my graduate-level, land-use-planning students to illustrate this point. We brainstorm and debate the meanings, settings, and purposes of open space, in order to prepare a land-use plan for open-space lands at the fringe of our city. The typology that develops usually swings widely between several perceived dichotomies—public/private ownership, functional/aesthetic purpose, urban/rural land use, natural/human-made elements, open field/tree cover, and visual/physical access. To the ecologically minded, open space implies a level of environmental integrity. To others, it is simply an aesthetic issue. Some think of neighborhood parks, and some think of productive farmland at the edge of town. Open space can comprise vast swaths of greenspace in urban areas, as in Figure 1.1, but it can also be small, seminal pieces in the center of the city, as shown in Figure 1.2. The constructs in people's minds around the idea of open space are wide ranging and often conflicting.

Likewise, the professional literature on open-space planning is often ambiguous and confusing. Some authors have crafted definitions that help readers understand what they mean by open space in specific locations or for specific research issues. Many focus closely on recreation. For example, Karen Payne uses the recreational focus: "Open space, or green space, can be thought of as a mix of traditional parks and reserves, hiking or biking corridors, scenic vistas and other areas that provide for informal recreation and natural resource protection."[18] Anne Beer usefully defines greenspaces based on their spatial and environmental qualities: "Greenspaces are 'places'—areas of land with mainly unsealed surfaces within and around the city—these 'places' carry human activity as well as plants, wildlife and water and their presence influences quality of life, as well as local

Fig. 1.1 Ottawa's Central Experimental Farm provides a large expanse of open land very close to the central city. (Photo by the author.)

Fig. 1.2 Civil War Memorial Fountain on Public Square in Cleveland, Ohio is a small island of green open space at the heart of the city. (Photo by the author.)

air and water quality."[19] While this definition highlights environmental processes, the nonprofit National Wildlife Federation's definition ironically omits the most ecologically important lands from its definition of open space: "Open space is undeveloped sites that don't meet the criteria for natural areas because of human disturbance, but still provide habitat, scenery and other benefits. Open spaces can include areas such as farm land, recreational areas and utility corridors."[20]

Hollis and Fulton classify open space as land conserved for

1. production (e.g., working lands)
2. human use (e.g., recreation)
3. high-value natural areas (e.g., national parks) and
4. natural systems (e.g., ecosystems).[21]

According to this definition, open space often means land with nonurban activities. However, this meaning leaves out many landscapes that people clearly value as open space—public and private urban lands, including cemeteries, empty lots, streamsides, community gardens, and schoolyards.

Increasingly, urban design and planning critics address this open-space ambiguity head-on. Beer and others cite an "increased level of confusion concerning the role of greenspace in cities: whether it was an aesthetic issue, an ecological issue, perhaps something more."[22] Similarly, Jane Holtz-Kay asks, ". . . what exactly is this thing called open space, this creed of the wild or wide-open spaces that makes the nation wax lyrical? . . . But why the phrase 'open space'? Why a concept that seems more a void for free-for-all pavers and ballpark proponents than a promise for the future. Can't we find a less vacuous phrase?"[23] Lisa Nelson and Andrew Kalmar illustrate how this confusion hinders our effectiveness on landscape-scale issues. They maintain that water quality, wildlife habitat, agricultural productivity, and recreational opportunities are all connected to the preservation of open space, but that the public is largely unaware of the many connections between these activities and their relevance to open-space planning.[24]

To make those links more apparent, and to help structure the open-space idea, several authors have expanded the definition of open space beyond parks and recreation, to embrace and prioritize alternate forms of urban open space. For instance, Catherine Thompson asks what should be expected of open space in the twenty-first century and advocates a more flexible approach, which she calls 'loose fit' landscapes.[25] Similarly, Quayle and Driessen van der Lieck describe "hybrid landscapes," spaces like beaches, community gardens, and greenways that mix the processes and forms of both public and private landscapes.[26] And Mark Johnson describes the "open-ended environment": a landscape "that is neither an empty vessel nor one that is a deterministic composition."[27] All three authors relate public open space to ideas of democracy and social equity. "What remains true for public open space, and for the urban parks in particular, is that they are the places where democracy is worked out, quite literally, *on the ground,* and therefore, the way such spaces are designed, managed and used demonstrates the realities of political rhetoric."[28]

To build on these ideas we need to know more about how the public perceives, uses, and values open space.[29] Social values about open space vary, depending on whether we are talking about the protected land in a private cluster development, a multi-jurisdiction public greenway, a preserved farm, a brownfield site, an urban square, or a small community garden. Yet it is startling how many times these places are lumped under the broad term "open space," even though different social groups use and appreciate open space in very different ways. In fact, one line of scholarship examines the influence of ethnicity, generational status, and social class variables on recreational preferences.[30] Citing Lee's work, Carr states that "recreation sites are rarely perceived as free spaces without social definition. Rather, individuals seek outdoor areas occupied by others they perceive as similar enough to themselves to feel at home or that they belong. One of the most basic elements of a social definition of a site is the ethnic composition of the people occupying it."[31]

So it is clear that, like the term "landscape," open space has diverse dimensions, definitions, and proponents. The two words "open space" cannot, in fact, integrate the inherent complexity of the field. And open spaces, especially when viewed at the scale of metropolitan regions, are truly complex systems. Homer-Dixon identifies six factors that define complex systems, all of which pertain directly to open space embedded in an urban structure. He claims that complex systems

1. Are made up of a large number of entities, components or parts. Systems with more parts are generally more complex. For open-space networks, these components are open-space sites, social groups, transportation corridors, and a host of other entities.
2. Contain a dense web of causal connections among components. The more causal connections, the more complexity. The causal connections among open-space networks involve, among other things, political processes, citizen perceptions and preferences, ecological processes, and economic impacts.
3. Exhibit interdependence among components. An example for our purposes, elaborated

in the following chapters, is the success that comes from collaborations among organizations working toward open-space goals.

4. Are not self-contained, but rather are affected by outside variables. For instance, open-space protection in a given municipality or urban region is affected by political and economic variables at state and federal levels, by environmental processes outside the city's boundaries, and by social changes that transcend the region.

5. Have a high degree of synergy among components—the whole is more than the sum of the parts. The synergy among open-space components is the purview of ecology itself. The whole of any natural system is inherently more than the sum of its soils, vegetation, climate, and so forth.

6. Are nonlinear. A change in the system can produce effects that are not proportional to its size. A small shift in priorities within a city department can have disproportional effects on support for open-space landscapes.[32]

Open-space systems are composed of a myriad of interacting and interdependent entities, from humans and wildlife to natural features and built structures. They inherently engage complex causal connections, both ecologically and socially. Peter Calthorpe and William Fulton express the challenge of layering open-space land (which they call preserves) over the myriad of other urban priorities: "Preserves are perhaps the most complex and controversial building blocks of a regional design: complex because they include so many different elements, locations, and potential uses; controversial because the means of saving the land and the economic effects are hotly debated."[33] Categorizing types of open spaces is one heuristic device for helping us understand this complexity.

Typologies

Because the term "open space" is an ambiguous one, scholars and practitioners have long devised schemes to understand the connection of open land to the built environment.[34] Urban scholars have devised morphologies that define the structure and processes of urban places, including the unbuilt spaces. Some scholars, especially over the last couple of decades, have grappled with what Anne Spirn calls the "deep structure" of cities and related that concept to both open-space planning and new growth.[35]

Typologies based on scale, uses, or natural features can help structure open-space complexity, for the purposes of communication, use, and planning. The typologies help define the types of open-space components, as well as their connections and interdependencies. A number of approaches have been used. A hierarchy of scale is a straightforward and commonplace strategy. For instance, Stanley Tankel, former planning director of New York City's Regional Plan Association, presented such a categorization in the 1960s.[36] His classification of urban open space, shown in Table 1.1, is based on ascending scales from the street to the region. This nested scheme is common in the parks-and-recreation literature and is often employed by park agencies as quotas for various types of parks. The classic quota system allots a minimum acreage of each type of open space per 1,000 residents, as illustrated by the average open-space standards in Canada (Table 1.2). The quantification focus of park quotas estimates the number of tennis courts for a certain population, but such

	Scale or level	Present examples of open space (Land)	(Water)
STREET	Building site	Yards, courts (i.e., sites less buildings)	
STREET	Group of Buildings	Rights-of-way, streets, piazzas, residential commons, tot lots	
COMMUNITY	Neighborhood	School grounds, playgrounds, small parks (<10 acres)	Ponds, streams
COMMUNITY	Municipality	Parks (10–100 acres), playfields	Ponds, streams
COUNTY	Group of municipalities	Parks (100–1000 acres), golf courses, minor conservation areas (flood plains, watersheds, wildlife)	Lakes, rivers
REGION	Metropolitan region	Parks (> 1000 acres), large conservation areas, major water bodies, private farms, woodland and other land on the urban fringe	Oceans, great rivers
REGION	Megalopolis	Coastline, mountain ranges, milksheds	Oceans, great rivers

Table 1.1 Stanley Tankel's categorization of open space, based on ascending scales of urban development (Adapted from Stanley Tankel, "The Importance of Open Space in the Urban Pattern," in Lowdon Wingo, ed., *Cities and Space: The Future Use of Urban Land* (Baltimore: Johns Hopkins University Press, 1960)).

Area	Acres per 1,000 population	Service Radius (miles)	Size (acres)
Tot-lot	0.25 to 0.5	1/8 to 1/4, usually 1/4	0.6 to 2.0 (usually 0.5)
Parkette (vest-pocket park)	0.5	1/8 to 1/4	.06 to 1.0 (usually 0.5)
Neighborhood park (playground, local park)	1 to 2	1/2 to 3, usually 1	1/4 to 20 (usually 6)
Community park (playfield)	1 to 2	1/2 to 3, usually 1	4 to 100 (usually 8 to 25)
City park (municipal, subregional park)	5	1/2 to 3, usually 2 (or 1/2 hour driving time)	25 to 200 (usually 100)
Regional park	4 to 10	20 (or 1 hour driving time)	25 to 1,000 (usually 100 to 250)
TOTAL	11.75 to 20		

Table 1.2 Average open-space standards across Canada. (Adapted from Canadian Ministry of Culture and Recreation.)

quotas are limited by not taking into account nontraditional forms of open space, environmental aspects of natural areas, or the landscape structure of open-space systems. It particularly fails to address ease of access from individual homes.

However, Tankel also offered a more subtle interpretation of open space for metropolitan areas. He distinguished between the kind of open space of which people are aware versus the kind of which they may be unaware but which nevertheless affects their lives. The former has three functions—it is used, viewed, or felt—and the latter does urban work or helps shape development patterns. He admits that "it is a rare bit of open space which does not perform many of these roles. And each category encompasses a wide variation in scale."[37] This approach to categorization focuses on the open-space user. Similarly, Woolley discusses a tripartite classification, based on the users' points of view and not on those of the planner. Based on the concept of "home range," she discusses domestic, neighborhood, and civic open space, based on distances from users' homes and on social encounters, suggesting levels of familiarity, sociability, and anonymity.[38]

Nature is another lens through which open-space types can be seen. An excellent example is Hough's model based on environmental value and sensitivity, which he correlates with levels of maintenance and intensity of use (Figure 1.3). Wildness is, therefore, a useful way in which to model urban open space.

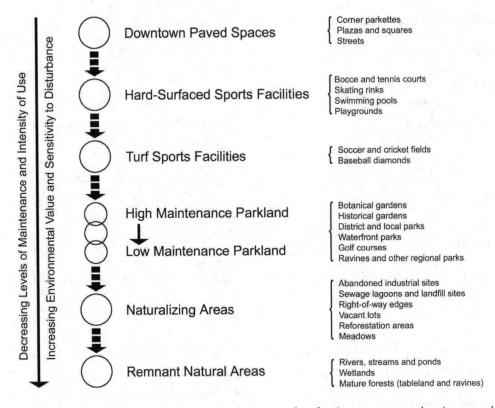

Fig. 1.3 Michael Hough's typology of open space, depicting scales of maintenance, use, and environmental value. (Adapted from Michael Hough, *Out of Place: Restoring Identity to the Regional Landscape*, New Haven: Yale University Press, 1990.)

Other systems are based on land use and ownership. Beer expressly includes both formally designated open space and other "actual" open space in her model (Figure 1.4). This view captures the imagination in a new way, recognizing that vineyards, roadsides, allotments, and other landscapes are indeed valuable open spaces.

Beer's work on open space begins to explore the structure of open space, including as

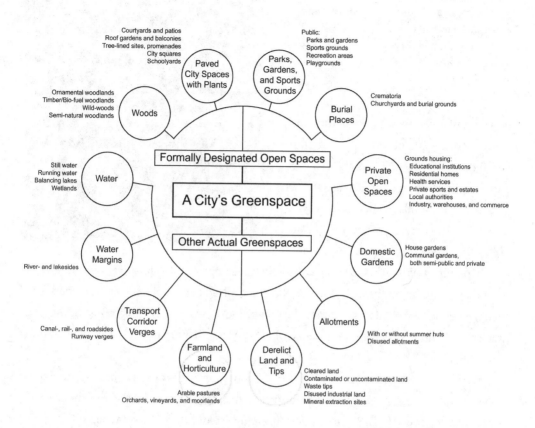

Fig. 1.4 Anne Beer's model of urban open space. (Adapted from Anne R. Beer, 2000.)

open space everything that is not impervious. A figure/ground study of a town or city would create the pattern of open space versus impervious space if parking lots and roads were included as built. Figure 1.5 shows a hypothetical example; white space represents unpaved urban land from which an open-space system might be created. This can then lead to modeling the *structure* of the greenspace—its form, scale, and connectivity. For instance, this diagram shows two adjoining, but distinctively different, patterns of urban open land. This approach transcends the public–private dichotomy by including home gardens, industrial grounds, and institutional landscapes as part of the valued open-space system.[39]

Similarly, Swanwick and colleagues developed a hierarchical typology of urban greenspace that focused on the relationship of open space to buildings and gray, impervious space.[40] They defined green versus gray space in the urban area and then created a

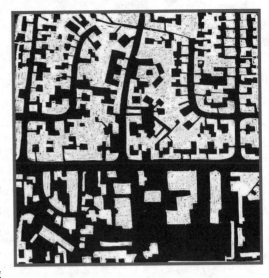

Fig. 1.5 Figure-ground study where buildings and paved surfaces are shown in black and unpaved urban land shown in white. There is a stark difference in amount and pattern of open land in the bottom and top portions of the diagram.

typology of greenspace based on function. They use concepts of amenity, function, and habitat as three main categories (see Table 1.3). Linear green spaces are shown as a fourth set. Similar to Beer and her colleagues, Swanwick et al. assert that "strategic approaches to green space planning clearly require a different and more comprehensive approach to classifications and definitions than the more traditional approach that has evolved in the field of park and open space management. They need to recognize the vital importance of the whole range of different green spaces within urban environments, whether or not they are publicly accessible or publicly managed."[41]

The city of Davis, California, also uses a functional approach for acquisition of rural open space around the city's edges. Working on a plan to help them categorize and rank open space, city leaders developed a scheme to create a shopping list for future land purchases. Categories include agriculture, biological and natural resources, urban fringe, community separators, and land that preserves scenic views. The first four categories include about 25,000 acres, and the agriculture category alone creates a 1-mile-wide greenbelt around the city.[42] From another perspective, many jurisdictions create ranking schemes for open-space land, often used as a funding tool by which applicants can accrue points for their open-space resource. For instance, the Pierce County, Washington, "Open space–public benefit rating system tax program," gives five points each for high-priority resources such as critical salmon habitat and wetlands, three points each for medium-priority resources such as agricultural lands and aquifer-recharge areas, and one point each for low-priority resources such as historic landmark sites, scenic view points, and archaeological sites. Bonus points are offered for public access, conservation easements, sites within designated urban growth areas, and sites that create linkage with other open-space parcels.[43]

Randall Arendt's work corroborates the need for careful open-space ranking in the context of new suburban development. He promotes codes that are specific about what consti-

ALL URBAN GREEN SPACE	Amenity Green Space	Recreation Green Space	Parks and gardens Informal recreation areas Outdoor sports areas Play areas
		Incidental Green Space	Housing green space Other incidental space
		Private Green Space	Domestic gardens
	Functional Green Space	Productive Green Space	Remnant farmland City farms Allotments
		Burial Grounds	Cemeteries Churchyards
		Institutional Grounds	School grounds (including school farms and growing areas) Other institutional grounds
	Semi-natural Habitats	Wetland	Open / running water Marshes and fens
		Woodland	Deciduous woodland Coniferous woodland Mixed woodland
		Other Habitats	Moors and heaths Grasslands Disturbed ground
		Linear Green Space	River and canal banks Transport corridors (road, rail, cycleways and walking routes) Other linear features (e.g., cliffs)

Table 1.3 Swanwick and colleagues' typology of urban green space (adapted from Carys Swanwick, Nigel Dunnett, and Helen Wooley, "Nature, Role and Value of Green Space in Towns and Cities: An Overview," *Built Environment*, 29 (Number 2, 2003): 94–106.)

tutes open space in new neighborhoods. "Some municipalities might value woodland habitat above farmland, while others might prioritize fields, pastures and meadow above forests. Still others might rank historic and cultural resources at the top of the list. Although this kind of provision is one of the most important features of subdivision objectives, it is frequently the one that is most lacking."[44]

These schemes are useful. No one typology is sufficient alone, given the complex nature of urban open space; it is important to use multiple lenses. However, while constructive in a number of ways, few of the typologies really address the *ecological structure* of the environment. Landscape ecology, based on a taxonomy of patches, corridors, and matrices, is the basis for a more structural view of open-space systems.[45] Where previous schemes organize scale, naturalness, or land use, the simple scheme in Figure 1.6 places open spaces in relation to each other and to people, based on a system of hubs, sites, and links at a regional scale. This way of viewing open space has profound implications for how the landscape is studied, planned, and developed. This model can be applied at a range of scales, can address a gradient of naturalness, and can incorporate varied land-use contexts.

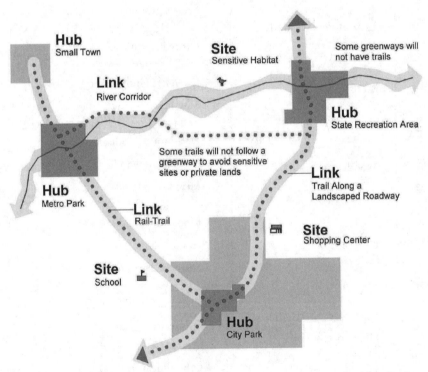

Fig. 1.6 Hubs, sites, and links as components of connected open space systems based on landscape ecology. (Adapted from Rails-to-Trails Conservancy of Michigan, "Southeast Michigan GreenWays," 1998.)

These diverse contextual settings remind us that urban open space needs specialized techniques for evaluation and categorization. D. A. Goode, writing about British open-space planning, emphasized that "established criteria for assessment of nature conservation value are not, in fact, particularly relevant for urban nature conservation. Criteria such as naturalness, diversity, rarity and size, used to assess the value of sites as potential nature reserves, are measures of intrinsic interest, but do not take account of either social factors or the local context of the site, which may be significant factors in an urban setting."[46] Landscape ecologists use four main characteristics to assess urban and suburban landscapes: large patches of undisturbed natural vegetation, natural vegetation along watercourses, heterogeneous distribution of natural patches, and connectivity between patches.[47] Connectivity is one crucial measure for assessing both ecological and social values.

Connectivity

Ecologists tell us that protecting isolated natural areas is not nearly enough. "There must also be linkages in the landscape that allow movement through the potentially hostile world of human settlement to the islands of undisturbed habitat. That makes connectivity important. An environmentally viable landscape has patches that are close or directly connected to other patches."[48] There are two main theoretical motives for connecting open spaces across metropolitan areas. The first is ecological; the second is *human*.[49]

The concern is with connections not only among ecosystems and landscapes but also between people and elements of the built environment. As discussed earlier, open space is being planned and funded in hundreds of towns and cities; likewise, connectivity among disparate open spaces is being planned and implemented with nearly the same vigor. And it is happening at all scales. Short corridors of a few hundred feet or less are being built, embedded within systems that are connecting entire river systems across hundreds of square miles. Numerous scholars and practitioners have made the case for connectivity persuasively and thoroughly.

Ecology

For ecologists, it is imperative to implement natural areas in a connected web at large scales. The concept of biodiversity summarizes many of these environmental goals. Biodiversity is "the variety of living organisms, the genetic differences among them, the communities and ecosystems in which they occur, and the ecological and evolutionary processes that keep them functioning, yet ever changing and adapting."[50] Ecologists have shown that high ecosystem diversity supports high species diversity. Unfortunately, even though the habitat network concept is well established, most conservation efforts are still

1.1 Landscape Ecology

Several disciplinary areas have emerged in recent decades to help inform the natural systems and landscape-change nexus. Research in landscape ecology, conservation biology, restoration ecology, and ecosystem management is forwarding the science of landscape change and the practice of landscape planning. However, we are only in the first stages of applying the knowledge from these disciplines. Landscape ecology is especially important for understanding landscape dynamics and for informing the way we design and plan landscapes at all scales.

Landscape ecology helps explain structure, function, and change over space and time in heterogeneous landscapes.[1] It uses a taxonomy of patches, corridors, and matrices for understanding landscape patterns and processes (Figure 1.7). Landscape ecology is concerned with both the biophysical and the societal causes and consequences of landscape heterogeneity. A broadly interdisciplinary field, its roots are primarily in geography and biology. According to the International Association of Landscape Ecology, core themes for the discipline are the following: spatial pattern or structure of landscapes, ranging from wilderness to cities; relationships between patterns and processes in landscapes; relationship of human activity to landscape pattern, process, and change; and effect of scale and disturbance on the landscape.

Landscape ecology offers a way to relate environmental phenomena to a wider context, assisting in a logical zoning of space and in phasing of landscape change over time. In the landscape planning process, landscape ecology can be used in two main ways—as an evaluative tool and as a basis for deliberate landscape change. As an evaluative tool, a landscape ecological perspective can foster a more thorough consideration of change in three-dimensional space. This approach surpasses typical two-dimensional site analyses by layering landscape components into structural wholes that form the basis for species' orientation in space: patches, corridors, and matrices. This evaluative approach serves as a design net—a reminder that understanding of a site is grounded in space *and* time.

As a form-generating tool, landscape ecology offers concepts that address human well-being, as well as that of other species. It helps delineate site selection schemes in space and phasing schemes through time. In addition, it incorporates an understandable landscape vocabulary for communicating planning decisions and design solutions.

Nowhere have the principles of landscape ecology been used so thoroughly as in the study and design of natural areas. Usually these applications are made in remote natural settings where human influence is minimal. However, ideas from landscape ecology are increasingly being applied to the delineation, conservation, and management of natural areas in diverse cultural landscapes, including metropolitan open-space corridors. Semi-natural reserves, and even urbanized areas, are currently a particular focus for landscape ecological research.

---

[i] Richard Forman and Michel Godron, *Landscape Ecology* (New York: John Wiley, 1986).

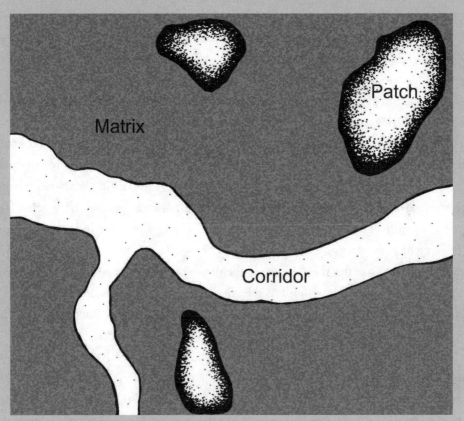

Fig. 1.7 Landscape components from landscape ecology theory: patches, corridors, and matrices.

relatively local, emphasizing isolated preserves, where protected lands are a fragmented patchwork, threatened by exotic species, edge effects, and increasing human disturbance and encroachment. The solutions generally incorporate two spatial effects—size and connectivity. However, as Soule and Terborgh have shown, implementation of large core areas and connectivity across the landscape is daunting: "On-the-ground realization of a program of large core areas and landscape connectivity will . . . require research, planning, and bold advocacy at unprecedented scales."[51]

Open-space corridors provide one critical form for achieving connectivity. The importance of conservation corridors was proposed in the 1970s and continues to receive wide attention from ecologists, planners, and policymakers. Corridor planning is a popular strategy in conservation planning, particularly for protecting biodiversity.[52] "Corridors are a hot topic, perhaps even a fad, in conservation planning these days. Planners and environmentalists from county to federal levels are busy drawing 'greenbelts' and other habitat corridors into their designs, sometimes with only a vague awareness of the biological issues underlying the corridor strategy."[53] Daniel Smith and Paul Hellmund's seminal book *The Ecology of Greenways* skillfully documents how connected open space satisfies ecological goals, bringing more specificity and empirical evidence to corridor planning and design.[54]

Conservation biologists see corridors as "linear habitat embedded in unsuitable habitat . . . that connects two or more larger blocks of suitable habitat and which is proposed for conservation on the grounds that it will enhance or maintain the viability of wildlife populations in the habitat blocks."[55] However, the role of corridors in biodiversity planning is also controversial. Rosenberg and others make a critical distinction between corridors for movement routes and corridors as habitat. "Linear patches have often been equated with biological corridors, but in fact, linear patches serve two different functions: as movement pathways and as habitats for resident species . . . Evaluation of the corridor function of linear patches should include the three stages of successful dispersal to a target patch through a corridor—finding, selecting, and moving successfully through it."[56] In addition, they show that corridors have diverse functions, shapes, and contexts. While some definitions of corridors emphasize movement, others stress form.

Although conservation biologists agree that wildlife species evolved in well-connected landscapes and that connectivity can enhance the population viability for species, there are also downsides to corridors.[57] Reed Noss has summarized the advantages and disadvantages clearly.[58] On the positive side, connectivity can potentially increase immigration rates to a conservation reserve in a positive way. Connectivity can also provide a range of benefits for animals by providing foraging area, predator escape cover, and a mix of habitats for species. It can also provide alternative refuges from large disturbances such as fire.

On the other hand, connectivity can also potentially lead to negative effects from immigration rates, facilitate the spread of fire and other disturbances, and increase exposure of animals to hunters, poachers, and other predators. In addition, riparian corridors can sometimes fail to enhance the dispersal or survival of upland species. They may also lead to increased costs and competition with more conventional land-preservation strategies.

Although many benefits of connectivity are documented, connection is clearly not a panacea for conservation. Despite the ambiguity, though, it is clear that corridors are often beneficial. Noss claims that "many of the potential disadvantages of corridors could be avoided or mitigated by enlarging corridor width or by applying ecologically sound zoning regulations."[59] For him, the most compelling reason to think carefully about landscape corridors is that pre-settlement landscapes were interconnected and that connectivity has declined with human settlement.

A number of scholars have documented the principles by which corridors should be protected and planned. For instance, A. C. Henry and colleagues offer the following guidelines:

1. Benefits of corridors are maximized by working at large spatial scales, for instance in watershed planning.
2. Continuous corridors are better than fragmented ones.
3. Wider corridors are better than narrow ones.
4. Structurally diverse corridors are better than those with simple structures, and diversity should be considered both horizontally across the landscape and vertically within layers and heights of vegetation.
5. Two or more corridor connections between patches are better than one.
6. Natural connectivity should be maintained or restored.[60]

The ideal width of conservation corridors is probably the most debated issue. In addition, it is a dimension that landscape planners, trying to apply landscape ecology principles, desperately need to know more about. Although many planners have searched for scientific answers about the ideal widths across different ecosystems, land uses, and corridor types, finding definitive answers is difficult. Species have different requirements for habitat; likewise, they have different requirements for corridor width. Generally, wider corridors, in the range of hundreds of feet or more across, are better for ecological soundness.[61]

Although the exact role of corridors in urban landscapes, as well as their optimum sizes, remains ambiguous, it can be claimed that the ecological importance of connectivity should be the baseline on which other open-space benefits are built. According to ecologists Rosenberg and colleagues, "because greenways are increasingly popular as means of improving urban and suburban living environments and may themselves serve as important habitat, biologists should work with urban planners and community groups to design greenways that contribute to urban wildlife conservation and education, rather than arguing whether greenways function as corridors."[62] Working with community groups is particularly important in order to incorporate humans into the realm of ecology.

Human Ecology

Landscape ecology and human ecology together provide critical information for connected open-space planning. Human ecology studies the relationships between parts and wholes, addressing how humans interact with each other and with the components of their environments. As Frederick Steiner suggests, as a discipline human ecology may be the key to the study of regions in all their complexity.[63] Connection is one part of the way regions function. It is not only good for wildlife, water quality, and other environmental features and processes—it is also good for people. This is a fundamental concept from human ecology, human geography, and the other social sciences.

Ample literature supports the idea that an urban landscape with high connectivity is more accessible, more humane, and indeed more democratic. Connected urban areas allow exchanges among various social groups, democratizing the city in a spatial way. A connected urban landscape fosters mobility, visual interest, and efficiency. Humans need to easily access services and amenities at the neighborhood and city scale, and this access should not all be dependent on cars. The walkable, connected city is one that helps foster sound human-ecological health.

Urban and landscape planners need to pay particular attention to the connected fabric of the city. Frederick Steiner writes eloquently about the important link between human ecology and landscape planning.[64] Several of his main arguments are built around the nature of connection for humans in the built environment. Gerald Young, an eminent human ecologist, asserted that planners "*must* consider the area being planned as a system, must understand its connectedness, its interrelatedness with its own parts and those exterior to it, must understand the flow of people, energy, and materials into and out of it, must understand the design essentials based on environmental characteristics and human needs. But they do not."[65] However, planning does not always have this ecological basis. Most planning has been done without realizing these human ecological principles. This gap is partly bridged by systematically assessing the open-space structure of metropolitan regions, including its connection to communities.

A study conducted by the Trust for Public Land (TPL) is an excellent illustration of a human ecological approach in open-space planning.[66] Fifty of the largest U.S. cities were surveyed to find what goals are used as maximum distances any resident should live from the nearest park. Findings showed that only eighteen of the cities had any goal in this regard, and that standards varied from as close as one-eighth of a mile to as far as a mile. There is no commonly accepted standard for acceptable distance. TPL contends that distance from open space is an important measure and perhaps more significant than total acreage of parkland. Los Angeles, for example, ranks fifth among large cities in acreage of parkland, but half of that land is relatively inaccessible. TPL ranks five cities highly by this criterion, three of which are used as case studies in this book: Denver, Colorado (three to six blocks); Minneapolis, Minnesota (six blocks); Long Beach, California (one-quarter mile in high-density neighborhoods); Seattle, Washington (one-eighth mile in high-density neighborhoods); and Chicago, Illinois (one-tenth mile to a pocket park).

Connectivity at the Metro Scale

Increasingly, whole urban regions are in the economic, ecological, and cultural spotlight. Just less than 50 percent of the world's population lives in cities; this percentage is expected to grow rapidly. Almost 80 percent of the U.S. population lives in metropolitan areas. And the conversion of land for urbanization is outpacing population growth. Cities are no longer compact; they sprawl in spiderlike patterns that abut wildlands.[67] And the points of abutment are critical. Burch notes, in reference to a scalar range from urban vest-pocket parks to entire wilderness areas, that "wildlands are separated from the larger social and ecological world by a thin membrane of institutional and normative patterns."[68] These membranes or edges are important zones for connecting open space with larger urban and rural landscape patterns.

Connectivity has been widely discussed in the context of city regions in recent years. New information networks change peoples' lives and the places they live. Global markets, wireless technology, cellular communication, and all manner of other digital devices connect us. Open-space connection at the scale of the region shares some of the same goals—bringing people together. It retains the old-fashioned physical dimension—creating space for an integrated spatial realm. Given the importance of connectivity in planning open-space systems, the scale of concern has widened dramatically in the last couple of decades. In fact, a dozen states have implemented state greenway programs. Pennsylvania,

1.2 Human Ecology

Human ecology is the study of the relationship between human communities and the environment, incorporating both the biological and the social sciences. It is a part of general ecology, not separate from it.[1] Landscape ecology and human ecology share the same ecological roots and a somewhat parallel conceptual evolution over many decades from several disciplines—most notably, biology, geography, and sociology. Catton defines human ecology simply as the study of ecosystems that involve humans. The ecosystem is widely used as the main concept for human ecology, and Catton uses three large categories for human ecology: (1) ecosystems in which humans are a very dependent part (the realm of ecological anthropology), (2) ecosystems dominated by humans in varying degrees, and (3) ecosystems so strongly dominated by humans (cities) that human autonomy and self-sufficiency can easily be misperceived. [2]

The academic origins of human ecology usually refer to early twentieth-century studies of urbanism and to the Odums' ecology and ecosystems work.[3] Young has claimed that it is in sociology that the concept of human ecology is most strongly established, that it is where the idea of human ecology began, and where there is the strongest and most unbroken tradition.[4] Park and Burgess are often credited with introducing the term, although the real origin of the idea is contested.[5] According to Young, "the city as a fit subject for ecological analysis is found prominently in the early works of the Chicago school of sociological human ecologists."[6] He claims that one theme runs through human ecology all along its course—"organization" as a fundamental principle. "At least one part of the organizational concern of sociological human ecologists has been with how aggregates of people have organized themselves in space: spatial analysis has played a prominent part in the development of human ecology."[7]

Human ecology is so broad that its application takes many forms. It has been used as a planning perspective, particularly in Europe.[8] Young claims that any field that manipulates the environment is applied human ecology since it affects the well-being of people, relationships of people to the environment, and behavior patterns. He claims that planning is, more than any other field, applied human ecology. Frederick Law Olmsted was one of the first students of applied human ecology, applying its tenets to open-space planning in the nineteenth century.[9] Another great landscape architect, Ian McHarg, defined human ecological planning.[10] He pointed out that if humans were accepted as part of ecology and ecology were accepted as part of planning, then one word—planning—would suffice for three.

[1] William R. Burch, Jr., "Human Ecology and Environmental Management," in J. K. Agee and D. R. Johnson, eds., *Ecosystem Management for Parks and Wilderness* (Seattle: University of Washington Press, 1988).
[2] William R. Catton, Jr., "Foundations of Human Ecology," *Sociological Perspectives*, 37 (Number 1, 1994):75–95.
[3] See the many contributions of Eugene Odum and Howard Odum to the science of ecology in the mid- to late-twentieth century, for instance, Eugene Odum, *Ecology: A Bridge Between Science and Society* (Sunderland, MA: Sinauer, 1997).
[4] Gerald Young, "Human Ecology as an Interdisciplinary Concept: A Critical Inquiry." *Advances in Ecological Research*, 8:1-105. (1974).
[5] Robert E. Park and Ernest W. Burgess, *Introduction to the Science of Sociology* (Chicago: University of Chicago Press, 1921).
[6] Young, "Human Ecology," 1974, p. 14.
[7] Ibid., p. 16.
[8] Herbert Sukopp, "Urban Ecology--Scientific and Practical Aspects," in J. Breuste, H. Feldmann, and O. Uhlmann, eds., *Urban Ecology* (Berlin: Springer-Verlag, 1998).
[9] Burch, "Human Ecology and Environmental Management," 1988.
[10] Ian McHarg, "Human Ecological Planning at Pennsylvania," *Landscape Planning*, 8 (1981):109–120.

for instance, has decided to focus government efforts on the connectivity of its open spaces. The state's program, begun in 2001, seeks to create a network of greenways across Pennsylvania, linking open space, natural landscape features, scenic, cultural, historic, and recreational sites, and urban and rural communities. Greenways are being used as one tool to achieve sustainable growth and design livable communities. The plan's authors believe that a statewide network will result in a "green infrastructure" and provide a new connectivity within and among Pennsylvania's communities. Goals are also to promote healthier lifestyles, increase recreation and transportation opportunities, and strengthen connections to cultural and historic places.[69]

Pennsylvania, although progressive, is not alone in the pursuit of large-scale connectivity. For example, Florida's greenway concept plan, adopted in 1998, is shown in Figure 1.8. The plan networks the entire state, connecting ecological hubs with recreational and environmental linkages. Dozens of metropolitan areas, often as large as or larger than the state of Rhode Island, are actively trying to connect their open spaces into urban webs of green. For example, planners in Seattle reviewed nearly fifty plans involving the city and found that the word that comes up over and over in the plans is "connection."[70]

Where towns and cities once considered greenway connections along rivers and other linear features, now webs of connected open space are being planned for entire metropolitan regions. They include whole river systems, transportation corridors, adjoining jurisdictions, and rural fringe areas. Increasingly, cities and their regions are planning for *regional systems* of open space, motivated by more systems-oriented approaches to urban ecology.[71] These systematic efforts are driven by environmental concerns, by growth-management efforts, by increasing interjurisdictional planning, and by larger landscape approaches to conservation and urban planning.

There is some confusion about regionalism as applied to open-space planning. While the outcomes of large-scale connected open space are ecologically desirable, the political and social scale is both less certain and more difficult. The debate over an appropriate scale for public projects is not a new one, and the efficiency of regionalism is controversial. Detractors have claimed, for instance, that regional government is not a remedy for spatial problems, and that while large metropolitan governments can best address some problems, most problems are best solved at more local levels.[72]

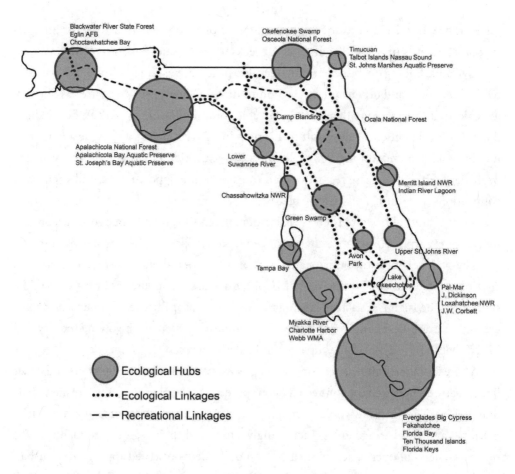

Fig. 1.8 Florida's greenspace and greenways plan. (Adapted from Florida Department of Environmental Protection and Florida Greenways Coordinating Council, "Connecting Florida's Communities with Greenways and Trails," 1999.)

However, open-space protection (as one public good) is an area where planning and implementation at the regional level are effective in both ecological and humanistic terms. In fact, success stories abound—from Denver to Chattanooga and from Austin to Toronto. Apart from the ecological benefits, people may actually perceive and use linear corridors across large metropolitan areas. Arguing for the perceptual benefits of a regional approach, Kevin Lynch states: "I mean to take the peculiar position that the experiential quality of the environment must be planned for at a regional scale . . . since people now live their lives at that scale."[73] For better or worse, people live their lives at even larger scales now than they did in 1976 when Lynch was writing. They traverse longer distances for work and shopping, and it can be hypothesized that they use a far larger array of open spaces in larger spatial realms. Where a house adjoining a golf course was once the ideal, people now value housing that adjoins walking and biking trails to access distant landscapes.

Moreover, connectivity for metro regions demands that open-space design and planning be carried out simultaneously at multiple scales. One paradigm for thinking across scales is the concept of hierarchy.[74] Open-space systems can be seen in a nested hierarchy, where small neighborhood trails are part of larger citywide systems, which in turn are part of larger regional networks. There is no single or correct scale at which to examine or plan open-space networks. They are parts of urban ecosystems, and ecosystems have no clear boundaries.[75]

Spatial Forms of Regionally Connected Open Space

Greenways, greenbelts, and parkways are all used for planning connected open spaces, but each has distinctive characteristics and benefits. While parkways and greenways are certainly not interchangeable spatial phenomena, both provide long, green corridors on the landscape. Greenbelts, on the other hand, are not necessarily linear but provide a buffering function around the edge of urban areas that can incorporate linear elements. Figure 1.9 depicts the prototypical spatial configurations for greenways, greenbelts, and parkways on a hypothetical landscape. Trails may or may not be incorporated in all three types of open land.

Parkways

Many of the historic parkways in North America provide important open-space amenities. However, scholarly analyses of the parkway as a distinct urban form are sparse. In searching for concise treatments of parkways in the classic texts and contemporary planning books, one is often directed to see streets, see roads, or see national parks. However,

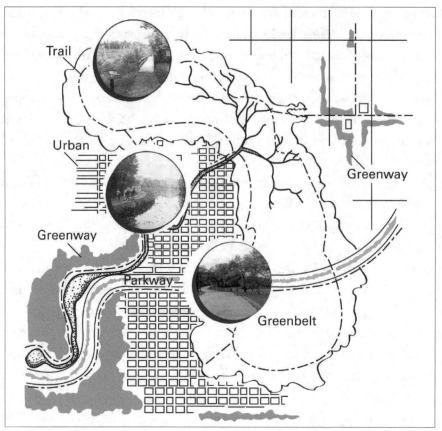

Fig. 1.9 A hypothetical image of greenways, greenbelts, and parkways in a city and adjacent countryside. Trails may or may not be incorporated in all three types of open land.

parkways have a distinct and fascinating history as an American urban open-space form. In addition, since the 1930s parkways have been created and managed within the National Park Service system, providing attractive connections between parks and as destinations in their own right.[76]

As Newton writes, "It is doubtful that any single type of park area has been more widely misunderstood and misinterpreted than the parkway. The confusion is hardly to be wondered at when one considers with what free and easy imprecision the term 'parkway' has been used. Unfortunately, it has even been employed by real-estate developers in recent years as a sort of status label."[78] Newton describes early parkways more accurately as boulevards with limited access. Parkways designed in the growing twentieth-century cities were meant for comfortable driving in pleasant surroundings, with alignments of gentle curves and low speeds; visually they were meant to be a natural part of the countryside. The parkway's broad swath was often roomy enough for pathways and other recreational features (see figure 1.10). They were meant not only to beautify the city but to reduce environmental hazards and enhance transportation options within the city.

A 15-mile stretch of the original Bronx River Parkway in New York City, completed in 1923, is generally regarded as the first true parkway in the United States.[78] "It was only with the completion of New York's Bronx River Parkway after World War I that the modern parkway came into being with its clear set of distinguishing characteristics. The term now denoted a strip of land dedicated to recreation and the movement of pleasure vehicles (passenger, not commercial, automobiles)."[79] Parkways were primarily conceived for transportation; whatever benefits they may have had as connected greenways had more to do with scenic views from cars than other purposes and integrative potentials were often unrealized. According to Cynthia Girling and Kenneth Helphand, "parkways have great potential to integrate recreational and open space functions; unfortunately, however, most are image without substance, offering no more than 'entry statements' and a ceremonial greening of the street."[80]

Fig. 1.10 A parkway scene in Ottawa, Ontario, with wide, green right-of-way, scenic curves, and separate non motorized path. (Photo by the author.)

Greenbelts

Greenbelts, in contrast to both greenways and parkways, are swaths of natural or open land surrounding cities or towns, protected in part to control or guide growth. They often contain a mix of public land and privately held land on which development restrictions are placed. Originating in the Garden City Movement of the early twentieth century in Great Britain, greenbelts were meant to control urban growth by protecting a ring of undeveloped land, often forested or agricultural, around the city. Where greenways follow linear features in the landscape, often radiating through cities, greenbelts are less structured by rivers or other natural features and take a belted form encircling the urban region. In some cases their forms are quite arbitrary. Greenbelts remain a planning strategy and land-use policy in Great Britain, where they are used to check unrestricted sprawl, prevent neighboring towns from merging, assist in protecting the countryside, preserve historic values, and promote urban regeneration.[81] Historically, greenbelts are perhaps the most prevalent approach to shape urban growth with open land. In contemporary use, greenbelts are one mechanism for providing open space near residents, as used in Ann Arbor, Michigan, or Boulder, Colorado. For Boulder, the greenbelt helps buffer the Rocky Mountain Front from the encroaching urbanized region (Figure 1.11).

Many analyses have concluded that greenbelts have failed to control growth or to protect natural features, although they have sometimes resulted in other benefits; in fact many early greenbelts have now been converted to urban development.[82] According to Whyte's greenbelt analysis, "the arbitrary boundaries that look so tidy on a map are extremely difficult to hold on the ground. The kinds that work follow the idiosyncrasies of the land; the ridges and valleys, and especially the streams and rivers."[83] Even with these limitations, the greenbelt idea is still being promoted.[84] It provides the public with a simple land-preservation concept to relate to. Greenways may overcome some of the disadvantages of greenbelts.

Greenways

The greenway idea, a renewed landscape concept from the nineteenth and early twentieth centuries, has swept across North America as one solution to landscape connectivity. According to William Whyte, "Linkage is the key. Most of the big tracts in our metropolitan areas have already been saved, or they have already been lost. The most pressing need now is to weave together a host of seemingly disparate elements—an experimental farm, a private golf course, a local park, the spaces of a cluster subdivision, the edge of a new freeway right-of-way."[85] Leaders in Toronto see greenways as a simple way to link existing greenspaces, thereby increasing open-space usefulness for both people and wildlife.[86]

Fig. 1.11 Aerial image of Boulder, Colorado from the 1930s. Much of the land surrounding the city has since been developed. However, the area between the city and mountains is now Boulder's greenbelt. (Photo by the Denver Photo Company, courtesy of the Denver Public Library Western History Collection.)

Charles Little credits the term "greenways" to Whyte, from Whyte's monograph *Securing Open Space for Urban America*.[87] Robert Searns, in his paper defining eras of greenway planning, claims that the roots of greenways go back several centuries. He sees greenways as an adaptation of humans to their environment—"a response to the physical and psychological pressures of urbanization."[88] A nationwide push for greenways was spurred by the 1987 President's Commission on Americans Outdoors, which linked greenways with American pride, patriotism, and spirit: "Greenways . . . have the potential to be this country's most important land-based effort for conservation and recreation in the next several decades . . . And, if greenways truly capture the imagination and boldness of the American spirit, they could eventually form the corridors that connect open spaces, parks, forests, and deserts—and Americans—from sea to shining sea."[89] While greenways may not always seem so patriotic, they offer a range of amenities.

Greenways are linear open spaces along natural or human-made features such as rivers, ridgelines, railroads, canals, or roads. They are planned, designed, and managed to connect and protect ecological, scenic, recreational, and cultural resources. A greenway may include trails, or it may be a conservation corridor without recreational access. Greenways receive wide attention as landscape connectors for conservation, recreation, and transportation in the built environment. They are sometimes referred to by other names, such as extensive open-space systems, ecological infrastructures, wildlife corridors, or habitat networks.

Some cities have implemented impressive greenway networks. Others continue to develop comprehensive greenway plans, attempting to weave together those diverse urban elements that Whyte valued over thirty years ago. Meanwhile, urban planners are increasingly hoping that connected landscape corridors provide more than recreational opportunities. They are promoting metropolitan greenway networks that help shape urban growth, contribute critical environmental values, and, indeed, *place* economic development and neighborhood revitalization.[90]

Greenways are unique landscapes. As long linear features, they are often developed on a complex mosaic of public and private lands. They traverse property lines, natural features, and other public infrastructure (see Figure 1.12). They transcend jurisdictional boundaries and sometimes even state lines. Greenway development usually includes aspects of both creating new spatial forms and protecting existing resources. For these reasons, implementation is difficult. Cross-jurisdictional cooperation is imperative.[91] When multiple, isolated segments are implemented by various local agencies and organizations, the result is often competing, conflicting land-use policies and narrow plans that fail to take into consideration the greenway in its entirety. Lack of coordination can result in the degradation or even loss of the greenway and its component resources.[92]

Since many citizens' groups, municipalities, and organizations have decided to create and protect greenways in their communities, practical information about design, planning, and implementation has been needed. Given their unique scope, complexity, and audience, understanding how greenways and greenway networks are realized is crucial. Charles Little's book *Greenways for America* has been particularly influential in depicting historic and contemporary greenways, their planning processes and constituents.[93] Flink and Searns subsequently published a helpful volume with applied advice on greenway planning processes.[94]

Empirical evidence of greenway impacts is also critical if the phenomenon is to secure the needed support, funding, and attention. Social scientists have therefore analyzed the human dimension of greenway planning, asking important questions about use, percep-

Fig. 1.12 Seattle's Burke-Gilman Trail is an example of a greenway converted from a former rail line, one of the most popular in the United States. An 11-mile section of Burlington Northern track was converted in the early 1970s. Now the greenway is 27 miles long, extending out into King County. (© 2005, Rails-to-Trails Conservancy.)

tion, and economics. An influential study by the National Park Service documented economic impacts, showing that greenways have positive effects on property values and other economic indicators.[95] Other scholars have described greenway users' characteristics and perceptions, particularly documenting intensity and pattern of use and its variation across greenway types.[96] Paul Gobster showed that trail location, especially relative to users' homes, influenced frequency and type of use.[97] He concluded that local rather than regional trails should be the basic framework for metropolitan greenway systems.

The environmental effects of greenways have also received close attention, particularly connecting to the landscape ecology literature. In addition to Smith and Hellmund's *The Ecology of Greenways,* research by other scholars has focused on ecological impacts of connected corridors.[98] These contributions have shown that greenways can positively affect water quality, habitat, and other environmental assets.

A few researchers have focused on implementation and the larger planning framework within which greenways dwell.[99] Jack Ahern's contributions have integrated greenways with wider planning issues, arguing for open-space design as a strategic method for comprehensive landscape planning.[100] However, little research has focused closely on the institutional setting for greenway development, especially at regional scales. And the linkage of greenway corridors into larger metropolitan networks has received only spotty attention. Many of the regional greenway systems have been planned only over the last decade or two, and systematic implementation (let alone evaluation) has only begun in most cities.

So we know a good bit about how to achieve greenways and other corridors on the landscape, including the planning methods, participants, funding, and logistics. And the physical form of connectivity has been analyzed and classified. The various forms that connected open space takes are, of course, only part of the story; function is another critical variable. The "form and function" discourse is not a new one. However, regardless of whether form or function leads, the functionality of greenways and other open-space networks is at the heart of the matter.

The Functions of Connected Open-Space Networks

Greenways, and open space more generally, must serve specific functions. For contemporary open-space projects, success will of course depend on the objectives the projects are setting out to serve. As background, Searns defines three generations of greenways and their objectives: Generation One greenways, up to 1960, consisted of boulevards and parkways, whereas Generation Two greenways, from 1960 to 1985, were trail-oriented recreational greenways and linear parks providing access to rivers and abandoned rail lines. Generation Three greenways, since 1985, are multiobjective greenways that include wildlife protection, water-quality concerns, education, recreation, and other goals.[101] Searns describes how the greenways movement has become more sophisticated and comprehensive in serving multiple needs and connecting to diverse urban contexts. Still, the most common objectives of most greenway systems are recreation, conservation, and/or nonmotorized transportation. In most places, the protection of ecological quality is a particularly strong motivator. Economic development and growth-management issues are less likely to spur greenway planning at the outset; however, these are sometimes secondary effects that are later connected to implementation. Similarly, scenic quality and historic preservation are mentioned less often, but are sometimes important long-term benefits of greenways.

The new frontier for urban open-space planning lies in having multiple objectives. Natural-features protection and restoration will, like the restoration of neighborhoods, be central to successful implementation strategies for urban greenways. In reference to this new generation of greenways, Searns writes that the latest thinking "addresses more complex issues and reflects more sophisticated thinking about environmental issues."[102]

The natural and social functions of connected open space are additive. The more functions that a landscape provides, the greater its worth to the system. However, this complexity is also one of the challenges of these new projects. For instance, a small urban park that provides a children's playground, basketball courts, and large, older trees may be more valuable than a pocket park with a fountain. Another greenway concept claims that the functions are nested, that connected open space is multifunctional but should be based on an ecological framework that takes precedence in open-space planning. An ecological system that protects regional diversity could form the framework of a regional greenway system. In this approach, the determining factors are ecological, forming the basis on which other functions are added (such as recreation or transportation). This approach is a 180-degree departure from traditional open-space planning.[103] The concepts of greenstructure (as it is called in Europe) and green infrastructure (the North American term) provide the framework for ecology as a basis for connected open-space development.

European Greenstructure

For some time, European scholars and planners have been investigating, planning, and implementing landscape plans based on connected open-space networks. This work has advocated a more serious approach to open space as the city's critical infrastructure, specifically promoting an approach called greenstructure—a multiobjective approach that uses ecology as a base.

Beer and colleagues explain that greenstructure planning "emphasizes the multifunctional nature of greenspace within the land-use planning system and demonstrates that there are many reasons to take its planning and enhancement more seriously."[104] They argue that greenstructure should have equal weight with other city infrastructure in the planning process and be adequately financed. "What is still lacking in most cities is a 'vision' for the role of greenspaces; an understanding that greenspaces form a greenstructure, which can be used as a resource for the benefit of inhabitants and to enhance sustainability."[105] They see a functional urban greenstructure as important to quality of life for residents as is the city's "gray" infrastructure (roads, sewer lines), and that this significance needs to be recognized in the planning and financing systems. They recommend urban greenstructure plans that are citywide but have enough detail to be included into local plans.

Similarly, greenstructure plans have been created and implemented in the Netherlands for a couple of decades. These types of plans are defined as "a coherent package of objectives, principles and priorities for the desired quality of green areas in the public domain throughout the whole municipal territory, leading to proposals for sustainable development, with agreements about shared responsibility and finances."[106] Greenstructure plans depict physical interventions in the urban landscape using open space as a framework. Tjallingii describes the defensive and offensive stances of those working in open-space planning and advocates a more integrative working relationship between the open-space and development sectors.[107] He also notes a shift from thinking only about quantity and distribution of greenspace (hectares per 1,000 residents) toward considering a green strategy with emphasis on the quality of open space and its structural role relative to other land uses. Indeed, the amount of open space in a neighborhood or city doesn't indicate much about its environmental soundness.

Green Infrastructure

The progress being made in Europe provides an interesting background to green infrastructure planning in North America. Green infrastructure is synonymous with greenstructure but is being used specifically in the context of exploding urban growth in American cities where the economic, social, and political conditions are quite different from those of Europe. The term "green infrastructure" has been used recently with almost the same frequency and enthusiasm as the term "smart growth." Indeed, the two are often used in the same breath. Like greenstructure, green infrastructure is perhaps the most promising direction for a more holistic definition of open space. In fact, Ed McMahon of the Urban Land Institute makes a compelling case for new terminology, replacing the term "open space" with "green infrastructure", claiming that this shift in nomenclature gives more specificity and value to the meaning of open land.[108]

Mark Benedict and Edward McMahon endorse the use of green infrastructure for proactively shaping new growth, defining green infrastructure as "an interconnected network of green space that conserves natural ecosystem values and functions and provides associated benefits to human populations . . . Planning utilizing green infrastructure differs from conventional open space planning because it looks at conservation values in concert with land development, growth management and built infrastructure planning."[109] Their principles create a compelling argument for change, where green infrastructure is designed and planned as a critical public investment before development occurs. It would provide the framework for conservation and development, engaging key partners and diverse stakeholders. Their model stipulates, furthermore, that green infrastructure creates key linkages, functions across jurisdictions at multiple scales, and is grounded in sound science and planning theory.

While green infrastructure presents a persuasive case for taking open-space planning more seriously, so far the literature *promoting* green infrastructure as a planning approach outweighs the literature that critically *assesses* its potential and impact. Ample evidence exists for the ecological soundness, centered on the need to curtail fragmentation, protect biodiversity, and improve water quality. Unfortunately, many local communities protect open space with little regard for the needs of wildlife and ecosystems.[110] In addition, there is little examination of how the green infrastructure approach fits within real political and social contexts, the concept as a community planning strategy, or the fiscal effects of greening the gray urban infrastructure. According to Kostyack, "understanding which policy tools are working is extremely difficult because there are no universally accepted measures to protect green infrastructure. Biologists, urban planners, policymakers, and others must agree on these measures of success and gather the data needed for meaningful comparisons. Otherwise, we face a future where open space and other protection programs spend vast sums yet fail to deliver on their promise of conserving our natural heritage."[111] Green infrastructure offers the most systematic approach to protecting open space and evaluating land-use decisions.

Conclusion

Urban residents, suburban commuters, farmers, politicians, and environmentalists are all increasingly distressed about open spaces being paved over. However, literature on open-space planning shows that open space must be more than open and must offer more than space.

Protecting and designing meaningful open space that enhances landscape ecology and human ecology is a tall order. The results must be ecologically sound, and they must be beneficial to people. That combination is difficult, partly because we have scant evidence on the effect of managed recreational use on habitat quality in urban contexts.[112] And one patch of open space cannot do it all for any given community, unless it is not only large but also uniquely situated. So we need creativity in putting together open-space systems that, like intricate puzzles, create a whole that is greater than its parts. In her critique of standard approaches, Holtz-Kay writes, "Forgotten is the fact that defined space, visionary space—not 'open space'—makes the pulse race and the place pulse."[113] To create these visionary spaces, designers and planners need to be very specific about what open space means, how local residents value it, and how it is connected into functional networks for city regions.

2

Learning from City Stories:
Ten Case Study Comparisons

The city is a fact in nature, like a cave, a run of mackerel or an ant-heap. But it is also a conscious work of art, and it holds within its communal framework many simpler and more personal forms of art. Mind takes form in the city; and in turn, urban forms condition mind.

—*Lewis Mumford[1]*

We learn from the stories of places. They reveal patterns and processes that are useful not only for understanding one place but for anticipating what might be experienced and accomplished elsewhere. Chapter 1 explained that open-space connectivity is worth pursuing at metropolitan scales and that, indeed, many places are attempting to fit open spaces into larger patterns that achieve environmental and social goals. Ten cities in North America have grappled with open-space connectivity in assorted ways and for diverse purposes. While each story is unique, there are themes that cut across the cities and inform efforts in other places.

Ten City Open-Space Stories

The ten case studies of Canadian and U.S. cities in the Part II portfolio, mapped in Figure 2.1, are central to this volume:

Fig. 2.1 Map of ten case study cities in Canada and the United States.

- Toronto, Ontario
- Calgary, Alberta
- Vancouver, British Columbia
- Ottawa, Ontario
- Chicago, Illinois
- Denver, Colorado
- Portland, Oregon
- Minneapolis–St. Paul, Minnesota
- Cleveland, Ohio
- Milwaukee, Wisconsin

This list of ten is, of course, not an exhaustive inventory of the cities planning and implementing innovative open-space networks at the metropolitan scale in North America. Dozens of cities qualify. I do not claim that these are necessarily the most successful examples; indeed, the measures of success vary widely. Rather, these cities shed light on many of the challenges and opportunities faced in a wide range of settings.

The cities chosen in this study are located in the northern United States (with Denver the farthest south) and southern Canada. From the former Rust Belt to the Rocky Mountain Front to the Pacific coast, they all have unique open-space stories to tell, sometimes revealing successes of implemented networks and in other cases exhibiting great potential that is just now coalescing toward regional open-space visions. Some of these places are renowned examples of greenway system design, such as Portland and Denver. Others are well-known for their stellar park systems but not necessarily for the connections among them—the Twin Cities, Milwaukee, and Cleveland.

The ten cities have the following factors in common regarding connected open space:

- *Network or system.* They have incorporated a web of linear open spaces, often along rivers and streams, but along other natural and human-built corridors as well.
- *Regional scale and multijurisdictional scope.* The networks encompass multiple political jurisdictions (e.g., counties), rather than existing wholly within one town or county (with exceptions of some Canadian cities with very large urban and rural areas within one jurisdiction).
- *Multiple functions and objectives.* The networks have been planned for multiple purposes, such as ecological soundness, alternative transportation, or recreational amenity. Although each city is used to illustrate one function primarily, all of them have diverse goals that include both competing and compatible objectives.
- *Implementation.* These case study regions have begun the implementation phase, at least in part, and have passed beyond the planning stage.

Why use the metropolitan region as a unit of analysis? Existing greenway literature primarily uses the river corridor, neighborhood, or municipality as a unit of analysis for connectivity. The creation of individual corridors is well documented. Moving the scale of concern up to a systems level has advantages for visualizing a bigger picture. A number of urban scholars have argued that the city must be addressed in its regional context, that "urban form is an expression of the natural and cultural history of a region."[2] Frederick Steiner writes, "A regional view can enable cities to cope with change. Imagine living in

New York City in the mid-nineteenth century, or Chicago early in the twentieth, or Los
Angeles in the middle of the twentieth . . . None of these great cities stood alone; each
depended on a larger region for water, food, and other vital supplies. These regional cities
prospered when that connection was reinforced. They floundered during times when those
essential ties weakened."[3]

Comparing spatial planning in one nation with those of another helps us understand
change processes that are simultaneously global in importance and local in context.[4]
Examining four Canadian and six U.S. cities reveals political, cultural, and environmental
differences that impact open-space connectivity within cities of the two nations. Canadian
and U.S. cities share many approaches to urban planning and design, yet both subtle and
overt distinctions come into play and provide instructive lessons. Several Canadian cities
have developed impressive greenway networks with creative combinations of local and
regional coordination. Conversely, U.S. experiences in open-space planning have great relevance to Canadian planners, since political and economic conditions are similar and U.S.
planners have advanced greenway design dramatically over the last twenty years.

Cities are paired in Chapters 3–7, using case study comparisons to help answer questions about how open-space connectivity is accomplished. The ten metropolitan areas have
some key aspects in common, as well as some relevant differences. Like most cities built at
the confluence of rich water and terrestrial ecosystems, they have important natural assets.
For instance, they are all located on water bodies—rivers, the Great Lakes, or the Pacific
Ocean. Populations in the core cities range from around 300,000 to nearly 3 million; however, the Metropolitan Statistical Areas (Census Population Areas in Canada) are much
larger, from 1 million to 3 million in most cities, with Toronto and Chicago representing
very large metropolitan regions of 5 million to 9 million (Table 2.1).

The number of local jurisdictions operating within the urban regions directly affects
the connected open space. These jurisdictions are primarily cities, towns, and counties
in the United States (although park boards and other special districts are also involved).
For Canada, counties are not generally a pertinent level of government in urban areas.
Calgary is an example of a Canadian unicity approach, where land is annexed into the city
at its edges as the city expands. Only one municipality is relevant for open-space planning
in the developed areas of both Calgary and Ottawa. At the other end of the spectrum,
Chicago open spaces are overseen by a complex array of municipalities, park districts, and
forest reserves, with over 260 units involved. In fact, Chicago has the largest number of
separate jurisdictions of any city on the continent involved in open-space planning. In
addition to the wide range of local municipalities involved in these metropolitan areas, the

City–Metro region	Population (2000) city	Population metro region	Land Area	Counties in metro region	Major water body(ies)
Vancouver	545,671	1,986,965 (CMA)	1,112 sq mi	N/A	Strait of Georgia Pacific Ocean
Ottawa	774,072	1,063,664 (CMA)	2,796 sq mi	N/A	Ottawa and Rideau Rivers
Milwaukee	596,974	1,500,741 (MSA)	1,460 sq mi (PMSA)	4 (MSA)	Lake Michigan
Toronto	2,481,494	4,682,897 (CMA)	2,279 sq mi	N/A	Lake Ontario
Calgary	878,866	951,395 (CMA)	1,963 sq mi	N/A	Bow River
Minneapolis–St. Paul	382,618–287,151	2,968,806 (MSA)	6,063 sq mi (MSA)	13 (MSA)	Mississippi River
Cleveland	478,403	2,148,143 (MSA)	2,707 sq mi (PMSA)	5 (MSA)	Lake Erie and Cuyahoga River
Denver	554,636	2,179,240 (MSA)	3,761 sq mi (PMSA)	10 (MSA)	Platte River
Portland	529,121	1,927,881 (MSA)	5,028 sq mi (PMSA)	7 (MSA)	Willamette River
Chicago	2,896,016	9,098,316 (MSA)	5,062 sq mi (PMSA)	14 (MSA)	Lake Michigan and Chicago River

CMA=Census Metropolitan Area (Canada)

CMSA=Consolidated Metropolitan Statistical Area (U.S.)

MSA=Metropolitan Statistical Area (U.S.)

PMSA=Primary Metropolitan Statistical Area

Table 2.1 Population, land area, local units of government, and major water bodies among ten case study cities.

U.S. cities span from three to thirteen counties, sometimes crossing functionally across
state lines, as in Chicago, the Twin Cities, and Portland.

Comparative Case Studies

Case studies are the heart of this book. By documenting and comparing different cities, we
can see the most successful approaches to protecting open space. Additionally, case studies reveal how open-space planning works in real-life contexts. Mark Francis defines the
case study, particularly applied to design and planning, as "a well-documented and systematic examination of the process, decision-making and outcomes of a project that is
undertaken for the purpose of informing future practice, policy, theory and/or education."[5] Case studies are particularly effective when "how" or "why" questions are posed.[6]

Open-space planning and implementation are highly complex. Case studies can reveal
themes, explain intricate dynamics, and answer questions about how and why things happen as they do in city regions. Case studies are also useful for turning anecdotes and gen-
eralizations into concrete documentation, bringing to light successful projects that can be
replicated elsewhere.[7] The case studies presented in this book are meant both to describe
and to evaluate how open-space connectivity is accomplished in selected places, thereby
drawing out generalizable themes.

Looking *across* these cases is as important as looking *within* them. According to Francis,
"it is often in the looking across multiple case studies with an eye toward synthesis and
patterns rather than the individual case study that common themes and principles can
be identified."[8]

Following established methodological techniques for qualitative research, a set of data
collection sources was used to develop in-depth cases.[9] These included the use of secondary sources such as historic documents, planning reports, and legal material. Research visits were made to each city, in order to conduct interviews, access historical resources, and
tour open-space corridors. Spatial data were also consulted, in order to understand the
location and pattern of both planned and implemented open-space landscapes.

Key informant interviews were an important source of evidence, revealing vital information on the main research questions. In selecting interviewees, referrals were sought
from people knowledgeable about open-space planning, both at national and international
levels and at specific case study sites. Between five and fifteen interviews were conducted
in each city. Interviewees were project managers working on open-space planning within
public agencies, citizens' groups, or nonprofit organizations. For the validity of findings,

multiple sources of evidence were used, a chain of evidence was established, and key informants were asked to review drafts of the case study reports. The identities of informants are not used in the book.

Research Questions and Hypotheses

This work is not simply about open-space planning; rather, it focuses on the *outcomes* of open-space planning. How and why are greenways and other connected open spaces implemented, beyond the planning stages? Figure 2.2 depicts a simplified image of how greenways come into being. The diagram emphasizes diverse actors and objectives. Specifically, it shows the relationships among objectives that motivate open-space networks, the organizations involved, and the subsequent purposes served. In other words, it asks not only the prototypical questions of how and why, but also the questions of who, where, and when. The questions are naturally interrelated. History (*when*) affects contemporary participants (*who*), which in turn impacts motives (*why*), programs (*how*), and spatial form (*where*). The outline of research questions, below, is reflected in the structure of each case study chapter in Part II.

Historic Precedent and Spatial Form

What is the history of city form that has affected the reality and potential of connected open space, particularly as that history impacts the way connectivity is now being addressed? For each city, the history of open-space planning is briefly explored and the physical change in connectivity is assessed over time. The tangible outcomes of open-space planning and implementation take shape in diverse ways, typically in bits and pieces through time and space. What is the physical outcome? Some cities focus their efforts on linear greenways, whereas others are retrofitting parkways, greenbelts, and other landscapes. One hypothesis is that where a connected open pattern is already nearly intact, due to enlightened planning many decades ago, it may be possible to retrofit that pattern to accomplish new needs, whether for water quality protection, nonmotorized transportation, or other benefits. For some places, ingrained landscape structures exist on which to design functional open-space corridors, such as along abandoned railroad lines, historic boulevards, or industrial waterfronts.

The ten cities of this study contain rich narratives about the evolution of urban form. All ten were incorporated in the mid- to late-nineteenth century, with Cleveland and Chicago, the older U.S. midwestern cities, at one end of a timeline and Vancouver and

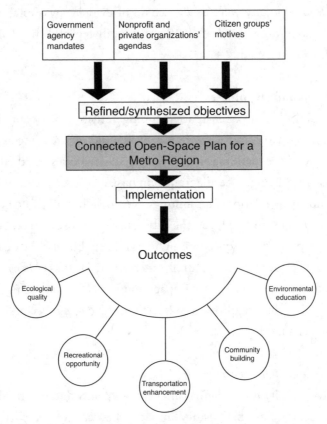

Fig. 2.2 Simplified model showing multiple agencies and organizations involved in greenway planning, working toward unified objectives, and producing a connected open-space plan. Once the plan is implemented, a variety of outcomes are usually expected.

Calgary, the newer western Canadian examples, at the other end. During an important period of progressive planning efforts early in the twentieth century, new park commissions were active in Milwaukee, Minneapolis, Cleveland, and Chicago. Particular individuals influenced many of these cities, directly shaping the urban framework and creating open-space patterns that are visible and useful today. Some of them were public officials whose impacts were profound—Charles Whitnall in Milwaukee, Theodore Wirth in Minneapolis, or Robert Speer in Denver. Others were consultants whose names are ubiquitous in the history of city planning and landscape architecture—the offices of Frederick Law Olmsted Sr., Horace Cleveland, Harland Bartholomew, and Daniel Burnham.

Institutional Structures and Collaborative Ties

Institutional structure refers to the relevant agencies, organizations, and citizens' groups and their system of interaction. Achieving an open-space network necessitates an effective institutional structure, including strong leadership and intergovernmental cooperation. These factors have been important in cities across North America. In structuring this study, I hypothesized that visionary thinking is critical, along with the leadership and cooperative structure to carry out the vision. The cities that have achieved open-space networks across metropolitan areas have been guided by strong resolve about the benefits of greenspace and its contribution toward community health.

Given the complex, large-scale nature of greenways, greenbelts, and other open-space systems, they are planned and implemented by a wide array of public and private organizations. Although grassroots effort has been the hallmark of the greenways movement, achieving connected open space beyond the individual corridor and at the scale of metropolitan regions takes both top-down and bottom-up work. Indeed, the multitude of government agencies, nonprofit groups, and corporations is sometimes staggering, particularly in cities as large as Toronto or Chicago. Table 2.2 summarizes the historic and contemporary open-space plans that are discussed in more detail in Chapters 3–7. The ten cities, incorporated between 1834 and 1893, have been strongly influenced by historic open-space plans, most from the early twentieth century. Early in the twenty-first, most of these cities are working from open-space plans completed in the 1990s by a range of public and private organizations.

How are these entities organized? Who are the participants and their agendas? What is the role of leadership and intergovernmental collaboration? To reveal these issues, key informants were asked a series of questions:

- What levels of government are involved in open-space planning?
- What level has primary responsibility? What level provides funding?
- Who has taken an important leadership role?
- What government agencies are involved?
- Has agency influence changed over time? Are agencies that traditionally did not consider open-space connectivity now integrating it in their agendas?
- What is the facilitative role of government?
- What is the nature of transjurisdictional cooperation?

Government agencies are critical facilitators in developing greenway networks. However,

City/Metro region	Incorporated	Influential historic open-space plans	Primary contemporary metropolitan open-space plan
Vancouver	1886	Harland Bartholomew Plan (1928)	Vancouver Greenways and Public Ways Plan (1992) and GVRD
Ottawa	1855	Holt Report (1915) Jacques Gréber's Plan for the National Capital (1950)	No unified open-space plan at the metropolitan scale
Milwaukee	1846	Charles Whitnall's Milwaukee County Master Plan (1923)	No unified open-space plan at the metropolitan scale
Toronto	1834	Toronto Harbour Commissioner's Plan (1912); first to recommend protecting waterfront land for public use	Regeneration—Royal Commission on the Future of the Toronto Waterfront (1991)
Calgary	1893	None that address large-scale open-space planning	Urban Parks Master Plan (1994)
Minneapolis–St. Paul	1867/1854	Horace W. S. Cleveland plan for the Grand Rounds (1883)	Department of Natural Resources Metropolitan Greenprint
Cleveland	1836	Cleveland Metroparks (1917)	No unified open-space plan at the metropolitan scale
Denver	1861	Mayor Robert W. Speer's open-space plans (1907–1918)	Northeast Greenway Corridor (2004)
Portland	1851	Frederick Law Olmsted's Parks Plan for City of Portland (1903)	Metro's Greenspaces Master Plan
Chicago	1837	Daniel Burnham's Plan of Chicago (1909), commissioned by the Commercial Club of Chicago	Northeastern Illinois Regional Greenways Plan: Northeastern Illinois Planning Commission and Openlands Project (1992)

Table 2.2 Dates of city incorporation, influential historic open-space plans, and contemporary metropolitan open-space plans for ten case study cities.

an important variable in greenway implementation is the level of government involvement and the nature of transjurisdictional cooperation. The primary local, regional, and state / provincial organizations involved in open-space planning for the ten cities are shown in Table 2.3. A complete list of participating agencies and organizations would be unwieldy; those shown here are the primary planners and implementers. All ten cities have active participation by local jurisdictions; however, the extent of regional government influence is less pronounced, with only three metropolitan areas—Vancouver, Minneapolis–St. Paul, and Portland—having influential regional governance. Other cities, like Milwaukee, have input from regional council-of-government organizations that have little or no regulatory power. Toronto's Conservation Authority has the ability to own and manage land, but lacks broader regulatory power. Likewise, the influence of state and provincial agencies is mixed, with the U.S. states being far more involved in open-space planning, funding, and acquisition than their provincial counterparts. Nonprofit organizations generally play more central roles in U.S. open-space planning than they do in Canadian cities. Part III synthesizes the structure of these institutional configurations, suggesting different models and predicting their usefulness to other cities.

The extent and nature of collaboration among public and private open-space planners, advocates, and citizens varies. In order to expand connected open-space networks effectively, it is critical to learn what partnerships and coalitions are operating. Increasingly, public–private partnerships are making these projects viable—boosting the enthusiasm, visibility, and funding that move efforts from *plan* to *land*. These partnerships vary in composition, scope, and longevity. In order to assess the roles of both public and private entities, interviewees were asked these questions:

- What private partners exist for this project?
- How do public and private groups collaborate?
- What is the role of open-space advocates, neighborhood groups, and citizens?
- Are nonprofit environmental organizations an important aspect of the project's success? In what way?

Drivers of Connectivity: Motives, Intents, and Goals
In many metropolitan areas, the open-space corridor concept is stretched tight between two main drivers—ecological quality and social amenity. In plan after plan, a list of benefits and objectives is laid out, from environmental education to water quality to human health. Cities are

City/Metro region	Local jurisdictions	Regional government	State/provincial or federal agencies
Vancouver	City of Vancouver and 20 other local municipalities	Greater Vancouver Regional District	N/A
Ottawa	City of Ottawa (functions as a regional government due to its size and mix of land uses)	N/A	National Capital Commission
Milwaukee	Milwaukee County and other surrounding municipalities and counties	Southeast Wisconsin Regional Planning Commission	State of Wisconsin Department of Natural Resources
Toronto	City of Toronto (functions as a regional government due to its size and mix of land uses)	Toronto and Region Conver- Conservation Authority	Province of Ontario, Waterfront Regeneration Trust (quasi-public organization)
Calgary	City of Calgary	N/A	Province of Alberta
Minneapolis– St. Paul	City of Minneapolis, City of St. Paul, and other counties and cities	Metro Council	Minnesota Department of Natural Resources
Cleveland	City of Cleveland and Surrounding jurisdictions, Cleveland Metroparks Cuyahoga County Planning		

City/Metro region	Local jurisdictions	Regional government	State/provincial or federal agencies
Denver	City of Denver and surrounding local cities and counties	Denver Regional Council of Governments	State of Colorado
Portland	City of Portland and surrounding municipalities and counties in Oregon and Washington	Metro	N/A
Chicago	City of Chicago dozens of other cities and counties, County Forest Preserves, and Park Districts	Chicago Area Transportation Study, Northeastern Illinois Planning Commission	Illinois Department of Natural Resources

Table 2.3 Primary agencies and organizations directly involved in connected open-space planning across ten case study regions. This table does include non-profit organizations, which are prominent open-space advocates and leaders in many metropolitan areas.

just now sorting out the complexity of creating linkages on the physical landscape and at the same time satisfying these multiple (and often competing) demands. This is a complex endeavor.

What motives are really moving agencies and organizations to seek connectivity across the urban landscape? Is it environmental integrity or some other social, political, or economic goal? In fact, it is nearly always a combination. And sometimes one objective, like recreation, needs to be prominent in order to gain widespread support for tackling another issue, such as environmental health. So, given that the motives are compound, how are the interacting, and sometimes competing, motivations over open-space connectivity being worked out in contemporary projects? To find the answers, we asked interviewees the following questions:

- What are the main objectives driving the open-space connectivity efforts?
- What is the big vision and how was it formulated?
- Have objectives changed over time?

- How are competing goals or objectives reconciled?
- What are the issues that most constrain innovation and creativity?
- Is the green infrastructure concept being used as an ultimate objective?

Complex city regions often have objectives distinct among the different scales of planning. Local jurisdictions seek to serve residents' requirements for housing, education, recreation, and other needs. This differs somewhat from regional entities, which address large landscape-level problems—environment, transportation, and economic development. Therefore, it is likely that the open-space planning and implementation being accomplished at different scales will vary and that objectives will mismatch, if not collide. A follow-on question then: How are these varying motivations leading toward or away from coordinated efforts in connected open space?

Another prediction is that the goals for open-space projects in general, and connected ones in particular, are changing. These projects, in order to be funded, supported, and implemented, often need to multitask. Whereas in the past, recreation or transportation could be a dominant intention for these projects, recent efforts are much more complicated. For instance, nonmotorized transportation was the heart of funding for greenway projects, largely through federal transportation funding, in the United States throughout the 1990s. To move toward green infrastructure planning, which many cities are attempting to do, the canvas will need to widen to incorporate issues of public health, ecological quality, and neighborhood revitalization.

Chapters 3 through 7 explicate five interrelated functional themes for connected open space: ecology, recreation, transportation, community, and green infrastructure. It is important to realize that they are not mutually exclusive, and the Part II chapters explore the interactions. Each chapter is organized around one main approach (or suite of functions) of open-space planning. For each city, however, the objectives that drive open-space programs are always more complicated, and, as shown in Chapter 1, motives are nested. Indeed, this complexity is explored in each chapter using real places and their actual opportunities and constraints.

These chapters are ordered to create a structural design that builds from the broad to the more specific and back again. In other words, ecology is used in Chapter 3 as a foundation for all other open-space connectivity goals. Following that, Chapters 4 through 6 explore specific cultural goals that may be overlaid onto an ecological framework. Then Chapter 7 puts these diverse objectives back together within the scaffold of green infrastructure, an emerging paradigm for thinking about urban form, sustainability, and connectivity.

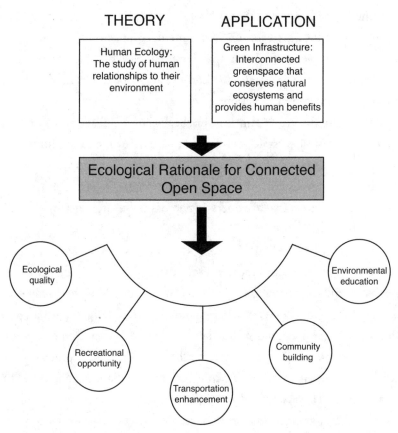

THEORY

APPLICATION

Human Ecology:
The study of human
relationships to their
environment

Green Infrastructure:
Interconnected
greenspace that
conserves natural
ecosystems and
provides human benefits

Ecological Rationale for Connected
Open Space

Ecological
quality

Environmental
education

Recreational
opportunity

Community
building

Transportation
enhancement

Fig. 2.3 A model of theory and application in connected open-space planning using ecology as a foundational goal.

ECOLOGY: HOME

Ecology is used as an umbrella context under which all other open-space motivations are clustered, as illustrated in Figure 2.3. The subtitle "home" implies the importance of human ecology and urban habitat as a wellspring from which to build networks of open land. Across the continent, cities are striving to merge issues of sustainability, biodiversity, and environmental health into many aspects of civic enterprise. Instead of thinking that people are secondary in an ecology-first agenda, human ecology shows us that people are part of ecology and that environmental quality is a prerequisite to all other human endeavors.

Chapter 3 highlights cities where an ecological agenda is crucial in connected open-space planning. Chicago and Toronto set the foundation for the other case study chapters. Their open-space planning, implementation, use, and impacts are complex and vast. Both cities have efforts devoted to watershed protection, urban greening, and protected corridors across multiple jurisdictions. However, at the heart of much of the open-space work being done in both city regions is a profound goal of environmental protection and enhancement. Both cities have developed a diverse set of objectives for open space, and these are built on a foundation of environmental goals. Chicago and Toronto are at the forefront of ecological open-space planning for their respective nations.

These cities are also the most daunting; the sheer size of Chicago and Toronto prevents detailed examination of open-space networks. It would be an overwhelming task to catalog all of the organizations and initiatives under way regarding connected open space. Rather, this chapter explores the large multijurisdictional open-space initiatives, and the collaborations among them, that are operating across these large metropolises.

RECREATION: WELL-BEING

Recreation has long been one leg of the traditional three-legged stool of greenway objectives (with conservation and transportation). Concerns for human well-being, for peoples' leisure-time places, have been important since park planners began designing urban parks in the nineteenth century. Over the past decades, there has been a dramatic renewal in the health-enhancing aspects of recreation activity and the shape of places to accommodate it. It is fitting that we have come full circle on the connection of spatial design and health. One of Frederick Law Olmsted and Calvert Vaux's primary goals in designing their famous nineteenth-century urban parks was the health of city-dwellers. Over nearly four decades of design work, they addressed health, safety, and aesthetics in a range of open-space contexts.

More than a century later, environmental conditions for most of North America's city-dwellers are vastly better than in Olmsted's time. Even though dramatic basic improvements have obviously been made for most city inhabitants, we now are beginning to realize the more subtle effects of an automobile-dependent life. A new renaissance is under way, where the connection of spatial design and human health is being explored in housing, the workplace, and, indeed, all facets of the design of human settlements. An important part of this endeavor is getting people outdoors to walk, work, play, and move through open space.

In Chapter 4, Ottawa and Milwaukee are used as prototypes for cities where recreation is, or has been, a primary driver behind greenway planning. Planners who valued the recreational benefits of well-connected, environmentally healthy landscapes structured both cities earlier in the twentieth century. How has this motive stood up in recent decades, and how can it be overhauled to incorporate the myriad of other benefits that connected open space is expected to provide today? These cities show that historic frameworks for connected open space, designed over a half century ago for humanistic goals, have important elements to contribute to modern open-space networks. They also show that the sometimes conflicting, sometimes compatible relationship between recreation and ecology is an unsettled one in open-space planning.

TRANSPORTATION: MOVEMENT

Connected open space in metropolitan areas is partly triggered by the need for people to be on the move, and is also influenced by new knowledge about healthy lifestyles. Alternative transportation, primarily cycling, has been a primary driver of networked open-space systems.

It is estimated that about 80 percent of urban open space is in the form of streets, so the transportation connection is an important one for open-space planning. The potential for transportation routes to satisfy other open-space needs is often overlooked. According to Helen Woolley, "the fact that streets impinge upon urban life as routes, locations for services, frontages to both residential and business properties and often are the boundary between public and private life is often ignored by professionals, politicians and decision makers."[10] And when transportation is the focus—for example, in cycling routes—the implementation of long-distance greenways and parkways has entailed pragmatic getting-from-here-to-there goals, rather than incorporating any sense of environmental soundness. Bike trails and bikeways abound in our urban settings. Do they qualify as connected open space? Do they provide the other benefits that accrue to green corridors designed for multiple purposes?

In many cases, the answer is yes. The provision of corridors for walking and cycling reduces the use of automobiles, having direct environmental benefits aside from the important health effects. In some cases bikeways are routed in ways that provide a range of other open-space amenities. However, the transportation motive probably conflicts with environmental goals more than any other pairing.

In Chapter 5, Calgary and Denver, cities situated within wide-open spaces and covering great land areas, are used to illustrate how nonmotorized transportation is achieved through greenway planning and implementation. Both cities are excellent models for successfully integrating pathways and trails into the urban fabric even though their environments are often not green and their climates are harsh. They differ in institutional structure, urban history, and open-space leadership, but the corridor outcomes in both cities have a similarly high level of support, use, and popularity.

COMMUNITY: NEIGHBORHOOD AND SOCIETY

A basic tenet of human ecology is the concept of community. Open spaces in built envi-ronments reflect their community settings through design, management, location, and use. Landscape architects and other designers have shown that a sense of community can be fostered through manipulating spatial environments. The neighborhood community garden is an often-used example, as are the promenades, plazas, and other gathering areas that bring people together and encourage interaction. Community gardens speak volumes about neighborhood pride. They provide one context where the public realm provides space for social interaction to be played out.

Open spaces are increasingly used as community-building tools. For some cities, the benefits of neighborhood revitalization, citizen empowerment, and community health are foremost in thoughts about landscape connectivity. Open-space connections can be empowering neighborhood elements, as depicted in Vancouver's neighborhood greenway program. In Chapter 6, Vancouver and Portland exemplify efforts at building neighbor-hood identity, illustrating city history, and mobilizing citizens' efforts through greenway design and implementation.

GREEN INFRASTRUCTURE: CITY FUNCTION AND THE SHAPE OF GROWTH

Cleveland and the twin cities of Minneapolis and St. Paul are used in Chapter 7 for exploring comprehensive objectives that move open-space planning toward green infra-structure objectives. Cleveland is used as a potential test site for green infrastructure development, and the Twin Cities as a metropolitan region that is currently implement-ing these concepts.

Chapter 7 depicts the evolution of greenway planning toward green infrastructure planning, a shift that has its base in the merging of human well-being and environmen-tal goals. While human ecology and landscape ecology show that this merger is logical and beneficial, it has only recently been assembled holistically in the green infrastructure idea. "It has only been in the last ten years that an urban focus for environmental con-cerns has emerged around 'people-centered' environmental issues such as health, environ-mental quality and consumer behavior issues such as energy and water and household level recycling. Now for the first time, the human built environment is the primary focus of attention. For the first time, responsibility for environmental issues falls within the professional realm of urban designers."[11]

On the other hand, the ideas of green infrastructure are not totally new. But they have been reframed to help us think about the gray and the green surfaces, the mundane underground pipes, and the aboveground roads and utilities in a new way. Anne Spirn showed this nearly twenty years ago: "The pathways along which energy and materials flow through the urban ecosystem are also the routes along which pollutants disseminate and where energy is stored and expended . . . Many American cities, however, share two major problems: the deterioration of urban infrastructure, including water supply and sewage treatment systems, and the decline of inner city neighborhoods. A comprehensive view of urban nature could contribute to the restoration of both."[12] As Mark Benedict and Ed McMahon have argued, communities need to upgrade and expand their network of open spaces, woodlands, and other natural areas just as they do their roads, sewers, and utilities.[13] But beyond that, they need to integrate the two realms. The Twin Cities and Cleveland help depict how green and gray networks might be pursued not only at the same time, and with the same urgency, but also in the same place.

Conclusion

The five case study chapters in Part II build a platform for conclusions about open-space connectivity. Part III draws out the lessons learned from examining these ten cities across the continent, considering their different histories, social fabrics, and geographies. It shows how some contemporary open-space corridors are living artifacts of early-twentieth-century urban design and planning.

In addition, the case studies provide evidence for a typology of institutional structures for connected open-space implementation, showing how different levels of government participate. Part III deals centrally with issues of leadership and vision, not only by individuals but by organizations and agencies. Another thread running through the case studies weaves together facets of collaboration, coordination, and citizen involvement. Part II provides the basis for diagramming and diagnosing, in Part III, the way governmental and nongovernmental entities interact in open-space programs, and how neighborhood and citizens' groups affect implementation.

Finally, Part III pulls together the lessons learned about motives and outcomes. The objectives for developing and protecting open-space corridors change over time. While the three-legged stool of recreation, transportation, and conservation has supported greenway efforts across the continent, it is rare that each leg is equally weighted. Furthermore, modern open-space corridors are expected to provide many other benefits—from environmental education to neighborhood enhancement to water quality protection. The new frontier lies in multiobjective projects. Natural features protection and green infrastructure planning will, like the restoration of neighborhoods and communities, be central to successful implementation strategies.

Part 2

Connectivity and Human Ecological Planning

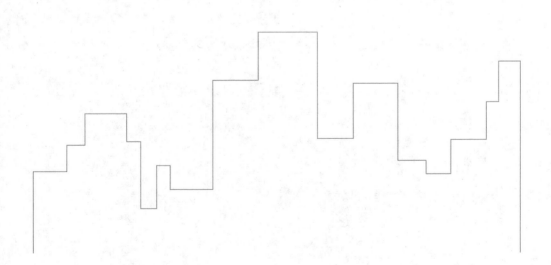

3

Ecology—Home:
Toronto and Chicago

Ecological design . . . is the careful meshing of human purposes
with the larger patterns and flows of the natural world and the
study of those patterns and flows to inform human actions.

—*David Orr*[1]

Ecological function should be the foundation for all other objectives in connected open-space planning, where human ecology is considered in tandem with landscape ecology. This assertion is not hard to justify, based on what we know about ecology—
both from the perspective of the damage that has been done by human development and
from the perspective of the restoration efforts succeeding on many fronts. Furthermore,
an optimistic outlook would hold that other objectives often coexist with environmental
soundness. On the other hand, the meshing of environmental goals with recreation, transportation, and other human needs is an unsettled situation at best. Chicago and Toronto
illustrate this complexity. They help show how ecological health is being used as a motivator for connectivity and how it interacts with other goals. And they depict the ways that
organizations and agencies work in partnership for environmental objectives.

Toronto and Chicago: Historic and Geographic Context

Toronto and Chicago have legendary histories and reputations as great cities on the Great Lakes. In their separate ways, they are iconic cities on the continent, offering all of the cultural, commercial, educational, and business opportunities imaginable. As major urban powerhouses for their respective nations, both cities are built on layers of cultural ideas, immigrant settlement, raw natural resources, and economic power. Over the past eight years, the United Nations has placed Canada as number one on its Human Development Index. The index combines cost of living, adult literacy, job opportunities, life expectancy, and school enrollment. And Toronto is one of Canada's most livable cities, where the cost of living is much lower than in American cities, education standards are high, and crime rates are low. Chicago, by comparison, has one of the highest costs of living among American cities. It has been characterized as a sophisticated global city—"the city that works" is working across the globe, both in its worldwide influence and in its international citizenry. It is also a gritty, working-class city. And the Chicago region contains one of the most ethnically diverse populations in the United States, with over a hundred ethnic backgrounds found in the city region. Their distinctive cultures are evident in Chicago's unique neighborhoods and cultural landscapes.

Toronto: Dramatic Natural Features Frame Canada's Largest City

Toronto's urbanization had its beginnings in the eighteenth century, with tiny settlements along waterways and lakes. In about two hundred years the settlements along Lake Ontario have grown to be the largest urban area in Canada, now home to 2.5 million people. The population growth is one of the fastest in North America, expanding at nearly 100,000 people per year. Population is expected to be 6.8 million by 2021. Toronto was, for many decades, a model of compact development served by rail transit. That has changed dramatically, with scattered development now served by highways. The city is one of the largest urban agglomerations on the continent, when contiguous areas of New York State are included. The Greater Toronto Area (GTA) includes the City of Toronto, four regional governments, and thirty-one other municipalities (Figure 3.1).

The embracing arms of the Oak Ridges Moraine, the Niagara Escarpment, and the Lake Ontario shoreline frame the Toronto region of 250 square kilometers. Many of the comprehensive plans and reports about the future of Toronto's physical landscape, especially in the last twenty years, are consistent in proposals for an ecosystem approach to planning the Greater Toronto Area. They all voice concern for the Oak Ridges Moraine, Niagara

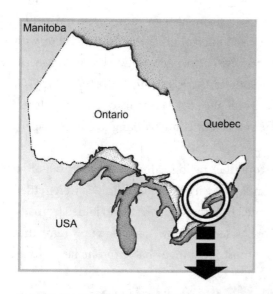

TORONTO
ONTARIO

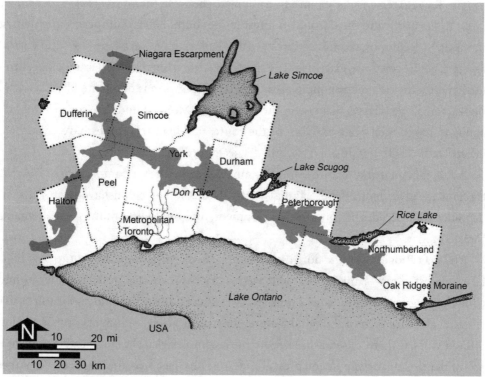

Fig. 3.1 The metropolitan Toronto region.

Escarpment, river valleys, and Lake Ontario waterfront as the region's primary natural landscapes. Furthermore, the plans recommend an interconnected landscape system, with access to regional trails, and the need for cooperative partnerships to implement long-term greenspace conservation.[2] Given these rich resources, there is no single agency in the GTA responsible for providing land-use planning guidance or overseeing open-space development. Rather, a number of organizations and activities are working to connect open-space land across the municipalities.

The physical form of the Toronto metropolitan region is linear, the merging of an amalgamation of settlements along Lake Ontario. A string of communities were settled along the north shore of Lake Ontario, separated by farms and forests and joined by roads, railways, and lake shipping routes. Those forests, farms, and wetlands are now remnants; the communities have merged to become almost indistinguishable in one large urban metropolis linked by superhighways.

The Toronto region falls within a transition area between the Great Lakes–St. Lawrence forest to the north and the Carolinian forest to the south. Before European settlement, it was mostly deciduous and mixed forest, with small wetland tracts, meadow and coastal habitats. Forest cover was extensive. The rivers that flow from these larger upland features further structure the metropolitan area. The Toronto region is dominated by a series of well-defined river valleys that rise in the Oak Ridges Moraine and flow south across till plains to Lake Ontario. Over much of the route, the main tributaries have cut deeply incised valleys with floodplains that broaden as the streams flow south.

All of these natural features, and the nine watersheds that comprise the GTA, are threatened. Over half of the original wetlands in the bioregion have been filled or degraded over decades of Toronto's development. And only a fifth of the region remains forested today.

The Oak Ridges Moraine north of Toronto is a 100-mile-long ridge of rolling hills, lakes, and streams—running east and west—that stores water in deep underground aquifers. It varies in width from 2 miles to 14 miles and is the headwaters for thirty-five rivers. A significant environmental feature, formed by glacial sediments during the last million years, it is one of Ontario's largest, most complex glacial remnants. Portions of it are under serious development pressure, despite the fact that the moraine recharges groundwater and contains some of the GTA's most important wetlands and forests.

To the west of Toronto, the Niagara Escarpment is a natural ridge running along southern Ontario for about 450 miles, north and south, from the Bruce Peninsula to Niagara Falls. The escarpment is a ridge of gently tipped rock with a long gradual slope on one side and steep cliff on the other. The Escarpment was recognized as a World Biosphere Reserve by the United Nations in 1990, due to its unique natural features. It is the most prominent topographical feature of the southern part of Ontario, and is the headwaters of several rivers and an important area for groundwater recharge. Largely forested, the corridor has a rich agricultural heritage, with vineyards, orchards, and farming. A number of spectacular waterfalls include Niagara Falls at the escarpment's southern end, where Frederick Law Olmsted Sr. was instrumental in establishing the international Niagara Park.

The Lake Ontario shore is the other major natural feature in the GTA. The City of Toronto, with 29 miles of lakefront, has been separated from the lake for all but industrial uses for over a century. In the 1850s the first developments along the shoreline began cutting residents off from the lake. Then railroad and industrial uses expanded through the early part of the twentieth century. The central waterfront was turned over almost completely to port, transportation, and industrial land uses, built on land created by fill (Figure 3.2). The Toronto Harbour Commissioner's Plan of 1912 was the first to recommend protecting waterfront land for public use. But not until 1967 was a comprehensive plan developed for public waterfront parks. Meanwhile, the Gardiner Expressway, an elevated highway that parallels the waterfront, completed the separating wedge.

Fig. 3.2 City of Toronto, viewing westward along Lake Ontario waterfront. The Docklands are visible in the foreground. (Photo courtesy of Toronto Economic Development Corporation.)

Chicago: Defending Shoreline, Rivers, and Prairies from Explosive Growth

Chicago adopted the motto "Urbs in Horto" (City in a Garden) on its City Seal in 1833. Historically, Chicago grew both up and out, expanding into existing greenspaces. As it did in many cities, the turn of the twentieth century brought new ideas about the relationships between city, countryside, and nature. Planners began thinking of ways to bring the country to the city, in the form of parks, to ameliorate the effects of an increasingly industrial and commercial city.[3]

Chicago's open spaces are remnants of that legacy, led by the legendary architect and city designer Daniel H. Burnham. His 1909 Plan for Chicago, commissioned by the Commercial Club of Chicago, is considered one of the most famous city plans of the twentieth century. Chicago's World's Columbian Exposition in 1893 set the stage for the 1909 plan. Burnham's often-repeated advice to "make no little plans" extended to protection of open-space land. Among its many recommendations, the Burnham plan focused on the shore of Lake Michigan (Figure 3.3) and a large network of natural inland landscapes preserved in public parkland. Subsequently, the political will and economic resources were garnered for setting aside greenspace along Lake Michigan as well as the inland forest pre-

Fig. 3.3 Chicago's Lake Michigan waterfront, viewing northward, showing Grant Park along the lakeshore. In contrast to Toronto, much of the lakeshore is in public, open-space use. (Photo by Alex McLean.)

serves of Greater Chicago. The 18-mile Lakefront Path along Lake Michigan and 70-acre Grant Park are the crown jewels of that legacy. Since then, thousands of acres of open space have been purchased and protected in the Chicago region. Today, about 200,000 acres are formally protected as conservation land, although adjacent development and other pressures have compromised the ecological quality of much of it.[4]

The Chicago region is a six-county area surrounding the City of Chicago, which lies within Cook County. The larger metropolitan area, which includes parts of northwestern Indiana and southeastern Wisconsin (Figure 3.4), covers 3,800 square miles, 265 different municipalities, and 1,200 separate tax districts. The City on the Lake is formed from prairie land that, according to Chicago Wilderness, is one of the best concentrations of prairie and oak woodlands existing anywhere. And the quality, although deteriorating, is surprising. An inventory of natural features conducted by the state of Illinois in 1978 showed that only 0.07 percent of Illinois land was in a healthy state, but that 25 percent of those lands were in the Chicago metropolitan region. In addition to the Lake Michigan waterfront running north–south at the eastern edge of the region, a number of rivers— the Fox, DesPlaines, DuPage, Little Calumet, Chicago, and Kankakee—carve through the prairie and savanna landscape.

Like the rivers in Toronto, and in many other North American cities, Chicago's rivers are important ecological and cultural resources. They represent two centuries of settlement, commerce, and industry. Sister rivers, the Chicago and Calumet, have particularly important histories. They were joined together by canals to form an inland network of waterways. The Illinois and Michigan (I&M) Canal was completed in 1848, creating the first navigable waterway from the Great Lakes to the Mississippi. The Chicago Sanitary and Ship Canal replaced it in 1900 and reversed the flow of water away from Lake Michigan. A 100-mile-long corridor of industrial, farming, and recreational landscapes is found along the canals. Congress designated this region the Illinois and Michigan Canal National Heritage Corridor in 1984, managed as a "partnership park" of the National Park Service.

Together, Chicago's rivers and canals are important ecological and recreational assets, with great numbers of birds, fish, and other species inhabiting them. Layers of history are visible along these corridors. The buildings, canal remnants, and bridges tell the tales of settlement, shipping, and industry over the decades. Preserving the historic structures, and reusing them in new ways, has helped vivify a sense of place over time.[5]

The sources of environmental concern for the Chicago region's natural landscape have been documented: they boil down to degradation and development.[6] The land that is already protected is degrading in quality due to subtle and overt management decisions

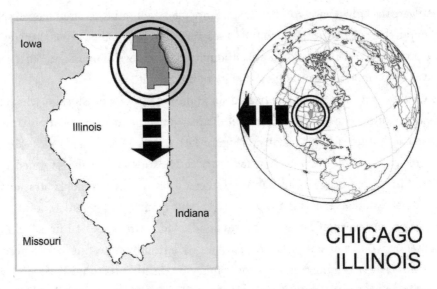

CHICAGO
ILLINOIS

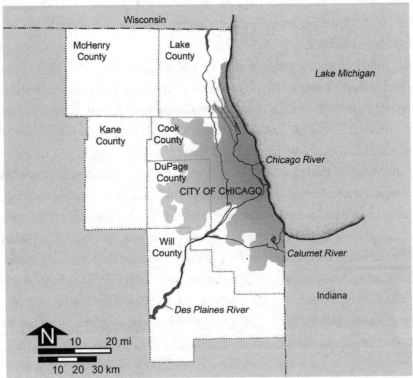

Fig. 3.4 The six-county Chicago region, where gray tone depicts urbanized area.

and use patterns, as well as influences from neighboring sites. And development is rampant on lands surrounding many protected landscapes. Chicago has become one of the worst U.S. metropolitan regions for sprawling, low-density development and uncoordinated land use. The city is growing outward, fanning from the central city at a rate that is almost unprecedented in American urban history. From 1970 to 1990, the Chicago metropolitan area grew only 4 percent in population, but land used for housing and commercial development increased 46 percent and 74 percent, respectively. Meanwhile, more than two thousand manufacturing sites lie vacant.[7] Population in the outer counties of the Chicago region is projected to increase 70–100 percent by 2020; the corresponding potential increase in developed land is overwhelming. Chicago is built on a fertile prairie. According to the American Farmland Trust, the region has lost 15 percent of its farmland just in the past decade. This loss represents some of the most threatened agricultural land in the country.

Collaboration for Planning Ecological Open-Space Networks

Ecological goals are woven into a matrix of collaborative work at many levels in Toronto and Chicago. For Toronto, no one map expresses the vision of connectivity across the metropolitan landscape, as does the greenways and water trails map for Chicago. However, well-known leaders and innovative organizations in both cities have seized on the opportunity to build environmental soundness into city planning. The work of the Royal Commission on the Future of the Toronto Waterfront and Chicago Wilderness helped their respective cities turn a corner on awareness, action, and hope about urban ecology and the need for ecosystem-based planning for connectivity and other goals. Also in both places, the importance of working across multiple scales has been essential to the success of regionwide efforts. The organizations and agencies engaged in open-space planning are configured in very different ways for Chicago and Toronto, but collaboration is the unifying theme.

Toronto: Ecosystem-Based Planning Starting at the Waterfront

The open-space story for the Greater Toronto Area has many dimensions and layers, with a strong basis in ecological purpose. Land-use planning in Canada is a provincial responsibility. The province creates broad policy frameworks that the municipalities use to implement on-the-ground decisions through their Official Plans. A new City of Toronto was amalgamated from seven municipalities on January 1, 1998. Overlaying it, and the five jurisdictions around it, the Toronto and Region Conservation Authority has authority over the nine watersheds that comprise the GTA. And at a more detailed level, new activities on the City of Toronto's Central Waterfront distill and intensify efforts for connection and environmental improvement.

Local municipalities are the main implementers of open-space protection and enhancement. The planning environment in the Toronto region is generally stronger and more progressive than in most U.S. cities, historically supporting high-density development, mass transit, public housing, and transit-oriented development.[8] The City of Toronto, in its new Official Plan, focuses specifically on connectivity through the linkage of parks and open spaces into a city network. The City of Toronto has over fifteen hundred named parks on almost 20,000 acres. Of that, an estimated 72 percent are considered natural heritage lands, including valleys, ravines, woodlots, and waterfront land. More than 12 percent of the total urban area is comprised of municipal parks and Conservation Authority lands.[9] According to Suzanne Barrett, the city has made major changes in its planning philosophy and practice over the 1980s and 1990s, including campaigns for beautiful places, sustainable transportation, affordable housing, and a dynamic downtown.[10] Greenways have become a popular movement at the local level in Toronto, where a significant demand has been established for trails and other connected open space. The Royal Commission on the Future of the Toronto Waterfront stimulated many of these activities.

PLANNING THE FUTURE OF THE TORONTO WATERFRONT

The Royal Commission on the Future of the Toronto Waterfront conducted a study in the late 1980s and early 1990s that proposed developing greenways within a 10,360 square kilometer area known as the Greater Toronto Bioregion.[11] Its nine principles for the waterfront—clean, green, accessible, connected, open, useable, diverse, affordable, and attractive—have been used time and again in the intervening years. Former mayor David Crombie, later a federal politician, was the visionary leader behind the Toronto waterfront focus and was extremely influential in the success of this project.

The Royal Commission, convened by the Canadian government in 1988, introduced urban ecology concepts as well as the ecosystem approach to planning. According to Ray Tomalty and colleagues, when the commission published its interim report *Watershed* in 1990, it marked a new stage in the history of ecosystem planning in Canada.[12] Until the 1990s, ecosystem planning was little known outside academic circles. Unlike sustainable development, the ecosystem management concept was not used to guide development. "The strength of Crombie's report was that it seemed to gather up all the positive ideas for change under one relatively simple concept—the ecosystem approach—and then deliver it to a receptive public."[13] In the commission's publication *Regeneration*, it outlined the following holistic characteristics of an ecosystem approach, which proved to be the catalyst for many new open-space approaches:

- Includes the whole system, not just parts of it
- Focuses on the interrelationships among the elements
- Understands that humans are part of nature, not separate from it
- Recognizes the dynamic nature of the ecosystem—a moving picture rather than a still photograph
- Incorporates the concepts of carrying capacity, resilience, and sustainability—suggesting that there are limits to human activity
- Uses a broad definition of the environments—natural, physical, economic, social, and cultural
- Encompasses both urban and rural activities
- Is based on natural geographic units such as watersheds—rather than political boundaries
- Embraces all levels of activity—local, regional, national, and international
- Emphasizes the importance of extant species other than humans and of generations other than our own
- Is based on an ethic in which progress is measured by the quality, well-being, integrity, and dignity it accords natural, social, and economic systems

Strong leadership was critical in Toronto. As commissioner for the Royal Commission, Crombie provided the leadership and enthusiasm that sparked the entire project, especially its emphasis on ecosystems and their accessibility. An emphasis on environmental quality led to the greenways theme. According to the commission, a green strategy was visualized for the entire watershed, physically linking the waterfront to the river valleys, which, in turn, would link to preserved headwater areas. A continuous trail system would guarantee public access throughout.[14]

The Toronto greenway concept was articulated in *Regeneration*. It proposed a two-tiered system with arterial greenways that establish an interconnected framework across the region and local connectors within each community (Figure 3.5). It proposed an interregional greenway system totaling 560 miles, based on watersheds. The Waterfront Trail proposed in *Regeneration* was intended to link 34 major parks, 74 small waterfront parks and promenades, 40 significant natural habitats, and 25 marinas. Linkage patches include wetlands, woodlots, Environmentally Sensitive Areas, and Areas of Natural and Scientific Interest.

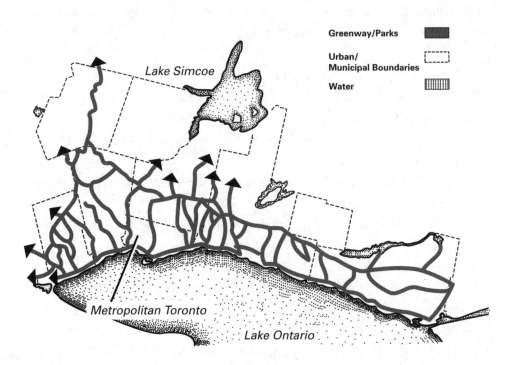

Fig. 3.5 Connected greenway plan promoted by the Royal Commission on the Future of Toronto Waterfront. (Adapted from Royal Commission on the Future of the Toronto Waterfront, *Regeneration*, 1992.)

Five working groups fed information and recommendations into the process of designing *Regeneration*: access and movement; housing and neighborhoods; parks, pleasures, and public amenities; environment and health; and jobs, opportunities, and economic growth. For instance, the access and movement group recommended a transportation framework based on nine network elements regarding movement at and to the waterfront, including a network of trails and walkways, a bicycle network, and other transportation connections. One group, looking at several of Canada's greenway projects, saw the Toronto plan as the most ambitious because it moved from an urban design approach to ecologically based planning.[15]

CONNECTING THE WATERFRONT

The Waterfront Regeneration Trust (WRT) is one of the main coordinating mechanisms for open-space planning in the GTA. WRT replaced the Royal Commission on the Future of the Toronto Waterfront in 1992 and was established to implement the commission's findings. Its goal is simple and powerful: "Our goal is to make sure people can get to the

3.1 Oak Ridges Moraine Protection

The Oak Ridges Moraine is one of the few remaining large greenspace corridors in Ontario, despite more than 4 million people living around and within it. Covering 190,000 hectares, it is still over 30 percent forested, containing a unique kettle and knob topography (Figure 3.6). Its exceptional combination of environmental, geological, and hydrological systems makes the moraine a vital ecosystem for southern Ontario. It is one of the most important landscapes for providing connected open space in the Greater Toronto Area. A prominent geological landform, the Oak Ridges Moraine extends nearly 100 miles east from the Niagara Escarpment to the Trent River. More than 100,000 people reside within the moraine, and it provides drinking water to another quarter million. Moraine land is 90 percent privately owned, and the eastern part is particularly vulnerable to development pressure.

Fig. 3.6 Aerial view of the Oak Ridges Moraine, showing encroaching residential development. Note: the aerial photograph 'flattens' much of the true topography of this region. (Photo by Lou T. Wise.)

Even before the Royal Commission's reports advocating ecosystem approaches, an influential group called Save the Oak Ridges Moraine (STORM) Coalition was advocating an ecosystem framework for protecting the moraine landscapes. STORM and other groups appealed to the commission during its work, arguing that the waterfront could be rehabilitated only if the Oak Ridges Moraine was protected, given that the moraine serves as the region's headwaters.[1]

Citizen action in the late 1980s motivated Ontario's government to name the moraine a provincially designated significant area in 1990. Subsequently, a provincial planning study was completed, supported by many private interests. Although the provincial government did not adopt this plan, a package of strategies, including legislation, regulation, and institutional creation, was put into place in the early twenty-first century. In 2000, more than 450 scientists signed a statement calling for protection of the moraine. The Oak Ridges Moraine Protection Act was passed in 2001, creating a six-month moratorium on development. The Oak Ridges Moraine Conservation Act was passed in the same year, and the Oak Ridges Moraine Conservation Plan was released in 2002. It is an ecosystem-based plan that creates urban boundaries around Settlement Areas (8 percent of the moraine), protects Natural Core Areas (38 percent) and Natural Linkage Areas (24 percent), and sets aside agricultural land in Countryside Areas (30 percent). A number of public and private groups, in addition to STORM, pursue conservation, recreation, and funding goals. These include the Oak Ridges Trail Association and Oak Ridges Moraine Land Trust. In addition, the Oak Ridges Moraine Foundation funds public education, research, monitoring, and the moraine-wide recreational trail. The province initially allocated $15 million to the foundation.

Open-space connectivity as a driver for landscape form is an important part of the moraine plan. "The Ontario Government's vision for the Oak Ridges Moraine is that of a continuous band of green rolling hills that provides form and structure to south-central Ontario, while protecting the ecological and hydrological features and functions that support the health and well-being of the region's residents and ecosystems."[2] In addition to ecological goals, one objective is to provide a continuous recreational trail through the moraine. The purpose of the Natural Linkage Areas is to provide a network of corridors to connect the Natural Core Areas in forested areas, wetlands, and along river valleys.

These areas must be a minimum of 2 kilometers wide, and permitted uses include existing single residences and agricultural uses, low-impact recreation, lands for flood and erosion control, areas managed for fish and wildlife management, and accessory uses such as bed-and-breakfasts or home businesses.

The Oak Ridges Moraine Plan is similar to the Niagara Escarpment Plan, originally approved in 1985 and updated several times since. The Niagara Escarpment Commission maintains the escarpment land as a continuous natural environment, limiting development of private lands. It includes a system of more than a hundred public parks. The Bruce Trail, which was created by a private association, links many of them. The land-use controls along the Niagara Escarpment are noteworthy, with strong development controls that would probably not be politically feasible today.

Like the Niagara Escarpment Plan, the moraine plan includes the use of specific land-use designations and permitted uses. Differing from the Niagara Plan, which established a separate provincial agency and planning system, the moraine plan is implemented by municipalities in a system whereby the local units' official plans must eventually conform to the provincial plan. This new management approach is notable for a number of reasons.[3] It provides the following:

- Legislation that is area-specific and prescriptive at a provincial level and carried out at a regional and municipal level
- Ecosystem-planning approach supported by substantial research to support plan development
- Public ownership of key areas
- Catalysts for smart growth throughout Ontario

[1] Ray Tomalty, Robert B. Gibson, Donald H. M. Alexander, and John Fisher, "Ecosystem Planning for Canadian Urban Regions," Report, ICURR Publications, Toronto, November 1994.
[2] Oak Ridges Moraine Policy Team, "Oak Ridges Moraine Conservation Plan," Report, Ontario Ministry of Municipal Affairs and Housing, 2002, p. 3.
[3] Parliamentary Commission for the Environment, "Superb or Suburb? International Case Studies in Management of Icon Landscapes," New Zealand, 2003.

water, and that the water is worth getting to."[16] In 1999, WRT was transformed from a governmental organization to an independent, nonprofit organization. It works toward the same objectives but is supported by grants and private funds rather than public money. The Province of Ontario reorganized in the late 1990s and downsized many operations that were not mandatory to achieve large-scale provincial mandates. WRT's was one of the entities determined fit to "go it alone."

While the WRT has no power or authority to set policy, it does have the ability to hold land. It considers the interface of land and water, and supports watershed groups that are conducting land-use initiatives. It acts as a facilitator to bring parties together, develop agreements on waterfront objectives, coordinate funding proposals, report on progress and challenges, and promote appropriate conservation and use of the waterfront. Its approach is based on the interactions of ecosystems and human communities, focusing on natural rather than political boundaries.[17] WRT's work is based on a series of principles: make the waterfront a community priority; look beyond political boundaries; set the stage with good planning; use milestone projects to build momentum; design with heritage in mind; add value with connections; make it happen with creative partnerships; secure strategic public investment; and attract private resources.

The area of interest for the waterfront greenway extends inland to the first major barrier along the lakeshore, whether a railroad bed, a highway, or other feature. Along the lake, the area of focus is primarily the waterfront along its entire north shore from Niagara-on-the-Lake to Gananoque, a distance of over 250 miles. A secondary focus is on trail and network development projects upstream from the primary waterfront area.

The unique service of the WRT has been to identify, encourage, and facilitate communication between different sectors and government agencies on a project-by-project or committee-by-committee basis. The trust's work is based on collaboration among all levels of government, conservation authorities, service clubs, community groups, businesses, and industries. The Lake Ontario Waterfront Trail is the backbone of WRT's work. In 1995, WRT opened the trail and prepared the Lake Ontario Greenway Strategy (LOGS), aimed at connecting hundreds of parks, historic and cultural sites, wildlife habitats, and recreation areas. LOGS is a broad conceptual framework currently used as a planning guide.[18] It sets a broad conceptual framework for completion of the greenway, since the responsibility for implementing greenways does not rest with any single agency. Rather, each of the agencies, municipalities, and community groups reviews its own area of responsibility and actions to ensure that it is contributing in a positive way to achieve the vision and objectives of the strategy.

Ultimately, municipalities that own and manage the various segments of the trail run the Waterfront Trail. Working with Greenways Advisory Committees in separate geographic areas, WRT helps organize schedules, priorities, and deadlines. Federal and provincial agencies, conservation authorities, and municipalities are encouraged to incorporate LOGS into their planning and regulation. Ontario's academic institutions are asked to assist in the research and monitoring. The organization has also helped facilitate innovative cooperative agreements with private industries for Waterfront Trail easements. The relevant municipality maintains the trail, but industrial owners provide the land.

The municipalities are also responsible for public involvement on a project-by-project basis. WRT funds only projects with significant public involvement. The organization is deeply embedded in the public participation process, using an informal and grassroots method. According to interviewees, the challenge of this approach is that it is a "people-powered activity." WRT has been effective partly because it lacks regulatory power; people therefore feel less threatened and are more inclined to listen to good information and ideas. WRT decided from the beginning to accomplish its objectives by influence and not by control. Its methods work when knowledgeable people take the time to become deeply involved.

LOGS implementation is based on three primary mechanisms. First, LOGS uses planning and regulatory mechanisms, including environmental impact assessments, waterfront legislation, watershed strategies and plans, remedial action plans, and integrated shoreline management plans. Second, it emphasizes stewardship, including management of public land, land acquisition by public agencies, and landowner contact. And finally, LOGS prioritizes funding incentives, including matching grants and attracting private funds to waterfront projects. The plan outlines a two-tiered implementation strategy based on arterial greenways along major geographic features and local connectors within each community.

WRT has found a strong demand in the greater Toronto region for trails, and municipalities eager to provide them. A lot has been done relatively quickly due in part to corporate support; for instance, CIBC bank has contributed $1.25 million to the trail. The 740-kilometer waterfront greenway is two-thirds complete; some of it already existed, but critical connections have now been made (Figure 3.7).

Figure 3.8 shows the Waterfront Trail and its connections to other regional inland trails. Ten waterfront parks have been revitalized to date through the program. By 2004 the WRT had linked 280 miles of Waterfront Trail, linking 182 parks and natural areas, 170 marinas and yacht clubs, 152 arts and cultural heritage attractions, and 37 major annual waterfront festivals.[19] User surveys done in 1997 and 2002 confirm the public's overwhelming support for a continuous trail along Lake Ontario; in fact, 14 percent of trail users commute on it regularly. WRT set broad objectives—economic, social, and environmental—from the beginning, and they have set the stage for land-use planning in municipalities today. One major sign of progress toward these objectives is that there has been a change in public and municipal expectations in terms of development along the waterfront setting. The new standard is for developers to provide public access to the water's edge, provide the waterfront trail, and build stormwater management controls. Developers find that they, in turn, can make higher profits in the housing market from these measures.

The biggest challenges to WRT projects are funding for capital projects, internal capacity to provide more services and maintain an ongoing presence, and the growth-management challenges that can be ameliorated only with regulatory authority. The Waterfront Regeneration Trust has had tremendous influence as an advocate, clearinghouse, and collaborator for the Lake Ontario Waterfront. It has, indeed, helped many people get to the water, and, in more places than ever, the water is worth getting to.

Fig. 3.7 A section of the Waterfront Trail east of downtown Toronto in the Beaches neighborhoods. The 2-mile-long boardwalk is bounded by several parks along Lake Ontario. The sandy beaches themselves have been popular open spaces since early in the twentieth century when parkland began to be acquired for public ownership. (Photo by the author.)

Fig. 3.8 The Oak Ridges Moraine and Niagara Escarpment region is called the Golden Horseshoe. This map depicts its inland and waterfront regional trails system.

OPEN-SPACE CONNECTIVITY AND WATERSHED PLANNING

While the work of the Crombie Commission and, later, the Waterfront Regeneration Trust has focused principally on the waterfront, the Toronto and Region Conservation Authority (TRCA) focuses on inland watersheds. The TRCA is a regulatory agency established in 1957 under the Ontario Conservation Authorities Act. The TRCA is one of thirty-eight Conservation Authorities in Ontario, created to address landscape problems left primarily by mining (deforestation and erosion). The organization is a key participant in developing inland greenways along stream corridors and is a focal point for creating connectivity.

The TRCA approach is articulated clearly as an ecological one, promoting strategic development that avoids natural heritage areas, water resources, rural amenities, agricultural land, and recreational settings. It sets out to manage renewable natural resources for the region and to implement conservation activities in the nine watersheds (35,000 acres) of the region. One-third of Ontario's population lives within the authority's area of jurisdiction.

TRCA funding sources are split between the province and municipalities. They are further supplemented with other government grants, user fees, contract services, and donations. The authority then funds local organizations working for watershed regeneration, such as projects on the Don and Humber rivers and the Lake Ontario waterfront.

A watershed focus is prominent in Toronto. The authority is involved in two main ways in watershed planning. First, it acts as an adviser and consultant to local municipalities, working with the City of Toronto; Regional Municipalities of Durham, Peel, and York; the Township of Adjala-Tosorontio; and the Town of Mono. The unique role of the TRCA is to develop monitoring information and to set guidelines for appropriate land use and development. Municipalities rely on the authority's expertise in reviewing plans and commenting on development proposals. For example, TRCA reviews local subdivision plans, weighing in on development proposals that could impact environmentally sensitive areas.

Second, the authority participates in watershed planning as a landowner, stakeholder, and land manager. It has authority to purchase, sell, or lease land, to create structures (such as reservoirs), and to alter stream flows. As the largest property owner in the greater Toronto region it can purchase real estate to fulfill its mandate, at times turning land over to local governments. It advocates for and implements watershed management programs and flood protection measures. The TRCA policies are particularly aimed at maintaining well-defined river valleys as public open space, where possible.

The resource areas of specific concern for TRCA are the river valleys, the Lake Ontario waterfront, Oak Ridges Moraine, and the Niagara Escarpment, each of which the authority recognizes for important ecological and recreational use. In its approach to these landscapes, the authority's mandates have changed over time from flood control, risk management, and erosion control in the 1940s and 1950s, to restoring the waterfront for both human and wildlife habitat in the 1970s to 1980s. It has gradually included more social objectives in watershed planning activities through the 1990s and into the twenty-first century.

For open-space planning TRCA uses both carrot and stick approaches—giving advice and support, but also regulating land use. It supports local nonprofit groups, like the Task

Force to Bring Back the Don River, organizing human labor and skills to complete site-specific projects. It works on trail development throughout the city and region. Collaborations occur with several municipal and provincial agencies, nonprofit organizations, and community organizations that deal with land management and use.

The Toronto Waterfront Aquatic Habitat Restoration Strategy is the TRCA plan for the Lake Ontario waterfront from Etobicoke Creek to the Rouge River, extending up estuaries of rivers and creeks. As in the Waterfront Regeneration Trust's work, an ecosystem approach is central. It seeks to ensure that waterfront revitalization, in its many forms, incorporates improvements to aquatic habitats as a critical aspect of creating a more livable waterfront. One of eight guiding principles for the plan is ecological connectivity, stressing the importance of physical and biological relationships among near-shore, watershed, and lakeside ecosystems. The TRCA strategy connects to a range of other efforts on the waterfront, including the Waterfront Trail. Similarly, the Terrestrial Natural Heritage System Strategy, drafted in 2004, is designed to increase biodiversity by increasing the amount and quality of forest and wetland habitats throughout the GTA. It calls for 30 percent of the land base to be in natural cover to achieve environmental targets. Currently, 17 percent of the land base meets that criterion. Again, connectivity is a primary approach. "The more connected (through direct linkage and proximity) that habitat patches are to each other, the more effectively ecological functions operate across the whole landscape, and the better the opportunities to support viable populations of species of conservation concern."[20] The strategy documents negative impact to the natural system, including the negative results of increases in trails and overuse of trails, and associated invasive species.

The biggest test to the TRCA is the magnitude of growth in the Greater Toronto Area. Challenges include maintaining watershed health while attempting to manage growth. The sheer scale of urbanization is an enormous challenge, and the authority is lucky to even maintain the current health of the watersheds, let alone improve them. A proactive, versus reactive, mode of operation is one important strategy. For instance, with new regional inventories and plans in place, instead of dealing with decisions on a parcel-by-parcel basis, the authority can now justify linkages that small parcels make toward the context of a broader systems framework. This supports the importance of large-scale vision and small-scale action working in tandem.

At a very large scale, the TRCA is collaborating with efforts to link a much larger swath of the Lake Ontario waterfront called the Golden Horseshoe (see Figure 3.8). This is an area circling the western end of Lake Ontario, from Niagara Lake to Rice Lake. One of the fastest growing regions in North America, it is the economic engine of Ontario and much of Canada.

A greenbelt is proposed for the region, including the Niagara Escarpment, Oak Ridges Moraine, and the fruit-growing region along Lake Ontario. A Greenbelt Protection Act was proposed in 2004. TRCA is also the facilitator, with WRT, for implementing the Metro Toronto and Region Remedial Action Plan (RAP), covering six watersheds draining into Lake Ontario. This effort overlaps with and supports proposals for open-space connectivity, particularly through waterfront habitat creation, development of new parks and trails, and improved stormwater management. Initiated by an international agreement between the United States and Canada, the RAP process has created a top-down stimulus for regeneration that, again, supplements and legitimizes site-level projects. In polluted areas, the RAP process supports watershed planning and promotes multifunctional projects such as greenway corridors.

CENTRAL WATERFRONT REVITALIZATION

A smaller-scale project, in land area, is one of the most important for Toronto's connectivity, due to its prime location and huge cost. The city's thirty-year plan to revitalize 2,000 acres of the central waterfront will create 500 acres of public parks and open spaces, 40,000 residential housing units, and over 7.6 million square feet of commercial space in an area that has suffered significant environmental degradation from industrial uses.[21] The land is at the city's doorstep (Figure 3.10). The project will cost over Can$17 billion, with public funding from city, provincial, and federal governments, and a large portion from the public sector. In 2002 the plan won an international award from the Waterfront Center in Washington, D.C., which praised its focus on not only environmental improvements, but on transit, urban intensification, and connectivity.

The vision for overhauling the central waterfront has many layers of history, planning, and analysis. Long a blemish on the city landscape, the area is cut off from the downtown, making the waterfront inaccessible, ugly, and blighted. In 1976, the firm of Wallace, McHarg, Roberts and Todd completed an influential plan for the waterfront, which focused on environmental resources. The current effort, now funded by all three levels of government, is brought about by the Toronto Waterfront Revitalization Task Force, made up of financiers, planners, and designers. A superagency was created to control the land and oversee development.

Based on a business plan that was created for the area, *Our Toronto Waterfront,* four projects jumpstarted the effort—the extension of a north–south street leading to the waterfront, improvements to Union Station, soil remediation in the port area, and an environmental assessment of plans for the regeneration of the Don River mouth. In its comparison of Toronto and cities across the globe, the task force identified four situations unique to Toronto. The area of land in need of revitalization is unusually large. The city

3.2 The Don River

The Don River is Toronto's symbol of reconnection. The Don River headwaters are in the Oak Ridges Moraine and its mouth is at Lake Ontario within the city. Canada's most urban river, the Don flows 24 miles and is one of Canada's most degraded rivers even though large amounts of the river valley and stream have been put into public ownership. For over two hundred years the river valley has tolerated urbanization, industry, deforestation, and pollution. Eight hundred thousand people live within the 140-square-mile watershed. The Don once flowed into the Ashbridges Marsh, a 1,500-acre lacustrine marsh that contained an astounding wildlife population, but was turned into a port industrial area. Early in the twentieth century, the wetland was filled; the Don was channelized into the Keating Channel in the 1950s. As landscape architect Michael Hough wisely states, "the river has become a gap between places, not a place itself."[1]

Fig. 3.9 Mouth of the channelized Don River in central Toronto. The photo is taken east of the Don River and looking southwest across to the Inner Harbor and the Toronto Islands. An environmental assessment is underway to examine flood protection and naturalization options for the Lower Don, including the Keating Channel to the inner harbour. (Photo courtesy of Toronto and Region Conservation Authority.)

A citizens group, the Task Force to Bring Back the Don, has been instrumental in mobilizing for rehabilitation of the river. "[It] has been able to articulate conservation, recreation, nature and the city in ways unknown to the traditional public works and conservation authorities in City Hall . . . Drawing on the strength of visible changes to the Don Valley, canoeists, visionaries, social utopians, and dreamers continue to construct an urban ecological narrative."[2]

The ecological reconnection of the Don to Lake Ontario is now a major focal point for the central city (Figure 3.9). In 1992, the TRCA created a Don Watershed Task Force, comprised of elected representatives as well as members of the general public, municipalities, agencies, and environmental groups. Its mandate was to develop a "management plan strategy" or regeneration plan for the entire watershed, using an ecosystem approach.[3] It created seven sub-watershed plans and six concept site plans, as well as a list of forty steps to regenerate the watershed.

The plan, currently being implemented, has a basis in connectivity—not only in reconnecting the river to the lake in a natural way, but in creating a network of green corridors that link natural areas in the uplands and in the river valleys and that creates a continuous watershed trail system between Lake Ontario and the Oak Ridges Moraine.

The Don River Watershed Report Card indicates that salmon are once again accessing the river, new lands are coming into public ownership and protection, the Lower Don is being transformed, and over 130 new regeneration projects have been started in the watershed. Public support, including volunteer help, is at a higher level than ever.[4] However, concerns abound. The TRCA reports that the collective actions of agencies and organizations are falling short of an effective ecosystem approach. The great majority of the regeneration projects are small-scale—planting a few dozen trees here, creating a wildflower garden there. The cumulative impact of these small projects may not be useful until they are supported by larger-scale ecosystem restoration projects that improve the river's water quality and reduce the destructively high peak flows.[5]

---

[1] Michael Hough, "Looking Beneath the Surface: Teaching a Landscape Ethic," in Kristina Hill and Bart Johnson, eds., *Ecology and Design: Frameworks for Learning* (Washington, DC: Island Press, 2001).

[2] Roger Keil and Gene Desfor, "Ecological Modernization in Los Angeles and Toronto," *Local Environment,* 8 (Number 1, 2003):27–44.

[3] Metropolitan Toronto and Region Conservation Authority, "Forty Steps to a New Don: The Report of the Don Watershed Task Force," 1994.

[4] Toronto and Region Conservation Authority, "Don River Watershed Report Card," 2000.

[5] Ibid.

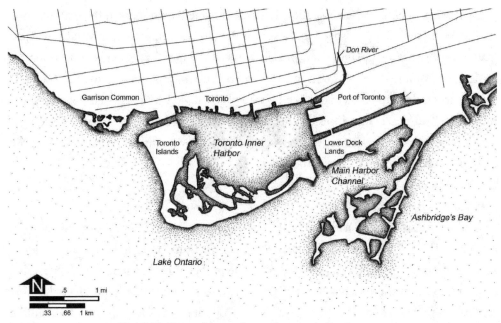

Fig. 3.10 Toronto's central waterfront revitalization area.

is nearly alone among the world cities for still possessing such widespread land abandonment so close to its downtown core. A very large proportion of the land is owned by one government or another. And finally, lands are vacant to a degree that is highly unusual compared with other waterfront cities. The plan sets out common themes—the desire to accommodate nature and parkland, the need to reconcile the imperatives of the environment, human settlement, and economic activity, and the need for coordinated public and private investment and cooperation among three levels of government.

Similar to parallel activities along the expansive waterfront, and activities at the watershed level, the central waterfront plan stresses natural linkages, such as supporting the notion of restoration at the mouth of the Don River. Increasing public open space is a large part of the plan. The visionary plan defines six major development initiatives, one of which is "building a waterfront for public enjoyment." It includes the Green Border, along the entire length of the central waterfront, including walkways, parks, promenades, piers, and other public open space. It is part of, and linked with, the larger Waterfront Trail and would add over 450 acres of new public open space. Environmental quality is another of the six initiatives, linking directly to the Task Force to Bring Back the Don, TRCA, and others working on this strategic river landscape.

There is no comprehensive spatial plan for connected open space at the regional level for Toronto. Notable open-space successes for the city are centered on pivotal landscape features—the striking upland, river, and lakefront landscapes that inspire commitment by leaders, decision makers, and citizens. It is interesting that the focus remains clearly on these features, by and large, and is not necessarily dictated by a particular governmental hierarchy. And nearly all of these projects involve collaborative partnerships, many of which have ecosystem planning as a basis. Chicago's story is similar in many respects but distinct in evolution, focus, and scale.

Chicago: Open Space That Works

Chicago is an excellent place to see open-space protection efforts and organizations in action, working for innovative urban–nature connections. Throughout the six-county metropolitan region, land acquisition during the past century has significantly helped to protect the region's natural resources.[22] But enormous effort is still needed, given that current trends threaten to double the size of the metropolitan area and consume 1.25 million acres of open land in the next three decades. Political fragmentation is staggering, especially compared with Toronto's regional political structure. The Chicago region has thirteen hundred units of government, more than any other U.S. metropolitan area, and it has about four times the population of Toronto.

For Chicago, the framework for open-space planning is largely centered at the county level within the Forest Preserves and Park Districts. Since 1913 the Forest Preserves have levied tax dollars to "acquire . . . and hold lands . . . and to restore, restock, protect, and preserve natural forests and said lands . . . in their natural state and condition . . . for the purpose of the education, pleasure, and recreation of the public."[23] Most districts hope to protect 10 percent of their county's land, and some like Cook and DuPage have reached that goal. Others have thousands of acres yet to purchase.[24] A number of initiatives are creating larger, multijurisdictional efforts for open-space planning.

CHICAGO GREENWAYS

The greenways phenomenon is an important part of open-space planning for the Chicago region. The Northeastern Illinois Regional Greenways Plan takes in six counties in and around the Chicago metropolitan region. The plan was developed through a partnership with Openlands Project and Northeastern Illinois Planning Commission (NIPC). This partnership sponsored local-level workshops and design charrettes around the idea of a regional greenway system. The resulting input was used to develop the Regional Greenways Plan,[25]

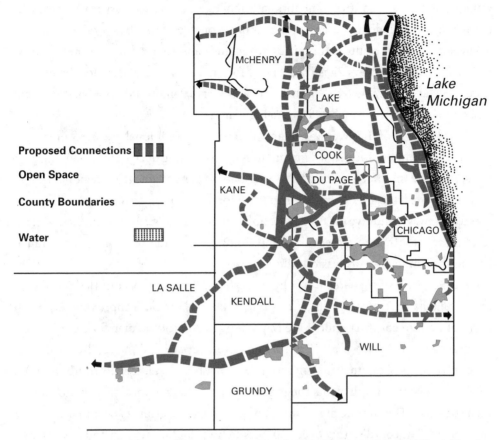

Fig. 3.11 Concept plan for Chicago open-space connections. (Adapted from Northeastern Illinois Planning Commission and Openlands Project, "Northeastern Illinois Regional Greenways Plan," September 1992.)

adopted in 1992 and updated in 1997 and 2000 (Figure 3.11). Today one of the plan's primary goals is linking existing municipal trails by "filling in the gaps." Other important participants included the National Park Service and the State of Illinois Department of Natural Resources.

NIPC was created in 1957 by the Illinois legislature to lead comprehensive planning efforts in the northeastern part of the state. It serves the local governments of the region by providing information, working toward regional cooperation, and developing policies on regional issues. The commission lacks taxing or regulatory authority, but does provide important coordination functions within a highly fragmented land-use environment.

Openlands Project was founded in 1963 as an independent, nonprofit organization to advocate for public open space in northeastern Illinois. It has protected over 45,000 acres of land in the Chicago region for parks, greenways, and urban gardens. "Openlands' vision for northeastern Illinois is a landscape that includes a vast network of land and water trails, tree-shaded streets and intimate public gardens within easy reach of every city dweller. It also includes parks and preserves big enough to provide natural habitat and to give visitors a sense of the vast prairies, woodlands and wetlands that were here before the cities."[26] Its greenways division is one of four main emphasis areas for the organization. Openlands was involved, for instance, in preservation of Midewin Tallgrass Prairie, a 19,000-acre complex connected through greenways.

The objectives of the greenways plan are to preserve additional greenway open space; preserve and improve the quality and biodiversity of existing open space, including greenways; improve the effectiveness and use of trails; expand the existing regional trail system and create linkages; expand the region's efforts to protect, restore, and utilize water-based greenways; improve the transportation benefits of trails; sustain and strengthen the funding base for trails and greenways; and continue the tradition of innovative trail and greenway planning in northeastern Illinois.

A 1994 "State of the Greenways Report" showed that all six counties and the City of Chicago had actively implemented parts of the 1992 plan.[27] Approximately 50–100 miles of new greenway corridors are in place as a result of the plan, bringing the total of existing greenways to nearly 700 miles of river ways, abandoned railroad beds, and other greenways. Despite planning activity at a regional level, as in Toronto there is no central agency that implements the greenways plan. Rather, local jurisdictions implement projects. The complexity of this region's plan arises from a coordination issue— the challenge of coordinating over 260 jurisdictions and more than 150 Park Districts and Forest Preserves. However, Northeast Illinois Planning Commission and Openlands Project serve as important facilitators, similar to the Waterfront Regeneration Trust's role in Toronto.

Even with these successes, the lack of a regional implementation structure presents some challenges. While there is a greenway priority list within the greenways plan, many of those projects listed as priorities have local issues that stall implementation. In the meantime, other greenways are pursued, not necessarily in an optimum sequence. Perhaps this incremental and nonlinear process is inevitable in a city as large and diverse as Chicago. It also highlights that, while the plan was adopted at a regional level, the implementation is accomplished not regionally but locally.

Even so, Chicago's big vision has stayed alive and active over the past decade. The 1997 plan update triples the size of the proposed network and doubles the trail component from 1,000 miles to 2,000 miles. It includes a separate water-based trail system and delineates a focused action plan for implementation.[28] Given the size and magnitude of the task, it is a constantly moving target. Planners report that it is difficult to keep track of how much has been accomplished across the region and a challenge to update the plan as often as needed.

Openlands Project strategically pursues and facilitates several greenway projects each year in order to implement the regional plan and ensure that greenway efforts stay active. For instance, the Salt Creek Greenway, built in phases, is a connector trail that passes through thirty-five jurisdictions. The coordination effort for this project was enormous, as it involved property belonging to forest preserves, park districts, and Cook County. The Illinois Department of Natural Resources (DNR) administers primary funding for the greenways program on a case-by-case basis. The DNR uses the regional greenways plan to determine funding, such as supporting projects that will link landscapes within the overall greenway plan. The regional greenways plan was incorporated into the Illinois transportation enhancement guidelines, which facilitated early implementation success. The most difficult, and at the same time most successful, part of the greenway funding process has been ensuring that federal transportation enhancement funds are secured annually. The combinations of federal and state programs contribute major funding; approximately $40 million has been committed in three rounds, which will build 17–20 percent of the proposed trail system in the next few years.

To supplement these sources for open-space financing, several of the counties have created their own foundations; for instance, in DuPage County, this effort was fostered by the Forest Preserve. Other private funding has been obtained from the MacArthur Foundation and the Conservation Fund. However, support from the state is critical. The Department of Natural Resources is very supportive of the Northeastern Illinois Regional Greenways Plan and has provided funding for stream protection measures that federal funds would not support. The state is recognizing the importance of greenways and is focusing grants not just on ball fields but toward connected networks. To this end, a greenway project rates higher in the state's evaluation system than will ordinary park development and thus will receive priority funding.

As in Toronto, urban rivers are a prime focus. There is increasing recognition of the importance of stream corridors to greenway planning in the region. In the late 1990s, NIPC, Openlands, and other lead agencies developed a regional water trails plan, a companion to the regional greenways plan, which recommends a system of nearly 500 miles of water trails for canoeing and kayaking (Figure 3.12). It also plans about 160 established and proposed access and portage sites, almost all on land that is publicly owned. An example is Openlands' planning for a greenway along the west branch of the DuPage River, in partnership with the DuPage County Forest Preserve. During the 1990s, Openlands was active in planning a land-based greenway along the river corridor. Now that the local units of government are organized

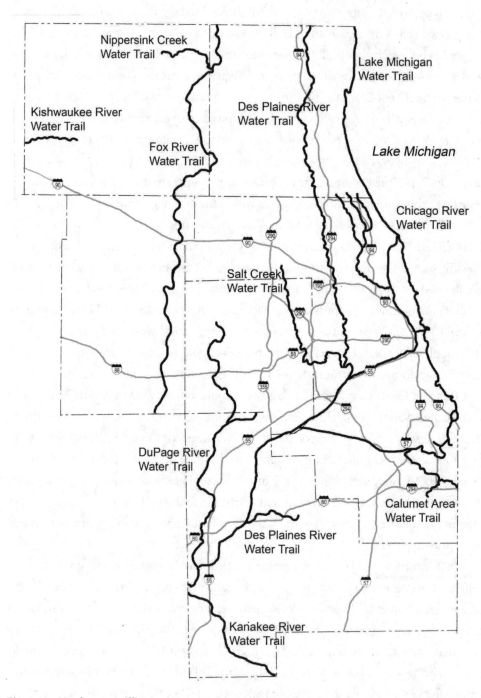

Fig. 3.12 Northeastern Illinois regional water trails. (Adapted from Northeastern Illinois Planning Commission and Openlands Project, "Northeastern Illinois Regional Greenways and Trails Implementation Program," 1997.)

3.3 Chicago River Trails

One may see barges, pleasure boats, commercial tour boats, water taxis, canoes, and kayaks on the Chicago River from one vantage point, while cyclists and pedestrians move along its shore on new riverfront trails. The Chicago River is an important corridor for greenway planning within the framework of the Chicago Greenways Plan (Figure 3.13). It is one of the longest and largest corridors of open space in the region. The crown jewel is the Riverwalk along Wacker Drive on the Main Branch in Chicago's Loop.

Fig. 3.13 Chicago River in downtown Chicago. (Photo by Anne Evans, Courtesy of the Chicago Architectural Foundation.)

The river was severely neglected and contaminated for more than a century. The first meat-packing plants and lumber mills located on the river in the early nineteenth century, and the river was used as an open sewer for many decades.[1] Especially since the 1970s, the integrity of the river has been improved dramatically.

Wildlife has rebounded since the 1980s; the river is a commonly used flyway for migratory birds. The city and community groups have created installations to improve fish habitat at six locations on the river and more than 8,500 feet of publicly owned riverbank has been restored. The city completed an inventory that maps the conditions of riverbanks in the city and assesses habitat values. This will be used to guide continued habitat improvements. These efforts are complicated by the fact that nearly half of the riverbank is in private ownership and about half of its banks are constructed seawall. Private owners are responsible for maintaining their portions of the riverbanks, which can be costly. The city has created a program that assists landowners with repairs and gives incentives for natural restoration.

A $1.5 million special congressional appropriation forged a partnership between federal agencies for coordinating river projects in the Chicago metropolitan area. Local and federal agencies have pumped over $4 billion into water quality improvements over the past twenty-five years. A collaboration of public and private organizations created a Chicago Rivers Demonstration Project to enhance the river through community-based activities.[2] Its companion publications, *People and the River* and *Nature and the River,* funded by the National Park Service Rivers, Trails, and Conservation Assistance Program, help depict the natural and social values of the river for Chicagoans.

Chicago Mayor Richard Daley, as one of his many greening initiatives for Chicago, has backed a long-range plan to turn the Chicago River into Chicago's second shoreline. The Chicago River Development Plan, completed in 1999, envisions parks, trails, and recreation areas along Chicago's inland waterfronts. A continuous multiuse trail along the entire river is one part of that vision. The plan subdivides the river into nine reaches, with nine different geographic characteristics. Across the nine reaches, twenty-two opportunity sites were identified, where specific development recommendations are outlined. Components include paths and greenways, public access, habitat enhancement, recreation, and economic development.[3] In 2002 the Chicago Park District completed a master plan for the river, creating strategies for increasing and improving public open space, followed in 2005 by the Mayor's Chicago River Agenda, a vision for improving water quality, protecting nature and wildlife, balancing river uses, and enhancing community life.[4]

A new 30-foot setback requirement for all new development along the river is a powerful tool for implementing Chicago River's many plans. It allocates space for a public path along the river and helps orient new development toward, rather than away from, the river. Since then, thirty-six new private developments have created over 12 miles of riverwalk, with trail connections made beneath seven bridges. The city has acquired 32 acres of public open space along the river downtown, and at least 46 more acres are planned. A detailed set of design guidelines and standards depicts expectations for development in three zones from the river's edge—riverbank zone, urban greenway zone, and development zone.[5]

Chicago has used impact fees to fund some parkland along the river. Open-space impact fees charge new residential developments for developing open spaces. Within the city, this regulatory measure has raised $23 million since 1998. Chicago's impact fees range from $313 to $1,253 per dwelling unit, depending on location, and have collectively raised enough to buy twenty-one parks on 17 acres.[6]

The nonprofit group Friends of the Chicago River has been instrumental in grassroots advocacy projects over the past twenty-five years. It promotes public access to the river and organizes river improvement projects. Projects have been implemented partly by using the unskilled labor of local youth, thereby providing environmental education and training. The work of the Friends of the Chicago River has been subsidized heavily by small grants from the Urban Resources Partnership, a federally funded program that brings together multiple interests for urban revitalization. The Chicago River is a focal point for regeneration of open spaces in the Chicago metropolitan area, an open-space story unfolding quickly through the commitment of a wide range of government and private participants.

[1] Libby Hill, *The Chicago River: A Natural and Unnatural History* (Chicago: Lake Claremont Press, 2000).
[2] Dave Wallin, "Resident Use and Perception of the Chicago and Calumet Rivers," Report, Chicago Rivers Demonstration Project, Friends of the Chicago River, and National Park Service Rivers, Trails, and Conservation Assistance Program, 1995.
[3] City of Chicago, "Chicago River Corridor Development Plan," 1999.
[4] City of Chicago, "Chicago River Agenda," June 2005.
[5] City of Chicago, "Chicago River Corridor Design Guidelines and Standards," 1999.
[6] Peter Harnik and Jeff Simms, "Parks--How Far Is Too Far?" *Planning*, December 2004.

for implementing the greenway, Openlands has turned its attention to the water, creating popular paddling facilities within its water trails program.

CHICAGO WILDERNESS AND OTHER REGIONWIDE INITIATIVES

The Chicago Region Biodiversity Council, now known as Chicago Wilderness, is a coalition of over 150 government, scientific, civic, and environmental organizations that coalesced to protect natural communities in the Chicago region. The coalition drafted the nation's first biodiversity recovery plan for a major American city in 1999. Their Biodiversity Recovery Plan is a national model of urban ecological planning, creating a comprehensive vision for connectivity, among other goals. One of the first activities of the coalition was the creation of an Atlas of Biodiversity that details the geology, human history, and biological richness of the region.

Chicago Wilderness is both place and people. It is a system of places and an organizational collaboration. "First and foremost, Chicago Wilderness is an archipelago of 200,000 acres of protected natural lands stretching from Chiwaukee Prairie in Wisconsin, through the six counties of northeastern Illinois and Goose Lake Prairie southwest of Joliet, to the dunes of northwestern Indiana—including the plants and animals that live on the land . . . and the people."[30] Its geographic scope is somewhat larger than the six-county Chicago metropolitan region.

The project began with twenty-eight new conservation projects, funded by the U.S. Forest Service, including creation of the Biodiversity Recovery Plan itself. The plan sets quantitative targets for resource protection for the region. For instance, the plan recommends that about 50,000 to 100,000 acres of healthy forest complexes in the region be preserved. Other targets are set for savanna, prairie, and wetlands. The Recovery Plan creates separate but connected goals for the entire landscape, ecosystems, individual species, and people. One landscape vision is a network of protected lands and waters that will preserve habitat for a complete spectrum of living things that form the region's natural communities. A second vision includes habitat greenways—wide swaths of natural land—that will connect sites, opening paths to allow for migration and dispersal between formerly disconnected reserves. An example is restoration work along the North Branch of the Chicago River, where degraded prairie communities within fifteen Cook County Forest Preserve sites are being reestablished (Figure 3.14).

These connectivity goals are being furthered by green infrastructure planning within the Chicago Wilderness agenda. A Chicago Wilderness Green Infrastructure Vision began in 2004. Its aim is to create a visionary map of the region that depicts both existing green infrastructure as well as opportunities for expansion, restoration, and connection.

Chicago Wilderness is similar in breadth to the Toronto and Region Conservation Authority. Both are concerned with broad-scale issues of ecological health, connectivity of natural systems, and sustainable urban form for their respective cities. Both help organize large numbers of volunteers for ecological restoration. However, their focus is slightly different—biodiversity in Chicago versus watersheds in Toronto—and they have distinct origins, authorities, and mandates. Although they have similar abilities to forge large plans and to facilitate broad coalitions, TRCA's work is done within the confines of a government agency. Even so, its authority and mandate are innovative by U.S. standards. Chicago Wilderness, on the other hand, is a private coalition that is based on collaboration among its members. According to Mary Kate Hogan, "not since the early 1900s when Daniel Burnham introduced his plan for integrating parks and greenways around Chicago, have groups collaborated on such an innovative conservation initiative . . . Through Chicago Wilderness, conservation groups are recognizing that their efforts should be interconnected, much like the ecosystems they're trying to save."[29] In the domain of natural features protection, the organization is filling a gap in regional governance—a gap that is not filled by a strong regional government with regulatory authority.

Fig. 3.14 Chicago Wilderness volunteers work on restoration along the North Branch of the Chicago River on a Cook County Forest Preserve site. (Photo courtesy of Chicago Wilderness.)

3.4 Chicago Lakefront

Chicago Wilderness has trained attention on one set of gaps that exists in Chicago's open-space network—the Lake Michigan shoreline. The city's 18.5-mile-long Chicago Lakefront Path is one of the most heavily used linear open spaces on the continent, with 60 million visits per year (Figure 3.15). It includes beaches, volleyball courts, baseball and soccer fields, and playgrounds, in addition to the wide, hard-surface trail. It enjoys great views of the Chicago skyline, widening for concert venues and other city amenities, such as Chicago's new Millennium Park. Unlike Toronto's more fragmented lakefront, Chicago's lakeshore is remarkably intact. Most of Chicago's 29-mile lakefront is already parkland, but gaps remain north and south of the central city.

The Chicago Park District is working with Openlands, Audubon, and other groups in a land-use-planning and park-planning project for the northern gap. The Park District is increasingly questioning the enormous effort that is required to maintain constructed water-front edges. Softening those lakeshore edges may be a priority in the future, including dealing with drainage flowing perpendicular to the water's edge. The city is studying the feasibility of creating a continuous lakefront park system from Evanston to the Indiana border.

Fig. 3.15 Heavy pedestrian and bike use along Chicago's Lake Michigan lakefront. Photo looking south toward Chicago's Loop. (Photo by Larry Deck.)

South of the city, a connected, accessible lakeshore from Chicago all the way to Michigan is an even bolder visionary idea. It would take a tremendous amount of time and money, but could be one of the greatest urban greenways in America.

According to Chicago Wilderness, biodiversity health is greatly compromised, not just along the shoreline in the city of Chicago itself, but across the lakeshore. Habitat loss due to the degradation and development of the shoreline is generating increased interest in ways that the lakefront can accommodate both people and nature simultaneously along this linear corridor. The lakeshore is characterized by high bluffs along the north shore communities; low marshes in the middle, near central Chicago; and dunes at the Indiana end. Lakeshore natural communities include beaches, foredunes, and high dunes. According to the Chicago Wilderness Biodiversity Recovery Plan, many natural beaches still exist, although most cannot function normally. Foredunes are particularly vulnerable and have been destroyed around the city as a result of hardening the coastline and other factors.

Chicago Wilderness highlights some areas, like Chiwaukee Prairie north of the city, where ecosystems of freshwater wetlands and dunes illustrate what the city's lakefront once looked like.[1] At the opposite end, Indiana Dunes National Lakeshore south of the city protects 15,000 acres along the southern shore of Lake Michigan. Chicago Wilderness frames the task as connecting the dots along the shoreline between those two hubs, to bring the lakefront "back from the edge." Meaningful restoration of the shoreline to an ecologically sound greenway is an enormous task involving all land uses, multiple levels of government, and massive funding mechanisms.

---

[1] Chicago Wilderness Web site, www.chicagowilderness.org, quoting Illinois State Geological Survey's Michael Chrzastowski.

Another enterprise, emerging from Chicago's business community, is striving to create a vision for the larger Chicago region. The Commercial Club of Chicago, the same private organization that sponsored Burnham's famous 1909 Plan of Chicago, published *Chicago Metropolis 2020* in 1999.[31] Its creation within a private group of business leaders, rather than a public agency, is its most unusual and refreshing aspect. It won the Daniel Burnham Award from the American Planning Association in 2004.[32] The effort addresses the six-county Chicago region and describes the region's main problems, including issues of sprawl, land use, and competing jurisdictions. It promotes the idea of stronger regional governance to manage housing, transit, and other services. Alternative scenarios were envisioned for the year 2020. A "business as usual" scenario was created, along with corresponding visionary scenarios addressing six main factors—education, economic development, taxation, governance, transportation, and land use and housing. Within the latter category, open-space protection and planning are strongly supported.

As in Toronto, a few key leaders are critical to the success of these ventures. George Ranney Jr., president and CEO of Chicago Metropolis 2020, is one important leader, as is Elmer Johnson, a member of the Commercial Club and author of *Chicago Metropolis 2020: Preparing Metropolitan Chicago for the 21st Century*. Prestigious advisers to the process included Alan Altshuler, Harvard professor; Anthony Downs, The Brookings Institution; Myron Orfield, Minnesota state legislator; and David Rusk, former mayor of Albuquerque. The firm of Fregonese and Calthorpe was also instrumental.

Of particular relevance to open-space planning, the plan promotes more walkable neighborhoods and business districts, with pedestrian and bicycle access. Decrying the destruction of open space, Chicago Metropolis 2020 argues for the restoration and protection of the region's prairies, woodlands, and wetlands. It claims that the plan would spare some 300 square miles from development, roughly the area of one of the six counties! Two-thirds of new households would be within walking distance of a park or open space compared with fewer than half in the "business as usual" scenario. The gain is clearly attributable to connected corridors of open land, which can be accessed at many points by many people. The plan strongly endorses the Regional Greenways Plan and its goal of creating a 4,300-mile system of stream- and water-based greenways. Similarly, it specifically supports the Chicago Wilderness partnership for natural habitats.

A primary recommendation of the plan was the creation of a new organization—Chicago Metropolis 2020. The new organization is implementing the ideas from the report, mainly by collaborating with other organizations. For instance, it was a participant in realizing a merger between the Northeast Regional Planning Commission and Chicago Area Transportation Study (CATS). In 2005, Illinois governor Rod Blagojevich signed into law a bill that creates a Regional Planning Board for Chicago, whereby transportation and land-use planning will be coordinated by one agency.

The Chicago Area Transportation Study has been an important regional actor for urban connectivity. It develops the region's long-range transportation plan and provides technical assistance to communities and public agencies. Pedestrian and bicycling planning is a growing priority in Chicago transportation planning. The Soles and Spokes Plan currently under way will be the first comprehensive pedestrian and bike plan for northeastern Illinois, recommending policies and projects to improve the safety, convenience, and frequency of walking and cycling throughout the region. CATS planners hope that improved infrastructure for walking and cycling will help address congestion, pollution, social equity, public health, and quality of life.[33]

CATS released the Existing Conditions and Regional Trends report in 2004 that carefully documents, for the entire Chicago region, issues of physical activity, air quality, and safety for nonmotorized travel. It also helps depict the demographics of who is bicycling and walking in northeastern Illinois. It analyzes the degree to which the region is bikeable and walkable and summarizes relevant policies impacting pedestrian and bicycle transportation. The findings from this study are being applied, even before the Soles and Spokes Plan is completed—for instance, in the creation of a pedestrian safety program and in the allocation of funding resources according to Trends report findings.

Chicago Wilderness, Chicago Metropolis 2020, and Chicago Area Transportation Study each have a different genesis and perspective, from natural restoration and protection to economic development to transportation efficiency. But all three are concerned with the public realm of the city and its sustainability, livability, and functionality. These regional efforts are actively involved with the various units of government within the region, such as the open-space initiatives by the City of Chicago itself.

CITY SPACE: CITY OF CHICAGO

Of the many jurisdictions in the Chicago region, the City of Chicago is a principal participant in open-space planning. The support and promotion of Chicago greening by Mayor Richard Daley are striking; he has created a model of powerful leadership for livable, green urban landscapes, and Chicago has become a model among American cities. The Chicago Park District particularly has an illustrious history of park design and protection.[34] In addition, the Department of Planning and Development is actively involved in the greening of Chicago. CitySpace is a joint effort of the park district and planning department, with the Forest Preserve District of Cook County, and the Chicago Public Schools, to address open-space opportunities for the city. After four years of study and planning, CitySpace was launched in the mid-1990s. The study inventoried open land in Chicago, found a surprising number of vacant parcels available in the city, and subsequently recommended large quantities of it for open-space design and planning. The Chicago Community Trust, a local foundation, supported the development of the initial plan with a grant of $400,000.

Three main initiatives were started. The NeighborSpace Program is an urban land trust that supports community-based management of small parks, gardens, natural areas, and other open spaces. Although a private nonprofit, 90 percent of its support is from the public agencies. Started in 1996, NeighborSpace owns forty community open spaces and many more are in the review or acquisition process. The Campus Park Program is a $50 million, five-year program to create parks on public school grounds. The project focuses on removing pavement from playgrounds, sometimes converting whole city blocks in order to mitigate heat island effects, improve aesthetics, and provide safer play spaces. The project has so far removed hundreds of acres of asphalt at about a hundred public schools. The Chicago River is the third focus area for CitySpace (see Chicago River sidebar).

It is nearly impossible to understand, in one sweeping view, the connected open-space opportunities, challenges, and outcomes in a city region as large as Chicago's. The ecological issues alone are confounding and difficult. However, it is clear that the spatial plan for connectivity, now in place for nearly fifteen years, is a strong organizing structure for both trans-jurisdictional projects and small neighborhood efforts. Many other factors are critical—the umbrella provided by Chicago Wilderness, the leadership of city initiatives, the foresight of the corporate community, and the funding priorities at the state level. The overlapping goals across these entities, all pointing toward the importance of ecological health, cannot be underestimated for the future of protected and connected open lands in the Chicago region.

Ecology as Thrust for Connectivity

Both Toronto and Chicago have made spectacular progress toward landscape connectivity based on a foundation of environmental soundness. For Toronto, the Royal Commission's work provided a clear turning point for ecosystem-based planning for the region. Landscape architect Michael Hough of Toronto describes it well in an update of restoration activities for the city:

> One of the most important design issues of the 21st century involves the concept of continuity in the landscape, one that functions to maintain biological diversity and recreational networks throughout the urban region . . . Today it has become a concept inspired by the science of landscape ecology. It's a broad vision for establishing an interconnected system of protected areas within, and beyond the urban regions, and has obvious application to the Toronto region's valleys and overall geomorphology. Restoring linkages where they have been disrupted, reintroducing woodland connections between valleys on plateau land are key strategies for the future, from both an ecological and recreational perspective.[35]

It is interesting that Toronto, even though a smaller metropolitan region than Chicago, has fewer spatially explicit visions that integrate landscapes across the region. Chicago has a vast army of organizations, agencies, and funding to make spectacular progress toward connected open spaces that promote environmental integrity. These are pulled together spatially around the regional greenways vision and the biodiversity plan. The natural resources themselves have never been so well publicized and coveted by the citizenry. This contrast may be due, in part, to the very strong geomorphological features in Toronto that create an inherent organizing structure for landscape connectivity; efforts for the Oak Ridges Moraine, Niagara Escarpment, urban rivers, and Lake Ontario Waterfront create a primary scaffolding for open-space planning. In Chicago, the numerous decision-making jurisdictions are more prominent than is an overall landscape structure. As a result, a concept plan that shows deliberate linkages across the landscapes of these many jurisdictions is even more vital. That has been provided in the form of the regional greenways vision, water trails plan, Chicago River rehabilitation, and Lake Michigan lakeshore efforts.

Hierarchies of scale define ecological systems and the activities of ecological planning. These interacting scales are particularly germane in creating linked open-space lands across metro areas. For instance, in Toronto, TRCA objectives are carried out over three scales of concern—the landscape, vegetation communities, and plant and animal species. At the landscape scale, each patch of natural habitat in the region is ranked according to a range of landscape criteria, including size, shape, and surrounding land use. Then closer scale work is done to address specific communities and species.

Like Chicago, Toronto's greenway system is planned at a regional level but is decentralized to local jurisdictions for implementation. In both cities, the importance of the overall vision at the watershed or regional scale was clearly emphasized by interviewees. For small-scale work in Toronto, the TRCA's watershed plans have given credibility and validity to decisions at the site scale that would otherwise seem unjustified. Ruliffson and colleagues found the same phenomenon for Chicago, where "support from a broad-based plan, like the NIPC Greenways Plan or the Chicago Wilderness Biodiversity Plan, can assist in establishing a project's significance by showing how a site, or even a method of site management, fits into the larger scheme of land protection."[36]

The organizational structure for Toronto's connected open space efforts is somewhat more straightforward than Chicago's. And its evolution is an interesting story for thinking about approaches in other cities. It is remarkable that the Crombie Commission did not start with the greenway theme up front in its work, but rather the emphasis on environmental quality led to the greenway theme. Furthermore, it is significant that *Regeneration* presented the ecosystem approach not only as the scientific answer to environmental ills, but to the problems of urban sprawl, competing political and agency jurisdictions, and economic inefficiencies. A combination of persuasiveness, timing, and power let the idea germinate and grow.

A critical distinction can be made between Toronto and Chicago in efforts toward open-space planning. The institutional structure surrounding Toronto's open-space planning is organized relationally rather than hierarchically, specifically relating to targeted natural features. This relational structure, with various organizations active in different geographic contexts and in diverse ways with each other, seems to be very adaptive. It responds to changing levels of participation, motivations for participation, composition of participants, spatial scope, and knowledge.

For Chicago, the system is more hierarchical among the various decision-making bodies in the region. However, that hierarchy is also being influenced and even deflated by the work of Chicago Wilderness. That organization, really a consortium of organizations, has shown that a structure of cooperative governmental and nongovernmental organizations with one big idea can spark vast opportunities for collective action. As Ruliffson and colleagues have described for Chicago, different organizations, like plant and animal species, fill different niches in the open-space planning ecosystem. Chicago Wilderness has helped the region visualize these relationships. "Explicit cooperation between the counties and other government agencies has led to extensive trail networks throughout the Chicago region and beyond."[37] Even so, the lack of commitment by some local officials, or the paucity of advocacy groups, is problematic in certain areas.

An enormous amount of open-space planning and implementation needs to be done in both cities to even keep up with the rate of environmental fragmentation from sprawl and other impacts. It is a daunting challenge to tackle the repair of the natural structure of Toronto and Chicago as they expand in population, as city infrastructure declines, and as funding evaporates. Many open-space opportunities are lost in an environment of explosive growth. And it is particularly challenging when other goals and needs for open space are considered simultaneously.

One of the main challenges of ecological soundness as a foundation objective for connected open space is its inherent conflict with other needs. WRT found this for Toronto, where the conflict between recreation and nature is a recurring theme, creating an area of tension for their open-space work. In Chicago it is a concern at all levels of open-space planning—how do recreation, transportation, historic resources, and other needs layer upon a network of environmentally sound open spaces? Chapters 4 through 7 address these tensions.

Recreation—Well-Being: Milwaukee and Ottawa

The fundamental lesson, to summarize, is that open space has
to have a positive function. It will not remain open if it does
not. People must be able to do things on it or with it—at the
very least, to be able to look at it.

—*William Whyte[1]*

Recreation provides the positive function that city-dwellers desire. It is critical
to the development of greenways and other connected open space. Recreational demand
generates the money, support, labor, and passion that get people behind open-space projects. Long before environmental activism, the need for leisure space is what drove park
development in the late nineteenth and early twentieth centuries. In recent decades, greenways have built on that legacy. This momentum is fueled by a growing awareness about
the connection between human health and the shape of urban open space; greenways are
one of many avenues for promoting healthier lifestyles. They are based on movement, on
distance, on going somewhere. At the same time, the protection and enhancement of ecological values is a primary concern of greenways work. Unfortunately, human access to
natural sites, particularly through more active forms of recreation, often decreases environmental integrity. Human disturbance particularly compromises wildlife and their

habitats. So the balance between providing human access to connected open space and protecting environmentally sound corridors is a thorny one.

"The development of greenways without the recreational element is extremely diffi-cult," explained one Milwaukee planner. Cities are just now sorting out the complexity of creating and linking greenways on the physical landscape and at the same time satisfying these competing demands. Although recreation and environmental protection are often incompatible or conflicting goals, recreational access sometimes facilitates ecological stew-ardship and environmentally sound outcomes. Recreational use spurs environmental con-cern, which can result in the protection of more land for both objectives.

And the exact opposite approach has been taken. Recreation can be a residual effect, after environmental soundness. In Boston's Back Bay, for example, Frederick Law Olmsted advocated that a "natural" water body, instead of an engineered flood storage basin, would be an amenity. He was mainly concerned with improving water quality and preventing flooding, with secondary goals of recreation and transportation.[2] Primary or secondary, recreation is a critical motivator for open-space planning. Milwaukee and Ottawa help illustrate trends and tensions inherent in recreation as a reason for connected open space.

Milwaukee and Ottawa possess open-space systems that are at the same time mature in historical precedent and embryonic in contemporary potential. Like a number of cities across North America, both cities boast a strong focus on parkways and rivers. These cre-ate clear open-space frameworks, already in place. The parkways incorporate multiple greenway objectives and provide diverse forms of linear recreation and transportation. One main lesson from these cities is that where the connected open pattern is nearly intact, due to foresighted planning decades ago, it may be possible to retrofit that pattern to accomplish new goals, whether through restoring environmental quality or integrating new recreational corridors. An existing historic framework is an enormous asset on which to build contemporary open-space corridors.

Milwaukee and Ottawa: Historic and Geographic Context

While dozens of cities in North America are attempting to implement connected open-space networks, many are working with sparse existing open-space resources. However, some metropolitan areas, like Milwaukee, Wisconsin, and Ottawa, Ontario, have impres-sive historic frameworks on which to build. Although neither city is well-known for pro-gressive, contemporary greenway planning efforts, both Milwaukee and Ottawa have remarkable historic corridors, especially in parkways and recreational trails planned along urban rivers in the early twentieth century. Despite these assets, contemporary collaboration around regionally connected open space is spotty, greenway objectives have changed over time in important ways, and coordinated open-space planning is just beginning. Both cities seem poised for integrated greenways programs, accelerated by recreational demand, innovative experimental projects, increasing environmental awareness, and growing institutional capacity.

Milwaukee and Ottawa are modest, second-tier, midsize cities; both have a blue-collar industrial heritage. Milwaukee, the largest city in Wisconsin, is twentieth in a size ranking of U.S. cities with 597,000 and 940,000 residents in the City of Milwaukee and Milwaukee County, respectively.[3] Ottawa's origins in lumbering and other resource extraction contrast with its status as the national capital. The city symbolizes the nation's identity and draws tourists from across the continent. Its population was 774,000 in 2000, with over a million residents in the greater Ottawa–Gatineau metropolitan area.[4]

These metropolitan areas have achieved well-connected networks of urban and suburban open space, strongly influenced by planners' early visions of parkways and greenbelts. This chapter describes the urban histories that created frameworks for open-space planning in Milwaukee and Ottawa, long before the contemporary greenway movement began. The importance of large-scale and long-term city plans is explicated, especially relating to parkway and greenbelt design nearly a century ago. These historic themes inform contemporary greenway efforts under way in both cities, particularly as they relate to recreation.

Milwaukee: Charles Whitnall's Progressive Era Parkway Network
Milwaukee has a rich history as a working-class, industrial, and ethnically diverse city on the shores of Lake Michigan (Figure 4.1). In the nineteenth century, the city was linked with the United States and the world through the construction of harbor facilities at the confluence of Lake Michigan and three rivers—the Milwaukee, Kinnickinnic, and Menomonee (Figure 4.2). As in many American industrial cities, the land along these urban rivers was owned and utilized by shipping and railway companies. Raw industrial landscapes developed along the rivers in the oldest parts of the city. The relatively fast and inexpensive railway and waterway transportation attracted industrial and commercial businesses and significantly influenced the development of the city into a major urban center.[5] While its strong river network shapes Milwaukee, its physical structure is even more determined by the geometric section and township land-division scheme common in most midwestern cities. The three rivers lie within a gridded landscape matrix, as does the surrounding countryside.

Fig. 4.1 The city of Milwaukee on the Lake Michigan shore, viewing northward, and showing extensive greenspace between the city and lakeshore. (From the American Geographical Society Library, University of Wisconsin–Milwaukee Libraries.)

In the mid-nineteenth century Milwaukee grew as a commercial port, followed by its transformation after the Civil War to a manufacturing leader. In the late nineteenth and early twentieth centuries, Milwaukee grew spread out from Lake Michigan and the rivers' confluence in a radiating pattern (Figure 4.3). Early in the century, concern about the city's suburban development was already growing. An assistant engineer of the sewerage commission noted with some exasperation in 1926, "About three years ago, a distinct change in the usual growth of various communities took place. Instead of the gradual radial growth out from the established population centers, numerous new centers were formed, scattered throughout the area, apparently for no other reason than a good real estate agent and a fine view."[6] Now, eighty years later, the land-use pattern in the Milwaukee region resembles that of many large U.S. cities—increasingly dispersed suburban development at the outskirts. Between 1950 and 1985, a 47 percent increase in urban population was accompanied by a 227 percent increase in land committed to urban use.[7]

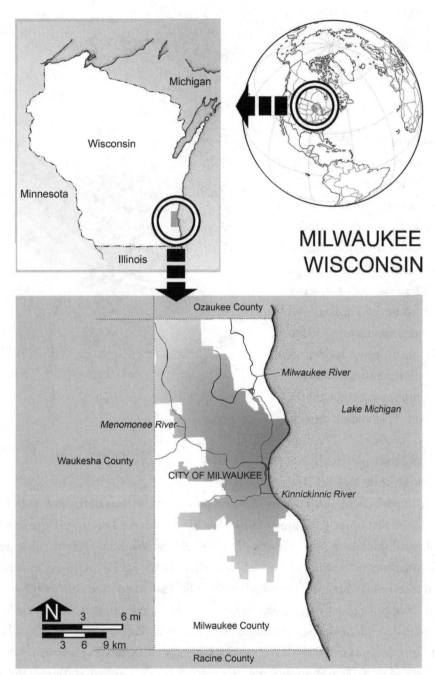

Fig. 4.2 Milwaukee, Wisconsin regional location within Milwaukee County. Gray tone depicts main urbanized area.

Fig. 4.3 Growth of the city of Milwaukee
from the mid-nineteenth century to the
present. (Adapted from Bayrd Still, *Milwaukee the History of a City*, North
American Press, 1948.)

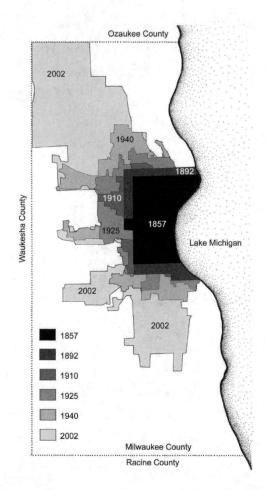

The story of Milwaukee's open
space is rooted in the history of its
park system during the Progressive
Era of the late nineteenth and early
twentieth centuries, including many
years of socialist control and influence. Historian William Clausen
describes "the existence of an active
and alert group of citizens who
adopted national planning ideas,
translated them into a local program of action which was sensitive
to local conditions, and fought for
the adoption of planning at the city,
county and state levels."[8] The purchase of land for parks and parkways is one of their legacies. The
first lands for parks were purchased in 1890 and promoted as "lungs of the city," with special emphasis at that time on the upper Milwaukee River. They were motivated by a combination of socialist ideals and the aesthetic principles of City Beautiful, a reform movement
in North American architecture and urban planning from the late 1890s through the early
twentieth century. City Beautiful was based on the belief that grand streets and noble public
buildings could bring order, dignity, and beauty to the built environment, thereby mitigat-
ing impoverished, blighted cities. It was linked to American Progressive Era ideals, which
began in American cities in the 1890s and lasted through the 1920s. Reformers sought changes
in labor and fiscal policies at all levels of government; rethinking the physical fabric of the city
was one outcome. Human health and space for leisure were foremost concerns.

Pressure for a municipal park system developed in the 1880s and, in 1889, resulted in the
state enabling legislation for a system of parks and a park commission to govern it. Soon the

need for parkland reached beyond the city limits, but the city lacked authority to buy land outside its jurisdiction. Again, permission was sought and granted at the state level for building parks outside of the city. Milwaukee used other innovative planning strategies as well. The parks were financed by the city almost from the beginning, in contrast to other cities where planning began as an activity of wealthy patrons and private organizations. In addition, the city's planners relied on local expertise for technical direction rather than on the handful of prominent planners, architects, and landscape architects who produced most urban plans.[9]

Around the turn of the century, park planners began purchasing numerous sites along the Milwaukee, Menomonee, and Kinnickinnic rivers. Thus began the open-space network in place today, which interweaves environmental goals and accessible open space. These planners believed that the protection and, indeed, the restoration of the natural drainage patterns were vital to public health. Forested lands adjacent to streams were valued for runoff absorption, sustaining groundwater levels, and ensuring an even stream flow.[10] Frederick Law Olmsted Sr. was consulted on park design and suggested a network of linear parks for Milwaukee, probably envisioning protected urban riparian systems similar to those he designed in Boston and elsewhere. The parkway idea, combining aspects of early environmental corridors, was an influential factor in Milwaukee County's park planning as early as 1906, even though the first parkway plan was not created until 1924.[11]

Charles B. Whitnall is recognized as the father of Milwaukee's open-space system. As a charter member of the city's Public Land Commission and the county's Park Commission (both begun in 1907), he led two of the metropolitan area's most important planning bodies. He worked on land-use and parks planning for over forty years, until the mid-1940s, with a passion for progressive socialist ideals. According to John Gurda, "Whitnall was the dominant figure in regional planning for an entire generation . . . He foresaw the day when Milwaukee would become a decentralized 'regional city' consisting of a specialized urban core ringed by a host of 'subsidiary centers' spreading fifteen or twenty miles out into the countryside."[12]

Whitnall's 1923 master plan called for 84 miles of "parked driveways" following the county's rivers, creeks, and lakeshore (Figure 4.4). At the time, the parks created a figure eight around Milwaukee County that touched every suburb and dozens of city neighborhoods. It was an ambitious plan that dealt not only with public recreation but also with wetland protection, flood control, stream bank restoration, sanitation, and environmental education. When seen in light of expanding twenty-first-century greenway objectives, this plan was decades ahead of its time. Whitnall set an unusual value on both environmental and social goals in his plan, particularly anticipating the recreational needs of the growing city. His plan was farsighted in its scope—expanding far out from the existing city—and in its sensitivity to natural features.

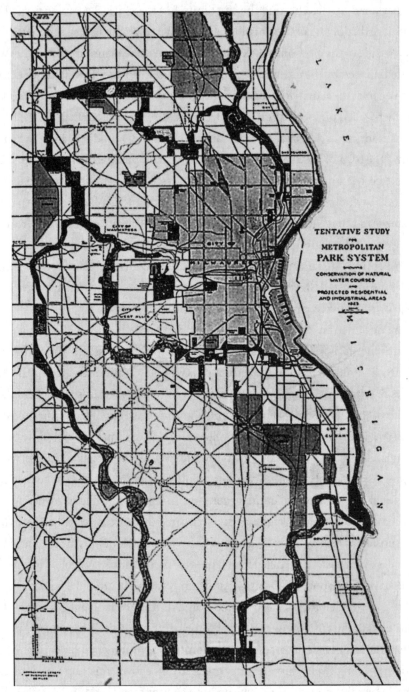

Fig. 4.4 Charles Whitnall's 1923 master plan for the Milwaukee County park system. Black pattern depicts proposed park system. (From John Gurda, *The Making of Milwaukee*, Brookfield: Burton & Mayer, Inc., 1999.)

Whitnall's highway and park maps created the blueprint for local land-use planning in Milwaukee. They provided specific and rational guidelines to development in the outlying reaches of the county. In addition, Whitnall established two policies that influenced land-use planners for many decades: buy land well in advance of need, and develop land with utmost respect for native contours and vegetation.[13] The origins of Whitnall's ideas are not entirely clear. According to William Clausen, "[Whitnall] combined the aesthetic values associated with early landscape architects with a surprisingly sophisticated understanding of natural systems and an active socialist's concern for the mass of people in congested cities. Add to this his untiring devotion to public life and you have an individual who translates uncommon vision into concrete accomplishments."[14]

Early on, Milwaukee County was the more aggressive partner in open-space protection, compared with the city, and in the 1930s the City of Milwaukee turned over its entire park system to the county. (The city also owned some gems in the system: Lincoln Memorial Drive, a 3-mile parkway completed in 1929 after many years as a landfill, was one of the best stretches of urban lakefront on the Great Lakes.)[15] The county had purchased over 1,977 acres of parkland by 1930, and laid the foundation for a connected greenway system based on Whitnall's design.

Ottawa: Jacques Gréber's Greenbelt and Parkway Vision

The presence of the federal government infrastructure in Ottawa has influenced the city's shape since Queen Victoria chose it as the nation's capital in 1858. Canada's capital sits atop a 150-foot limestone cliff, Parliament Hill, in what was a mere lumbering town in the nineteenth and early twentieth centuries. As the 1915 plan explained: "It lies on the banks of a great and beautiful river, the Ottawa, and has direct communication by water with the mighty St. Lawrence . . . Two subsidiary rivers flow into the Ottawa near the site of the capital, the Gatineau, which comes through a picturesque valley from the north, and the Rideau, which reaches the Ottawa from the south. Two striking waterfalls, the Chaudiere and the Rideau, lie within the borders of Ottawa."[16]

Figure 4.5 shows an historic bird's-eye view of the city and its prominent rivers. The city is situated in the Great Lakes–St. Lawrence bioregion, with a rustic mixture of forests, farmlands, and water. Ottawa's preeminent planner, Jacques Gréber described the Ontario–Quebec border gracefully: "The flat lands on the Ontario side and the nonchalant courses of its rivers make, with its pastoral scenery, striking contrast with the Quebec side, its undulating hills riddled with lakes, traversed by turbulent streams and covered by thick growths of trees."[17]

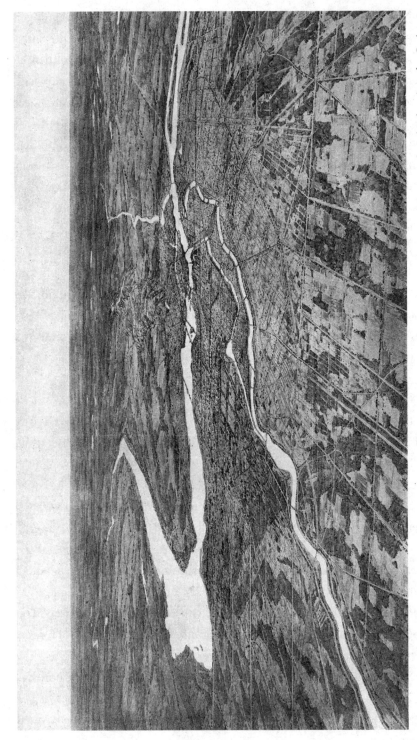

Fig. 4.5 Bird's-eye view of the Ottawa/Hull area in 1915, looking northward. The Ottawa River runs east and west across the drawing, the Gatineau River flows south into the Ottawa River, and the Rideau River flows north into it. The Rideau Canal is the western arm. (Rendering by Jules Guerin, landscape artist, from the Federal Plan Commission of Ottawa and Hull, "Report of the Federal Plan Commission on a General Plan for the Cities of Ottawa and Hull," 1915.)

Like Milwaukee, Ottawa lies at the confluence of three rivers (Figure 4.6). The story of those rivers defines the city's early history. The Ottawa River is used as a provincial boundary, separating the cities of Ottawa in Ontario and Gatineau in Quebec. Unlike the Milwaukee urban landscape, Ottawa's shape is less geometric; urban areas fan out from the Ottawa River in a more organic way. Ottawa has so far rejected the grandiose City Beautiful promenade to Parliament Hill, although that urban design approach has been considered and argued for nearly a century.[18] Instead, Ottawa is an intimate, human-scaled city. In fact, it was settled not as a prominent world capital at all, but as a mill town, converting lumber from the surrounding forests to wood products, dominated by the railroads needed to transport these products broadly. "The city had been laid out on no plan, and it developed on no plan. Industries grew up where they would. The railways carried on activities mostly as they liked."[19] The development of the Rideau Canal, a 124-mile system of channels, dams, and locks, helped shape the city and its economy.

Late in the nineteenth century, Lady Aberdeen, wife of Lord Aberdeen and an early feminist and social activist, promoted the idea of a planned capital. At least four city plans were subsequently completed in the first half of the twentieth century, including the 1903 plan by American landscape architect Frederick Todd, advocating the idea of a capital *region* (not merely a city) structured in a linked network of small urban parks, larger suburban parks, and very large conservation areas on the outskirts.[20] Subsequently, the 1915 plan, referred to as the Holt Report, recommended several spatial and administrative changes, including the creation of a federal district similar to the one developed for Washington, D.C.; zoning of industrial areas at the outer sections of the city; relocation of railways to the periphery; development of central plazas and parks; and acquisition of land on the Quebec side of the Ottawa River as a natural forested backdrop for Parliament Hill.[21] In addition, the Holt Report recommended parkland for a city of 350,000 people, although the population at that time was a fraction of that. Like Whitnall's later plan for Milwaukee, the Holt Report foresaw an expanding need for recreational landscapes for Ottawa's growing population. The plan included 3,000 acres of parkland, with a playfield of 7 to 10 acres within about a half mile of every resident—a plentiful supply even by today's standards.

As in Milwaukee, open-space connectivity was envisioned even then. The 1915 Holt plan recommends "connection of parks by means of parkways and the making of the park system continuous and comprehensive . . . the numerous waterways should be extensively used, not merely for business, but also for recreation. Few cities offer better facilities than Ottawa offers for pleasure upon the water."[22] The Ottawa Improvement Commission (predecessor to the National Capital Commission) had promoted parkways even earlier.

OTTAWA
ONTARIO

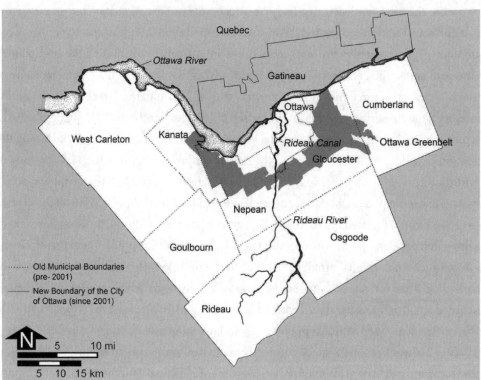

Fig. 4.6 Ottawa, Ontario region showing the greenbelt in gray tone.

4.1 The Rideau Canal

The Rideau Canal, the oldest operating nineteenth-century canal in North America, is an allegory to the evolution of recreational corridors (Figure 4.7). It links lakes and rivers by canals over a 124-mile route from Ottawa to Kingston, including twenty-four dams and forty-six locks. Its original purpose was to provide a safe supply route between Montreal and the Great Lakes, bypassing the St. Lawrence River. After the War of 1812, Lieutenant Colonel John By supervised two thousand men to build the canal system, planned as a wartime supply route. Officially opened in 1832, the canal was lauded as one of the greatest engineering feats of the nineteenth century and today is a featured centerpiece of Ottawa.

The area of the Rideau was wilderness when the canal was built. Many workers died of malaria during its construction through mosquito-infested swamps. After its completion, the Rideau became a busy commercial route from Montreal to the Great Lakes. But when most commercial water traffic reverted to the St. Lawrence by midcentury, the Rideau Canal's heyday ended. Over the last part of the nineteenth century, however, the canal system remained an important local transportation system and by the turn of the twentieth century had become an important tourist area for hunting, fishing, and boating. Hotels and cottages sprung up along the route. Since then, there has been massive expansion of recreational facilities and uses along the canal. As a site of national historic significance, the canal system attracts thousands of visitors each year. In 2000, it was designated a Canadian Heritage River by the Minister of Canadian Heritage.

Ottawa's section of the Rideau is the first 5 miles, maintained for over thirty years as a winter roadway of ice in the middle of the city. Billed as the world's longest skating rink, the canal is packed with skaters, including people commuting to and from work, from late December to late February, depending on weather. In spring, summer, and fall the canal is favored for canoeing and motor boating, and the pathways alongside it are well used by joggers, walkers, and cyclists. The canal looks much like it did in the mid-nineteenth century with its limestone locks, hand-turned cranks, wood-frame lock-master houses, and stone supply buildings. The maintenance of this corridor as a recreational, historic, and cultural landscape is a springboard for other connected open-space planning in the city of Ottawa and its region.

Fig. 4.7 Skating on the Rideau Canal near central Ottawa, with Parliament Hill in the background. (Photo by Ken W. Watson.)

Nearly its first formal task was to build two parkways, one replacing industrial uses along the Rideau Canal and one bringing visitors into the parkland east of the city.[23]

This focus on recreational parkways is a lasting legacy for the city. Eleven parkways were planned in the Ottawa and Hull region. At that time there were already 850 acres of parks and parkways in the city, in addition to the Central Experimental Farm, which still exists as an important open space in the heart of the metropolitan area (Figure 4.8).

Thirty-five years later, many of these ideas were proposed again in the plan of Jacques Gréber, now considered the architect of Ottawa's open-space system. Unlike Milwaukee, with its grassroots planning, Ottawa sought out the internationally known French architect and urban planner to design the nation's capital. There were three distinct aspects of Gréber's plan: (1) a description of the capital area; (2) an analysis of its main spatial problems; and (3) a prescription for a new type of capital.[24] While much of Gréber's plan was not implemented, many of the open-space components were.[25] Nancy Pollack-Ellwand observes that the elements of the plan that "relate better to improved human existence in the city were readily embraced, such as open spaces, organic forms, and more modest scales."[26] A vast system of protected green open spaces

Fig. 4.8 Ottawa's Experimental Farm provides rural open space very near the central city, represented here by a pastoral lane amidst farm fields. (Photo by the author.)

was designed, in the form of parkways, large park nodes, and nature preserves (Figure 4.9). Like Whitnall's plan for Milwaukee, the parkway concept focused on the city's river system. Some parkways were built; for those that were not, open-space corridors were retained. Unlike Whitnall's vision, Gréber's plan intended the parkways to be very urban and not necessarily well connected. The scenic nature of the parkways was no doubt meant to be experienced in a leisurely way from the automobile. Connectivity for walking or cycling was not preeminent.

At the heart of the Gréber plan was the notion of a large greenbelt surrounding the city of Ottawa, similar to Ebenezer Howard's Garden City concepts for Great Britain. This became Gréber's main legacy in the physical form of the city. The greenbelt was meant to include an area that could accommodate a half million residents. The inner limit was chosen based on providing municipal services economically. The greenbelt would encompass areas of great natural beauty. Although limiting sprawl, it was meant to include building sites, especially for government and other institutional buildings.[27] The greenbelt was seen as an urban-growth boundary and a physical separation between urban and rural land uses, people and functions, thereby protecting rural life and preserving the natural environment. It was not envisioned that the greenbelt would connect to the parkways, as the greenbelt was far from the city at that time. (One parkway has since been extended to the eastern part of the greenbelt along the Ottawa River).

The National Capital Commission (NCC), formed in 1959, was the key agency in implementing the Gréber plan. The commission is a Crown corporation whose mandate is to plan and assist in the development, conservation, and improvement of the National Capital region in keeping with its significance as the seat of the Canadian government. Part of that mission promotes Ottawa as a green capital, representing a green nation. The commission has no authority over local units of government, and since no effective local zoning plans existed at mid-century, expropriating land was the most expedient means to amass the acreage needed to create parks, parkways, and other capital improvements. Therefore, the NCC hastily acquired strategically located lands on both sides of the Ottawa River over a fifteen-year period, allowing it to implement the Gréber Master Plan.[28] From 1946 to 1960, the NCC purchased some eighteen hundred properties, totaling about 6,249 acres, for the Ottawa River Parkway, Rideau River Parkway, Western Parkway, and Eastern Parkway, and today there are over 25 miles in six parkways in the urban area of the capital region.

However, the greenbelt idea did not catch on easily, and strong criticism of it hindered progress toward implementation.[29] The greenbelt was controversial from the start, and from 1945 to 1958 very little progress was made. Subsequently, 589 properties were purchased for

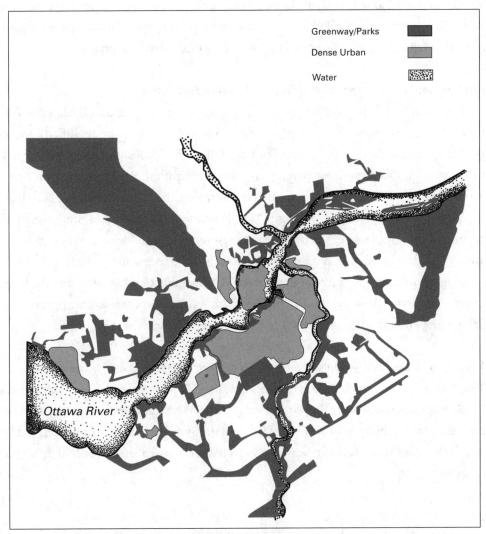

Fig. 4.9 Jacques Gréber's open-space plan for the National Capital region (Adapted from Jacques Gréber, Plan for the National Capital, Ottawa: National Capital Planning Service, 1950.)

the main landmass, accounting for nearly 24,500 acres newly in National Capital Commission ownership. By the end of 1960, this land-buy had cost Canadians $39 million.[30] Greenbelt opposition came from farmers, landowners, speculators, and local units of government on the urban fringe, who foresaw that the wave of building expansion in Ottawa was likely to engulf them, but that the federal government would offer lower prices than would the free market.

Despite the opposition, the greenbelt eventually circled the entire metropolitan area, encompassing about 44,000 acres in a 25-mile arc averaging about 2.5 miles wide, and only

5 miles from Parliament Hill in places. Among its many purposes, recreation has been especially important, particularly in more passive forms. It has proven to be a unique planning achievement—probably one of the only successful urban greenbelts.

Contemporary Open-Space Systems in Milwaukee and Ottawa

How has Charles Whitnall's connected open-space system matured over the last half century? What contemporary open-space initiatives have built on or modified Jacques Gréber's vision for Canada's capital? For both Ottawa and Milwaukee, open-space networks were motivated by interwoven goals, where recreation played an important part. Michael Hough, a distinguished Canadian landscape architect, puts recreation in its place for contemporary open-space planning: "The primary purpose of parks, since their 19th century beginnings, has been to provide places of recreation and leisure. While these will always remain as an essential ingredient of civic life, the recreational needs, values, and make-up of urban people are changing. There is an emerging trend toward parks that serve many purposes besides recreation."[31] Indeed, in Milwaukee and Ottawa other purposes are being interwoven in various contexts and at a range of scales.

Milwaukee: Elements Awaiting Assembly for a Connected Open-Space System

Today, three main agencies are active in Milwaukee's open-space planning. Milwaukee County continues to be an important steward of Whitnall's open-space legacy. The regional planning body, Southeastern Wisconsin Regional Planning Commission, and the state of Wisconsin have also forwarded connected open-space visions, although in quite different ways.

THE OAK LEAF TRAIL

The Oak Leaf Trail, owned and managed by Milwaukee County, is the modern version of Whitnall's figure eight around the Milwaukee metropolitan area and creates the scaffolding for the city's greenway network (Figure 4.10). The county has been astute in setting aside river corridors and other valuable land for protection throughout its nineteen municipalities over several decades. The Oak Leaf Trail is now a 92-mile trail that connects county parks through a combination of dedicated trails, bike routes, and other recreational land along parkways.

The original routing for a paved bike trail through the parkway system was developed in 1939 by a group of bicycle enthusiasts. It loosely traced Whitnall's figure eight. In the 1960s and 1970s pressure built again, especially from the biking community, to create more off-street trails through undeveloped parklands. The county began funding and imple-

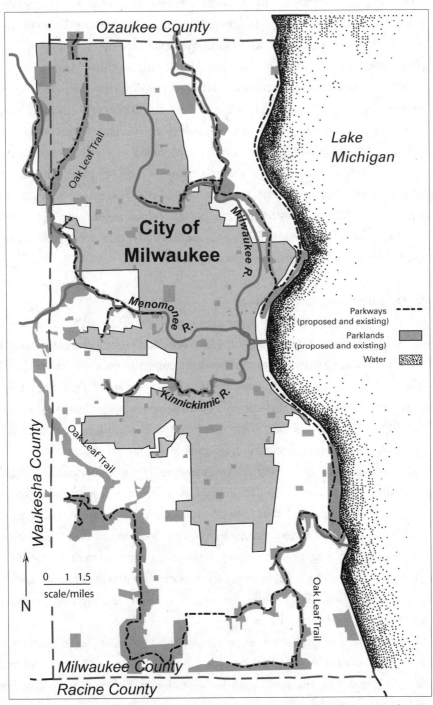

Fig. 4.10 Parks and parkways in Milwaukee county. The Oak Leaf Trail is shown as the connected linear system in a rough figure eight around the county.

menting off-road sections designed to support multiple recreational uses—jogging, in-line skating, bicycling, and cross-country skiing. Milwaukee County's 1972 plan proposed almost 1,976 acres of new parkway land that included extensive trails.[32] Bicycling groups continue to be active participants in corridor planning for the southeast Wisconsin region.

In 1990, the parkways encompassed over 7,413 acres in a dozen parkways varying from 12 acres to 4,000 acres each. Recent plans call for county acquisition of lands that continue to link the parkways and protect primary environmental corridors, and the Oak Leaf Trail is being expanded in some locations, including a couple of rails-to-trails projects that will connect to the existing network.[33] The system is composed of 140 parks and parkways totaling nearly 15,000 acres. Over time, the objectives of the system have broadened significantly from recreation; nonmotorized transportation has also become an important focus. However, some county parklands are being sold, so advocates worry that the trend for county corridors is not going in the right direction.

REGIONAL ENVIRONMENTAL CORRIDORS

The Southeastern Wisconsin Regional Planning Commission (SEWRPC), a "Council of Governments" organization, does much of the background planning for greenway corridors. The County Parks Commission helps fund the commission and uses its planning services. The 1991 Parks and Open Space Plan and 1989 Inventory of Vacant and Under-utilized Riverine Land have been particularly influential; each has given spatially explicit recommendations for nearly 1,000 acres of new open-space acquisition, with keen attention to opportunities presented along riparian lands.[34]

At the scale of the seven-county southeast Wisconsin area, the Southeastern Wisconsin Regional Planning Commission's plans for environmental corridors have also influenced connected open-space planning. Theirs is an example of applied landscape ecology at the scale of a large metropolitan region. Primary environmental corridors are created from elongated areas in the landscape, encompassing the highest quality elements of the regional natural resource base. They include the best surface waters, undeveloped floodplains and shore lands, woodlands, wetlands, wildlife habitat, groundwater recharge areas, and scenic, historic, scientific, and cultural sites.[35]

The identification and protection of environmental corridors in Wisconsin was inspired by the pioneering work of Philip Lewis, a landscape architect at the University of Wisconsin–Madison, who, for several decades beginning in the 1960s, promoted setting aside corridors of water, wetlands, and steep slopes to protect the most valuable recreational, scenic, and environmental lands.[36] For over thirty years, the Southeast Wisconsin

4.2 Hank Aaron State Trail

The Hank Aaron Trail will nearly complete Charles Whitnall's vision of linear parks along Milwaukee's river system. A critical open-space gap existed in downtown Milwaukee along the Menomonee River valley. In an ambitious urban-revitalization project the gap is being connected by the State of Wisconsin, using greenway design, river restoration, and brownfields development.

Beginning as early as the 1860s, as industrial development occurred in the Menomonee valley, the river was straightened and dredged and its wetlands filled. Tons of landfill and miles of sheet piling lined its banks. As manufacturing and rail transport declined, these lands were abandoned. Now the area contains one of the largest undeveloped sections of central-city land in America.

The new 7-mile urban greenway, in the heart of the heavily industrialized valley, will begin at a new state park at the Lake Michigan shore, run through densely populated and ethnically diverse neighborhoods in the inner city, and link up at the other end to the existing Oak Leaf Trail system. It will create accessible parkland for four neighborhoods, where about a hundred thousand children live with only minimal recreational facilities.[1] Its route passes next to Milwaukee's new professional baseball stadium, a major node in the redevelopment of the Menomonee valley (Figure 4.11). Even though the environmental motivations for the project are strong, recreation is a main priority, according to project managers.

Named after Milwaukee's most famous baseball player, the Hank Aaron State Trail is a collaboration of the Wisconsin State Department of Natural Resources, Milwaukee County, City of Milwaukee, National Park Service, business associations, and the Southeastern Wisconsin Regional Planning Commission. The White House Millennium Council designated the trail as Wisconsin's Millennium Legacy Trail.[2] The state leads the project and will own and manage the trail after completion; it runs a well-established state trails system, heavily weighted toward trail-based recreation. The Hank Aaron Trail is more complex. It is the only urban trail in the Department of Natural Resources system and is justified by a diverse set of rehabilitation goals in the degraded urban valley.

Initially, people thought the idea of a trail in this run-down industrial corridor was ridiculous. It has taken years to build a coalition around the concept, but the project is now well funded and under construction. More than a half mile of sheet piling has been removed, riverbanks have been restored and riparian vegetation planted. A paved trail with interpretive signs and picnic pavilions is situated near the baseball stadium (Figure 4.12). Along other sections, concrete linings have been removed, wetlands created, and river-banks stabilized. Businesses have been key partners. For instance, Sigma Environmental, newly located in the Menomonee valley, incorporated one link of the trail into its prop-erty next to the river. It is interesting that, late in his life, Charles Whitnall predicted that the Menomonee valley would become "a beauty spot which, for Milwaukee, would be more important than Central Park is to New York City."[3]

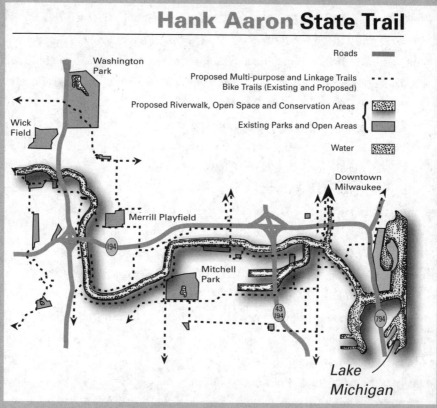

Fig. 4.11 Location of the planned Hank Aaron State Trail, running west from Lake Michigan through the Menomonee River valley in downtown Milwaukee.

---

[1] Tony Hopfinger, "Valley of Dreams," *Milwaukee Magazine,* 1996.

[2] The White House Millennium Council was President Clinton's initiative linking federal, state, and local govern-ments to create numerous projects celebrating the challenges and opportunities of the twenty-first century. The Millennium Trails project, in partnership with the Department of Transportation, Rails-to-Trails Conservancy, American Hiking Society, and National Endowment for the Arts, recognized, promoted, and stimulated the cre-ation of trails to "Honor the Past and Imagine the Future" as part of America's legacy for the year 2000.

[3] Hopfinger, "Valley," 1996.

Fig. 4.12 The new Hank Aaron trail runs near industrial and transportation facilities along the Menomonee River valley. A paved trail and streambank recovery project is shown here, next to Miller Park, the Milwaukee Brewers' new stadium (just outside this photo left of the river). (Photo by the author.)

Regional Planning Commission has sought to protect more than 347 square miles of environmental corridors in the region, about 15 square miles of which lie within Milwaukee County. Corridors are protected through a combination of land acquisition, land-use regulation, and policies to avoid utility-service extensions that support inappropriate urban development in the corridors.[37]

The 1997 Natural Areas Plan completed by SEWRPC found 447 key natural areas remaining in southeastern Wisconsin. Friends of Milwaukee's Rivers has pressured the regional agency to implement plans for protecting these natural resources. A watchdog group for rivers, Friends of Milwaukee's Rivers is a member of the Waterkeeper Alliance, a national coalition dedicated to protecting and restoring waterways. Its Milwaukee River Corridor Project, for instance, addresses the protection needs raised by the Natural Areas Plan in the Milwaukee River basin. The Friends group has also addressed residents' needs for physical access to the city's three rivers. Its Milwaukee Urban Water Trail, a takeoff on Chicago's water trail system, is addressing the lack of public access points along most of the Menomonee River. It has inventoried and mapped river access, including dangerous (and sometimes illegal) informal launching points for small human-powered craft. Its action plan will ultimately depict gaps, needs, and strategies for improving access to Milwaukee's rivers.

There is no overall vision for connected open space in the Milwaukee region, even though southeastern Wisconsin is seen as a national model for its delineation and protection of environmental corridors. There is no map that integrates recreational corridors, environmental corridors, and other open-space connections into an overall vision for regional open space. The Hank Aaron Trail, although only an 8-mile link across the city, may be the stimulus for this integration, given the collaboration that has been achieved across governmental levels, private enterprise, and the nonprofit community.

Ottawa: Diverse Network Comprises Greenways, Parkways, and Greenbelt
Both the City of Ottawa and the National Capital Commission plan and implement open-space land for the city. Public open spaces are divided into two main patterns: the greenbelt and the parkway corridors. Overlaying these systems, the greenspaces of the capital region are linked by about 105 miles of recreational pathways, managed by the National Capital Commission.[38] These connections are found both within and outside the parkways and greenbelt, linking numerous natural and cultural attractions. The wide, paved paths are designed for multiple users—walkers, joggers, cyclists, and in-line skaters—and often parallel the intact shorelines of the region.[39] The NCC began constructing them in the 1970s as high-rise living proliferated and traffic increased.

THE GREENBELT AND PARKWAYS

The impact of the greenbelt has been thoroughly analyzed since its creation. It is a paradoxical landscape. According to greenbelt planner Richard Scott, "with this greenbelt you ask ten different people what it is and you get ten different answers."[40] The city has grown up to and beyond the greenbelt boundaries, with three main satellite communities outside it (Figure 4.13). The city had reached a population of a half million in 1970 rather than Gréber's projection of the turn of the century.[41] So the greenbelt's contribution to

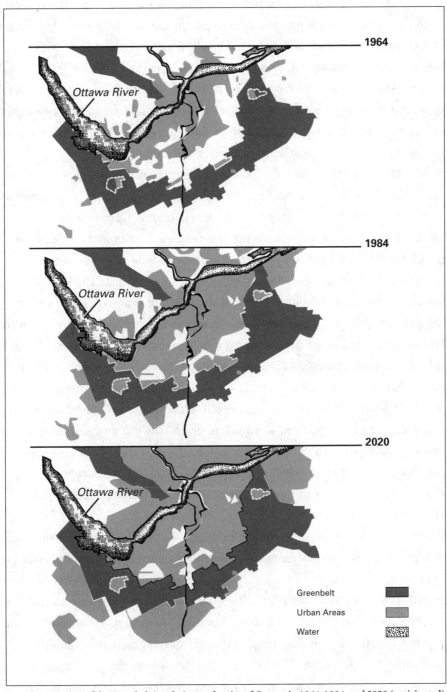

Fig. 4.13 Location of the greenbelt in relation to the city of Ottawa in 1964, 1984, and 2020 (anticipated). Three satellite communities that currently exist are shown in gray outside the boundaries of the greenbelt in the 2020 view. (Adapted from National Capital Commission, "Greenbelt Master Plan," 1996.)

urban structure has been more to separate satellite communities from the main urban area, rather than to constrain suburban development. Daniel Nixey evaluated the greenbelt's economic impact and found that it has had little effect on the density of existing and planned suburban development, or on suburban land markets.[42] Meanwhile, the greenbelt area has been expanded in recent years and, according to the *Greenbelt Master Plan* (1996), will continue to grow. Some greenbelt land is being sold, facilitating new land purchases. For every acre developed or sold, the NCC plans to add 4 acres of natural land.[43] Connecting ecosystems will be a main driver of new land purchases.

In 1991, the National Capital Commission commissioned an ecological study of the greenbelt.[44] The purpose was to examine the biophysical functions of the greenbelt and to show how an ecologically based vision could be used in future planning. The study examined natural features within and outside the greenbelt boundaries, and the degree to which the greenbelt protects them. Findings show that the majority of significant natural areas in the region are either not inside the greenbelt or at best only partially within it. In fact, greenbelt boundaries do not follow natural features, but appear to be based on other factors. A single wetland might be partly in the greenbelt and partly outside it. On the other hand, much of the land originally purchased for the greenbelt was previously farmed and so has been gradually managed for increased habitat quality. In fact, there are now recreational conflicts with bears, moose, and coyotes in areas that were formerly farmed.[45]

Despite the greenbelt's failure at containing the growing city of Ottawa, and its ambiguous ecological soundness, planners are quick to defend the greenbelt for the many assets it provides. Although it has not halted the city's growth at its border, it has provided a structure for urban form that brings nature closer to many urban residents, creates room for large institutional uses, and provides some level of environmental benefit. Given this evolution, the greenbelt now has an entirely new mandate, quite separate from curbing urban development. Even the development industries do not want the greenbelt degraded, according to interviewees, since many investments have been made that rely on the greenbelt's protection.

Evaluated by connectivity standards, the story is mixed. Ironically, to reach the greenbelt most residents and tourists must drive. The NCC is working to link various parts of the greenbelt together, to provide a unifying thread from an experiential standpoint. A system of continuous pedestrian and vehicular routes within the greenbelt was part of Gréber's original plan; unfortunately, only portions of it have been completed.[46] However, the 1996 plan incorporates a spine trail and connected spur trails throughout the length of the greenbelt. The Greenbelt Pathway, a continuous 38-mile recreational link, is currently being constructed and is part of a long-range implementation plan for NCC pathways (Figure 4.14).[47] Its objectives are to connect key visitor attractions and link with other pathways in the region; provide a unique rural experience; incorporate existing trails, forest access roads, and recreational pathways; encourage casual walking and extended hiking, cross-county skiing, and bicycle touring; sustain the atmosphere of a rustic farm lane in keeping with the greenbelt landscape; and address universal accessibility to key visitor attractions and segments of the pathway.[48]

According to NCC interviewees, the pathways provide the rationale for protecting both recreational and historic resources. In addition, the commission is interested in making greenway connections from the greenbelt to areas beyond the outer boundary. In addition, NCC is developing other environmental corridors outside the greenbelt. One main technique for getting corridors out into the countryside is by way of abandoned rail lines, of which there are many in the Ottawa region.

Fig. 4.14 The Shirleys Bay area in the western portion of the greenbelt, about a mile from the Ottawa River, the western terminus of the pathway. The 38-mile Greenbelt Pathway will span the greenbelt from east to west. About 9 miles have been completed. The pathway is designed to provide experience of the varied landscapes of the greenbelt, including natural areas and rural/agricultural landscapes. (Photo courtesy of the National Capital Commission.)

The NCC is still active in managing the parkways, providing scenic gateways into the city and toward Parliament Hill. The organization considers them to be "cultural landscapes," claiming that similar parkways could never be built in modern times. The NCC limits signage and lighting on the parkways, prohibits commercial vehicles, and restricts access to prevent congestion. It manages the parkway landscapes to enhance views toward the Ottawa River and other scenes. On Sunday mornings throughout the summer, many of the parkways are closed to cars, allowing walkers, cyclists, and in-line skaters to take over the paved routes. Some of the corridors that were saved as parkways remain open, and present tremendous opportunities for more open-space connections. Although the city controls this land, the NCC is working with the city to envision the functions that these corridors will have in the future.

CITY GREENWAYS

Greenway planning by the City of Ottawa has been somewhat complicated in recent years. The Ottawa metropolitan area was governed until 2001 by eleven municipal governments, of which the City of Ottawa was one. In addition, the Region of Ottawa–Carleton was created in 1969 to provide regional services for the metropolitan area. In 2001, all twelve of these jurisdictions were merged into a new City of Ottawa, aligned with the former Region of Ottawa–Carleton boundary and encompassing over 1,000 square miles (as seen in Figure 4.6), almost four times the size of metropolitan Toronto. Over 90 percent of the city is rural. The new city is now one of Canada's most geographically extensive urban areas, with about 28 percent of the city forested. In addition, about half of the soils in the rural areas of the city are suitable for agricultural production, and agriculture is a key element of the city's economy.[49]

In 1991, the City of Ottawa developed a greenway plan for the area within its old (smaller) boundaries.[50] The plan specified twenty corridors consisting of five components—environmentally sensitive areas, waterway corridors, linkages, major open spaces, and agricultural areas (Figure 4.15).[51] The greenway plan was incorporated into the Official Plan, the city's outline of how it wants to grow. Official Plans place an emphasis on land-use planning but also include economic, environmental, and social goals. About three-fourths of the land designated in the corridors is already owned or managed by public agencies. Connectivity is one important objective.[52]

Due to administrative and financial constraints, and because of the city's reorganization, the greenways plan stalled. The boundaries of most corridors have not yet been set, management plans have not been completed, and therefore none of the corridors are fully complete. In fact, the 1991 greenways plan did not have enough environmental information to make implementation feasible or to substantiate ecological need. Environmentally sensitive areas of the city had not been fully mapped. Subsequently, the Natural and Open Space Study was completed and approved in 1998.[53] It compares and classifies all natural and open-space land in the city, helps in reviewing development applications, and better defines the boundaries of the greenway system. The study recommends where *development, sensitive development,* and *no development* should occur, and targets fifty-seven natural areas for protection.

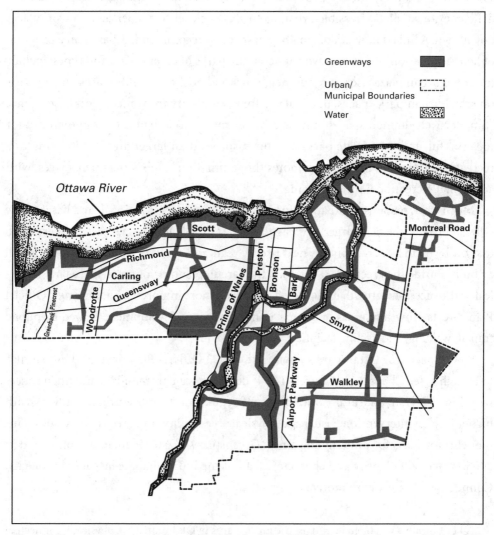

Fig. 4.15 Twenty greenway corridors planned for the former City of Ottawa, before consolidation with surrounding municipalities. (Adapted from City of Ottawa, Dept. of Engineering Works, "Land and Water Background Report: State of the Environment Reporting Program," 1993.)

With the greenway plan and the Natural and Open Space Study in place, the new city is poised for substantive greenways development, especially since acquiring large tracts of land in the Marlborough Forest southwest of the urban area and in other environmentally significant parts of the rural area. For the downtown section of the city, an award-winning Downtown Ottawa Urban Design Strategy 2020 was completed in 2004 collaboratively between the NCC and the City. It creates a shared vision of the downtown region and places a heavy emphasis on an interconnected network of open space. The plan found that, outside the open space provided along the waterways, there is a deficiency of smaller, accessible urban open spaces closer to residences and workplaces downtown. A linked network of small open spaces is recommended, based on a program of land acquisition. The plan advocates creating parks of diverse sizes and types, including small urban plazas, squares, and neighborhood pocket parks. It places an emphasis on small urban park spaces, particularly for their ability to connect with larger ones. "Smaller well-defined spaces may be a better means to enhance the opportunity for meaningful, active and safe parks and open spaces than larger areas."[54] Relating to a recreational mission, the plan promotes the "animation" of existing open spaces, with additional recreational programming.

Much work remains to expand efforts throughout its larger regional land base. A new Official Plan for the new, larger city was adopted in 2003. Ottawa's population is expected to grow by up to 50 percent in the next twenty years and about two-thirds of housing will be built outside the greenbelt. Therefore, the careful planning of open-space land is critical to the successful growth of the city. This is even more important since the new Official Plan directs growth to areas of compact and mixed-use development, served by public transit, walking, and cycling facilities.

Greenspaces for Ottawa are shown in the 2003 Official Plan on a gradient similar to Hough's (see Chapter 1) (Figure 4.16). It depicts a scale from more rural open spaces with high diversity, natural values, and self-regulation to more urban contexts with higher human intervention, visual and physical accessibility, and greenspace values. This model is the basis for undertaking a new Greenspaces Master Plan, to be completed in 2006, which will identify and characterize all of the individual greenspaces in the city. Connectivity is a primary motive:

> A key objective will be to identify those greenspaces in Ottawa that are physically connected, or that could be connected, in a Greenspace Network. The network includes natural features

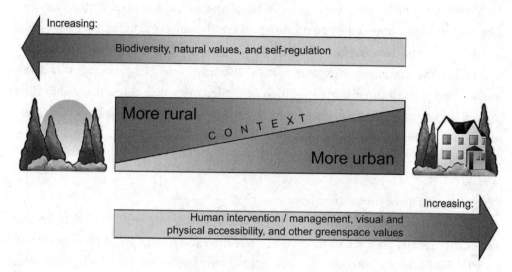

Fig. 4.16 Ottawa's gradient of open spaces, from rural to urban, including scales of natural values and human intervention. (Adapted from City of Ottawa, "Official Plan," 2003.)

and the linkages among them that maintain ecological functions and wildlife movement. It includes the open spaces that are accessible to the public, along pathways on the banks of rivers and through public school grounds. Recreational pathways as well as the river and stream networks help connect Ottawa's greenspaces. The Rideau and Ottawa Rivers, the Rideau Canal and other watercourses contribute extensively to the green and open quality of the Greenspace Network.[55]

The plan specifically addresses the balance, in the management of greenspaces, between protecting natural functions and providing recreational landscapes. It seeks to provide greater access to public greenspaces and more options for outdoor recreation and leisure. At the same time, it seeks to sustain natural systems—for example, by providing linked migration routes for species. To support the Greenspaces Master Plan, a technical study of natural features is under way for the most urban area of the city, which has identified 186 sites of importance. It includes woodlots, wetlands, and ravines of two acres or more. The sites are rated on nine criteria, one of which is connectivity. High ratings are given to sites that are close or adjacent to other natural features. When the Greenspaces Master Plan is completed, the Official Plan will be amended to accommodate its findings. This will most likely lead to acquisition policy, zoning, and development decisions.

Meanwhile, a unique form of open-space implementation is in place. Ottawa requires a Municipal Environmental Evaluation Report for all projects situated at or near environmentally important lands, including the greenway corridors identified in the 1991 plan. When the findings of this process show that adverse effects to a greenway corridor are likely, developments are modified or denied. Although a reactive rather than proactive method to guide development in important corridors, it is helping protect some lands for the time when the new city can continue the open-space vision in a more focused way.

Recreation as Thrust for Connectivity

For Milwaukee, protected greenway corridors were originally motivated by both recreation and environmental protection. Today, both recreation and nonmotorized transportation are vital motivators for connectivity work at the county level. And yet at the regional level, through the Southeast Wisconsin Regional Planning Commission, environmental quality objectives are driving the larger environmental corridor program. The two levels are not consistent or coordinated in any overall vision for connectivity, although recent efforts on the Hank Aaron State Trail are encouraging. This large project, through its many public and private partners, may serve as an important pilot case for collaborative work on restoring a connected urban fabric. Its contribution to the recreational needs for inner-city residents cannot be overstated; it illustrates the continued importance of urban recreation and the need for these objectives in open-space planning.

In many regards, Ottawa's greenway institutions seem to be moving in the same direction regarding motives and objectives. Both the National Capital Commission and the City continue to focus strongly on recreation as a key component, while integrating ecological protection in strategic ways. For instance, policies for Ottawa's new greenway system restrict development and emphasize linkages for environmental and recreation reasons over transportation and utilities. Collaborative possibilities between the NCC and the City have also improved; the federal government has only one municipality to work with, rather than eleven. Ottawa's historic framework, which was originally less ecologically based than Milwaukee's, is now being redesigned by the National Capital Commission and the City toward more environmentally sound outcomes.

These cities highlight important questions about recreation as a thrust for connected open spaces. Recreation is often seen as a one-time event—biking, in-line skating, walking—time that is discretionary outside work, school, or domestic obligations.

But "recreation" does not capture all the ways in which people enjoy and use open-space landscapes. Recreation is a solid term when we are talking about fields for soccer or beaches for swimming. But for other, especially passive, activities—even wandering around outside, thinking—the term is outmoded. The etymology of "recreation" is from the Latin *recreare* (to create anew, restore, refresh), meaning restoration to health. It signifies refreshment of strength and spirit as diversion after work. Spaces that refresh our spirits, that provide diversions from our hard work and problems, are not necessarily just spaces that entertain.

In the latter part of the twentieth century, vast sums of time, energy, and money were allocated to providing space for the latest sporting trend—whether fitness circuits, mountain biking trails, or skateboarding ramps. Some of these activities came and went. A broader program of recreation space also calls for spaces that are environmentally healthy, that delight, calm, and inspire. Many types of landscapes can fulfill this, particularly without special sporting specifications. The special niche for landscapes that connect is that they give us these amenities in places where we can walk home, or to school, or to work—in other words, to truly integrate recreation *with* the other parts of our lives. The skaters traveling to work on the Rideau Canal are a spectacular example, as are neighbors walking along the Menomonee River, overhearing the roar of the crowd as the Brewers play baseball. According to Tony Hiss,

> People need immediate places to refresh, reinvent themselves. Our surroundings, built and natural alike, have an immediate and a continuing effect on the way we feel and act, and on our health and intelligence. These places have an impact on our sense of self, our sense of safety, the kind of work we get done, the ways we interact with other people, even our ability to function as citizens in a democracy. In short, the places where we spend our time affect the people we are and can become.[56]

Furthermore, we now perceive fuzzier divisions between work and nonwork places and times, where many people are freer to structure the places and times of their work. In the future, this could dramatically alter the design of landscapes for very different lifestyles. For instance, as people telecommute from home, the provision of nearby nature for refreshment may be even more important in neighborhoods. According to those that monitor work trends, telecommuting has not caught on like it was projected to a decade or more ago. Among other challenges, many people working from home miss the community aspect of their workplaces. How can we create community, not just entertainment, through open-space design? Chapter 6 addresses this question directly.

Recreation is being integrated with other objectives in dynamic ways, and the case studies looked at so far show that multitasking is necessary for political and economic feasibility. The recreation–transportation connection is a natural one. For instance, Milwaukee's large connected system for biking is successful at using both on-street bike lanes and off-road routes that are integrated into environmental corridors. Integrating recreation with ecological goals is a striking trend. For a variety of reasons, one or the other may lead in funding initiatives or visionary planning, but the integration is where interesting things happen. Chicago Wilderness, for instance, relies heavily on a growing army of citizen volunteers who work to do management of natural areas. This is a prime example of alternative recreation—if one can count pulling out invasive plants on a local greenway all day as recreation! Here, discretionary time, some of it no doubt restorative to the volunteers themselves, is devoted to simultaneously restoring the natural landscape.

The recreation definition also highlights not only the restoration of energy and vitality but the restoration of health. When I was a child during the 1960s, my school, like hundreds across the county, started shaping us up. President Kennedy's Council on Physical Fitness had us out using the schoolyard for everything from 100-yard dashes to baseball throws. In addition, we left the schoolyard for the first time—jogging around the neighborhood, using local tennis courts, running on neighborhood tracks. President Dwight D. Eisenhower first established the council in 1956 after he learned that American children were less fit than European youth. In the twenty-first century, many people are even more concerned with the fitness of our youth, as dramatic statistics document obesity and sedentary lifestyles. The causes are complex. Many scholars are now working out the cause-and-effect relationships between the obesity epidemic and the physical landscape. But it is not hard to see that new housing developments often lack even sidewalks, much less restorative open-space trails along environmental corridors.

Providing recreational landscape space is vital in efforts to protect, plan, and connect open-space landscapes. The greenways movement has shown that recreation generates the enthusiasm, public interest, and funding for implementing projects. Corridors that connect recreational sites and hubs are particularly well used. It has also shown that new types of recreational use promote long-term care and management by the public, especially when broad definitions of recreation are used. Recreation connects inherently to transportation, education, ecology, and the other purposes of greenways.

5

Transportation—Movement: Calgary and Denver

Just as language has no longer anything in common with the thing it names, so the movements of most of the people who live in cities have lost their connection with the earth; they hang, as it were, in the air, hover in all directions, and find no place where they can settle.

—*Rainer Maria Rilke[1]*

Cities are known by their buzz—by the movement and excitement generated and maintained over days, weeks, and years by the steady flow of people. A big part of that motion is created, of course, by the automobile. But the cities that are deemed most vibrant and alive are ones where large numbers of people move around outside their cars in the public realm. From Manhattan to Montreal to Monterey this movement is important in cities across the continent, varying in amount, pattern, and purpose.

Chicago and Toronto are known for this buzz—the strident and sometimes snarled combination of motorized and nonmotorized movement. Unfortunately, in both of these large cities as in many others in North America, the neighborhoods outside the inner city are not particularly well served by nonmotorized means of transportation. Cities of all sizes are scrutinizing transportation options made possible in conjunction with connected open spaces. Calgary, Alberta, and Denver, Colorado, are two excellent examples of innovations in this respect. Both cities are primary transportation hubs for the Rocky Mountain west in their respective nations; they are each situated amid vast open landscapes where transportation and movement seem especially dependent on cars. However, with more than 500 miles of pathways and 160 miles of on-street bikeways within its boundaries, the City of Calgary boasts one of the most extensive urban pathway and bikeway networks in North America. In the United States, Denver is a national leader for greenway planning. Its 400 miles of greenways, parkways, and trails, supplemented by a superb park system, illustrate a number of lessons about the implementation of open-space connections that could be useful in enlivening other urban centers.

Calgary and Denver: Historic and Geographic Context
The official city Web sites for Calgary and Denver depict bucking broncos and stunning western scenery. These cities of the North American plains are both icons of western history, but a rugged ranching legacy is not all they have in common. Denver and Calgary are booming western metropolises with economies based historically on the earth's riches: minerals, oil, and gas. As nineteenth-century boomtowns they grew famous for their backdrop as gold rush prospectors and oil miners came and went. Denver is at the geographic crux of the United States, poised midway between Canada and Mexico. With the Rocky Mountains soaring to 14,000 feet behind it, Denver has grown to become a dominant force in the Rocky Mountain west, its urban center framed by Pikes Peak and Longs Peak. Calgary's backdrop is equally dramatic, with the Canadian Rockies lacing the horizon and the vast wilds of Banff National Park lying just to the west. Distances between destinations are great in both regions; from Denver the closest major city, Salt Lake City, is over 500 miles away. Calgary is relatively close to Edmonton (175 miles), but otherwise the Alberta prairie is vast and sparsely populated. Both cities enjoy warm Chinook winds in the winter between snowstorms, but even these can't temper Calgary's winters, where temperatures often drop to –40°F.

Denver is quite warmer and a far larger metropolitan region than Calgary, but both cities sprawl across the plains, bordered by the Rockies, but unfettered by other topographic barriers. In both places, development is explosive and obvious, visible for miles on the open land. Calgary sweeps across the Alberta prairie, occupying a vast land area of over 270 square miles. The city of Denver proper takes up a land area of 154 square miles, and the metro area is far larger: 500 square miles in 2000, up from 410 square miles in 1990. According to the Denver Regional Council of Governments, a build-out of about 1,100 square miles is foreseen, although regional recommendations suggest containing development to 747 square miles, and even this assumes a population growth to 3.2 million people.[2] The sprawl of human settlement creeps like a blight on the land. Historian Thomas Noel complains of Denver's commercial landscape: "the metropolis is littered with half-empty old strip mall stores, ugly boxes of short-lived discount stores, and elderly, struggling shopping malls."[3]

Calgary has grown to a city of almost a million in just over a century. Now at a population of 820,000, it is the sixth largest city in Canada. Its population doubled from 1947 to 1955 and then doubled again by the late 1960s. It has been the most rapidly growing city in Canada since the 1950s, with no signs of flagging. The city attracts thousands of newcomers each month. About 11 percent of Calgarians have migrated there within the last five years. The city gobbles land as it grows beyond its bounds, annexing into adjacent municipal districts.

Unlike Calgary's more consolidated jurisdictional structure, the metropolitan Denver region has over 300 special jurisdictions, including 65 cities and towns. Denver's metropolis engulfs six Front Range counties and continues to spread into surrounding areas. Over a half million people were added to the metro area between 1990 and 2000, a 29 percent increase. The city of Denver's population grew nearly 19 percent in the 1990s, reversing the 5 percent decline in the 1980s. Despite continuing decentralization and suburban growth, the Denver suburbs grew nearly twice as fast as the city itself in the 1990s. By the 2000 census, Denver's population stood at 550,000 with the entire Denver/Boulder Consolidated Metropolitan Area at nearly 2.6 million. By 2030, 1.2 million new residents are expected, and 800,000 new jobs created.

Calgary: Wide-Open Spaces on the Alberta Prairie
Calgary's urban form is strongly influenced by its natural legacy—by its place on the vast plains and at the confluence of the Bow and Elbow rivers, and by the cyclical economic growth fueled by natural resources. Deliberate planning of its open space is relatively recent here. Besides the main rivers, three other distinct waterways flow through the city—Nose Creek, West Nose Creek, and Fish Creek (Figure 5.1). The region as a whole has a dry climate, averaging only about 17 inches of precipitation a year, with only about 6 inches falling as snow, and the climate grows more arid as one moves south and east. Southern Alberta hosts a diversity of vegetation: dry short-grass prairie and a mixed native grass zone, a region of aspen parkland, an ecotone grading into grassland to the south, mixed-wood forest to the north, and mountain forests to the west. Ten human-made lakes, a major reservoir, and a large irrigation channel within Calgary contribute to the city's water resource.

Southern Alberta has a highly variable continental climate. Temperatures in Calgary range from highs of 90°F or more in summer, to lows of –40°F in winter. Warm westerly winds called

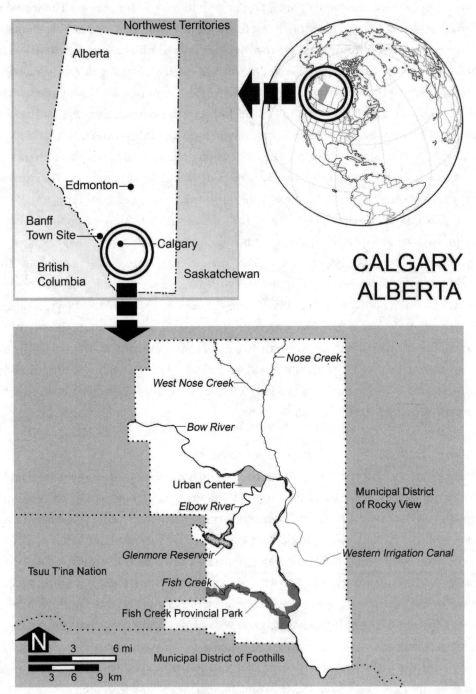

Fig 5.1 City of Calgary, Alberta and region.

Chinooks frequently blow through the mountain passes, periodically cracking cold winter temperatures, and preventing excessive snow cover. Even so, the cold climate prevents a lush, green environment. The pre-settlement landscape of this region was treeless; all of the trees currently found in Calgary and its environs have been planted, even those along natural waterways.

Prairie wetlands are a unique but threatened feature of Calgary's natural environment. In the 1980s it was estimated that 78 percent of Calgary's native wetlands had been lost to development. Today the estimate nears 90 percent. The urban expansion of Calgary continues to threaten significant wetland complexes—some that hold provincial and national importance as breeding grounds for waterfowl. In 1999 a wetlands inventory found about 14,000 wetlands in the undeveloped fringes of the city—likely to be disturbed by continuing urban expansion.[4]

The Bow River valley, lying along another important waterway, has been inhabited for the last ten thousand years. First Nation tribes subsisted here thanks to seasonal migrations of American buffalo herds. In the 1870s when Europeans hunted the buffalo to near extinction, the lifestyle of the tribes was disrupted forever. In 1875 a fort was established at the junction of the Bow and Elbow rivers, and farmers began to cultivate the fertile Alberta prairies. The plains to the west of Calgary are ideal for grain farming, and abundant native grasses have fed Alberta's world-famous beef for many decades.

The Canadian Pacific Railway arrived in Calgary in 1883; in the following year the town was granted the title of the first city in the Northwest Territories. In its early years, Calgary looked like most western towns—wood-frame houses and modest commercial buildings. A large part of the town burned in 1886, and a new building material was subsequently used—sandstone from the banks of the Bow River. The city soon became the center of Canada's cattle-marketing and meatpacking industries. The Calgary town-site is located near one of the only passages through the eastern wall of the Rocky Mountains—Kicking Horse Pass. This location contributes to Calgary's history as a launching point for the mountains and for British Columbia beyond.

From 1896 to 1914, settlers from all over the world poured into the region with the offer of free homestead land. The town of Calgary, incorporated in 1904, was predominantly supported by cattle ranching and crop agriculture until early in the twentieth century. The following year, Alberta became a Canadian province. Natural gas was discovered at about the same time, and Calgary experienced the first of several population booms, increasing by 400 percent from 1906 to 1911. In 1913 Thomas Hayton Mawson, an English landscape architect and town planner, was commissioned by the city to design a plan for future development. A proponent of City Beautiful ideals, Mawson made plans for a number of Canadian cities. His design concepts for Calgary were ambitious ("Vienna on the Bow") and unrealized.

Fig. 5.2 City of Calgary, with the Bow River in the foreground and the Rocky Mountain Front in the distance. (Photo by Mel Buschert.)

Just before World War I, huge reserves of oil were found near Turner Valley, and the city began its focus on oil and gas industries. Two tourist attractions also helped put Calgary on the map. In 1924 Banff National Park, 75 miles from Calgary, became an international tourist destination. And in 1930 the Calgary Stampede began—the "Greatest Outdoor Show on Earth." As a celebration of the cowboy and ranching culture, the Stampede is still a world-class showcase and tourist venue.

The economic boom-and-bust cycle associated with an oil-based economy has greatly impacted Calgary's development and character. One of the bust cycles occurred after World War I when the demand for oil dried up. A recession set in and many residents left to seek fortunes elsewhere. Calgary's biggest boom came in the 1970s after the formation of the Organization of Petroleum Exporting Countries (OPEC). OPEC restricted oil exports to Canada and the United States: the price of crude oil quadrupled, and the demand for Alberta's oil soared. At the peak of 1970s growth, three thousand people per month were moving to Calgary. The historic downtown was bulldozed block by block to make way for new development. Many of its historical landmarks were lost. The pace of development prevented any real master planning; little consideration was given to intentional urban design. Again, the boom cycle ended, when the early 1980s brought less reliance on Canadian oil and an international recession under way.

Since Calgary did not develop as a major manufacturing center, the river corridors were not degraded as in some industrial cities (Figure 5.2). Therefore, the history of Calgary's natural corridors is very different from Denver's, where the river corridors were far more industrialized. Deliberate open-space planning has not shaped the spatial form of historic Calgary the way it shaped those of early Chicago, Milwaukee, or Denver.

Denver: Queen City of the Plains

Denver's historic center is found where the South Platte River and Cherry Creek merge (Figure 5.3). The Colorado capitol building might be considered its modern heart, where the thirteenth step is reported to be at an elevation of one mile. The "Mile High City" was incorporated four decades earlier than Calgary (1861), established by a wave of prospectors in 1858 after gold was discovered at the South Platte–Cherry Creek confluence. The city built a network of railroads to accommodate newcomers, quickly making Denver the hub of banking, minting, supply, agriculture, and processing for a multistate region. Like the Calgary Stampede that came later, the establishment in 1906 of the Denver Livestock Exchange and National Western Stock Show created a destination for celebrating western life and commerce. Denver became the "Cow Town" of the Rockies. Boosters gave the city other less pejorative titles: Mile High City, Queen City of the Plains, and Gateway to the Rockies. Planners deliberately shaped aspects of the young city; the initial influx of people gave way to an era of steady growth that allowed for conscious construction of Denver as a multifaceted metropolis.

The South Platte River and Cherry Creek are prominent features of Denver's history. First the site of First Nation settlements, and then a railroad corridor and industrial magnet, the South Platte River basin is one of the most significant riparian systems in Colorado, providing not only water resources for the city of Denver but critical wildlife habitat. It is a lifeline for migratory birds of national and international importance. Despite its importance, decades of use and abuse maligned the Platte River. The industrial corridor is comprised of gravel quarries, sewage treatment facilities, and other industrial complexes. Gravel extraction has resulted in widespread destruction of wetland and riparian habitats, but has also created large lakes for migratory waterfowl. James Michener wrote in 1974 of the Platte as "a sad, bewildered nothing of a river. It carries no great amount of water, and when it has some, it is

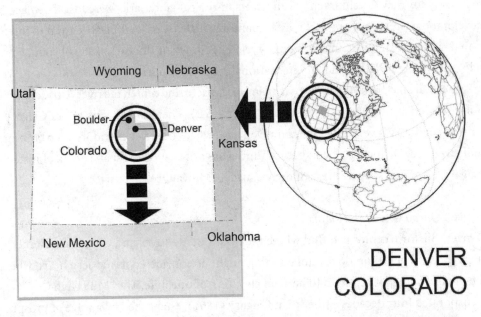

DENVER
COLORADO

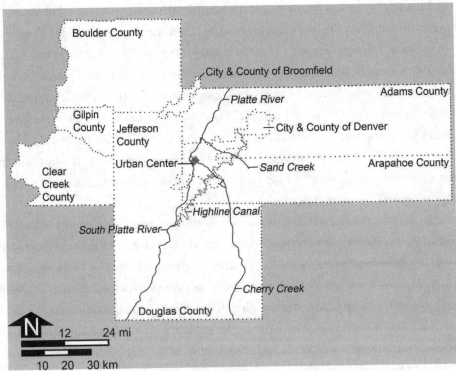

Fig. 5.3 The Denver, Colorado metropolitan region.

uncertain where it wants to take it. No ship can navigate it, nor even canoe it with reasonable assurance. It is the butt of more jokes than any other river on earth, and the greatest joke is to call it a river at all. It is a sand bottom, a wandering afterthought, a useless irrigation, a frustration, and when you've said all that, it suddenly rises up, aprils out to a mile wide, engulfs your crops and lays waste to your farms."[5] Although Michener certainly used poetic license, his account of the Platte River is backed by historical descriptions.

Denver's open-space chronicle is twofold: its parkway system was developed from the 1890s through the 1940s, and its mountain parks system was shaped from 1900 through the 1930s. As early as the 1890s, a few Denverites envisioned the city through a City Beautiful lens invigorated by ideas gleaned from the 1893 Chicago World's Fair. Robert W. Speer, mayor from 1904 to 1912 and 1914 to 1916, is credited with transforming Denver with City Beautiful aesthetic sensibilities and Progressive Era ideals.[6] He started a tree-planting program and created an office of city forester. He bought land along Cherry Creek, stabilized its banks, and foresaw a network of tree-lined parkways from the city center to outer residential neighborhoods.

Mayor Speer was motivated partly by Horace Cleveland's 1873 critique, which complained that midwestern and western cities, including Denver, failed to take advantage of their natural settings—"an outrage of common sense and beauty in dividing the land for profit."[7] A parkway system master plan was created in 1894 (Figure 5.4). Landscape architect Reinhard Schuetze and his successor S. R. DeBoer were instrumental in refining and enacting this plan, as were the Olmsted Brothers. The parkway vision was based on a hub-and-spokes network that linked parks, gardens, and neighborhoods.[8] In 1906 Mayor Speer hired landscape architect George Kessler and planner Charles Mulford Robinson, who envisioned a citywide system of boulevards and parks. They refined the parkway plan and started implementing it. Their plan spawned some of Denver's most successful civic spaces.

Speer's crowning achievement was perhaps the Cherry Creek Corridor, later named Speer Boulevard. Denver's first protected riparian corridor started with Speer buying land along Cherry Creek in 1907, ending another plan to reroute the creek into a sewer line. The creek began to be restored and maintained as Denver's first greenway. This laid the groundwork for the protection of Denver's river system many years later.

Another lasting legacy of Speer's conservation ethic was the 1912 founding of Denver's renowned Mountain Parks. The Mountain Parks were the most grandiose scheme of Denver's Progressive Era planners, creating public open space well beyond the city boundaries in neighboring Clear Creek, Douglas, Grand, and Jefferson counties. Frederick Law Olmsted Jr. was hired to plan the network, although implementing the plans required much

Fig. 5.4 Early bird's-eye view drawing of Denver, showing parkways stretching in straight lines toward the mountains. (From Thomas J. Noel and Barbara J. Norgren, *Denver: The City Beautiful and its Architects*, Historic Denver, Inc., 1987.)

effort and cooperation. An act of Congress was required to allow the city to buy federal land, the Colorado legislature needed to approve the city's purchase of land in other counties, and Denver's citizens had to approve taxation to pay for the parks. The forty-seven mountain parks, covering 14,000 acres and including twenty mountaintops, form a semicircle at the foothills of the Rockies along the western side of the city, a transition zone between urban development and the mountainous landscapes above the city (Figure 5.5). The parks encapsulate all of the region's ecosystems, from prairie to alpine tundra. Some were preserved for scenic views or watershed protection; Summit Lake Park is 60 miles from Denver and 8,000 feet above it. Important historic and cultural sites can be found as well; in the 1930s, beautiful stone structures were designed by the National Park Service and prominent Denver architects and built by the Civilian Conservation Corps. Maintaining the Mountain Parks has been an increasing financial challenge for the City of Denver. They remain an important resource. Where the parkways, such as Speer Boulevard, became one foundation for an urban greenway system, the Mountain Parks were a central piece in a broader network of open space for the entire metropolitan area.

Fig. 5.5 An aerial view of access roads built to Red Rocks Park in Jefferson County outside Denver. The photo was taken in the early 1930s. (Photo by Denver Photo Company, courtesy of Denver Public Library Western History Collection.)

Progressive Era planners wanted to create the biggest and wealthiest city in the Rocky Mountain west, and also the most beautiful. As in other cities of the time, long-range master planning was important for realizing these dreams. During the Great Depression, Denver Mayor Benjamin F. Stapleton and his manager of parks, George Cranmer, further implemented City Beautiful designs. They used New Deal funding and community help, particularly through the Civilian Conservation Corps and Works Progress Administration, to finish the Civic Center, extend the park and parkway system, and enlarge the Denver Mountain Parks system.[9]

Similar to Calgary, large oil and gas corporations fueled Denver's post–World War II growth. Forty-and fifty-story high-rise buildings sprang up downtown in the 1970s (Figure 5.6). Although Denver remains a hub for mining and oil exploration, this is now a smaller economic sector than at other times in history. Today, the city's economy relies on high-

Fig. 5.6 View of the Denver, Colorado skyline with the Rocky Mountain backdrop. (Photo by Ron Ruhoff.)

tech businesses and telecommunications. Federal government offices, such as the National Park Service's Denver Service Center, further support Denver's economy; the city supports the largest number of federal employees outside Washington, D.C.

According to Thomas J. Noel, a Denver historian, the city is obsessed with transportation systems, due to its relative isolation from other U.S. cities and its strategic advantage as a major transportation hub. This area of long distances and mountain obstacles has promoted a strong reliance on the automobile. Colfax Avenue, traversing Denver, Aurora, and Lakewood for over 30 miles, is reported to be the longest continuous street in America. In fact, Denver has one of the highest per-capita vehicle ownership rates in the country. In 1999, 98 percent of Denver area respondents indicated that their household owned at least one vehicle. Eighty-two percent drive alone to work.[10] But Coloradoans pay a price for this mobility, since roads and parking lots have carved up the metropolitan region, and automobile exhaust is the main cause of the brown cloud that visibly taints the Rocky Mountain air.

Open-Space Initiatives That Mobilize the Metro Regions

Calgary and Denver are not, overall, green places. However, both Calgary and Denver boast vital and extensive connected open-space systems, albeit in very different ways. Calgary has protected large sections of its river valley landscape as connected open space and claims 350 miles of regional and neighborhood pathways. Metropolitan Denver boasts over 400 miles of greenways and trails, over 300 designated parks comprising 5,100 acres, 100 miles of parkways, and 135 miles of hiking paths and bikeways. In both metropolitan areas, non-motorized transportation becomes crucial as the cities expand outward and automobile reliance, long a fact, is increasingly becoming a concern.

Calgary: Moving People on Pathways

The case of Calgary demands a reexamination of the whole greenway concept. As one planner explained, the term "greenway" has not really caught on in Calgary, although Calgarians are proud of their extensive pathway system. This highlights an important point: if greenways are only ecological, or if they are always green, then the river valley in Calgary is nearly the only example. However, more comprehensively, if they are landscape connections allowing people to navigate on foot or by bike, then Calgary's extensive pathway system is a striking example. The main story in Calgary is that these two types of systems—the river valley and the pathways—are programmatically separate although they physically connect.

Indeed, open-space planning is divided in the city. On one hand, Calgary has one of the most impressive nonmotorized path systems on the continent, bolstered by and founded on policy that forces developers to construct pathways in new housing subdivisions. The city has planned, funded, and implemented remarkable public land projects in the river valleys. On the other hand, these efforts have not been integrated as they might be. This points to the difficulty of satisfying numerous and competing objectives. Calgary's system is focused on promoting active lifestyles, perhaps at the expense of a strong environmental-corridor approach.

THE CHALLENGE OF OPEN-SPACE PLANNING AND RAPID GROWTH

Calgary has a unicity approach to city government, which arose in the 1950s in response to urban services needed in adjacent municipalities as Calgary grew.[11] At that time, several local municipalities were merged into one City of Calgary, with the logic that one economic and social unit can be more efficiently and effectively governed by one central municipal authority. This approach entitles the city to expand its boundaries, as needed, into rural municipalities. The city now borders the Municipal District of Rocky View, the

Municipal District of Foothills, and the Tsuu T'ina First Nation. While there is a clear line between Calgary and its Municipal District neighbors, that line steadily shifts outward (although not onto First Nation lands).

Suburban expansion, growth management, and open-space protection pose Calgary's biggest challenges (Figure 5.7). The city, largely created with a unicity approach, has not embraced a method that puts green infrastructure in place and then develops around it. An incremental means of growth, where the city annexes land as needed for growth, has made a coherent planning approach difficult. In the rapid growth areas, annexation takes place almost simultaneously with development so a regional planning perspective is difficult. Some regional planning is done between Calgary and its neighbors, including some open-space planning. However, a corridor approach has not been emphasized across borders.

The Urban Design Institute (UDI) is a powerful developers' organization in Calgary. The reactions of this group to various open-space issues often carry considerable weight with political forces. The City annually signs a Standard Development Agreement (SDA) with the UDI, detailing developers' obligations to provide public infrastructure and make financial contributions in the form of fees and levies. However, there is no all-encompassing growth-management planning for Calgary. This becomes problematic when conservation goals are wide reaching. For instance, prairie wetlands are currently a strong focus in the growing eastern half of Calgary. City planners are keen on creating and maintaining connections between these wetlands and the Bow River, but they lack the tools to protect these resources on private land.

The city currently uses two tools for acquiring public land and protecting it from development by giving it special status. Neither is particularly effective as an open-space conservation tool. Municipal Reserve requires that 10 percent of subdivision land be set aside in public ownership for schools, parks, and other needs. Most of the Municipal Reserve land is used to supply local and community parks. This policy does not specifically stipulate habitat protection, corridors, or nature protection as a part of this dedication. However, when the land for schools and other public uses has been satisfied, these lands are occasionally used for environmental protection.

A second category that limits development is Environmental Reserve status for land deemed unfit for development or unsafe, for instance, because of soil instability. It includes ravines, gullies, unstable slopes, or natural drainage courses, as well as floodplains, swamps, or land abutting lakes, rivers, and streams. Although the designation does not officially target ecological quality as a primary criteria (as the name would imply), these lands often hold environmental sensitivities. Environmental Reserve status is rarely used positively

Fig. 5.7 Exurban development spilling onto the prairie near Calgary. (Photo by Mark Ruthenberg.)

as a category to protect environmental values, though developers who own Environmental Reserve land usually transfer it back to the city. In some cases, pathways can be placed through these lands. However, public access is a controversial point in many subdivisions, and the location and character of pathways through them is a delicate issue.

From a systems point of view, an effort to tie these unbuildable Environmental Reserve sites together into a network is a sensible goal. However, this is difficult since developments are not necessarily contiguous. According to Parks Department planners, building a network of Environmental Reserve land is an objective, but they are limited by the need to react to developments as they are proposed. Given that, planners do not miss many protection opportunities that present themselves.

Open-space planning in Calgary is largely fueled by the public demand for paths. Developers tout nonmotorized paths as an attractive feature in new subdivisions. The fringe suburbs are being geared largely to active young families, so the amenity value of connecting to the larger pathway system is high. In sum, Calgary's pathway system is increasingly geared toward connecting all parts of the city, but the true ecological backbone is the river valley system.

5.1 Fish Creek Provincial Park

Fish Creek, located at the southern edge of the city of Calgary, was the first urban provincial park in Alberta and was one of the forerunners to the Urban Parks Program. It remains one of the largest urban provincial parks in Canada and hosts more than 3 million visitors annually. Including over 3,300 acres of parkland, it encompasses parts of both the Fish Creek and Bow River valleys (Figure 5.8). The park stretches about 12 miles from the Tsuu T'ina Nation in the west to the Bow River in the east (as shown in Figure 5.1). It includes diverse habitats, including wetlands, grasslands, spruce forests, and riparian woodlands. Home to many wildlife species, the area has also been an important site for humans for centuries. Over eighty archeological sites have been found in the park, revealing evidence of early buffalo jumps, native weaponry, First Nations campsites, and other artifacts. Humans are believed to have first settled in the Fish Creek valley around 6500 BC.

The Alberta government committed to fund Fish Creek Provincial Park in 1973, although protection was proposed as early as the mid-1960s. Most of the park has been left in its natural state; only a quarter of the land has been developed for outdoor recreation, including an extensive network of trails connecting to the citywide regional trail system along the Bow River. A management plan was done in conjunction with the city and adjacent landowners; strong connections between the park trails and city of Calgary

Fig. 5.8 Bridge across Fish Creek in Fish Creek Provincial Park. (Photo by Brett Sharkey, courtesy of Friends of Fish Creek Provincial Park Society.)

trails are one outcome. The Fish Creek trails are used about half-and-half by walkers and wheeled users. The park is heavily used as a commuting route.

Heavy rains flooded southern Alberta in June of 2005, washing away half of the Fish Creek trails and damaging the others. Seven pedestrian bridges over Fish Creek were destroyed and seven others damaged. Repairing this damage is a high priority. However, other long-range initiatives are under way. The park is being used as a destination for urban stormwater. Formerly, large storm sewers emptied water directly into Fish Creek. Four major wetland projects have been built to collect runoff from neighboring communities. Other ongoing initiatives include park expansion as land becomes available, and protection and enhancement of wildlife corridors within the park.

According to James Taylor and his colleagues, "Fish Creek . . . was unique in Canada because it was intended to function as a greenway within a major city while being funded and administered by a provincial government."[1] The ecological planning approach used for Fish Creek Provincial Park was advanced for its time.[2] It represents a great Canadian greenways success story.

[1] James Taylor, Cecelia Paine, and John FitzGibbon, "From Greenbelt to Greenways: Four Canadian Case Studies," *Landscape and Urban Planning*, 33 (Numbers 1–3, 1995):47–64, p. 52.
[2] Ibid.

PROTECTING THE RIVER VALLEYS: THE PROVINCIAL ROLE

The government of Alberta has been concertedly investing in urban parkland for nearly thirty years. In 1976, led by visionary Premier Peter Lougheed, the province initiated the Alberta Heritage Savings Trust Fund, established with oil and gas royalties. The premier saw the potential of these monies to benefit Alberta citizens, and providing urban parkland was one part of that agenda. The parks program was designed to buy land in river valleys throughout Alberta cities and towns and to keep these lands in the public domain. The first investment by the Urban Parks Program was in the Calgary and Edmonton river valleys. The province spent the money outright to acquire land; in Calgary this became the Fish Creek Provincial Park. Today, the fund has about Can$12 billion, with interest used primarily for capital projects. In addition to parks, the fund is used for libraries, scholarships, research, and health facilities.

In 1989 eleven Alberta municipalities became eligible to use over $82 million for development of urban parks as the result of the new Urban Parks Program. The purpose of the Urban Parks Program is given in its goal statement: "The establishment of significant areas of open space to ensure that urban populations have easy access to natural environments and the development of these areas to enable their sustained and unimpaired use for outdoor recreation."[12] Initially, five cities received funding, including $15 million earmarked for Calgary.

The provincial funding initiated an important process for river valley planning in the city, leading to adoption of the Urban Park Master Plan in March 1994. Prepared by the Citizens Advisory Committee for the City of Calgary, the plan includes an assessment of private lands that have potential as public parkland, and includes the valleys of the Bow River, Elbow River, Nose Creek, and West Nose Creek. The vision statement for the master plan strongly promotes connectivity by encouraging a continuous, integrated river valley park: "The River Valley Park System will include a continuous river valley pathway, not always adjacent to the river's edge . . . Appropriately designed park linkages will extend into adjacent communities, connecting school sites, community centers, recreational facilities, and urban open spaces."[13]

The plan divides the river valleys into five segments, subdivided further into planning units. Each is described and analyzed, proposed improvements are suggested, development priorities are shown in a matrix, and a spatial master plan of the entire segment is mapped. The plan also maps private and public land and sets forth additional funding strategies. A land acquisition matrix for each segment, broken down by planning unit, makes obtaining the land seem feasible. But city employees report that the plan has proven far too ambitious—for example, it calls for acquiring the entire river valley bottom and similar feats that require tools and funding beyond reach.

The role of the province has been quite significant in protecting urban open space in Alberta. Ironically, this has occurred simultaneously with the province's permissive policy on growth and the environment. The Municipal Act at the provincial level, which designates the municipalities' powers, contains no habitat conservation policy for urban areas. The province allows the municipalities to undertake land conservation projects but does not mandate it. Transportation and recreation have therefore been the drivers of open-space connectivity, whereas other goals have suffered.

CITY OF CALGARY: DUAL FOCUS ON NONMOTORIZED
TRANSPORTATION AND PARK HUBS

Connectivity is a strong and clear mandate at the city level. The 2002 Open Space plan creates a framework for regional pathways as means to connect communities to city and regional parks, natural features, commercial areas, adjacent communities and cultural attractions, as well as other pathways, bikeways, trails, and mass-transit stations. The plan promotes extending paths into each new community and employment area to ensure a continuous system. Local pathways are designed to connect to a regional pathway, as well as to link key destinations within neighborhoods.

As Calgary matured as a city, awareness of the river valleys heightened. The rivers became more valued as aesthetic, recreational, and wildlife resources. In the late 1960s, Calgarians began envisioning a system of connected pathways on which to travel throughout the city and access areas of unique natural beauty. The pathways program started in 1974 with a clear recreational focus, represented by the first completed section of the pathway through Confederation Park in the downtown area. Then paths were constructed along the Bow and Elbow rivers. Today pathways connect the rivers, Fish Creek Provincial Park, Nose Creek, West Nose Creek, the Western Irrigation District Canal, and the perimeter of Glenmore Reservoir. The latest City of Calgary Pathway and Bikeway Plan was adopted by the city council in 2000, and reflects a shift in objectives from recreation toward transportation.

The pathways system has expanded dramatically. In 1994, 185 miles of pathways were in place. In 2005, over 310 miles of pathways had been established, including 26 miles in the downtown area that are regularly maintained and cleared of snow in the winter (Figure 5.9). Thirty-two miles were completed in one recent year alone. The paths are

Fig. 5.9 Heavily used commuter route on a pathway only blocks from central Calgary. (Photo by Brian M. Brown.)

usually 12 feet wide downtown, and range from 5 feet to 8 feet wide in local areas. User counts have shown that 400 people per hour use the pathways in the downtown area, with traffic as high as 600 people per hour on one urban pathway. The potential for use is even greater, as Calgary continues to grow; pathway users are vocal about wanting missing pathway links completed.

The Pathway and Bikeway Plan contains a set of guiding principles relating to the planning, design, and management of the routes. The main objectives of the plan are to create conceptual and physical ties to regional and national pathway systems (such as the Trans-Canada Trail), to develop policy to support city negotiations with developers regarding pathway and bikeway construction, and to produce a comprehensive and networked pathway/bikeway plan.[14] It is divided into two separate systems, one for nonmotorized transportation and one for recreation. The Regional Pathway System is a citywide linear network providing paths for nonmotorized recreation and transportation. It is a multiuse system, with no particular user given priority. It is hard surfaced, typically asphalt, and located off-street. This system is subdivided into two categories: open-space pathways that run through parks, Environmental Reserves, or along riverbanks; and boulevard pathways that are located in road rights-of-way.

The local layer of pathways provides routes within neighborhoods and connects to parks, schools, and other local destinations. A bikeway system includes all roads in the city that are legally open to bicycle travel, whether or not separate bicycle facilities are included.

The pathways focus is aimed to promote healthy lifestyles; it is not particularly focused on environmental protection. According to the plan, "the City of Calgary is committed to being a healthy place to work and live. It recognizes the importance of walking, running, cycling, wheelchair use, skateboarding, in-line skating and all other non-motorized modes of movement as positive contributions to the urban fabric. These non-polluting modes have inherent value as viable, efficient and environmentally friendly means of both transportation and recreation. They facilitate healthy and active living, and contribute to overall community vitality."[15] The vision is one of interconnected neighborhoods linked by the pathway network and usable by all citizens.

Along watercourses there is more opportunity for the integration of environmental goals from the Urban Parks Master Plan. According to parks planners, wherever possible the pathways have been meshed with greenspaces for the most aesthetically pleasing routes possible. The older pathway infrastructure is primarily through park space. In recent years though, the linkages have become strikingly utilitarian, with goals of convenient access to the regional pathways from neighborhoods and less focus on environmental goals.

However, planners point out that, particularly in sensitive habitat regions, the pathways are an ecological boon because people tend to stay on them rather than trample indiscriminately through natural areas.

The pathways idea grows in momentum and authority as it continues to expand into new subdivisions and attract more attention from both planners and potential users. The pathway network has been instrumental in bringing different parts of city government together—sewer, roads, parks—for joint projects, such as new pedestrian overpasses. In addition, politicians can identify with the pathways as tangible artifacts of city planning and expenditures. Given the heavy use and popularity of the pathways, two important priorities have emerged in the budgeting process—increased snow removal on the paths, and filling the missing links (which will cost $8 million).

Under the authority of the Standard Development Agreement, developers are required to build regional pathways within developments during the construction process. This requirement makes a major contribution to the expansion of the pathways and ensures that each new community is connected to the existing system.

Monitoring, planned at 5- to 10-year intervals, is intended to give vital information for managing and planning the pathway system. The Pathwatch 2002 study team counted pathway users at thirty-nine sites and conducted interviews with a subset as part of a Calgary Parks initiative. A previous benchmark had been established in a 1994 survey. The results, especially those showing increased use, have been instrumental in leveraging funds for expanding the pathway system. Pathwatch 2002 showed that cycling was the most popular activity, followed by walking, in-line skating, running, and walking dogs.[16] Twenty-seven percent of respondents said they used the paths year-round, and 84 percent rated the pathway quality as "excellent" or "very good." Pathwatch 2002 also showed increased potential for conflict, where bicyclists, walkers, runners, and others coexist on the multi-use pathway system. Calgary Parks has had a considerable number of inquiries from retailers who want to use the results of the user counts in their business decisions, sometimes with the intent to move closer to a heavily used pathway.

In 2002, the Calgary Open Space Plan was developed to provide a single, comprehensive policy on open space.[17] The plan is a policy document; implementation occurs through more specific implementation plans—for instance, plans for stormwater management, sports fields, or urban forestry. Despite the plan's creation, there is no vision or leadership for implementation of a coherent ecological greenway system early in the twenty-first century. For Calgary, issues of connectivity are clearly about recreation and transportation, and there is little active work toward environmental connectivity, especially away from the river valleys. The plan shows a lack of support for a green infrastructure approach. For instance, one open-space category is Linear Parks, which are meant to accommodate pathway links. The plan discusses these as strong visual amenities but limits their ability to handle stormwater.[18]

Principles for planning open space for the city are central to the plan. Three are particularly concerned with mobility. First, and more generally, a systems approach is promoted for "creating a continuous and integrated open space system that takes advantage of both natural and constructed features." Issues include providing recreational opportunities at several geographic scales, protecting environmentally significant areas, and providing linkages to create a continuous pathway system. Second, the plan promotes access to open space for all Calgarians within about a five-minute walk. Third, it advocates coordination between open space and other land uses (such as housing or commercial uses) at all stages of planning, design, development, and management. Mixed use is encouraged, as are linkages between open space and other land uses. Road rights-of-way are shown as one area to provide linear recreation and transportation by accommodating regional pathways and sidewalks.

Despite the recent open-space plan, connected open-space planning by the City of Calgary is difficult. While the plan codifies policies, it also depicts a conceptual spatial plan for future open space (Figure 5.10). Unfortunately, city park planners are not optimistic about being able to conserve all of the open land shown on the map. Especially for the rapid-growth areas at the city's periphery, they have no substantive mechanisms or funding for greenspace protection and no mandate from the city or province to achieve the vision.

Furthermore, the split between protecting river and upland landscapes is quite pronounced in corridor planning. On the one hand, the city has worked hard to implement the Urban Park Master Plan along the river valleys, creating one of the largest nonmotorized transportation routes on the continent. Unfortunately, there has been little support for environmental corridors away from the rivers, and the pathway system has little connection to ecological systems. A recent effort in an area called McHugh Bluff is a promising exception (Sidebar 5.2).

In urban areas away from streams, Calgary's parks and nature preserves are, for the most part, planned as islands, or patches, rather than as networks. According to interviewees, if there is no obvious feature like a river or utility corridor, there is no corridor policy. There has not yet been a groundswell of activism regarding ecological corridors, although there is increasing public support for protection of the river corridor and development of pathways projects. Residents may not see the need for connected

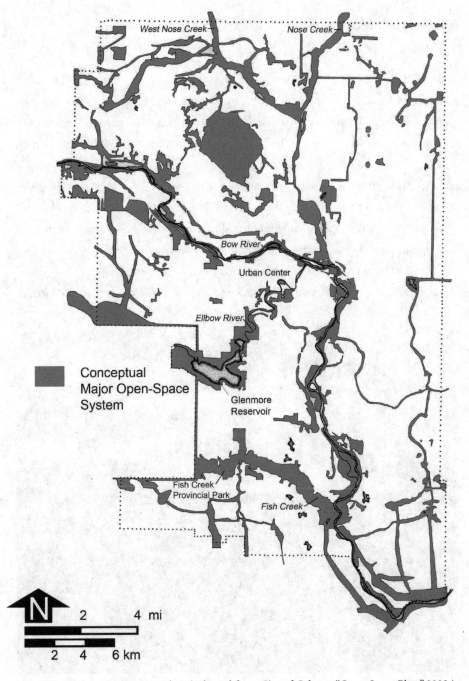

Fig. 5.10 Calgary open-space plan. (Adapted from City of Calgary, "Open Space Plan," 2002.)

5.2 McHugh Bluff

McHugh Bluff is an escarpment north of the Bow River from downtown Calgary. It is a signature park in Calgary's inner city and one of the few linear open spaces away from the river valleys. A road parallel to the top of the bluff serves as an important commuter route to and from the downtown core. The bluff overlooks the Bow River and the city beyond and is highly valued for this scenic vantage point (Figure 5.11). The bluff contains cycle and pedestrian paths, but its steep banks are badly degraded by soil erosion and other slope instability issues. A park user study found that use levels are some of the highest observed in any park in Calgary. This is an interesting finding, since McHugh Bluff is one of the only sizable linear natural areas in the city, other than the river and creek corridors.

The bluff has a conflicted history of human use. As far back as the 1930s, concern about seeping and slumping on the bluff led to efforts at stabilization, in the form of

Fig. 5.11 The view from McHugh Bluff toward downtown Calgary. (Photo by Chris Manderson.)

retaining walls and other structures. By the end of the 1940s, the city council allocated $1 million to install a gravel blanket over about a third of the bluff, which changed the entire nature of the hill. A visible city backdrop that was once forested became a barren landscape. In the 1950s and 1960s more armoring was installed, in addition to more gravel blanketing. McHugh Bluff was used as the location for Operation Lifesaver in 1957 during the cold war. This event was the largest civil defense exercise in Canada. In 1972, the first aesthetic concern was registered in city government: an alderman made a motion for assessing both the stability and the *aesthetic* factors in future work on the bluff. By the 1980s various community associations also became vocal about improving the bluff, beyond simply trying to keep it upright. An early 1990s concept plan for park improvements was created but never funded. The current efforts on the bluff follow from a 2001 decision by city council to work on the stability and aesthetics of the bluff, including the circulation system of paths and trails.

According to park planners, McHugh Bluff is one of the only places in the city where serious restoration planning is now being done. A 2003 restoration plan seeks to improve the area's appearance, reduce soil erosion, and facilitate the movement of cyclists and pedestrians to and from the downtown. It addresses long-standing concerns about slope stability, erosion, and trail proliferation. A secondary project is to formalize the current ad hoc pathway along the top of the bluff, creating a designed pathway parallel to the bluff's ridgeline. Restoration activities will include construction of stairs and fences, trail repair, native tree and shrub planting (including bioengineering techniques), trail closures, and interpretation about the restoration.

open space, since there is so much of it surrounding the city. The Parks Department does not have an ecological mandate around a landscape approach to open space. Instead, it focuses on the incompatibility of human access in environmentally sensitive areas, perhaps at the expense of integrative possibilities. The open-space plan discourages pathways through the city's natural areas, where residents often want access. According to interviewees, this is complicated by the fact that when the city does try to protect environmental values, the community often responds negatively. The current focus is therefore on managing current and critical problems, such as dealing with water quality issues and managing user conflicts, rather than connected open space.

Connected open-space integration by the City of Calgary could be prompted by concern for specific resources. In May 2004 Calgary became one of the first municipalities in Canada to approve a Wetlands Conservation Plan. The policy depicts priorities and best practices for wetland protection and outlines procedures to use in identifying and protecting wetland habitats. Implementation of the plan primarily takes place in the development approval process. Large projects are addressing wetland issues earlier in the development process, including issues of wetland mitigation, road design, and stormwater management. For instance, a policy plan is being created for the northeast region of the city, a 4,000-acre area with the highest density of wetlands in the city. In fact, 40 percent of the area is wetlands. This area is a testing ground for implementation of the new Wetlands Conservation Plan.

THE ROLE OF NONGOVERNMENTAL ORGANIZATIONS

The city government has been a major contributor to open-space planning for the Calgary metropolitan area. However, the nonprofit sector is playing an increasingly important role. Parks Foundation Calgary is an example, doing innovative work that supplements what the city can accomplish in connected open-space planning. It was established in 1985 by private citizens and has since invested $1.5 to $2 million annually in Calgary's natural environments. The foundation has contributed to $100 million worth of private and corporate fundraising for parks, river valleys, and amateur sports.

A key action in the organization's river valley focus was the creation of a River Valleys Committee (RVC) in 1991 to give advice to the city council on issues affecting the river valleys. The RVC now has a twenty-two-member executive board, three subcommittees, and over sixty member organizations representing various interests. Core activities include education about the value of the river valleys; facilitation of projects that protect, acquire, or reclaim river valley assets; input to policy and development plans that affect the rivers; and acquisition of river valley and watershed lands.

The RVC has promoted two approaches. First, it emphasizes a watershed planning approach aimed at preserving, reclaiming, and establishing habitat and wildlife corridors in the river valleys while monitoring and protecting water quality. Second, and more controversial, the organization has promoted green infrastructure planning. So far, the city has been particularly reluctant to embrace this approach. However, the committee is seeing a slow but steady increase in community interest. RVC programs have initiated cooperation and investment with the city.

As a result of an urban greening conference organized by the Parks Foundation, a land trust was proposed to focus on landscape connectivity for the metropolitan area. The land trust will potentially connect to the Mayor's Legacy Park Project, a $50 million project designed to develop city parks located outside the city. The land trust purchases would be made on lands within neighboring Municipal Districts that connect to parcels donated to the City of Calgary. This enterprise is controversial within the Municipal Districts, which often oppose Calgary buying land inside their jurisdictions. Permission is needed from the Municipal Districts to buy land in their jurisdictions if the land will be used for public purposes. A new land trust could help play an important role in negotiating these purchases.

Calgary has strong potential to connect its population to open-space options. In fact, it has in place a number of puzzle pieces just waiting for deliberate assembly. Its pathway system is extensive, well used, and accessible. The environmental protection of river valley landscapes, through both provincial and city initiatives, is a success story. The detailed Urban Parks Master Plan has been used extensively, especially as an extension of the broader framework of the city open-space plan. There is strong coherence around issues of water quality. However, challenges remain in broadening the transportation agenda to include other open-space objectives in trails planning, and especially to integrate water quality and transportation issues more holistically. The city's open-space planning resources must be balanced between the growth frontier at its edge and the needs of older neighborhoods. To that end, the older suburbs are being studied to assess the services, including open space, available in established neighborhoods.

An even bigger hurdle for Calgary is to begin shaping the form of new exurban development by open-space design. This is a huge leap from business-as-usual parks maintenance priorities. The protection of wetlands, now facilitated through substantive policy, may serve as a catalyst. Strong leadership, in the form of open-space and growth-management champions, will be needed to impact the shape of new exurban development in a sensitive way that marries the inherent qualities of the Alberta prairie landscape with development demands.

Denver: Greenways Chart the Waterway System

The Denver region has a long record of acquiring and protecting open space, some of it in urban areas and some of it in rural and natural landscapes, intended for the use of urban dwellers. For instance, in 1967, Boulder, Colorado, became the first city in the country to tax itself for buying and managing open space. Approximately 43,000 acres of land are protected through Boulder's open-space and mountain parks system. The Denver region is also gaining considerable attention for its innovative light-rail lines to ease traffic congestion, partly funded by a 2004 vote to increase the sales tax.

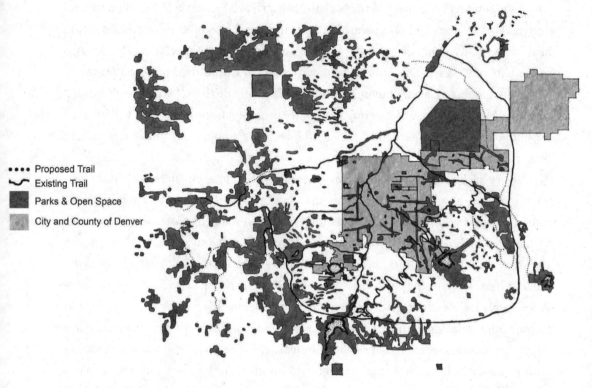

Fig. 5.12 Trail networks in the Denver metropolitan area.

Built on a legacy of parkways and mountain parks, metropolitan Denver boasts over 400 miles of interconnected trails and greenways (Figure 5.12). The foundation of Denver's system is the Platte River, where greenway efforts have yielded miles of bike and walking trails. The river's headwaters are in the Rocky Mountain Front Range, and after passing through mountains and foothills, it runs 10.5 miles through downtown, residential, and industrial areas of Denver (Figure 5.13), and through a number of other metropolitan area cities on its route to the Mississippi River. The Central Platte Valley is the heart of the system: the historical birthplace of the city, where the two waterways come together. It was once dominated by a network of rail yards that served the industrial and warehouse area as well as Lower Downtown—Lodo—a historic district that has been redeveloped into a mixed-use residential, commercial, and entertainment center.

The High Line Canal, owned and managed by Denver Water, is known as Denver's first urban greenway. The 66-mile canal, begun in 1879 to irrigate the dry urban region, winds through the east side of the city of Denver. A diversion dam on the South Platte River provides its water. The canal continues to deliver irrigation water to sixty-seven water customers along its route. In the 1960s, the road along its banks was opened to the public for walking, biking, and horseback riding. The canal has since become an important open-space resource for the metropolitan region. Since the 1970s, five recreation departments have struck agreements with Denver Water to manage recreational facilities along the corridor. They now oversee a network of more than 60 miles of continuous trails that connect neighborhoods, parks, and cities.[19]

CITY OF DENVER AND THE SOUTH PLATTE RIVER GREENWAY FOUNDATION
Since the success of the High Line Canal as an open-space resource, other greenways have been implemented along waterways in the Denver area. Mayor Bill McNichols created the Platte River Development Committee in 1974 to transform Denver's South Platte River. The river was literally used as a sewer during much of the twentieth century, as was often the case in many American cities.

Devastating floods occurred in 1965 and 1973, directing attention toward the river and its need for restoration. McNichols appointed Joe Shoemaker, three-term Colorado state senator, to chair a cleanup committee with nine other civic-minded citizens. The public originally responded with apathy and ridicule. But the work of the committee, now called

Fig. 5.13 The South Platte River Valley runs horizontally across the upper part of this aerial image of Denver, where much of the corridor is in industrial use but large areas remain open. (Photo by Dana Weniger and Andy Leach, By Land, Water, and Air.)

the Greenway Foundation, gained momentum over time. The South Platte River, once polluted, maligned, and forgotten, has since become one of the most successful greenway systems in the United States.

The process began when McNichols allocated $1.9 million in revenue-sharing funds
for the committee to start creating 150 miles of trails, boat launches, chutes, and parks in
four counties and nine municipalities. According to Shoemaker, "The river had never had
a budget, so it never had a constituency. When we approached the city for help, they
thought we were nuts, and the people said it was a joke to even call the South Platte a river
at all. That was what we were up against."[20] In addition to physical changes, the mind-set
had to change as well. The committee divided into four groups, each aligned with a section along the central 10.5 miles of the river that bisected the city. Each group quickly identified a "node" or park for its section. One of those was Confluence Park, where Cherry
Creek meets the Platte River—now one of Denver's most important civic spaces.

Revitalizing the river was done incrementally, by identifying nodes and then connecting
them, all the while working toward cleanup of the river and the floodplain itself. The committee located 440 places where pollution was being dumped directly into the river. Two hundred of the polluters stopped polluting voluntarily, and forty others were sued successfully on
behalf of the city.[21] Shoemaker refused the committee any official contract or authority.
Without any official powers, there were then no limitations on what the committee could do.
His maxim was "No power is all power," which became known as Shoemaker's Law.

With $780,000 in seed money from the Gates Foundation, the Platte River Devel-
opment Committee became the Greenway Foundation in 1977. It shifted from government to nonprofit status in order to control philanthropic funds and interest income.
Nonprofit status helped the organization avoid political delays and accept private funding. In its first seven years, the foundation raised $14 million, and built 10.5 miles of paved
trails, four whitewater boat chutes, and seventeen mini-parks over former dumps.

For the next ten years, the Greenway Foundation focus expanded to include greenways
and trails along tributaries to the South Platte including projects in the suburbs. Inspired
by the Greenway Foundation example, several similar entities were formed, including the
South Suburban Park Foundation and the Sand Creek Regional Greenway Partnership, to
successfuly pursue greeways in Arapahoe, Adams County, and others. Local residents began
to use the greenway system heavily. The cornerstone of the foundation's success has been
partnerships with willing public entities. The foundation does not own land; rather, its work
is based on the political will of the communities where it provides project support. It provides a means of accumulating both public and private funding, and an institutional con-

text that can help get things done quickly. The foundation sees itself as an ombudsman for the river, promoting river education, and organizing events to celebrate the river and protect the places it has helped build. In a number of areas the foundation's role has been reduced as local entities take up the work and no longer need a great deal of foundation support. This is framed as part of the foundation's success.

According to the foundation, the main drivers of the greenway movement in the Denver region are path usage, boating, and parks development. Paths are the most actively favored of the three. Nonmotorized transportation in all its forms is a main motive behind the popularity of open-space development. Denver's paths have become overcrowded in places, and new, separated paths are now being planned and built (separating pedestrian and wheeled traffic). As in Calgary, the path system is the most important aspect of the entire endeavor and drives many open-space projects.

In 1996 Mayor Wellington Webb appointed the South Platte River Commission and announced that further enhancement of the South Platte River Greenway was his top priority. The twenty-seven-member commission established goals in five areas: water, wildlife, open space and recreation, youth, and neighbors. One of the commission's goals is a 150-foot continuous wildlife corridor along the Platte River, with the reestablishment of native vegetation. The trail system along the river was upgraded and hundreds of acres of new parkland created. In 2000 a Long Range Management Framework was completed.[22]

Three main programs have helped achieve the commission's goals. First, the South Platte River, Cherry Creek, and other tributaries within Denver were designated officially as parks, assuring oversight and protection. Second, a new maintenance district was established for the river, tailored to the management needs of the river corridor. Third, the Greenway Foundation launched its campaign for the river—the Greenway Preservation Trust, an endowment program for education, employment, cultural events, and enhancements, with an initial goal of $5 million.

The most important funding source for open-space work in the Denver region is Great Outdoors Colorado (GOCO), administered through the state government.[23] GOCO directs hundreds of millions of dollars raised through the state lottery into open space, trails, and park projects. It has been a key to the success of the greenway systems in the state. Without this unifying factor and motivating force, the Denver region would not have made nearly as much progress as it has to date. GOCO funding is directed to several categories, including open space, legacy, trails, planning, wildlife, and local parks and recreation. Over $6 million was allocated for the South Platte River Project to the City of Denver and over $10 million to the Conservation Fund for the I-25 Conservation Corridor

Project. GOCO encourages multijurisdiction projects in its competitive grant selection process, which has fostered increasing cooperation in recent years.

The Platte River Greenway has become a focal point, not only for open space, but as a catalyst attracting housing, a theme park, an aquarium, and magnet businesses (Figure 5.14). The Central Platte Valley (CPV), in close proximity to downtown Denver, is one neighborhood that has been impacted positively by the greenway. The CPV is a 120-acre area that was the site of rail yards, warehouses, and viaducts, then garbage dumps. Now it features entertainment landmarks, including the largest outdoor skate park in the United States and 90 acres of parks along the South Platte River. According to Bill Mosher, president of the Downtown Denver Partnership (a nonprofit business organization), a plan that features open space will be critical for the CPV as it continues to be redeveloped. He advocates open-space planning as an important draw for the residents who will eventually live in the more than three thousand housing units being planned for the area.[24]

According to Robert Searns, a Denver greenway planner and author, "the Greenway Foundation's partnership with city government was largely based on goodwill and a common mission—to get the greenway built." He says the phenomenon in Denver is noteworthy for its lack of formal planning and credits a combination of power and leadership by both Shoemaker and McNichols. Together they got things done quickly. "Another factor is the simplicity of the original greenway concept. River cleanup, small parks, boating

Fig. 5.14 Kayakers at the confluence of Cherry Creek and the South Platte River in downtown Denver. The South Platte River Greenway parallels the river. (Photo by Robert Searns.)

improvements, and a continuous trail from city limit to city limit were easy to understand and hard to oppose . . . The system took on a life of its own, spreading, replicating, and integrating into the nation's most extensive regional urban greenway network."[25] In addition to spreading across the region, not only did efforts evolve to include trails, but substantive efforts were made to rehabilitate creek banks—to create space for the meandering urban stream and for natural renovation.

The river cleanup has led to social transformations. According to Colorado historian Thomas J. Noel, "Arapaho Indians had camped along the river, later followed by busted prospectors, broken down cowboys, homeless homesteaders, poor immigrants, and downsized capitalists."[26] Homeless people who traditionally squatted in the South Platte river bottoms have been displaced, their paths along the river converted to paved trails lined with condominiums, upscale businesses, and landscaping. The lower socioeconomic groups who used the river valley have been pushed elsewhere. Some of the housing along Denver's waterways is now the city's priciest.

DENVER'S GAME PLAN FOR A CITY IN A PARK

The city of Denver still has an important role in open-space connectivity. The city strives to be a "city in a park," according to its 2003 Game Plan, created by the Denver Parks and Recreation Department.[27] The innovative plan maintains a strong theme of connectivity and open-space access. The plan was created through a two-year public participation process that emerged with a fifty-year vision for transforming Denver. Three primary scales are used: neighborhood scale and just beyond; citywide scale, which addresses connections, civic space, and urban waterways; and mountains-to-plains, which addresses regional open space, trails, and mountain parks.

At the neighborhood scale, Denver's standard of a park within three to six blocks of each residence seems ambitious. Furthermore, the city's standard is six *walkable* blocks, which takes into consideration barriers like highways, railroad lines, and streams. According to the Trust for Public Land, this is one of the best proximity standards in the United States.[28] About 90 percent of the city's 550,000 residents already live within the mandated six blocks of the city's 6,200 acres of parkland. Linear connected open-space land will help further accessibility goals. For newer, denser subdivisions, Denver's standard mandates that no house can be more than three blocks from a park. This requirement helps compensate for smaller private landscapes in denser developments. The plan contributes to a new way of conceptualizing green space, calling for two hundred gravel-covered elementary and middle school grounds to be redesigned to provide parkland in neighborhoods.

In complementary work, Colorado's Department of Transportation (DOT) is starting to work with city and county health departments to explore grassroots efforts to combat both obesity and road congestion through nonmotorized corridor design. One DOT program is called Safe Routes to School, which distributes funds for bike racks, connecting trails, and other infrastructure to improve and maintain safe routes for children to walk or bike to school. It sets up advisory committees composed of teachers, parents, law enforcement officers, and students.

On the citywide scale, the Game Plan focuses strongly on connections. The goal is to develop a clearly connected system of public open spaces. This will mean strengthening the connections between the downtown and surrounding neighborhoods. It will also entail increasing open space in the downtown itself, as the downtown population is expected to grow from just over four thousand people at the turn of the twenty-first century to over forty thousand by 2025.[29]

Outside the downtown area, the Game Plan focuses on a network of green streets with adequate sidewalks and street tree canopies, as well as citywide off-road regional trails. Green streets will connect parks to schools, recreation centers, and neighborhood centers. When surveyed in 2001, Denver residents said that improving connections and access were priorities. "Our parks and trails are great, but we can't get there," residents frequently commented at public open houses. Starting with the existing parkway system, the new plan will retrofit other residential streets as green streets. This will mean manipulating the width and continuity of sidewalks and tree lawns (the area between curb and sidewalk), and reworking the spacing of street trees.

Residents requested more recreational trails like the High Line Canal and Cherry Creek Trail to connect parks with longer cycling and walking loops. Off-street trails will ideally be located closer than one-half mile to each major residential area. Missing trail links will be bridged and strengthened where they connect to major regional and metrowide trail systems. The current system offers 51 miles of pathways, most of which are paved, forming a web through the city. The recommendations for strengthening this system include separation of cyclists and pedestrians, use of utility easements for nonmotorized use, linking established bikeways, improving road crossings, and connecting to transit points. Furthermore, the "City in a Park" vision includes Denver's urban waterways as a circulatory system for transportation, conservation, and recreation.

The city of Denver, beyond the neighborhood and civic scales, sees itself as a hub in a larger regional system of trails, natural areas, and mountain parks. Indeed, Denver's park system spans five ecosystems across 100 miles, from prairies to mountain peaks. Hundreds of miles of additional connected open space could be needed and used as the metropolitan area of the Front Range approaches three million people.

THE LARGE, REGIONAL GREENWAY VISION

The Denver Regional Council of Government (DRCOG) is an umbrella organization involved in open-space planning at the larger metropolitan scale. Like most councils of government, it has only limited authority to help shape land use and growth patterns, but promotes a regional perspective on issues facing the metropolitan area. Mobility and transportation are key components of its agenda. DRCOG does regional planning for the nine-county metropolitan area (fifty-one cities), including planning for development, water quality and wastewater, air quality, roads and transit. One part of the regional plan is the open-space system for the region.

DRCOG inventoried and mapped all existing local, state, federal, and NGO open-space areas in 1997 and again in 2004. City, county, special district, and federal lands already comprise about 26 percent of the 5,000-square-mile Denver region. Its 1999 open-space plan advocates that another 100 to 600 square miles be protected in the region before 2020[30] (Figure 5.15). Open-space land is categorized in the plan in six forms: natural resource land; environmental hazard and development constraint areas; outdoor recre-

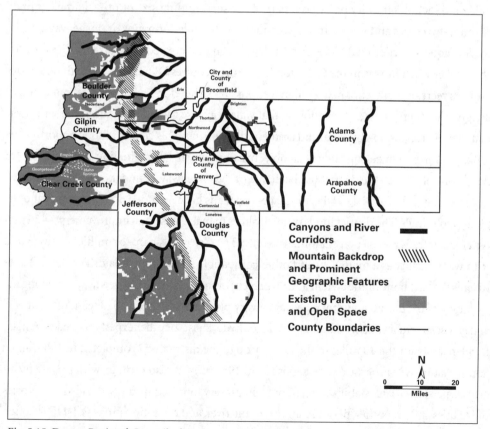

Fig. 5.15 Denver Regional Council of Government open-space plan.

ation lands; agricultural resources; prominent geologic, geographic, and cultural features; and open-space land that can shape patterns of urban growth. More than 1,200 square miles with these open-space values are identified in the plan. About half lie within 5 miles of the region's 2030 growth boundary and are particularly valued for protection.[31] While the DRCOG is a helpful agent in the open-space planning process, it is not where projects typically get led, motivated, or controlled. Its transportation-enhancement funding, funneled from the federal government, is critical but does not provide the main leadership focus for connected open spaces.

The Denver Urban Drainage and Flood Control (DUDFC) district, like DRCOG, operates across the entire metropolitan area. Unlike the council of government, it has a strong influence on the planning and management of connected open spaces. The district was established by the state legislature in 1969 to assist local governments in the Denver region with multijurisdictional drainage and flood control problems. The district was an early participant in addressing the river system and jointly funding connected riparian projects, starting in the 1970s. It has tax-base funding to carry out its work. It covers an area of 1,600 square miles and includes the city of Denver, part of the surrounding six counties, and parts or all of thirty-two cities and towns. It oversees about 1,600 miles of major drainage ways.

A unique aspect of DUDFC is that the legislation that created the district, written by Joe Shoemaker when he was in the Colorado legislature, requires DUDFC to make flood control projects recreationally enhancing whenever possible. Therefore, the district is mandated to design in partnership with recreation so that waterways are more flood-safe at the same time that they are recreationally useful and aesthetically pleasing. This creates unique opportunities for combining engineering and social objectives, an unusual combination in the context of flood control. In fact, the district has been one of the Greenway Foundation's best partners.

Since the early 1970s, DUDFC drainage-way plans have included access routes that double as public trails. The district funds municipalities to make these trail improvements—50 percent for soft trails and 25 percent for paved ones. The district is set up for multiobjective work, with water quality as a main goal and other compatible functions overlaid. The South Platte River is the backbone of the system and 90 percent of the Denver area's greenways are along the river and its tributaries and drainage ways. Every project is planned with a team of engineers and landscape architects, in addition to wetlands hydrologists or other experts as needed. A master plan study for the 40 miles of the river through the district was completed in 1985, and a South Platte River Program was established in 1987. Efforts also include, with private property owners, riverbank stabilization, floodplain preservation acquisitions, detailed inventories of facilities and properties, periodic surveys of the river, and recreation projects. DUDFC often serves as project manager for these efforts, as they hold the money to make them happen. The district has some similarity to the Toronto and Region Conservation Authority in this regard.

The Denver Urban Drainage and Flood Control district is clearly the most actively engaged agency at the regional level for open space in the Denver metropolitan area. However, subregional projects are increasingly important, as exemplified in the Sand Creek Regional Greenway (see Sidebar 5.3). Another new initiative is important: the Northeast Greenway Corridor is a project emerging from a regional leadership committee composed of state, city, and county leaders in Adams County, Aurora, Brighton, Commerce City, Thornton, and the city/county of Denver. In 2004 the committee announced a plan to create a network of trails, greenbelts, and open space. The network will span 150 miles connecting Denver to Brighton, Aurora to Commerce City, and all four cities to the Rocky Mountain Arsenal National Wildlife Refuge.

Former Colorado attorney general Ken Salazar, now a U.S. senator, leads the project. During his tenure as attorney general, Salazar began to resolve outstanding claims against the U.S. Army and Shell Oil for cleanup of the Rocky Mountain Arsenal, a contaminated site just northeast of Denver. The site, now the Rocky Mountain Arsenal National Wildlife Refuge, consists of 17,000 acres that were used as a major chemical weapons production site and major supplier during World War II. As the largest open space in the Denver urban region, its cleanup has been a visible and active project over a number of years. Salazar brought together the northeast government entities in a coalition of mayors and county commissioners to plan open-space projects that would use settlement monies to help resolve off-site impacts of the contamination. The emphasis is on connections through greenways and other open-space projects. The coalition has outlined tens of millions of dollars in projects, all revolving around open-space needs in that section of the metropolitan area. The project would extend the South Platte trails to the Rocky Mountain Arsenal Wildlife Refuge and protect large open-space areas to prevent the cities from growing together, in this area where development is rampant. The entire Northeast Greenway Corridor effort will take a number of years to complete and require $200 million in contributions, with $60 million needed in the first phase.

Several aspects of the Denver greenway story are particularly instructive. The extent and use of the corridor network for transportation, as in Calgary, is remarkable. However, like Calgary, the rapid suburban growth across the open plains is an enormous challenge for achieving open-space connectivity in the Denver region.

Many factors have contributed to the successes so far. First, the adroit leadership of Mayor Speer, and subsequently Mayor McNichols and Joe Shoemaker, laid the foundation

5.3 Sand Creek Greenway

The northeastern area of Denver has traditionally been underserved by parks. This area consists of Commerce City, Denver, and Aurora, a subregion with mixes of industrial use and low- to moderate-income neighborhoods. However, the area is growing and changing, propelled by rapid development and investment. The Sand Creek Regional Greenway is an effort to participate early in the redevelopment process in order to protect and restore Sand Creek, a tributary of the South Platte River, before opportunities for parks and greenways are forgotten or overlooked. The Sand Creek Regional Greenway Partnership is a nonprofit group focused on raising funds to implement a master plan done in 1997 for the 14-mile greenway and to increase use and awareness of the greenway.

A special focus of the organization is to create a trail with one continuous identity, not three different ones as it crosses the three diverse jurisdictions. This consistency is a strong focus, as is creating recreational opportunities and protecting natural ecosystems. For example, the area is rich in bird diversity, providing habitat for eagles, egrets, great blue herons, and kingfishers. This environmental quality is balanced with off-road transportation links made possible through the greenway. One strategy for accommodating these multiple goals has been creating park hubs along the greenway, so the creek corridor itself does not need to absorb all of the human use. A key piece is envisioning larger parks that connect to the greenway.

In the early 1990s residents began to recognize that the area would change dramatically. A handful of visionaries recognized Sand Creek as a blighted drainage with great potential. Much of the creek was in private hands and highly contaminated. Most people did not even realize the waterway was a perennial creek. Local residents took particularly strong leadership roles and pulled together people to work on the project. The worst section of the creek was in Denver, where it was channelized. When the Denver residents sought cleanup funding, they found that similar activity and interest was under way in Aurora and Commerce City. After a series of public meetings and a planning grant from the state, the project coalesced. Subsequently, councilwomen from all three cities were very active in the project, as were staff members from each of the park departments.

The Sand Creek Greenway traverses the 4,700-acre former Stapleton International Airport site, where 10,000 new housing units and 30,000 new jobs will be located when the Stapleton Development Plan is implemented. In June 2002, 13 miles of the greenway were opened. Construction efforts are still under way through all three cities, as they work to get on-road portions rerouted and to carry out other improvements along the entire corridor. Transjurisdictional cooperation has been excellent, fueled perhaps by a multi-million-dollar legacy grant from Great Outdoors Colorado that prioritizes this type of collaboration. This is all the more remarkable, though, given that the three cities are quite diverse. Aurora is a magnet for residential growth and Commerce City is a traditional industrial town, reborn as a destination for parks and open space. A number of business partners have also been critical, some of which went beyond their regulatory requirements for creek cleanup. The three cities have created a wish list of projects along the greenway, totaling $5–6 million. The partnership is working to acquire those funds.

for open-space connectivity in the city. Second, partnerships between the city and its non-profit collaborators have been highly influential. The transformation of the Greenway Foundation from city agency to nonprofit organization, similar to the evolution of Toronto's Waterfront Regeneration Trust, is an administrative model that could be used elsewhere. Third, the role of the Denver Urban Drainage and Flood Control district, similar to the Toronto and Region Conservation Authority, is useful at implementing open-space projects at the scale of the metro region.

Fourth, the grassroots escalation of the greenway concept is remarkable in Denver. Robert Searns calls it a "virus" concept, based more on "lead and follow" than "command and control." One municipality tries something and then the others follow along on the success. One example is the countywide open-space purchases, led by Jefferson County. Jefferson County has 150 miles of trails in the foothills west of Denver. Its open-space sales tax, begun in 1972, preserved 30,000 acres. Jefferson County was one of the first counties in the United States to create a program of this kind; now all of the counties in the Denver region have followed suit. The ideas were noticed, emulated, and repeated across the region. Today, open space is quite well funded in many Denver cities and counties, even in a conservative political climate. Locally funded programs continue to be renewed by voters due to a sense of urgency about growth and land consumption.

Finally, goodwill across jurisdictions is an important ingredient in Denver, where adversarial thinking across political boundaries seems to be diminishing. Shared community visions about connected open space have catalyzed a number of projects. These attitudes have spread to the development community, where new developments are expected to have a system of greenways and trails. There is a record of cooperation, as multiple towns and cities have sometimes pooled their resources for bigger projects, such as the greenway along the South Platte River. Towns have spent money on projects in other towns, realizing that each town will eventually benefit from the overall project. This collaboration is partly lubricated by money from the drainage agency and from GOCO. Funding can motivate collaboration when those collaborative incentives are built in.

Transportation as Thrust for Connectivity

A central motive for connecting open-space lands is enabling the movement of people through the landscape. Transportation objectives often drive open-space connectivity, and funding for this objective has been critical. Many U.S. cities would not have gotten greenway programs off the ground without federal transportation-enhancement dollars that specifically fund nonmotorized transportation.[32]

Linear corridors are inherently about movement, not only of people but of animals, water, and other materials. But there are important complexities, and indeed contradictions, in the way transportation moves open-space networks for cities. In both Denver and Calgary transportation is a strong motivator, from local greenways that provide neighborhood walking routes to long-distance commuting on systems hundreds of miles long. In both places, the greenways are heavily used and strongly supported, largely for their transportation value.

Transportation can be a barrier to or facilitator of open-space connectivity, depending on the mode of transportation, location of the corridor, and its size. The negative effects of roads on ecological integrity have been documented in the landscape ecology literature.[33] Road corridors are known to be detrimental to wildlife habitat, water quality, and ecosystem health. Providing alternatives to auto traffic is beneficial on many dimensions, not the least of which is environmental. However, trails and pathways are not always benign ecologically. Trails through sensitive areas, like recreational uses, can compromise habitat integrity and other natural values. Calgary parks planners are cognizant of this conflict, avoiding public access entirely in some of the city's best natural areas.

The conflict between motorized and nonmotorized transportation is inherently problematic. Dan Burden, an advocate for walkable communities, has summarized the tension well by claiming that cars need quantity and pedestrians need quality. Innovative solutions use other linear infrastructure, like sewer lines, abandoned rail lines, and utility corridors to route pedestrians away from roadways. Both Denver and Calgary provide excellent models for successfully integrating pathways and trails into the urban fabric. As nonmotorized routes become more prevalent and heavily used, theoretically there should be less need for extending and widening roads. However, an important question is often difficult to answer: How many cars will be taken off the road by building nonmotorized routes? The answer is important for helping solve the ratio of streets and roads to paths and trails.

Another approach embraces streets and roads *as* greenways, such as in Denver's green streets plan. In Seattle, where downtown residents are projected to increase by 60,000 in the next twenty years, the greenway plan "follows the path of least resistance, the streets and patches of green that make up the 30 to 40 percent of downtown land already owned by the city."[34] The city's open-space strategy moves from a focus on traditional parks and plazas to an urban ecosystem approach focusing on city streets. Vancouver, as discussed in Chapter 6, has followed a similar philosophy.

A "complete streets" movement is gaining momentum in a number of cities. A complete street is one that works not only for motorists but also for bus riders, bikers, pedestrians, and people with disabilities. The goal is to make all streets useful for diverse modes of transportation, not just the ones designated as bikeways, greenways, or parkways. The Bureau of Transportation Statistics estimates that about one-quarter of walking trips take place on roads without sidewalks or shoulders and that bike lanes exist for only about 5 percent of bike trips. Some cities are paying attention, especially as the link between walking and health gains speed. For instance, a 2004 San Diego sales tax measure will generate $14 billion over forty years for building and improving complete streets.[35]

Using streets as greenways makes sense from the standpoint of destinations. People want to travel through all parts of the city, so planning must account for a range of topographical settings, not just along waterways. Greenways have traditionally followed rivers and streams; a new era of open-space connections will connect uplands to the river valleys and to each other. And for systematic transportation goals, nonmotorized connections will be made to light-rail and other mass-transit stations. For instance, Denver has the opportunity to create stronger relationships between its new regional light-rail lines and its greenway corridors. Some of this is yet to happen, since there has been such a strong focus on waterways.

What do greenways and other connected corridors really mean in these types of environments, especially away from waterways? For Calgary and Denver, they are not often green and they are not always warm and inviting. It is very difficult to reintroduce green in the Calgary and Denver environments, where climate and the natural ecosystems of the regions present a different palette of colors and forms. Therefore, our ideas of what greenways look like, along streams and away from them, change dramatically from one region to another. In addition, it is clear that trail activities do not have to rely on warm weather. Anchorage, Alaska, has one of the largest urban trail systems (250 miles) within its city limits for biking, hiking, dog sledding, and equestrian use.

Mobility is valued in our modern societies more than ever. Recent decades have seen strong priorities placed on assuring access to our public spaces by all citizens. This goal has been successfully realized in the open-space planning arena, where more and more people can use their legs, bikes, wheelchairs, skateboards, horses, and skis to move around their neighborhoods and across entire cities. But many connections are missing; some cities are far behind in making these travel corridors possible. People are demanding alternative access opportunities and are starting to emerge from their cars. The alignment of transportation with recreational, ecological, and community goals is not precise but is often compatible. In addition, there is a powerful intersection where human health and fitness concerns intersect perfectly with ideals of environmental soundness and landscape health. We should be able to continue to make our open-space networks move North American populations outside their cars, enhancing the buzz of city life.

6

Community—Neighborhood: Vancouver and Portland

We abuse land because we regard it as a commodity belonging
to us. When we see land as a community to which we belong,
we may begin to use it with love and respect.

—Aldo Leopold [1]

Open space helps enhance community—humans' connections both to the natural community and to each other. The process of building greenways and other open-space connections can be a powerful catalyst for creating a stronger sense of community. The open-space stories of Vancouver, British Columbia, and Portland, Oregon, illustrate a number of exciting objectives and outcomes. Their use of the greenways idea for environmental protection, recreation, and nonmotorized transportation is quite forward-thinking. Additionally, Vancouver and Portland are models that illustrate community as a distinct objective of connected open-space planning. In each region the residents enjoy the outdoors and are vocal in protecting and shaping their outdoor spaces.

Vancouver and Portland, unlike the mountain cities explored in Chapter 5, are fair-weather cities. Like Calgary and Denver though, they are popular destinations for tourists and new residents alike. Vancouver and Portland each have just over a half million residents living in metropolitan areas of nearly 2 million.[2] Connected open-space corridors in the Vancouver region are products of efforts early in the twentieth century and again more recently. Its contemporary greenways program was designed to enhance the public realm in a way that brings neighborhoods, and the people in them, together. In Portland, a robust and well-funded open-space program at the regional level is complemented by committed efforts at the local level that bring nature and people together. Through their greenway plans both cities have fostered stronger communities and connections to the outdoor environment.

Vancouver and Portland: Historic and Geographic Context

The third-largest city in Canada, Vancouver possesses one of the few deep-sea ports on the Pacific coast of North America and is Canada's major west coast port. Facilities for container ships, cruise ships, and other maritime businesses (fishing, boat-building) are important parts of the city's historic and contemporary life. Beyond its commercial assets, the city is consistently rated one of the most livable cities in the world by international surveys. Although it was described as "a setting in search of a city"[3] in 1979, more recently it has blossomed into one of the most attractive cities in North America.

Vancouver's popularity has also caused problems. Half of the people living in British Columbia are concentrated in the Vancouver metropolitan region, which comprises less than 2 percent of the province. Forty thousand new residents move to the area every year. Unlike many North American cities, Vancouver has a large base of central-city residents. Around 50,000 people currently live in downtown Vancouver; by the year 2020, it is predicted that 100,000 will live downtown and that 175,000 will work there. But the city is mostly built-out. Only an 89-acre piece of former industrial land bordering False Creek remains as the last large piece of undeveloped waterfront property in the central city. In 2010 Vancouver will host the Winter Olympics, which will dramatically affect development in the entire region.

Like Vancouver, Portland enjoys a mild climate within a spectacular rain forest. This pleasant climate is one of many reasons that Portland is also consistently rated as one of North America's most livable small cities. The city is located 78 miles from the Pacific Ocean at the confluence of the Columbia and Willamette rivers, with postcard views of the Cascades. Mt. Hood, 60 miles to the east, is the tallest peak in Oregon's Cascade Range. Known as the Rose City, Portland boasts an extensive 37,000-acre park system (including 5,000-acre Forest Park), beautiful rose gardens, waterfront promenades, and a classical Chinese garden. A walkable city, with particularly short, people-friendly city blocks,

Portland also has extensive cycling paths. One of the best is located along the downtown waterfront.

Portland has been facing the competing pressures of growth and land preservation for decades. By 2040 an estimated 1.8 million people will live in the three-county region overseen by the regional government, Metro. Among U.S. cities, Portland is the poster city for progressive growth management. Connected open space has been one aspect of this agenda. Governors Tom McCall and Robert Straub in the 1970s were early promoters of the greenways concept, and many of Portland's open-space successes are outgrowths of that foresight. The Willamette River corridor was declared a greenway in 1967, long before most urban river initiatives began in the United States. More recently, Metro has sought to protect and set aside open space, natural areas, habitat, and recreation areas throughout the entire region.

Vancouver: Impressive Open-Space Settings

It is no accident that Vancouver is Canada's equivalent of Hollywood. Although many factors contribute to the film industry's location in Vancouver, setting is essential. Vancouver's physical setting is spectacular (Figure 6.1). The metropolitan region consists of twenty-one municipalities, bordering the United States on the south and nestled toward the Coast Range

Fig. 6.1 Vancouver skyline, with forested Stanley Park and protected shoreline of English Bay in the foreground. (Photo by Maurice Jassak.)

Fig. 6.2 Region comprising the Greater Vancouver Regional District.

on the north (Figure 6.2). Sited dramatically between English Bay, Burrard Inlet, and the Fraser River delta, the region possesses a rich aboriginal history spanning thousands of years. It has two distinct geographical districts: the Coast Mountains on the North Shore and the Fraser Lowland, with gently rolling uplands and wide, flat valleys. Prior to European settlement, the region consisted primarily of mature stands of western hemlock, western red cedar, and Douglas fir on the mountains and estuarine marshes in the river delta.

The city of Vancouver is surrounded on three sides by water. It is shaped like a sideways mitten with the thumb peninsula pointing northwest. On this peninsula lie the downtown, the West End residential neighborhood (with the highest population density in Canada), and the 1,000-acre Stanley Park. The rest of the mitten has residential neighborhoods, with vibrant neighborhood commercial streets and scattered industrial facilities (particularly along the Fraser). The city is fairly young; it was built largely between 1900 and 1940. In recent years, Vancouver has become a model for urban planning.[4] The lack of freeways in the downtown core greatly affects Vancouver's urban form and is striking in comparison to most U.S. cities, which have been struggling with the scarring effects of central-city freeways from the 1950s onward. Conservationists defeated a proposal that would have cut freeways through the heart of downtown Vancouver in the 1960s. Now, the Trans-Canada Highway is the only freeway within the city limits and several miles from the center.

City residents enjoy a temperate rain forest climate, proximity to vast natural areas, and splendid views of sea and mountains. Of course there has to be a downside: the average annual rainfall is about 44 inches. The record for days of rain in a month is twenty-nine days, set in 1953. Even so, the climate is rarely severe and is often wonderful. However, Vancouver has other, more pressing problems, from a growing homeless population to increasing traffic snarls. Even though the region is not highly industrialized, it has serious air and water quality problems.

Vancouver and the surrounding cities were built within the delta of the Fraser River. The river runs 870 miles from the Rockies to the Pacific Ocean. Most of the Fraser Valley was covered in old-growth forest in pre-settlement times, with areas of grasslands and peat bogs in the delta area. The Fraser Valley was extensively logged from the 1880s onward as settlement moved east through the valley. The Fraser is the third-largest river in Canada and supports the world's largest salmon run. The 1.5 million salmon that swim up the river system enter it at the city of Vancouver. The massive delta, some of it now diked, is composed of sedimentary deposits built up over eons. Soils are glacial till, sand, and clay—superior well-drained soils for forests and agriculture. The largest anchors of Vancouver's natural area patches include Burns Bog, at nearly 10,000 acres the largest domed peat bog in North America and one of the largest in the world. Others are Pacific Spirit Regional Park, Burnaby Mountain Conservation Area, and Stanley Park. The region is on the Pacific flyway, with 1.5 million waterfowl passing through seasonally.

The history of land acquisition and urban development in Vancouver differs significantly from that of American cities, such as Seattle just across the border. The first buyers in Seattle were private citizens; in Vancouver they were often public officials. In the nineteenth century, lumber mills, starting in 1863, were built on Burrard Inlet and lined the waterfront into the twentieth century. In addition, the Canadian Pacific Railway shaped Vancouver's history and at one time owned more than a quarter of the city.

Vancouver has a long history of extensive urban plans going back to the late nineteenth century. In 1888 Vancouver created a Park Board and the protection of Stanley Park was its first action. This act laid the foundation for land protection in the city. Subsequently, urban planning was advocated early in the twentieth century. Thomas Adams's 1915 essay *Report on the Planning of Greater Vancouver* called for comprehensive planning for the city and neighboring municipalities. He advocated a "city-functional" approach, "with a thorough analysis of social, economic, and physical conditions in which each part of a city was designed to serve a particular purpose . . . and an overall layout that encouraged links between functions."[5] The establishment of the Vancouver Town Planning Commission in 1926 marked the beginning of formal city planning. Harland Bartholomew and Associates, a St. Louis firm that planned over fifty other North American cities, many of them in the midwestern United States, created Vancouver's earliest plan.

"Few cities possess such a combination of nearby natural resources, a splendid harbor, a terrain ideally suited for urban use, an equable climate and a setting of great natural beauty." These were the words Harland Bartholomew used to describe Vancouver as he embarked on the city's first urban plan in 1928.[6] His praise was even more unreserved: "It is suggested that, scanning the world over, it would be hard to find a city which, in addition to being practically the sole ocean port of half a continent, inhabited by a progressive and increasing population, has on its outskirts a river valley of great agricultural possibilities, with a hinterland rich in minerals, lumber and raw materials for manufacture, and adjoining at the moderate distance of five hundred miles the greatest granary in the world. Can any city claim an equal situation?"[7] Although never officially adopted, the Bartholomew plan of 1928 was the city's blueprint for decades. A number of pieces were implemented—industrial uses along the Fraser River and False Creek, apartments in the West End, and the city's grid layout. The wide boulevards are also a Bartholomew legacy. His plan was designed for a city of a staggering 1 million at a time when the city population was less than a quarter of that.

The Bartholomew plan, like other City Beautiful plans, greatly emphasized aesthetics, based on visual coherence, scenic variety, and civic grandeur.[8] A more practical emphasis on the city's functions—housing, commercial, and industrial—led to Vancouver's first zoning bylaws. Bartholomew emphasized using streets to provide aesthetic experiences as residents moved along them. His plan highlighted Vancouver's waterfront location by recommending a scenic drive starting at Stanley Park, skirting English Bay, and continuing around Point Gray to the north arm of the Fraser River in Burnaby.[9] He emphasized that the pedestrian deserves primary consideration above automobiles, even though the plan responded very directly to the novel allure of car travel in the city. Nearly eight decades later Vancouver is, indeed, a walkable city where bold views of the city are complemented by local open space and where the greenway movement is focused on streets and neighborhoods.

Bartholomew recommended an aggressive plan for setting aside land for recreation and enjoyment. The plan is remarkable in the urgency it placed on protecting parkland in a period of rapid population increase. Bartholomew claimed that development could come later, after protection. He advocated that for a number of years large portions of city funds be used to buy new parks, playgrounds, parkways, waterfronts, and beaches. He recommended pleasure drives to connect large parks. These were to be built in the form of boulevards with straight, formal lines and parkways following meandering ways along streams and through irregular landscapes.

The entire English Bay shoreline should be parkland, according to Bartholomew. He found that only 30 percent of the shore was in public lands, whereas 100 percent should have been. He scolded the city for its lack of foresight and proclaimed, "There is no matter of greater urgency than that of undertaking a systematic and determined campaign of waterfront acquisition along such lines as are laid down in the plans following."[10] His plan spelled out nine specific recommendations, in spatially explicit terms, for achieving this protection, as well as many design standards and routes for boulevards.

His thorough survey of recreational spaces in the city documented everything from schoolyards (found lacking) to waterfront resources (judged vulnerable). He found that beaches and waterfront areas were rapidly rising in value and quickly becoming private holdings. Although his plan located heavy port, lumbering, and other industrial uses on portions of the waterfront (especially adjoining the deep-sea port in Burrard Inlet), he prioritized public access to the waterfront as highly as the port facilities. Summarizing Bartholomew's legacy, one historian stressed that he "blended City Beautiful concepts into the 'practical' school of planning through the use of legal and administrative techniques such as zoning."[11] As Bartholomew claimed in his plan, Vancouver would be remembered "by its ability to create and hold bits of sheer beauty and loveliness."[12] His confidence in the physical setting of Vancouver was clear; he thought the city could have shipping and industry on the water but also have recreation and public access along other waterways. The focus on community needs was strong in Bartholomew's plan and continues in open-space planning today.

Portland: River City on the Pacific Rim

The Portland metropolitan area spreads over three main counties around the confluence of the Columbia and Willamette rivers in northern Oregon (Figure 6.3). Its location between the rivers, the Pacific Ocean, and the Cascade Mountain Range is spectacular (Figure 6.4) Portland has remained a midsized commercial city; it never developed as a center of heavy industry.[13] Rather, its strategic port location became its major strength. The west coast of the United States developed rapidly in the late nineteenth century through capital and supplies channeled through port cities like Portland, Seattle, and San Francisco. In addition, Portland served as an important point of departure for overseas Asian trade, especially after about 1850. Founded in 1843, Portland was laid out in a simple grid parallel to the riverfront. The Oregon Steam Navigation Company became Portland's largest early company, focused on river traffic. It built wharves and warehouses on the river and moved thousands of people and tons of freight on the rivers. The company monopolized shipping and passenger travel from its inception in 1860 until the arrival of the railroad in Portland in 1883.[14]

By the start of the twentieth century, Portland had a commercial downtown, a bustling waterfront, and a successful trolley line. As railroad yards were built and the city became a west coast port for shipping grain and lumber, the banks of the Willamette were lined with foundries, sawmills, machine shops, flour mills, and meat-packing plants. Portland's favorable geographic location gave excellent access through the Columbia River Gorge to the "Inland Empire" between the Cascade Range and the Rocky Mountains, where agricultural production was enhanced by new irrigation systems. By 1914 the city was the third-fastest-growing midsized city in the United States, behind Los Angeles and Seattle.

In 1852 the first parks were acquired.[15] The urban parks effort in Oregon was furthered at the end of the century, when the state passed an act that allowed parks to be purchased by park commissions in cities with populations over three thousand. These commissions had the power to levy property taxes and had full control over city parks. Following the establishment of Portland's Board of Park Commissioners in 1900, the Olmsted Brothers

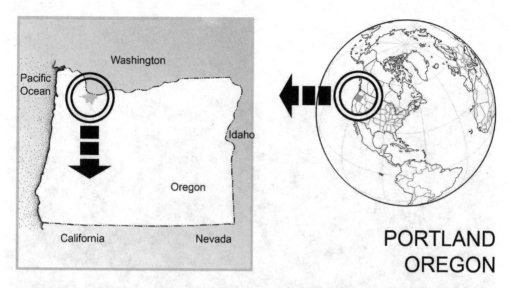

PORTLAND
OREGON

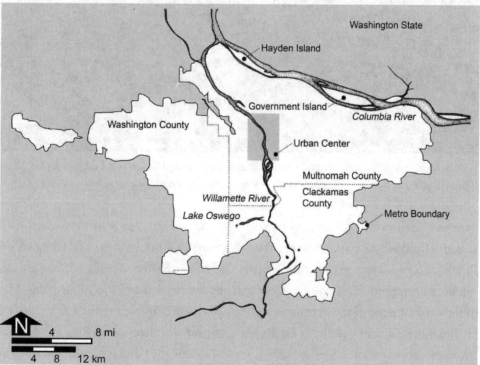

Fig. 6.3 Three-county urban region of Portland, showing Metro boundaries and Portland urban center.

Fig. 6.4 Aerial view of Portland skyline, with the Willamette River and Hawthorne Bridge in the foreground. (Photo courtesy of the City of Portland Stanley Parr Archives & Records Center.)

firm was hired to analyze park potentials in the city. Their 1903 report recommended a system of individual parks connected by parkways and boulevards. The Olmsted plan sought to take advantage of natural scenery, including the Terwilliger Parkway, five large "scenic reservations," and a 40-mile loop circling the city and linking public parks. Many of their recommendations were never realized; others were implemented many years later.

Emanuel Tillman Mische, a landscape architect who had worked for the Olmsted Brothers, was superintendent of parks from 1908 until 1914 and is considered to be one of the most influential leaders in Portland's park history. Just before Mische's tenure as superintendent, the Park Board led a successful campaign in 1907 for a bond measure to buy parkland and playgrounds. By 1913 the city had fifteen parks and thirteen playgrounds and had widened a few streets to boulevards. Primarily, the promotion of park planning came from business leaders who saw the opening of the Panama Canal as a growth stimulus for west coast cities. In 1912 the city approved a plan by E. H. Bennett, who had worked with Daniel Burnham. The plan emphasized riverfront and perimeter parks, and boulevards connecting them to greenspaces around housing and commercial areas. However, the city council never acted on the plan because property owners could not agree on how it would affect their property values.

By 1934 the Planning Commission created a comprehensive report on open spaces. It discovered ten thousand parcels of vacant land that were largely city-owned due to tax delinquency. The commission recommended that each district in the city should have a 40-acre park within walking distance of all residents. It also set a standard of 1 acre of city parkland for each 100 people, or 10 percent of the city devoted to parks. In 1936, the Planning Commission reiterated these goals with a "System of Public Recreation Areas" similar to the Olmsted plan, including a hierarchy of park spaces and a pleasure-drive system. In the 1940s, Robert Moses, New York City's Parks Commissioner, completed a public-works study for Portland that included many park improvement recommendations. He advocated purchasing more land for parks in the hills to the west, downtown, and along the waterfront. This plan, although not funded at the time, provided a blueprint for the growth of city parks for the next twenty years.

By the mid-1960s, the residents of Portland began to resist large-scale urban renewal projects. In Portland the demolition of mixed-use, working-class neighborhoods, many of them inhabited by African-Americans, provoked people to think differently. Mayor Neil Goldshmidt, elected in 1973, created an Office of Neighborhood Associations to bring local communities into the land-use planning process. By 1975, an alliance of neighborhood groups and downtown businesses defeated plans for a new freeway through east Portland. Neighborhood activism for open space also became an important force. For example, in 1969 a group called Riverfront for People staged a picnic for 250 adults and 100 children on a strip of derelict riverfront land on the Willamette. Subsequent work led to Riverfront Park's construction on the site, later named for Governor Tom McCall.

At the state level, 60 percent of logging jobs had disappeared between the mid-1950s and 1980. Despite these changes, or because of them, Portland has choreographed both a civic and an architectural renaissance downtown and, at the same time, an explosion of high-tech development in the suburbs.[16] The economy of the region has shifted from processing and shipping raw materials to producing consumer electronics and apparel (Portland hosts the Nike headquarters), and moving Asian automobiles for sale across

North America. By 2002 Portland became the largest auto-handling port on the Pacific Coast for Asian cars.

Contemporary Open-Space Systems Stimulate Community Cohesion
Both Vancouver and Portland possess remarkable community assets that are attracting increasing populations. At the same time, residents of both cities are extremely vocal in protecting their quality of life. For instance, citizens in both cities have successfully blocked freeway projects in their inner cities, in favor of more human-scaled development and resource protection. In recent decades, both cities have developed open-space programs tailored to create civic connection and social benefits.

Vancouver: Greenways Changing the "Way the City Thinks"
Planning for connected open space in the Vancouver region is carried out at several scales. First, several cities have discrete greenway programs. For instance, the city of Burnaby east of Vancouver is implementing a 46-mile urban trails system. However, the focus in this chapter is on the city of Vancouver, where greenway planning is done at two distinct scales, and is particularly aimed at community building. In addition, planning for open space at the larger metropolitan region is coordinated by the Greater Vancouver Regional District, which focuses on regionally significant greenway corridors and on a "Green Zone" of protected forest and farmland. BC Hydro, the regional power supplier, is also linking communities in the metropolitan region through open-space corridors.

CITY OF VANCOUVER GREENWAYS PROGRAM
It is telling that Vancouver's most famous symbol and its biggest tourist attraction is not an architectural or industrial marvel but rather Stanley Park. By park numbers or acreage, Vancouver is not long on parks compared with Seattle or Portland, even though the city promotes itself as a city of parks. But the actual numbers are compensated by popular Stanley Park and by the accessible and highly visible shoreline (Figure 6.5). Nature is close in Vancouver; this proximity to wilderness and water makes the actual acreages of open space less relevant. Over time there has been strong public and political priority on parks: funding for parks from both an independent parks board and the city has been fairly stable over time, without the dramatic reductions recently experienced in many places.

An emphasis on neighborhood planning began for Vancouver in the 1970s, with the creation of citizens' planning committees. Different approaches were used in each neighborhood, but the emphasis at the outset was on community participation in a two-way

Fig. 6.5 Open space corridor separating English Bay from the dense housing of Vancouver's West End. (Photo by the author.)

planning process. The legacy of community involvement continued over the subsequent decades and greatly influenced the city's planning efforts. For instance, Vancouver's 1995 City Plan resulted from broad citizen input.[17] The plan's progressive process was so innovative that the city won national and international awards, specifically for novel public processes involving thousands of citizens. A citizen consensus emerged around the notion of a city of neighborhood centers.[18]

In 1991 the mayor and city council appointed an Urban Landscape Task Force (ULTF), chaired by landscape architect Moura Quayle, to report on Vancouver's urban landscape. The task force was given a two-part mandate: find out what people in Vancouver value about the urban landscape, and recommend how best to manage, protect, and enhance it. The task force started with the notion that Vancouver had not articulated a vision for the public realm since the Bartholomew plan.

The final report, *Greenways–Public Ways,* approved by the city council in 1995, recommended the development of a citywide greenway network.[19] It created a broad vision statement for making green connections, enhancing and celebrating the public realm, strengthening neighborhoods, and focusing on physical design. The report recommended

establishing a greenway trust as a hybridized public–private institution for implementing the greenway–public way agenda. It provided an ambitious vision with fundamental
organizing principles for public space in the city, including enough specificity to prioritize project areas. The main landscape themes that run through the recommendations are
greenway connections, truly public places, democratic streets, ecological priority, and
neighborhoods that work.

The ULTF's work created the political direction and leadership to make greenways a
reality for Vancouver. Earlier in the 1990s, urban greenway opportunities had been catalogued. Since the city is nearly built out, few opportunities were found for natural-based
greenways, other than the shoreline, a ridgeline, and two pieces of intact ravines. Even at
the shoreline, port activities compromise public access to some portions of the waterfront.
(Since the 9/11 tragedy, there are more severe limitations on public access to port areas.)
There are also very few abandoned rail lines. However, the city's expectations were broader.
Planners started looking at parks and streets as potential greenway linkages and devised
a double system of both citywide and neighborhood greenway programs. The greenway
idea was transformed to rethink streets as more than transportation—as important spaces
for public life, including pedestrian experience, street beautification, public art, and traffic calming. The ULTF saw streets as a huge untapped resource, with the ability to enhance
neighborhoods. Greenways were one part of an effort to move people into the street. The
Bartholomew plan created the structure for that goal; its strong street grid enables one
to find routes through the city on small streets.

As Vancouver's greenway program began implementing *Greenways–Public Ways,* the
Vancouver Parks Board could have been a natural home for the program. The Parks Board
is an agency that works independently from City Hall and the city council. It is operated
by its own publicly elected Board of Parks Commissioners and is guided by the mandate
of a park standard: 2.75 acres of parks per 1,000 people. Since the Parks Board deals with
large user groups and large capital projects, it was not particularly interested in the greenway idea. The city Engineering Department then picked up the greenways ball, since it had
a larger staff that is accustomed to implementing small projects involving neighborhoods
and landowners. The Parks Board, meanwhile, remains active in managing waterfront corridors, which it largely controls.[20]

As this process has evolved for Vancouver, the greenways goal is community building
through travel and connectivity. Streets are the focus of greenways in Vancouver, and this
focus is reinforced by the program's home in the Engineering Department rather than the
Parks Board. Greenways in Vancouver are green paths for pedestrians and cyclists. They

can be waterfront promenades, urban walks, environmental demonstration trails, heritage walks, and nature trails. "Their purpose," the city declared, "is to expand the opportunities for urban recreation, to provide alternate ways to move through the city, and to enhance the experience of nature, community and city life."[21] The *Public Ways* portion of the plan's title targets those streets with commercial or retail opportunities. Although greenways are distributed throughout the city, the routes are concentrated in areas with greater population density and a higher number of natural destinations.

Vancouver's two-tiered system starts with a network of City Greenways, fourteen corridors totaling about 87 miles (Figure 6.6). About 50 percent of this system will use street rights-of-way. When done, a city greenway will be no more than a twenty-five-minute walk or a ten-minute bike ride from any residence. Because of the legacy of the seawall along English Bay, 30 percent of the network was already in place before the first city greenway was constructed. City Greenways are normally financed from the city's capital budget. Funding may also come from other levels of government, donations, nonprofit agencies, or business associations.

The goals of the City Greenways are to make walking more interesting, make cycling safer and easier, reduce vehicle impact, and make the city "greener." The program also connects closely to Vancouver's strong public arts program, managed by the Office of Cultural Affairs. When possible, public art is installed to make greenways more aesthetically appealing. The planning process starts with initial public meetings and the development of initial design concepts. Those designs are taken back to the relevant neighborhoods for further comment, and detailed designs are subsequently produced. Residents are then surveyed so that public opinions about the designs can be quantified. Cost estimating is then completed and construction carried out by city crews and/or contracted builders.

City Greenways are distinct from bikeways, of which Vancouver has an extensive network, although objectives sometimes overlap. Bikeways are intended to create safe and convenient bike transportation routes, often through traffic-calming measures. Greenways enhance the experience of walking or cycling with a wide range of improvements, including expanded parks, increased landscaping, public art, or drinking fountains. Bicycle commuters will also use the greenways system, and many sections of the greenways and bikeways networks overlap; recreational or very young cyclists may be safer and more comfortable cycling along greenways.

The second tier in the system, Neighborhood Greenways, creates smaller-scale connections with ideas initiated by local residents. These projects are smaller in scope, with shorter routes that are maintained by the community once completed. They connect local community amenities such as parks, schools, libraries, community centers, or shopping

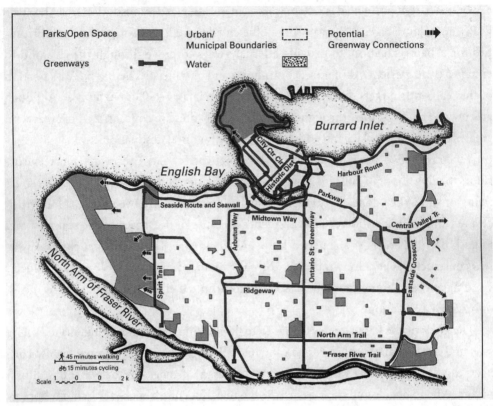

Fig. 6.6 Vancouver's fourteen citywide greenway corridors, identified and planned in *Greenways—Public Ways*. (Adapted from City of Vancouver, Urban Landscape Task Force, *Greenways—Public Ways*, 1999.)

streets. They are also meant to highlight places of special meaning, such as a group of heritage houses, an interesting street, or a corner store. Neighborhood Greenways epitomize the community-building motive of connected open space. They are specifically meant to reflect and honor the local character and identity of the neighborhood by providing opportunities to express the unique features of the area and adding new details and activities to the public landscape.

Neighborhood Greenways are partly funded by the city, supplemented by community funds or in-kind contributions. Nine have been completed so far. "We view these Neighborhood Greenways as partnerships between the community and the City," one report stressed. The community must take a leadership role. City staff helps in the design development and construction phases. A neighborhood greenway can take several years to complete as interest and energy fluctuates in the community. Long-term commitment by the community group is essential for success.[22]

6.1 Ridgeway Greenway

The Ridgeway Greenway was the first citywide greenway to be completed in Vancouver. It extends about 8 miles across the spine of the Vancouver peninsula, from Pacific Spirit Park in the west to the city of Burnaby in the east. The Ridgeway Greenway was designated as a pilot project when the greenways plan was adopted in 1995. The Ridgeway, as its name implies, lies on a long east–west ridge above the central city, with outstanding views toward the downtown and the northern mountains beyond.

The process for developing the Ridgeway Greenway was remarkable. Initially the principals of four large design firms came together for a design charrette to generate ideas. Subsequently Kim Perry was hired to create a concept plan. That plan was organized around six main ideas—walking, cycling, environment, art, special places, and calming traffic. The city took these six themes out to the neighborhoods along the proposed greenway. In a second public-involvement stage, the city held workshops to develop the ideas further. Neighbors were also asked if they would be willing to be involved in greenway planning and development. According to planners, one of the biggest keys to success in these workshops was the presence of uniformed officers, who helped diffuse worries about increased crime as an outcome of greenway development.

The Ridgeway Greenway, except for a mixed-use path in one park, takes advantage of the existing street (Figure 6.7). Pedestrians use the sidewalk, and cyclists share the roadway along traffic-calmed streets that include corner bulges, traffic circles, landscaped medians, street segments closed to motor vehicles, and bicycle gates. The entire route has been enhanced for pedestrian and cyclist safety and pleasure, including landscaping, seating, signage, and water fountains. Its route goes by one of Vancouver's most scenic overlooks and through both wealthy and modest neighborhoods. It passes by or through ten parks and a cemetery, and it intersects other city and neighborhood greenways. Public art, most with a cycling theme, is a striking feature of the Ridgeway Greenway, contributing to its sense of community and aesthetic experience.

Fig. 6.7 An intersection near multiple-family housing along the Ridgeway Greenway, showing a plaza area with seating, public art, bike racks, and a corner bulge for traffic calming. (Photo by the author.)

Garden Drive is one example where the project tested new design ideas and new community involvement techniques (Figure 6.8). Garden Drive, a short residential street in a modest neighborhood east of downtown, became one of the first successful traffic-calmed streets in Vancouver. The street was being used heavily as a shortcut to bypass busy arterial streets. The city worked in conjunction with about 150 residents to design traffic circles and corner bulges at intersections.[23] The residents chose to beautify their street in the process, and it is now a pleasant, pedestrian-friendly corridor that has brought the community together for further improvements in the public realm.

Two spin-offs of the Neighborhood Greenways program have gained remarkable momentum—the Green Streets program and Country Lanes. Green Streets offers Vancouver's residents the chance to become volunteer street gardeners in their neighborhoods by sponsoring a traffic circle or corner bulge garden (Figure 6.9). This not only creates a more colorful street but also encourages and promotes a sense of community pride and ownership that ultimately benefits the entire city. The program, which has

Fig. 6.8 Garden Drive streetscape, showing a large boulder serving as a round-about, and enhanced planting along the street. (Photo courtesy of Vancouver Greenways Program.)

recently been expanding, starts to break down the division of public and private. It encourages neighbors to know one another, to work together, and to help monitor public spaces.

Country Lanes is a program to retrofit lanes (alleys) to provide a more rural aesthetic and to reduce discharges to the city's storm sewer system. A demonstration project was completed in 2002. Country Lanes includes two narrow strips of concrete for vehicle wheels, with an area between and beside the strips of a planted pervious material that can support vehicles (Figure 6.10). The Engineering Department is still experimenting with these lanes to gauge cost, durability, and functionality. As in the Green Streets program, the community is heavily involved. Both Green Streets and Country Lanes can clearly be traced to the thinking that went into the Urban Landscape Task Force work. That effort asked Vancouverites to rethink "local improvements," the term describing how street renovation projects are funded. The task force urged more creativity in that process: narrower streets, traffic calming, green lanes, and streetside gardening are all direct responses.

Fig. 6.9 Green Streets project, planted and maintained by neighborhood residents. (Photo by the author.)

One city staff person claims that "greenways planning has made a huge difference in the way the city thinks." Others claim that the community-building aspect of the greenways program has been as important, or more important, than the physical greenways themselves. Greenways in Vancouver are not so much about routes as about how we move through the city and get people involved in their neighborhoods. The greenways plan has had many spin-offs that fit under the greening umbrella—for instance, traffic circles and other traffic-calming designs.

Through these experiments aimed at more community-friendly streets, the greenways program has taken on a type of research and development function in the Engineering Department. In some cases the greenways program has the opportunity to experiment (and to fail) where other branches of engineering cannot. For instance, the implementation of corner bulges started with the greenways program; now all new intersections automatically include them. Another example is infiltration bulges, where the corner bulges become small catchbasins for rainwater. The greenways program received an award for these installations, which are not only more environmentally beneficial but less expensive as well (compared with standard corner bulges). Greenway designing becomes a

Fig. 6.10 Prototype of Vancouver's Country Lanes program. (Photo courtesy of Vancouver Greenways Program.)

mechanism for experimentation without high risk. Where successful, these street improvements become standard practice.

The community-building characteristics in the city's Neighborhood Greenways program are echoed by the efforts of Evergreen, a national, nonprofit environmental organization that brings nature to Canadian cities through naturalization projects. Its work centers on three main programs: Learning Grounds transforms school grounds; Home Grounds targets home landscapes; and Common Grounds protects public open space. Evergreen works on capacity building among community groups, landowners, foundations, municipal governments, local land trusts, and the corporate sector to restore and manage parks and open spaces in urban areas. Their Nature of Cities project showcases tools that local government and community leaders can use to address nature in the public realm.[24] At the scale of the entire urban region, the Greater Vancouver Regional District provides similar services as a regional level of government.

GREATER VANCOUVER REGIONAL DISTRICT: REGIONWIDE GREENWAY VISIONS

The Greater Vancouver Regional District (GVRD) is responsible for the creation and support of community infrastructure. Incorporated in 1967, the GVRD is a voluntary federation of twenty-one municipalities and two electoral areas (University Endowment Lands and Bowen Island), which comprises one of twenty-seven regional districts in British Columbia. The GVRD's role is to deliver utility services like drinking water, sewage treatment, recycling, and garbage disposal in an economical and effective means on a regional basis. In addition, the GVRD strives to protect and enhance the quality of life, managing and planning growth and development through measures that seek to protect air quality and green spaces. The GVRD has a community-minded structure, with a board of directors made up of mayors and councilors from the member municipalities, on a representation-by-population basis.

Parks planning by the GVRD began with a 1966 plan to create a regional parks plan for the lower mainland region. Even then, there was strong support for a complete park system that included corridors linking protected areas. Of the forty regional sites identified in this plan, one-quarter of them were linear connections. However, connectivity goals were postponed for several decades as acquisition of regional parks took priority in rapidly urbanizing areas. Now, the GVRD owns and manages twenty-three parks, including three greenways, on over 27,000 acres.

Open-space planning in Greater Vancouver is a collaborative effort. The GVRD approach allows for assembly of funds from the whole region, which are then dispersed to small municipalities that would not otherwise be able to garner such monetary support for managing public lands. The GVRD is similar to Councils of Government in the United States, but since it has more power to implement projects and to own land, it is even closer in form to a regional level of government, as in Portland. Although the GVRD has considerable funding for land acquisition, operating budgets are slim. This is complicated by the fact that, until recently, the provincial act that authorizes regional districts stipulated that the districts could not spend money on land that they would not ultimately own. Since this was overturned, the GVRD is now able to spend money on easements and rights-of-way that will be owned and managed by the municipalities—a major improvement for the prospects of connected, linear open space at the regional scale.[25]

The GVRD's Livable Region Strategic Plan, first adopted in 1996, is recognized by the province as the Vancouver region's growth-management strategy. The plan identified a preliminary Park and Outdoor Recreation System, which included large, conceptual corridors for open-space connectivity (Figure 6.11). This "Green Zone" is not only a local benefit but also a central feature to open-space protection at the regional scale. The Green

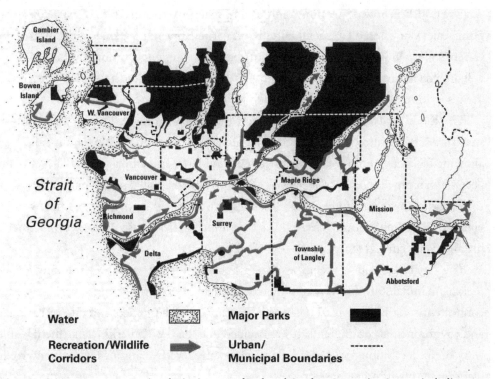

Fig. 6.11 Greater Vancouver Regional District map of Park and Outdoor Recreation System, including connected wildlife corridors. (Adapted from Greater Vancouver Regional District, "Livable Region Strategic Plan," 1996.)

Zone concept was envisioned in the 1960s but not implemented until the 1990s. The concept is far-reaching and offers protection to lands designated as community health lands (watersheds, floodplains), ecologically important lands (forested mountain slopes, wildlife habitat, wetlands, etc.), outdoor recreation and scenic lands (major parks and recreational sites), and renewable resource lands (agriculture and forestry).

Of the nearly half million Green Zone acres, most is in public hands—owned by the GVRD, the province, and the municipalities. Private land is largely agricultural—placed in the Agricultural Land Reserve (ALR) based on land assessment by the province and protected by provincial legislation on farmland protection. The ALR in British Columbia is the most comprehensive farmland protection program in Canada. The Green Zone has established an effective urban-growth boundary around the Vancouver metropolitan area in a way that has not dampened growth inside the boundary but has enjoyed a high level of endorsement from the region's residents.[26] Since adoption, only 0.03 percent of Green Zone land has been lost to urbanization.

The GVRD is now developing a more comprehensive regional biodiversity conservation framework based on a federal initiative. A cornerstone of the plan is protection of the Green Zone, allowing no further interior urban development. This biodiversity strategy will provide more specificity about Green Zone land use, provide an inventory of each segment's resources, and determine how each sector contributes to biodiversity.

The Biodiversity Plan will knit together the Green Zones and a new Green Infrastructure scheme into one framework and align objectives on multiple political scales, allowing for greater emphasis on connectivity and large-scale linkages. It will eventually become an umbrella concept for ecological restoration, integrated pest management, green roofs, and many other biodiversity initiatives. It will provide more than a framework; it will also be a compilation of case studies for municipalities to use in further implementing and connecting greenspace.

The City of Vancouver greenway project helped jumpstart greenway thinking for the region. An initial study of the region was completed in 1999, providing a general vision for connectivity on a broader level.[27] This study separated undeveloped land into recreational and environmental components. It was decided that the GVRD Parks Department would work on the recreational part of the plan and that the GVRD Planning Department would work on the environmental segment.

The Parks Department divided the region into five sectors and created a plan for each. For instance, a North Shore plan encompasses the districts of North Vancouver and West Vancouver, Bowen Island, the city of North Vancouver, and the village of Lion's Bay. The GVRD manages the public participation process and provides support for these plans. Two categories of greenways were created. Regionally Significant Greenways are corridors that local municipalities will implement and manage. Regional Greenways, in contrast, are managed by the GVRD. Criteria were developed and applied across plans for all five geographic sectors.

The scale of the plans made some sense. There are advantages to focusing on areas smaller than the entire metropolitan area but larger than individual municipalities. This stimulated the neighboring units of government to talk to one another about connectivity and to negotiate their communities' needs. Furthermore, incentives helped nudge their participation. Funds may be sought from the GVRD to implement improvements, such as bridges or signage, on Regionally Significant Greenways.

An analysis of the GVRD Greenway Program reveals some challenges of the planning-to-implementation process. According to Heather Wornell, "The Greenway Program would have benefited from a clear definition of success at its outset, in the form of well-defined and communicated goals and objectives and the development of performance indicators, to ensure that participants held a common understanding of program success."[28] In addition, because the Greenways Program is primarily a recreational initiative, divorced from environmental goals, it did not explicitly address the multifunctional prospects of modern greenway planning. In addition, little effort has gone into the assessment of sector plans once they are adopted—implementation was not even a clear criterion of success for the sector plans. Some municipalities have been strategic in promptly asking for implementation assistance after a sector plan is completed, but funds are not automatically made available. In addition, the process is fragile because there is no accountability or commitment about implementation.

Heather Wornell's recommendations for the GVRD address issues important for regional open-space planning in Vancouver and elsewhere. She suggests more defining departmental goals and objectives for implementation and assessment, including a process for measurable targets. This is especially critical since the GVRD has no real authority for implementing the category of Regionally Significant Greenways, which the local municipalities design and regulate. Direct annual funding to implement the sector plans would help clarify expectations, as would the creation of a greenway typology with design principles for different types of greenways. The criteria for selecting Regionally Significant Greenways have turned out to be too broad, as they sometimes capture lands that should really be part of the larger Regional Greenways system managed by the GVRD rather than by the local agencies. Furthermore, the GVRD currently lacks data on the number of planned Regionally Significant Greenways that have been completed.

Though improvement is always possible, the GVRD Parks Department has developed an innovative greenways technique that could have application elsewhere. Since the GVRD is responsible for supplying utilities, it is required to maintain access roads on top of underground lines. The green infrastructure concept is being applied in creative ways to create recreational paths with public access on top of underground utilities. The GVRD already controls access roads along streams and rivers, and thus has some control of how these corridors will be shaped and used.

The Delta–South Surrey Regional Greenway is an example: an opportunity to connect Vancouver, Richmond, New Westminster, Delta, and Surrey to one another and to the U.S. border. In collaboration with the City of Surrey and the Corporation of Delta, the GVRD is retrofitting a public-access greenway simultaneously as sewer twinning is installed (a second, parallel line being installed along the first). The gravel maintenance road will be a walking and cycling route; staging areas with washrooms and parking will complement the recreation area. Another similar pilot project was the Brunette Fraser greenway, a 9.3-mile corridor along a sewage and drainage right-of-way paralleling the Brunette River in Burnaby and New Westminster. According to greenway planners, it was a big step for the utility department to accept the idea of a greenway on their facilities, but now there is considerable enthusiasm. Collaborative possibilities are being considered for other GVRD rights-of-way.

BC HYDRO: THE ROLE OF REGIONAL UTILITIES

BC Hydro, British Columbia's Crown corporation electrical utility, is becoming an important player in the metropolitan greenways scene. It manages 10,500 miles of transmission line rights-of-way covering about 350 square miles of land. BC Hydro rights-of-way cross federally owned land, First Nations land, and private land holdings. These lands are used for a variety of uses compatible with power generation. BC Hydro lists appropriate uses as greenways, tree farms, parking and other commercial uses, recreation, wildlife habitat, residential gardens, grazing, agricultural uses, hiking, and equestrian trails. Although the land over which BC Hydro rights-of-way run is usually owned by other landowners, the utility works with those landowners to implement greenway corridors in selected areas. The company acknowledges that those corridors create edge effects, which can be attractive habitats for deer, black bear, eagles, and songbirds.

BC Hydro reviews proposals for innovative corridors compatible with public activities, and works with community groups and other agencies in enacting these projects. The company also encourages environmentally sustainable uses under transmission lines, such as habitat enhancement. Local governments, public agencies, and interest groups are seeking to link legal rights-of-way with established parks and trails and public-use facilities on the ground. Interest in these projects and the pressure to complete them is mounting.

The municipality of Surrey has been aggressive over the last twenty years in developing utility corridors using BC Hydro rights-of-way. The city has been successful in connecting fragments to produce linear corridors. The burgeoning greenway movement has resulted in efforts such as Serpentine Greenway in Surrey, a multiuse pathway to which BC Hydro contributed $50,000. A pathway for walking, in-line skating, jogging, and cycling, it also features informative kiosks that discuss not only habitat and wildlife but also the electric transmission system so crucial to the creation of the path in the first place. In Coquitlam, the Mundy Greenway is the first section of a larger right-of-way greenway system built with a similar framework. It is a multiuse pathway running along the edge of Mundy Park and includes a series of interpretive signs installed by BC Hydro in partnership with the city. When the larger system is complete, the greenway will be a 10-mile series of pathways located mostly within the utility corridors.

The Center for Urban Ecology, with BC Hydro, has been instrumental in both the Surrey and the Coquitlam greenway projects since the mid-1990s.[29] The center, administered through Douglas College and led by Valentin Schaefer, is largely supported by foundation and other grant funding. Its Green Links program, started in 1996, has used the utility corridor sites as demonstration projects to increase connectivity and biodiversity, as well as community involvement in support of these goals. The goal of Green Links is to create a corridor network that links habitat patches, with an emphasis on ecological integrity and environmental education rather than recreation. Native vegetation has been planted and invasive species removed as part of restoring 325-foot-wide utility corridors. The projects have relied heavily on funding that enabled youth employment programs that paid salaries for young people, 16 to 24 years old, to get hands-on experience in environmental stewardship.

Few cities in North America have gone further toward a seamless connection of diverse open spaces. The Green Links program has identified the opportunities for connectivity in a myriad of shapes and forms: stream corridors, utility lines, hedgerows, farm fields, cemeteries, golf courses, parks, backyard and balcony habitats, and school grounds. This exemplifies the type of broad thinking at all levels of government and across the private sector that has created momentum for open-space planning, particularly among younger generations. Perhaps the most striking measures of progress are the degree to which engineers, utility providers, and other professionals are taking part in greenway efforts, in addition to the engagement of local community members.

Portland: "Community in the City"

In only five years, 1992 to 1997, Portland's population grew by 131,000 people. It is expected to increase by a half million more people by 2017. This will create enormous pressure for basics like housing, and for infrastructure from sewers to schools. And, ironically, the more people in the area, the higher the demand for open space as well. There are direct and active efforts to protect open spaces in light of this growth. The birthplace of Portland's physical open-space network is the Willamette River; the vision can be traced to Governor Tom McCall's leadership from 1967 to 1975. The river is Oregon's longest— 187 miles, draining 11,500 square miles. The Willamette River spine has been an important building block for subsequent open-space planning in the city of Portland and the

Fig. 6.12 Governor Tom McCall Waterfront Park on the west bank of the Willamette River in downtown Portland. (Photo courtesy of Portland Parks and Recreation, Portland, Oregon.)

larger metropolitan region. McCall envisioned a revitalized river with a public greenway on its banks, reversing a trend of neglect and abuse of the river and its banks. The continuation of his conservation legacy has been ensured by the creation of Governor Tom McCall Waterfront Park, where millions attend festivals and events along the river's banks (Figure 6.12). The Willamette River Greenway Trail, when complete, will give access along the lower 40 miles of the most urbanized stretch of the river. The plans for a Willamette greenway are not new. In the early 1970s, the landscape architecture firms of both Lawrence Halprin and Robert Royston prepared visionary plans.

Citizen awareness of planning issues and growth management is as strong in Portland as in any American city, due to strong statewide land-use planning, including the implementation of urban growth boundaries and structured consensus-building processes.[30] Several agencies own and manage public open space in the Portland metropolitan region, including Metro (the regional government), the state of Oregon, and the cities of Lake Oswego, Gresham, and Oregon City. Within the city of Portland, two hundred parks are spread over more than 10,000 acres managed by the city. It is clear, too, that the culture and economy of Portland is strongly tied to the natural environment and that residents place a high value on enjoyment of the natural landscape, something that has become intrinsic to their city's identity.

CITY OF PORTLAND AND PORTLAND PARKS FOUNDATION

"The first summer I moved to Portland, I had two toddlers. I took them to the Grant Park playground almost every day. At the end of that summer I received a questionnaire on my doorstep from an urban studies professor at PSU [Portland State University] who was researching how community forms in neighborhoods. One of the questions asked, how many people in your neighborhood do you know by name? I counted up 80. I had met almost all of them at the park."[31] These are the words of Barbara Scharff, a northeast Portland resident and member of Portland's 2001 Park Vision Team. The city of Portland is known for both its greenness and its active outdoor community. Nearly 10 percent of the city is in parkland, and a remarkable three-fourths of that land is undeveloped and managed for natural resource values, like clean water and healthy forests. Portland boasts that Forest Park is America's largest urban forest; at nearly 5,000 acres it is more than five times as large as New York's Central Park. Portlanders have long made the connection between close access to nature and viable, lively neighborhoods. Surveys show that almost half of Portlanders spend some time every week in a park. City residents strongly support buying public open space and preserving habitat within the city and along the rivers.[32] They are particularly active in open-lands work.

During several years in the 1990s, Portland, under the leadership of Parks Director Charles Jordan, worked with the Project for Public Spaces, the Lila Wallace-Reader's Digest Fund, and the Trust for Public Land on an innovative project to engage the community in park work. Jordan inspired a more holistic view of parkland use, working particularly hard to engage underrepresented minority residents in environmental pursuits. Similar to Vancouver's greenway program, this project used park-building as a vehicle to get people involved in neighborhoods.

The project focused on four small urban park sites and one natural areas site, where the community had active involvement. The parks, formerly tax foreclosure sites in under-served neighborhoods, were blank slates for neighbors to scheme up ideas and desires to share with the Parks Department. The Parks Department stressed that neighbors would be expected to help build and maintain the parks. A project coordinator from the Parks Department helped organize the citizen involvement, as the coordination of efforts was an enormous task. But interesting synergies emerged. In one instance, sod was donated for a planting project. A local resident knew how to lay it and taught his neighbors; together they installed the sod. Neighbors stepped up to maintain the sites as well. The work rein-vigorated the communities and built skills and capacity among residents, but required active coordination from the city agency. Without coordinated planning and organiza-tional involvement, an initiative like this is usually doomed.

Unfortunately, this particular project was discontinued by Portland Parks as staffing and budgets tightened. Partnership between the community and Parks Department was difficult to sustain as leadership, funding, and priorities changed. The efforts of local res-idents are intrinsic to improving Portland's park deficiencies, but must be balanced by committed city involvement.

The Three Rivers Land Conservancy in Portland is an example of this success. The conservancy started a neighborhood Special Place program, modeled after Chicago's NeighborSpace program. Building on nascent desire for neighborhood involvement, they created a program whereby neighborhoods can propose funding for local open spaces. But first, the neighborhood must demonstrate strong community support. One group in southwest Portland has raised $218,000 to buy a half-acre site. The commu-nity successfully put the deal together. Most of the proposed projects have connec-tivity goals, for instance, landscapes connected to a high school campus or other com-munity feature.

These types of locally supported community programs are increasingly important given that the parks system is overused and underfunded. "Our parks and natural areas have never had as many visitors as they have now, but they are being loved to death—and many suffer from overuse," according to the city of Portland's Parks Vision.[33] Despite rousing efforts in some areas, many neighborhoods have few or no recreation facilities, and a parks inventory shows that all sections of the city have at least one type of parkland deficiency. For the area inside the region's urban growth boundary, it is estimated that only 62 percent of residents live within walking distance, one-quarter mile, of a park or regional trail.[34]

Parks Vision 2020 addresses the future of the city of Portland's park system. It was started in 1999 and completed in 2001, by a team of parks staff and city residents, with the participation of thousands of residents. The 2020 plan is based closely on the idea that community building happens through providing quality open spaces. It breaks the city into six subareas for addressing park and open-space needs. However, the plan's specificity as a policymaking tool may not be strong enough. While it underscores park needs and lays out a big vision, it may lack the force to affect actual outcomes.

The 2020 Vision recommends buying 1,870 acres of new parkland, including over 600 acres of habitat lands, thereby ensuring a basic neighborhood park within a fifteen-minute walk of each residence. It envisions a more robust urban forest along streets and in parks. One of several objectives in the vision is to create an interconnected system of trails, paths, and walks to make Portland "the walking city of the west." It calls for an additional 150 miles of trails, complementing the existing 150 miles that comprise the Parks Department's most heavily used resource. These additional linkages would connect parks, natural areas, and recreational facilities with neighborhoods, civic institutions, and commercial areas. They would include physical and visual access to the rivers and complete a 40-mile loop. A main goal of the plan is to develop parks that promote "community in the city," complete with public plazas, green connections along main streets, and programmatic partnerships with schools.

The Parks Department city partners include Metro, Portland Development Commission, and the bureaus of Planning, Environmental Services, and Water. An additional sixty-five different friends groups, corporations, community partnerships, and volunteers provide support. To help pay for new parks, Portland has levied a parks impact fee—the Park Systems Development Charge—since 1998, which offsets the costs of parkland for new housing development. This impact fee yields about $1,500 per residential unit, totaling $1 million per year for park capital improvements in the city. Other funding is sorely needed, since these funds cannot be used to improve existing parks, and can be levied only on residential development.

6.2 The 40 (140)-Mile Loop

The revival of the 40-Mile Loop idea started in 1977, with a new parks superintendent in the city of Portland. In that year, voters requested funds for regional parks and for beginning the Olmsted 40-mile loop. But the bond measure failed. In 1981 a private land trust was formed to raise money and acquire the necessary land. The subsequent planning brought together the park planning work of thirteen local jurisdictions, including city and county governments, Oregon State Parks Division, Port of Portland, Corps of Engineers, state and federal Fish and Game agencies, and public drainage districts.

When the loop is completed, it will be 140 miles long, rather than the original 40 miles

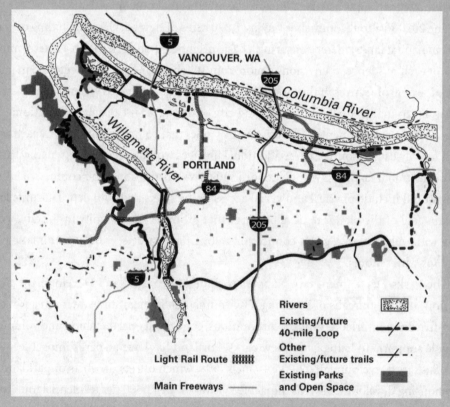

Fig. 6.13 Portland's 40-Mile Loop plan, showing other existing and proposed trail connections.

the Olmsteds envisioned for the once-smaller city. It will link over thirty parks in the Portland region along the Columbia, Sandy, and Willamette rivers, providing a central structure from which local, state, and regional trails can connect out to federal, state, and county recreation and natural areas (Figure 6.13).

One segment of this ambitious project is the Vera Katz Eastbank Esplanade, a 1.5-mile connection along the Willamette River (Figure 6.14). This section provides a link to the river for two different neighborhoods. It was completed at about the time that the 2020 Vision was unveiled. Designed by the landscape architecture firm of Mayer/Reed in Portland, the esplanade includes interpretive panels, public art, a demonstration project for fish and wildlife habitat restoration, and a 1,200-foot floating walkway.

Fig. 6.14 Vera Katz Esplanade on the east bank of the Willamette River. (Photo courtesy of Portland Parks and Recreation, Portland, Oregon.)

One recommendation coming out of the 2020 Vision was the establishment of the Portland Parks Foundation, which has already raised between $4 million and $5 million since being established in 2001. As a philanthropic vehicle for parks, the organization has two goals. The first is a parks expansion fund to ensure that all neighborhoods have access to parks and green spaces, with a focus on parks-deficient neighborhoods (20 percent of Portland's neighborhoods, according to the 2020 plan). The foundation has helped fund one city park. Second, the foundation aims to provide financial aid to organize recreation programming for low-income youth in the face of shrinking public funding.

A first step in implementing the Vision 2020 plan was to evaluate the ecosystem health, at the species level, of 7,000 acres of public park and natural-areas land. The inventory found that a good portion of the parkland is in good or fair stead, but that 23.7 percent is badly or severely degraded. The Parks Department is one of the largest landowners in the city, and it owns more pervious surface than any other owner, making the environmental quality of that land a primary concern. This focus on ecological values has broadened beyond existing landholdings to include a natural-areas acquisition strategy for the city. Since a serious mission of the Parks Department relates to citizens' access to nature, this effort fits perfectly with other, more traditional, parks and recreation objectives. This emphasis carries over into the categorization of park spaces. Park system planning focuses on settings and experiences rather than on traditional categories like "neighborhood park" or "tot lot." The settings include a spectrum from natural to highly developed, using human perceptions of naturalness rather than acreage for evaluating the system.

Since 1990, the city has acquired 750 acres of additional natural areas with funding from three main sources—Metro's Metropolitan Greenspaces program, Federal Emergency Management Agency (FEMA), and the Park Systems Development Charge. FEMA monies relate to flooding along Johnson Creek, to fund land acquisition in the floodplain to prevent flood-prone development. The Parks Department works closely with the Department of Environmental Services on these acquisitions. The Development Charge includes a small amount allocated to natural-areas acquisition (not necessarily contiguous to new development) and another allocation for trails.

Using priorities developed by the Oregon Watershed Enhancement Board, the Parks Department is working on a strategy to protect large intact areas, preserve biodiversity values, buffer current natural areas, and improve connectivity across a regional system. The connectivity focus is primarily on protected corridors along the Willamette and Columbia rivers, Johnson Creek, and a band of forest connecting Forest Park and the Tryon Creek State Natural Area. The natural area is the only Oregon state park within a major metropolitan area and is only minutes from downtown Portland. Specific natural-areas acquisition objectives are being developed in each watershed, with first-priority parcels identified, as well as more long-term targets. Although the city has traditionally approached natural-areas acquisition in an opportunistic manner, it now has a more comprehensive, long-term strategy.

METRO: REGIONAL PARKS AND GREENSPACES CREATE CONNECTION

Metro, Portland's unique elected regional government, asked the public in 1992 what values were most important for future planning. Portland residents responded with several key goals: a sense of community; preservation of natural areas, forests, and farmland; quiet neighborhoods with easy access to shops, schools, jobs, and recreation; the "feel" of open space and scenic beauty; and transportation efficiency including nonmotorized choices. It is striking that all of these community-minded goals connect in one way or another to the creation and preservation of connected open space.

Metro serves 1.3 million people over 460 square miles in Clackamas, Multnomah, and Washington counties and the region's twenty-four cities. Like the GVRD in Vancouver, Metro provides basic services to the metropolitan area, including transportation, garbage disposal, recycling, and waste-reduction programs. It operates the Oregon zoo and other institutional facilities and provides land-use planning services. One primary mission is regional growth management. Unlike the GVRD, Metro is an elected body, serving as a formal layer of government.

Metro has become a standard for regionalism continent-wide. It was formed in 1979 when voters approved a transition from an appointed council of governments (Columbia Region Association of Governments) to an elected level of government, funded primarily through user fees rather than taxation. In 1992 the voters approved a home-rule charter giving land-use and transportation planning responsibility to Metro. Local governments implement local planning, such as zoning, permitting, and neighborhood design. Metro's job is to make sure local planning is coordinated in the region in order to protect air quality, reduce traffic congestion, and preserve farm and forest lands outside Portland's urban growth boundary.

The case for Metro's regional coordination is persuasive. "A traffic problem in Beaverton is a traffic problem in Portland; Westsiders light rail will improve eastern Clackamas County's air quality. More efficient land use in downtown Gresham lessens the pressure to develop farmland in Hillsboro. Roads don't stop at city boundaries and water quality problems find their way from stream to river. By providing regional coordination and setting regional standards, cities and counties can achieve better coordination with the neighbors—and this benefits all of the region."[35] Neighborhood connectivity is one such standard, whereby maximum block sizes, minimum levels of street connection, and pedestrian amenities are mandated for new development by Metro.

Oregon state law requires that each city and county have a long-range growth plan that sets urban growth boundaries, uses urban land wisely, and protects natural resources. Metro has the authority to set and move the Portland region's urban growth boundary, which was adopted in 1979 and last extended in 2002. It is also authorized to implement planning and growth-management measures on a regional basis. Metro's work is supported by its 2040 Growth Concept, adopted in 1995, which projects accommodating about 720,000 new residents and 350,000 additional jobs in the region.[36] Oregon law also mandates an extensive citizen-involvement process as part of its land-use planning regulations.

Metro's work on open-space planning for the metropolitan region followed astute leadership by a few key individuals in the early 1980s. Mike Houck, an urban naturalist then with Portland Audubon, proposed a regional wildlife refuge and natural-areas system for the city. He became convinced that important natural areas were not getting enough protection through the regulatory land-use system. With other citizens, particularly those involved with jumpstarting the 40-Mile Loop, he promoted the idea with Metro. Metro helped organize a coalition to collaborate on greenspace protection across the entire region of Portland, Oregon, and Vancouver, Washington. A 1989 Metro inventory revealed increasing interest in having park and recreation opportunities close to home and brought community members together around the goal of open-space protection. At about that time a researcher at Portland State University conducted a mapped inventory of natural features relevant to open-space lands for the entire 1,925-square-mile area. The inventory showed that, of the 372,682 acres in the three-county region, more than a quarter were still natural areas. At that time it was also estimated that the region was losing an average of 2,360 acres of open space annually.[37]

Subsequent federal funding, at half a million dollars per year, was secured by Senator Mark Hatfield and helped create a partnership between Metro and the U.S. Fish and Wildlife Service (FWS). This was one of only two partnerships of this kind involving FWS in urban environments and led to Portland's Metropolitan Greenspaces Program. At first, the program supported inventories and mapping, leading to development of a greenspace plan in 1992. Metro sought to protect and set aside open space, natural areas, habitat, and recreation areas in an effort to preserve the high quality of life as the Portland region's population escalated.

In 1992, a $200 million open-space bond measure designed to protect those resources was rejected, at least partly due to lack of specificity in the bond measure package, for it did not outline the specific regional parks and greenways that would be acquired. However, through extensive education and outreach to the Portland metropolitan community, the second try at a $135.6 million bond measure was successful in 1995, with 60 percent approval. In 1995 there was a broader base of support, for instance, with the home builders' association on board. The primary goal was to purchase targeted natural areas, trails, and greenways. The funding from this measure enables the purchase and protection of critical pieces of the region's open spaces. Fifty-seven natural areas and thirty-four trails / greenways in the master plan were distilled to fourteen regional acquisition target areas and six greenway corridors—specific, large-scale sites, geographically distributed across the region.

Portland's Metropolitan Greenspaces program has used organized citizen involvement as part of its process from the beginning. Public involvement and education were particularly critical in the ultimate approval of the bond measure. Natural resource groups like Audubon, Friends of Forest Park, and Oregon Trout were helpful in identifying objectives and priorities, thereby leading to the authority to buy land. Land acquisition groups like the Trust for Public Land, The Nature Conservancy, and River Network helped refine goals and obtain acreage.

Three branches addressed the technical, political, and community issues of the greenway initiative. A Greenspaces Technical Advisory Committee provided technical assistance, while a Policy Advisory Committee, composed of local decision makers, worked on political feasibility. Finally, Friends and Advocates of Urban Natural Areas (FAUNA), made up of affiliated groups, provided leadership for regional coordination of neighborhood groups and nonprofit organizations. The Portland Audubon Society, with Mike Houck, was particularly instrumental in bringing FAUNA together. The final master plan contained results derived from the coordination of all three groups.

The cities within the boundaries of Metro and all four counties have passed resolutions of support for the Metropolitan Greenspaces Master Plan since 1990. Metro, the planning coordinator and key implementer of the program, has the authority to buy land and to

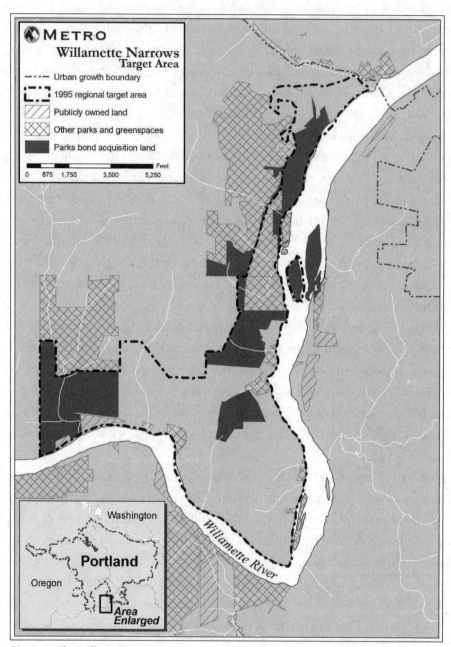

Fig. 6.15 The Willamette Narrows, part of the Willamette Greenway, is one of Metro's open space acquisition target areas. It includes numerous drainages, seeps, and wetlands in an area with limited development. These natural features, along with varied topography and habitats, makes the Narrows unique in the urban region. Metro has acquired 472 acres and seeks to buy 40 more. (Drawing courtesy of Metro.)

implement certain planning and growth-management measures on a regionwide basis. Simultaneously, Metro cooperates extensively with local jurisdictions. Metro's goals are to (1) coordinate the efforts of government and citizen groups to create a regional open-space system, (2) negotiate public access agreements, and (3) own and operate some of the acquired lands.

Subsequent to the passage of the 1995 bond measure, even more fine-tuning was needed for Metro to begin acquiring natural-area parcels. A refinement process was done for each of the twenty target areas to establish acquisition goals and objectives and specific geographic boundaries. Target areas were based on watershed, rather than political, boundaries. Management plans for all twenty target areas were adopted by the Metro Council, authorizing the purchase of certain properties that meet the goals, objectives, acquisition boundaries, and acreage targets. The emphasis is on protecting wildlife and stream corridors and on connectivity between hubs. Connections to schools and to federal and state lands were prioritized. The final acquisition priorities consisted of confidential maps showing ownership parcels.

Aiming to be competitive in the private market, Metro can buy land (or easements, water rights, or timber rights) in its "willing seller" program quite easily; if appraised values, environmental studies, and clean titles are documented, transactions can be completed on a cash basis. As an example, for one targeted area, nearly all of the land has been purchased after ten years of the program. One measure of the program's critical success is its ability to buy quickly, to bank land while it is still available (Figure 6.15). Surpassing the goal of 6,000 acres, 8,130 acres had been purchased for natural areas in 261 "willing seller" negotiations by 2005.[38] This includes over 70 miles of stream frontage and thousands of acres of wetlands, riparian areas, meadows, and forests. An outgrowth of FAUNA, the Urban Streams Council keeps public involvement alive through a watershed approach and a more biological focus beyond the urban growth boundary.

The greenspace program creates a typology of connected open spaces, including a regional web of parks linked by river and stream corridors and a system of trails. Plans call for a 950-mile network of regional trails, including water trails and greenways, 30 percent of which were complete by 2003. The linear open-spaces network is comprised of several parts: the six proposed regional trail corridors form the backbone of the system.[39] Second, water trails exist for canoes, kayaks, and other water craft. Third, greenways create corridors that "follow rivers and may or may not provide public access." They pro-

Fig. 6.16 Terwilliger Parkway and adjacent trail. Terwilliger Boulevard was first mentioned as one park-way route in John C. Olmsted's report to the Portland Park Board; it is now the only one completed for pub-lic use as envisioned. In 1959, Portland created a special design zone to protect the parkway's heavily wooded character. (Photo courtesy of Portland Parks and Recreation, Portland, Oregon.)

vide a swath of protected habitat along a stream with no public access, or allow environ-mentally compatible trails, viewpoints, or canoe launches.

Metro coordinates planning, funding, acquisition, design, development, construc-tion, operations, and management for regional trails.[40] Unlike local trails, regional trails are typically separated from roadways, are larger in scope, and straddle neighborhoods and towns. They specifically link parks, natural areas, and other trails, although some are destinations themselves. A number of them are now at least partially complete and open to the public—from Beaverton Powerline Trail, which, as its name implies, fol-lows an electric power line corridor, to Terwilliger Trail and Parkway, which partially runs along an historic boulevard, to the I-5 Bridge Trail Crossing connecting the

Portland trail system with Vancouver and Clark County trails across the Columbia River in Washington (Figure 6.16). A 2004 report on implementation of the 2040 plan showed that 133 miles of regional trails are now in place, in addition to 137 miles of water trails.[41]

In addition to the regional natural areas and greenways, Metro set out to fund a hundred local parks projects, spread across nearly each city, county, or park district, through a $25 million "local share" portion of the 1995 bond monies. The slogan for this portion of public funding is "People Places—Open Spaces," highlighting strong community-based goals. These acquisitions are funded by Metro grants and administered at the local level. By 2004, twenty local jurisdictions and park districts had bought open-space properties with these funds, totaling 445 acres. The city of Portland has received the largest share of monies in the local share program and collaborated consistently with Metro. The city was one of the only park providers that agreed to manage natural-areas lands purchased by Metro. However, with increasing financial cutbacks, the city may be more reluctant to take on management of more lands in the future.

Several challenges have emerged, even though the Metro greenspaces program is clearly a remarkable success story. Long-term maintenance is one hurdle for open-lands preservation. Metro has needed to accept management responsibility for most of the land acquired, although in many cases local municipalities are better suited to it. Also, developing public access and site amenities is often secondary to land banking, since holding these lands in public ownership is a critical priority. In addition, for the trails component, careful explanation of the benefits, limitations, and management of trails and greenways has been critical since these "lines on the map" are often contentious—the case in nearly every greenways program.

There have been some concerns about taking land off the tax rolls due to Metro purchases. This has been offset to some extent by increases in surrounding property values. Other tensions between Metro and local communities include designating land for development versus open space: Metro's designations and local community desires are not always aligned. Metro, holding most of the financial cards, is sometimes seen as a competitor rather than a collaborator that helps build capacity in the smaller jurisdictions.

Portland has extraordinary capacity for continued progress on open-space protection, due in large part to engaged and committed communities and leaders. Unlike many North American cities, it has lucid and convincing documentation of its open-space protection needs. Metro has identified 80,000 acres of regionally significant fish and wildlife habitat within its boundaries. Almost half of this acreage is high-quality streamside habitat. Coordinating its protection is both complicated and facilitated by regional government. At the city level, support fluctuates for further greenspace projects due to budgetary shortages. But there is widespread awareness of the acute need for parks, natural areas, and other open spaces. As Metro prepares to launch another greenspaces bond measure in 2006, it is seeking the advice of its veteran open-space leaders—Charles Jordan, Mike Houck, and others. It is likely that the community- and neighborhood-building collaboration for open-space planning will be tapped into and strengthened.

Community as a Driver of Connected Open Space

The term "community" has meanings both in physical space and in human experience.[42] "Sense of community" refers to the latter but has implications for the former. There are many social science theories about the connection between spatial pattern and sense of community, and about built work (such as new urbanist developments) that seeks to foster sense of community. However, the empirical evidence is too scanty to allow researchers to draw firm conclusions about the types of landscapes that foster sense of community.

Community is fundamental to human ecology. Social bonding and behavioral rootedness are evidenced in neighborhood attachment. Social bonding indicators include feeling part of the neighborhood and being able to identify neighbors, whereas behavioral rootedness refers to years of residency, home ownership, and prospects of remaining in the neighborhood.[43] City size and density do not significantly weaken a sense of local community sentiment. However, as Robert Putnam documented in *Bowling Alone*, a steady decline in sense of community has weakened social capital over the last few decades in America.[44] The causes are complex and far-reaching, from dependence on the automobile, to electronic communications, to suburban placelessness. Community open space—not always lack of it, but rather poor design, wrong location, or weakened ecological health—is one link in the complex phenomenon of diminished social capital.

Ray Oldenburg, in *The Great Good Place*, claims that community gathering places—third places—are critical for nourishing sense of community.[45] In his triad, first places are home and second places are work. He argues that the disappearance of third places in our culture—the corner store, neighborhood tavern, or café—has weakened our culture. For Barbara Scharff in Portland, a local park clearly provided the third place for her situation. It provided a setting for meeting her neighbors—a simple thing, but one that cannot be taken for granted in today's gated, internal-facing, car-dominated urban neighborhoods. Open spaces outside can help bring people together in non-threatening environments for a range of activities, benefits, and purposes. Research in Great Britain showed that the social meaning of public open space is a central concern, not only because well-designed open space enriches urban living, but because it gives opportunities for particular kinds of social interactions that cannot be found in other settings.[46] Allan Jacobs's book, *Great Streets*, depicts how streets contribute to social life: "In a very elemental way, streets allow people to be outside. Barring private gardens, which many urban people do not have or want, or immediate access to countryside or parks, streets are what constitute the outside for many urbanites; places to be when they are not indoors. And streets are places of social and commercial encounter and exchange. They are where you meet people—which is a basic reason to have cities in any case."[47]

Vancouver is a striking example for its use of the actual street as neighborhood-enhancing space, as exemplified in the city's definition: "Greenways are paths designed for pedestrians and cyclists that enhance the walking and riding experience and provide different ways to move through the city."[48] Greenways *are* streets in Vancouver. This definition has profound meanings for the way streets are built and existing ones improved. The frontier for street design may not be in building a better car-conveyance medium, but in creating roadways that foster community interaction and engaging residents in these designs.

However, as in many cities, contemporary greenway efforts get only partial credit, as historic planning laid previous frameworks for outstanding connected open space. Vancouver's impressive public waterfront, dating from 1911 when the city council decided to buy land on English Bay, complements the contemporary street/greenways as another linear layer in the public realm.

There is another main lesson from the Vancouver story and from experiments in Portland—the idea of supporting small neighborhood greenways as a second tier to city-wide efforts. While the larger city infrastructure enhances existing community, the neighborhood greenways are catalysts for community building. These environments are catalytic—open space creates community where the neighborhood creates open space. It is the difference between passively enjoying your neighborhood versus actively improving it. When neighbors propose, design, build, and maintain open-space land, physically building connections within their neighborhoods, community benefits are magnified exponentially. Volunteers can see the tangible effects of their contributions to the neigh-

borhood. The experience with these projects illustrates the importance of small experiments in the landscape and the importance of saying yes to residents' ideas.

This ideal is undeniably difficult and time-consuming, as shown in Portland's experiment. But using park-building as a vehicle to get people involved in neighborhoods also
makes use of skills that are not always present or prioritized in the typical municipal parks
department.

In Portland, Metro's Greenspaces initiative, though focused on large-scale planning
and land acquisition, reaches directly to community enhancement and even to the individual. An environmental education program involves about 10,000 people per year,
including 7,000 children. In addition, the Greenspaces program has awarded grants to over
160 community organizations to fund 300 habitat restoration and environmental education projects. In one year alone, 1,000 volunteers gave more than 12,000 hours to the
Metro Regional Parks and Greenspaces Department.

Metro's is the most important open-space vehicle in Portland and one of the most
impressive on the continent. Its work is admittedly at a scale that is not community centered. But the large visions that are created and facilitated by Metro bring spatial decisions
that filter back to the community and human scale. For example, Metro's open-space work
contributes to community enhancement by providing environmental education and by
improving open-space accessibility in areas of dense housing. Its grand vision of an urban
region that incorporates healthy open land gives communities access to nature. Separating
clusters of development and creating visible neighborhood edges fosters neighborhood
identity. Where cities have defined urban boundaries, as in Vancouver and Portland, the
civic realm is more defined, understandable, and functional—all factors that help cultivate sense of community.

7

Green Infrastructure—
Hardworking Systems:
Cleveland and
Minneapolis—St. Paul

In a world increasingly concerned with the problems of a
deteriorating environment, be they energy, pollution, van-
ishing plants, animals, natural or productive landscapes,
there remains a marked propensity to bypass the environment most people live in—the city itself…The underlying
disciplines that have shaped the city have little to do with
the natural sciences or ecological values. If urban design
can be described as that art and science dedicated to
enhancing the quality of the physical environment in cities,
to providing civilizing and enriching places for the people
who live in them, then the current basis for urban form
must be re-examined.

— *Michael Hough* [1]

225

The very foundations of urban form are, indeed, being reexamined. The connective tissue of city infrastructure is a main focus, where green infrastructure principles are being applied to roads, highways, water lines, canals, and sewer lines. Infrastructure is about work and function. It delivers people and basic necessities to the locations they need to be in order for a city to operate and its inhabitants to flourish.

But the forms these lines take on the landscape and in human perception matter greatly. Hardworking midwestern cities are interesting places to consider the myriad possibilities for green infrastructure to combine utilitarian functions with green ambitions. Places like Kansas City, Cincinnati, Pittsburgh, Toledo, and Indianapolis are known as no-nonsense industrial workhorses of the American heartland. They are also some of the places where the green infrastructure idea is gaining the most momentum, and where much stands to be gained by integrating green concepts. Cleveland and the Twin Cities of Minneapolis and St. Paul are not places where the concepts of green infrastructure have been extensively implemented, but rather locations where the possibilities are ripe and the pieces ready for assembly. Both Cleveland and Minneapolis pride themselves on their "emerald necklaces," a term first used to describe Boston's linked park system along the Charles River, designed by Frederick Law Olmsted.

Cleveland, Ohio, is a Rust Belt city in the middle of an urban renaissance. The city that spawned such industrial giants as Standard Oil, Sherwin-Williams, Du Pont, and U.S. Steel was recently rated one of "ten great places to take a hike in the big city."[2] Its emerald necklace of regional parks is one of the nation's outstanding systems. The many bridges spanning the Cuyahoga River are apt symbols for connection, a major theme of contemporary open-space work in the region. A number of agencies and organizations have proposed a more regional approach to the area's open-space resources and have promoted the green infrastructure idea. An impressive set of projects is already in place, fostered by an interesting mix of city, county, nonprofit, state, and federal open-space planning and management agencies and organizations.

The Twin Cities already have a connected open-space network made up of a core of parks and parkways designed in the early twentieth century. The Urban Land Institute recently ranked Minneapolis as one of the best park systems in the United States, and the region is often touted for the quality and quantity of its parks. The metropolitan region is one of the fastest growing in the country, despite its notoriously harsh winters, and its population is wealthier than Cleveland's. The Twin Cities' poverty rate is one of the lowest of America's large cities. The cities are known for pedestrian connectivity—indoors and out. As they do in Cleveland, numerous massive bridges form strong elements of the Twin Cities' urban structure. Beginning in 1962, Minneapolis and St. Paul created an extensive enclosed pedestrian skyway system, connecting buildings downtown through sixty-two second-story bridges. These are the largest such systems in the United States and one of the largest in the world. However, Twin Cities residents are remarkably active outdoors as well. The Grand Rounds, the Twin Cities' version of an emerald necklace, is the heart of the connected open-space network.

Cleveland and Minneapolis–St. Paul: Historic and Geographic Context

Cleveland and Minneapolis, though very different in character, history, and economy, share deep historic roots in progressive open-space planning. Both cities benefit today from the foresight of visionary planners of the early twentieth century who knew that protected open space reaching into rural parts of the region would be important for the future. William A. Stinchcomb is known as the father of the Cleveland Metropolitan Park Board. He laid the conceptual groundwork for what became the Cleveland Metroparks in Cuyahoga County in 1917, one of the first American metropolitan park districts. In the Twin Cities, connectivity, beyond the need for greenspace, is a part of the city planning legacy. The Grand Rounds, designed by Horace W. S. Cleveland, is a stunning example of early-twentieth-century urban planning. There has been strong grassroots support for parks and open spaces since the mid-nineteenth century in the Twin Cities.

Cleveland: Remake by the Lake

Cleveland is one of the nation's most striking examples of conversion from rust to green—from harsh industrial inheritance to livable urban fabric. The city remains the headquarters for many manufacturing and service industries, with the Cuyahoga River and Lake Erie as the primary natural features on which the region's economy was historically based. The river, dividing the city, was once the western frontier for the United States and has since served as an industrial workhorse for the nation. Gigantic lake carriers still ply the river, and massive steel mills line the shores near downtown.

Located at the transition zone between the Allegheny Plateau and the Great Plains, Cleveland is home to a population closing in on half a million. A wider ring including all of Cuyahoga County has a population of 1,380,800 and the still wider six-county metropolitan area accommodates about two and a quarter million (including Ashtabula, Cuyahoga, Geauga, Lake, Lorain, and Medina counties) (Figure 7.1).

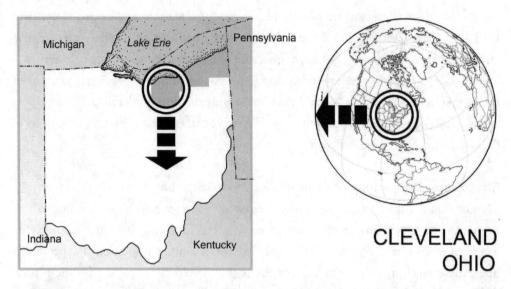

CLEVELAND
OHIO

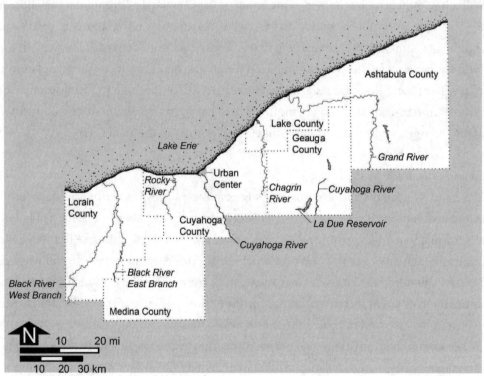

Fig. 7.1 The six-county Cleveland region.

Three main river valleys—Cuyahoga, Rocky, and Chagrin—and the Lake Erie shoreline create the physical framework of the Greater Cleveland region. But Cleveland's urban history is centered on a far smaller area at the mouth of the Cuyahoga River as it meets the lake (Figure 7.2). When Cleveland was first platted, the river's east and west sides were joined by ferries; now they are linked by high, fixed-span bridges and lower opening bridges that allow river traffic to flow up the Cuyahoga River. The dominant transportation corridors are now four interstate freeways crossing the valley.

Fig. 7.2 Downtown Cleveland on Lake Erie, with the Cuyahoga River winding through oxbows in the left half of the image. (Photo by Richard M. Wyner.)

The city's landscape features a wide river valley with steep slopes to the uplands. The bluffs that line the lake's southern shore have traditionally created an obstacle to integrating the lakeshore and the city, although the confluence of the Cuyahoga River and the lake is the natural point of connection. The Cuyahoga Valley is the backbone of the Cleveland region—75 square miles with unique natural, social, and economic assets. The Lake Erie shore has long served as a commercial zone and has been underappreciated in the Cleveland region's historic development.

The gray infrastructure of Cleveland is some of the most awe-inspiring in America. The view from the upland area in the downtown core of Cleveland is spectacular, with twenty bridges crossing the Cuyahoga River. This modern view is in striking contrast to the era when Cleveland was called "the mistake by the lake," with problems ranging from financial instability to race riots to pollution. The city became the butt of national jokes when Lake Erie was declared nearly dead and the Cuyahoga River was lit on fire. Cleveland is now hailed as an important American urban comeback story. The city, still industrial by nature, is capitalizing on the ability of industrial lands to contribute to community-based urban infrastructure. The public and private sectors have joined to reinvigorate down-town, the area known as The Flats along the river near downtown, and other urban dis-tricts. More than in many American cities, neighborhoods are organized and vibrant, with many historic ethnic neighborhoods that are intact and strong.

Cleveland's growth flourished after the construction of the Ohio & Erie Canal and, later, the railroads. The canal was constructed between 1825 and 1827 and provided a crit-ical transportation route for goods like wheat, flour, corn, and coal from Lake Erie to the interior of Ohio. This section was one link in an impressive continuous route that ran from the Atlantic seaboard to the Gulf of Mexico. The canal influenced agricultural and indus-trial progress across the region and beyond it. During the canal era, Cleveland grew from a little settlement to a thriving city. The economic effects of the canal were vital for the city, as it maintained the only weigh lock on the canal and controlled direct access to Lake Erie. Cleveland's first railroad, the Cleveland, Columbus and Cincinnati, began operating in 1851, and by the 1870s rendered the canal obsolete. The canal's remnants have, by and large, been obliterated within the city. (Other parts outside the city are still intact.) Even so, industrial development along former canal banks continued to grow in importance.[3]

The heart of Cleveland's urban open space is the four-quadrant area known as Public Square in downtown, set aside over two hundred years ago by Moses Cleaveland, who arrived in the area in 1796.[4] There was phenomenal population growth through the mid-nineteenth century—from only about a thousand inhabitants in 1830 to over 92,000 forty years later. During that time, as in many American cities, manufacturing became a central force of Cleveland's economy, spurring the demand for places to recreate and escape the city.

Cleveland was incorporated in 1836, and its first parks commission was established in 1871. Two years later the city issued a parks bond to purchase a hillside overlooking Lake Erie. However, the greatest era for parks creation in Cleveland was the 1890s, a time when critics complained that Cleveland lagged far behind other cities in its provision of park-land. In 1893 the state legislature enabled the creation of a more powerful parks commis-sion in Cleveland. Planned by Boston landscape architect E. W. Bowditch, seven large city parks were created on the outskirts of the city, some of them connected by parkways. This was the birth of Cleveland's emerald necklace.

By 1910 the city housed over a half million residents, and William A. Stinchcomb, the first director of the Cleveland Metropolitan Park Board, argued for the creation and maintenance of parks outside the city limits. In 1905 he served as a young engineer for the city and began developing his vision of the ring of parks around Cleveland's outskirts. He helped craft 1911 legislation that authorized county park boards in Ohio. Cleveland Metroparks was established in Cuyahoga County in 1917 (Figure 7.3). The Park Districts are independent government units with taxing ability. For fifty years Stinchcomb oversaw the development of one of America's first metropolitan park districts. With remarkable foresight, he wrote:

> I want to suggest the advisability of ultimately establishing an outer system of parks and boulevards . . . Through the valleys of Rocky River on the west, and Chagrin River on the east, lie some of the finest stretches of natural park lands to be found in the northern part of Ohio. While all this is now entirely outside of the city, it will be but a short time before they will be inside or very near the limits of a "Greater Cleveland" and it seems to me that such fine stretches of natural parkway should be secured for the benefit of the entire public before private enterprise or commercial industry places them beyond reach.

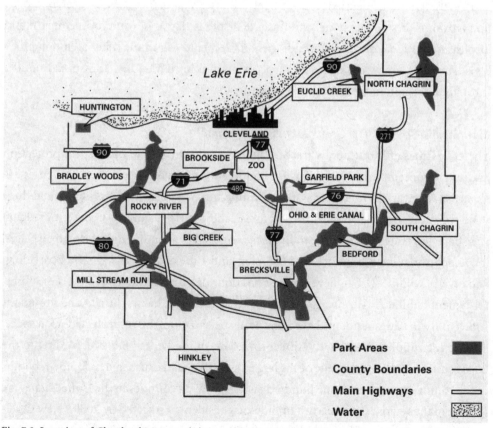

Fig. 7.3 Location of Cleveland Metroparks' ring of fourteen reservations (and zoo) in Cuyahoga County.

Stinchcomb, aided by a visit from Frederick Law Olmsted Jr. in 1915, created a master plan called *Cuyahoga County Park and Boulevard System* in 1916. It included a continuous parkway encircling the county and connecting to existing municipal parks. However, Olmsted Jr. and Stinchcomb apparently felt that the Cuyahoga River valley was already too industrialized for parkway use. Stinchcomb eventually did turn attention to the Cuyahoga, years after Olmsted's visit. He recommended that the Works Progress Administration (WPA) create a parkway from Public Square through the Cuyahoga River Valley to Akron; however, that vision didn't materialize until the twenty-first century and is now taking a very different shape.

During the Depression of the 1930s, the WPA and Civilian Conservation Corps (CCC) built many recreational facilities in the undeveloped Cleveland Metroparks properties. According to Diana Tittle, "by the 1930s, when thousands of Clevelanders took to the parks each night with their bedding, sleeping under the stars to escape the summer heat, the public's sense of ownership of the municipal parks clearly had been established."[5] By the 1960s and 1970s, the public decried signs of neglect in Cleveland area parks—litter, boarded-up restrooms and concessions, and untended sports fields. Beyond local concern and displeasure, national media featured stories on Cleveland's alarming water pollution problems. However, a new era of parks advocacy started in that decade and spread rapidly through the region in the late twentieth century.

Minneapolis–St. Paul: The Grand Rounds and Beyond

The Twin Cities of Minneapolis and St. Paul have a rich history of open-space protection and active contemporary programs for connecting the urban landscape. The cities are located at the heart of three river systems (Minnesota, St. Croix, and Mississippi) and three major biomes—boreal forest, hardwood forest, and prairie (Figure 7.4). The entire region was shaped by water and ice over millions of years. Lakes are numerous, formed by glacial movements that have left a rich and complex landscape of wetlands, riparian corridors, and diverse wildlife. Urban development has dominated an estimated 96 percent of pre-settlement habitat (Figure 7.5). Despite (or because of) a harsh climate and abundant snowfall, Twin Cities residents have historically been supportive of protected open space.

The metropolitan region, the fifteenth-largest in the United States according to the 2000 census, is experiencing one of the largest suburban and exurban development booms in the country. Seven of the one hundred fastest-growing counties in the United States are located in the region, with nearly a million new residents projected by 2030.[6] New development is rarely compact: population density in the metropolitan region decreased 17 per-

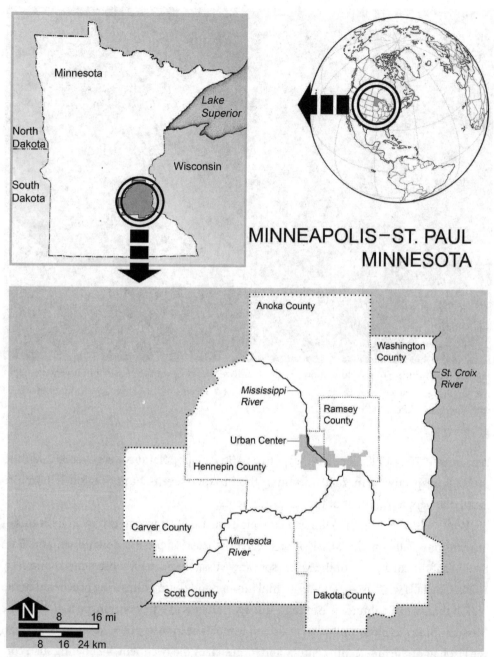

MINNEAPOLIS−ST. PAUL
MINNESOTA

Fig. 7.4 The seven-county Minneapolis–St. Paul metropolitan region. The central urban areas are shown in gray.

Fig. 7.5 The Minneapolis skyline, showing the West River Parkway on the Mississippi River, Hennepin Avenue Bridge, Third Avenue Bridge and Nicollet Island. (© Regents of the University of Minnesota. Used with the permission of Metropolitan Design Center.)

cent from 1970 to 1990.[7] The Minneapolis and St. Paul populations were over 382,000 and 287,000, respectively, in 2000, although the broader seven-county region is home to 2,642,000 people, one-half of the state's residents.

White settlements in the Minneapolis region are usually traced to two main locations—St. Anthony Falls on the Mississippi River northeast of today's downtown, and Fort Snelling at the confluence of the Minnesota and Mississippi rivers, constructed in the early 1820s. The falls were used as power to mill lumber and flour. Lumbering prospered in the region thanks to an abundance of high-quality timber and efficient transportation on the Mississippi River. Flour milling was also an important industry in Minneapolis through the last half of the nineteenth century and for much of the twentieth, incubating such corporate giants as General Mills, Cargill, and Pillsbury. Eventually, lumber mills and flour mills lined the river on both sides around and upstream of St. Anthony Falls.

By the mid-nineteenth century, the Rock Island Railroad was transporting travelers to the area by rail and steamboat, and settlers began flocking to the region's fertile farmland, abundant water, and thriving cities. Minneapolis now claims more bridges across the Mississippi than any other river community; the first permanent crossing of the river was in Minneapolis. In the 1920s and 1930s a series of reinforced concrete arch spans were built across the Mississippi River. Some are now listed on the National Register of Historic Places, and they continue to carry daily traffic.

The Minnesota Department of Natural Resources has found that within the 1.9-million-acre region, at least 133,000 acres (7 percent) are currently protected for recreational or habitat values. One protected area, the Minnesota Valley National Wildlife Refuge, is the largest urban national wildlife refuge in the country, at 14,000 acres.

The Twin Cities' Grand Rounds parkways system, designated a National Scenic Byway, encircles Minneapolis with 53 miles of parks, parkways, bike paths, and pedestrian paths. Twenty-two lakes fall within the city limits, as well as Minnehaha, Shingle, and Bassett creeks and the Mississippi River (Figure 7.6). Within the city of Minneapolis parks, there are about 39 miles of designated walking paths and about 38 miles of designated biking paths. The Grand Rounds originally circled Minneapolis; it now extends into St. Paul, the capital of Minnesota, whose downtown district is about 10 miles from the center of Minneapolis.

In 1883, the Minneapolis Board of Parks Commissioners was created by the Minnesota legislature, motivated by the proposals of Charles M. Loring, a Minneapolis miller and publicist. That year, landscape architect Horace W. S. Cleveland, a protégé of Frederick Law Olmsted, proposed to the board that a regional parkway and open-space system be created, following streams, wetlands, and lakes. He stated his vision in a 1899 lecture:

> I would have the city itself such a work of art as may be the fitting abode of a race of men and women whose lives are devoted to a nobler end than money-getting and whose efforts shall be inspired and sustained by the grandeur and beauty of the scenes in which their lives are passed. Nature offers us such advantages as no other city could rival, and such as if properly developed would exhibit the highest attainment of art . . .[8]

Like Charles Whitnall in Milwaukee, William Stinchcomb in Cleveland, and Robert Speer in Denver around the same time, Cleveland advocated that land be purchased in rural areas out from the city in advance of urban expansion. The president of the Minneapolis Board of Parks Commissioners, Charles M. Loring, is credited with implementing Cleveland's vision. The Grand Rounds can be considered the first truly complete American Emerald Necklace. According to the Minnesota Chapter of the American Society of Landscape Architects, the implementation of the Grand Rounds was so successful

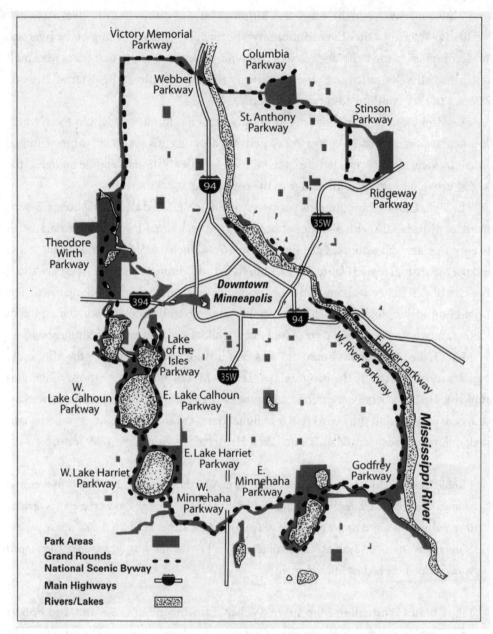

Fig. 7.6 The Grand Rounds Scenic Byway, showing numerous historic parkways.

because of "early planning and design followed by rapid and decisive implementation."[9] Cleveland was apparently aware that the land would need to be acquired quickly and construction expedited. By 1906 Theodore Wirth became the superintendent of parks, held that position for thirty years, and implemented many of the features of the Grand Rounds in place today. He championed the construction of active recreation facilities in the parks, particularly for water and ice sports.[10]

For fifteen years beginning in the early 1970s, Minneapolis landscape architect Roger Martin and his partners redesigned nearly the entire Minneapolis parkway system, implementing proposals that landscape architect Garret Eckbo had made in the 1960s. The parkways, which had been two-way commuter routes, were redesigned as narrower one-way routes with separated bike and pedestrian paths.[11] The redesign featured design elements that connect the parkway system aesthetically, including special lighting, benches, kiosks, and signage.

Sketches: Contours for Green Infrastructure Blueprints

Planning for open-space connections in Cleveland and the Twin Cities has taken a turn toward green infrastructure. Both city regions have achieved dramatic open-space systems, working at various scales and in diverse landscape contexts. In addition to their historic open-space legacies, they share the distinction of federal preservation programs along their rivers—a national park and heritage corridor along the Cuyahoga River and numerous federal protection strategies for the Mississippi, Minnesota, and St. Croix rivers. Collaboration is on the rise in both metro areas, as is broad regional thinking about sustainability.

Cleveland: Building on the Heritage Corridor's Solid Spine

Open space goes hand-in-hand with heritage in the Cleveland region, based on its Metroparks system, the nearby Cuyahoga Valley National Park, the Ohio & Erie Canal Heritage Corridor, the Lake Erie shoreline, and the dramatic industrial landscapes of the region. A vision for green infrastructure that integrates these historic landmarks and brings new functions to these important places is just taking root at a regional scale.

OHIO & ERIE CANAL HERITAGE CORRIDOR

The congressionally designated Ohio & Erie Canal Heritage Corridor has been a remarkable model of regional cooperation in the Cleveland region, spanning four counties— Cuyahoga, Stark, Tuskawaras, and Summit—and twenty-three communities along 110 miles of the Cuyahoga River valley. It is an exceptional example of the conversion from gray to green infrastructure, considered the most important regional-planning initiative in Cleveland for many decades. Ralph Regula, Ohio's senior congressman, is credited with securing legislation for the heritage corridor designation in November 1996. National Heritage Areas (including corridors) are a new type of national park, commemorating working, historic landscapes. They are meant to stimulate restoration, economic development, and renewal. Twenty-seven have been designated across the United States, most east of the Mississippi River.

The Heritage Corridor is often referred to as the spine of open space for the entire area, creating a physical setting for communities to consider quality of life, environmental restoration, historic preservation, and economic development. The corridor is created on public and private lands of all types—industrial areas, woodlands, commercial streets, and rural roads (Figure 7.7). Two large nonprofit groups were early and steady advocates for the Heritage Corridor designation—Ohio Canal Corridor in Cuyahoga County and the Ohio & Erie Canal Corridor Coalition at the southern end of the corridor.

One section of the Heritage Corridor has federal protection. The Cuyahoga Valley National Recreation Area was created in 1974, encompassing 33,000 acres. In 2000, it became Cuyahoga Valley National Park. When the Recreation Area was being planned, the towpath was discovered as an important amenity linking the entire region. The towpath was constructed 175 years ago as a part of the Ohio & Erie Canal, as a dirt path for leading the animals that pulled canal boats.

In 1993, the National Park Service converted 22 miles of the path to a multiuse Towpath Trail that will eventually traverse over 100 miles from downtown Cleveland into central Ohio (Figure 7.8). It has become the defining feature of the Heritage Corridor, a spine from which regional trail linkages branch off. The Towpath Trail is owned and managed by different organizations and agencies in separate sections. Seventy miles are now complete, mostly from the National Park southward; the remaining 30 miles are in various stages of planning and construction.

The Ohio & Erie Canal Association is the federally mandated management entity for the Heritage Corridor. The association oversees federal matching grant funds to promote local projects along the corridor. It drew up a management plan in 2000, covering the entire 110-mile corridor extending from Zoar, Ohio, north to Cleveland.[12] The focus is on reinvestment in historic settings, conserving the natural environment, supporting recreation, and attracting new development. The association estimates that $150 million will be needed in new funding to implement the plan.

The geographic scope of the corridor is complex, with a narrow ribbon created by the Towpath Trail and a broader boundary that includes a 500-square-mile planning zone. Areas within this "influence" zone are eligible to receive financial or technical assistance through federal funds established for the Heritage Corridor. The boundaries are intentionally drawn broadly to include the canal itself (and canal setting where the canal itself no longer exists), Towpath Trail, urban settings with close associations to the canal, rural and natural settings along the canal and along a Cuyahoga Valley Scenic Railroad Corridor, and scenic byways.

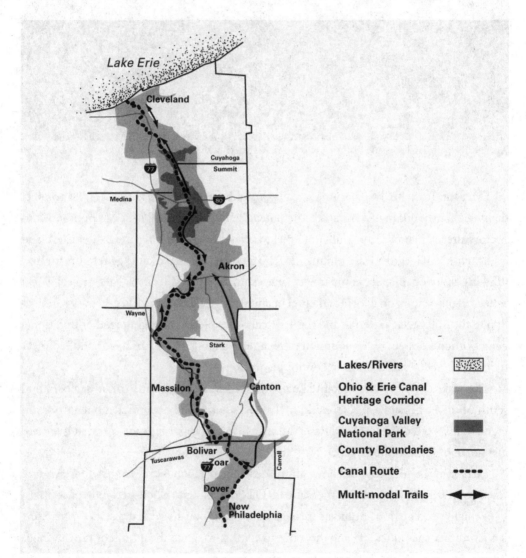

Fig. 7.7 Trail and canal routes through the Ohio & Erie Canal Heritage Corridor and Cuyahoga Valley National Park.

Fig. 7.8 Towpath Trail crossing historic Ohio & Erie Canal. (Photo by the author.)

Once the Towpath Trail became a reality, neighborhood groups scrambled to connect their neighborhoods to it. As Diana Tittle stated, "with thirty neighborhood spurs and connectors already planned, the trail's potential to spark the 're-greening' of Greater Cleveland is immense."[13] The greenways linking into the towpath are remarkable generators for new thinking about open-space connectivity. One example is the Mill Creek Falls project where a new neighborhood on a former mental hospital site includes a critical greenway connection to the Mill Creek Waterfall and the Towpath. This project brought together traditional neighborhood design, redevelopment of abandoned land, and riparian corridor connectivity into a successful economic development project.[14]

The task now is to continue the Towpath Trail in a continuous corridor north and south of the National Park. Cleveland Metroparks has already completed one important segment in its Ohio & Erie Canal Reservation, a former industrial landscape that is located just north of the Cuyahoga Valley National Park (see sidebar 7.1).

Farther north, the proposed Towpath route winds through 6 miles of urban Cleveland, where John D. Rockefeller started the Standard Oil Company and where steel mills once blazed in the night sky. The river meanders through oxbows for over twice that distance. Therefore, it is a complex and difficult feat to drive the Towpath through to the mouth of the Cuyahoga River at Lake Erie. About half of the river bottom is covered in heavy industry, but patches of forest still remain. An architecture critic, writing in the *Cleveland Plain Dealer,* described this segment well: "Today, the northern section of the valley is the forgotten geographic giant in our midst, a wide, flat-bottomed channel left behind by glaciers."[15] Revitalization of the river valley has potential to connect poor and minority neighborhoods and provide much-needed parkland, while celebrating the city's long industrial heritage. This would not be the first place where industrial landscapes have become popular tourist magnets.

In 2002 the Cuyahoga County Planning Commission published its *Towpath Trail Extension: Alignment and Design Study,* which solidified the 5-mile route and estimated the construction cost at $24–$48 million. A subsequent agreement helped solidify agency roles. Instead of Cleveland Metroparks in the foreground, the Cuyahoga County Engineer took the lead. The City of Cleveland will own most of the right-of-way, with the Cuyahoga County Engineering Department building the trail, and Cleveland Metroparks ultimately managing it. Where engineering departments are integrated and involved in projects like this, green infrastructure ideas that link the natural environment with utility services have a far better chance of being adopted.

The trail will soon run through Cleveland's industrial Flats area, the final one and a half miles of the river's journey, where steel mills and other heavy industrial use block easy access to the terminus at Lake Erie. The Flats has changed dramatically over the past twenty-five years. Now a nucleus of bars and nightclubs is mingled with the gritty remaining industrial facilities (Figure 7.9). Historically, local bars and restaurants served

Fig. 7.9 The west bank of the Cuyahoga river valley in the Flats area of Cleveland. The boardwalk separates night clubs and restaurants from the river. Across the river on the east bank, many buildings are empty and boarded up awaiting the city's transformation of the Flats region, including the extension of the Towpath Trail. (Photo by Robert Butler.)

7.1 Ohio & Erie Canal Reservation

The Ohio & Erie Canal Reservation is a textbook case of a successful public–private partnership. Cleveland Metroparks created the park, now the most urban of the fourteen-park system. The reservation opened in 1999 on 325 acres of bottomland on the Cuyahoga River, formerly owned primarily by industries, such as American Steel & Wire (now Birmingham Steel), who held lots along the river awaiting industrial use that did not materialize. That corporation's CEO, Tom Tyrrell, an avid runner familiar with heritage areas from living near one in Illinois, eventually donated land for the reservation. Other land was assembled with easements and leases. Eventually a number of public and private entities contributed land or easements, including American Steel & Wire Aluminum Company of America (ALCOA), BP America, Cleveland Electric Illuminating Company, the regional sewer district, and the Ohio Department of Natural Resources. Although Metroparks was at first hesitant, it accepted the property and created a centerpiece of the Metroparks system in the city. State and federal funding contributed to the $10 million project, including almost $2 million to construct the 4.3-mile segment of the Towpath Trail.

Some extraordinary collaborative groundwork was done throughout the 1990s to culminate in the successful realization of the Ohio & Erie Canal Reservation. The Towpath Trail project, initially driven by the Cuyahoga Valley National Park, was promoted by the advocacy group Ohio Canal Corridor, which saw the potentials for extending the trail all the way to Lake Erie. Even before the Ohio & Erie Canal Heritage Corridor was in place, Cuyahoga County completed a plan showing a pedestrian corridor through the river bottom to Lake Erie. The significance and opportunities for the corridor were mapped. At that time, a handful of people became advocates for the idea and convinced Cleveland Metroparks to become involved. Cleveland Metroparks managed the implementation of the 4.3-mile segment of trail to the edge of Cleveland's urban area on the north and the National Park to the south.

The Ohio & Erie Canal Reservation represents a success that *is* infrastructure in a green setting, not just plans to support it. The park's master plan was developed to tell the stories of "people at work, nature at work, and systems at work." The integration of these functions is visible. Trains pass overhead on a century-old, 130-foot-high trestle. Energy substations, petroleum tank storage facilities, and wastewater treatment plants are visible neighbors. A large green sewer pipe—the Southwest Interceptor—cuts across the valley bottom. Several streets pass through the reservation. Add to that the Cuyahoga River itself and several of the northernmost miles of the canal that still hold water, and you have nearly every imaginable infrastructure type. These "functional" factors contribute to making one of the most interesting and engaging new parks in the United States (Figure 7.10). People get married in the park's green verges. Its visitor center, designed to reflect the steel industry's pragmatic architecture, helps people understand the industrial and service systems at work, and highly creative interpretive facilities throughout the park do an outstanding job of linking the natural environment and the human history of the entire river valley. In its first year, the park attracted 300,000 visitors.

The reservation gives Metroparks a foothold in the city; since it acquires only land adjacent to its other holdings, Metroparks now has the possibility for other urban land purchases. A local Cleveland firm, Schmidt Copland Parker Stevens, developed a collaborative team for site planning, facility design, landscape architecture, and interpretation. The firm provided a continual thread of local context, as the larger team brought national expertise in public participation, industrial interpretation, environmental analysis, and ecological restoration.

Fig. 7.10 Ohio & Erie Canal Reservation, where passive recreation and interpretation interweave with industrial facilities in the background. (Photo by the author.)

the workers in the area, but the area has lost much of its former character. Now, with residential opportunities arising with the redevelopment of the Flats, and the Towpath Trail pushing northward and catering to families, Clevelanders are starting to rethink the commercial uses of this area.

This mix of the Heritage Corridor's commercial, recreational, and residential land uses is being considered south of the National Park as well. The Ohio & Erie Canal Coalition was established in 1989 as a private nonprofit to work on the development of the Ohio & Erie Canal Heritage Corridor. It now works in the region south of the National Park on organizational development and project management with ninety organizations—from other nonprofits to park districts. It focuses simultaneously on resource conservation and economic development. One success story in this southern part of the corridor is the city of Akron, where the canal is now a centerpiece of downtown revitalization, stimulating over $100 million in new development through the 1990s.[16]

COUNTY METROPARK DISTRICTS AND COUNTY PLANNING

Each of the eight counties in the Greater Cleveland region has a metropark district that oversees acquisition and management of county parkland.[17] Summit and Stark counties have been particularly progressive in thinking about greenway corridors. In Stark County, the Metroparks District initiated township-by-township meetings and identified trail opportunities. Enthusiasm then grew, particularly motivated by possibilities to connect to the Towpath Trail. As in Stark County, Summit County communities wanted to be connected to the Towpath, which generated enthusiasm and buy-in.

Cleveland Metroparks, the oldest and wealthiest Metropark District, serves Cuyahoga County. It is a separate government entity with taxing authority, governed by three commissioners who are appointed by a judge. In place since 1917 in Cuyahoga County (with small amounts of land in three other counties), Metroparks oversees Cleveland's Emerald Necklace, hosting over 50 million visitors per year. Its land area is divided across fifteen parks and a zoo, totaling about 20,000 acres mostly in passive recreation use. Cleveland Metroparks has won numerous prestigious national awards for park-system excellence.

Cleveland Metroparks has not placed a high priority on connectivity until recently. It has been active in curbing park overuse but has not had an aggressive land acquisition policy. The agency has consistently purchased land, as it becomes available, but only adjacent to its existing properties. Its newest park, the Ohio & Erie Canal Reservation, is a real departure in that regard, as it creates a critical linkage along the Ohio & Erie Canal Heritage Corridor.

There has been some effort toward coordination among the region's park districts. Early in the 2000s, the directors and staff of the districts met to discuss how to coordinate at the regional scale, and created the Northeast Ohio Regional Parks Consortium. This initiative, funded by the Cleveland Foundation and the George Gund Foundation, resulted in a mapped product depicting thousands of acres of land that might be conserved and over 1,000 miles of trails that could be feasible. Although the group accomplished some coordinated planning, it fell apart before achieving many tangible results.

The Cuyahoga County Planning Commission has been an important actor in connected open-space planning. It conducted an inventory of open space in the mid-1990s and found 32,200 acres of private and publicly owned open space. The commission created its Greenprint Plan in 2002, under the leadership of County Planning Director Paul Alsinas. This study is one of many that connect to green infrastructure goals. The plan advocates linking and improving the county's greenspaces with 20,000 additional acres of open space (6.6 percent of the county) linked by 330 additional miles of trails (115 miles existed in 2005). It recommends a network of natural corridors, based on natural geography, that link neighborhoods to each other and to the environment (Figure 7.11). A main focus is the three river valleys and the Lake Erie shoreline. The system builds on the existing park system and fills in those areas bypassed by earlier park development efforts.

Other recommendations are grandiose and visionary: 20 major scenic overlooks, 25 tributary watershed plans, 200 additional acres of wetlands, 5 bird sanctuaries, over 400 miles of greened roads and rights-of-way, and twice the number of community gardens.[18] A trails system is based on a series of three loops spaced approximately 5 miles apart across the county. In addition to finishing the Towpath Trail and connecting it to downtown, emphasis is placed on finishing the Emerald Necklace loop with a connection along the Chagrin River. Two other "chokers" would lie within it. An Inner Ring Loop would connect watersheds through some of Cleveland's older suburbs, where connections could include road improvements and easements along utility and institutional properties. The smallest, City Loop, would connect the city's oldest parks.

The Greenprint process was extensive and thorough, stretching over a year. Planners presented the vision to the community and found support there. Unlike the case of the Towpath Trail, in the Greenprint process there was no feasible way to delegate the completion of the vision. A structure is not yet in place to achieve the big green infrastructure goals that have been set out, even though the county embraced the agendas of the relevant organizations. County implementation is hindered by Ohio's strong local land-use control; counties can

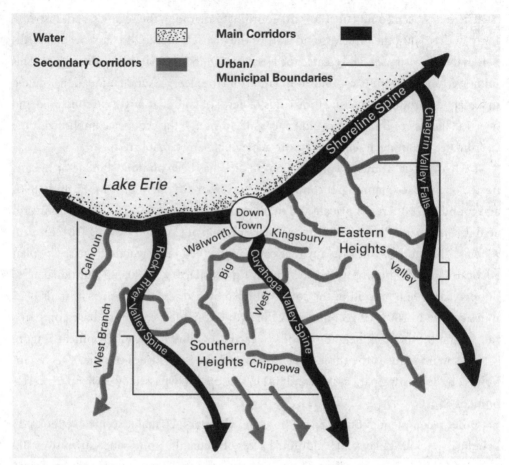

Fig. 7.11 Cuyahoga County Greenprint concept map, depicting primary and secondary greenway corridors in the Cleveland area.

advise and collaborate but cannot require land-use protection or change. Therefore, the county cannot take the type of leadership role that Metroparks or the city can.

CITY OF CLEVELAND

The City of Cleveland manages 1,400 acres of parks, most in active recreation use. Former Mayor Jane Campbell launched "Connecting Cleveland: The Lakefront Plan" in April 2002. The goal is to develop a community consensus for the future of Cleveland's lakefront, an 8-mile stretch along Lake Erie. The new plan depicts over 800 acres of new parks and trails, 175 acres of reclaimed road rights-of-way, and the elimination of 14 miles of ramps and roads. The overall project developed over the course of three main phases. The 2002 phase focused on visioning for connecting neighborhoods to the waterfront. A second phase in

2003 examined opportunities and assessed constraints to create a broad framework. That framework was approved by the City Planning Commission, leading to more detailed development plans for specific areas in Phase 3, when, in September 2005, the mayor unveiled the final Waterfront District Plan, depicting numerous projects that have already been completed as well as planning for an additional $395 million in lakefront projects that are currently under way.

Beyond the waterfront, the Connecting Cleveland 2020 Citywide Plan is the comprehensive plan for the future of Cleveland's neighborhoods. Its theme is connections. It updates the Civic Vision 2000 Citywide Plan, which was adopted in 1991. The Civic Vision 2000 plan was the blueprint for much of the civic and neighborhood development that took place in the 1990s. The 2020 plan intends to take the next step, particularly in connecting the dots between the individual projects. It proposes to connect each neighborhood to the region's assets and to connect residents to their neighbors.

PARKWORKS AND ECOCITY CLEVELAND:
VITAL NONPROFITS FOR CONNECTIVITY

The Trust for Public Land, which has been heavily involved in open-lands issues in the Cleveland region, analyzed Cleveland's open space and concluded that the city, like Portland, lacks sufficient greenspace to meet current and projected needs. Segments of the population are underserved, particularly neighborhoods close to the Cuyahoga River valley, and much of the open space that does exist is in poor condition. Two local nonprofit organizations have been particularly effective partners for open space and connectivity in the Cleveland area—ParkWorks on the smaller, site scale and EcoCity Cleveland at the regional scale.

ParkWorks (named Clean-Land Ohio until 1998) is a local NGO dedicated to improving and conserving the environment of Greater Cleveland and educating and motivating people to become environmentally responsible. It works on reforestation and beautification projects, including school yards and small urban gardens in the city. Clean-Land Ohio started as an effort to clean up the city's litter-strewn passenger rail corridors in the late 1970s and early 1980s. It works with the City of Cleveland and other partners to raise money for capital improvements in parks and to improve recreational programs. The city of Cleveland has thousands of vacant lots; ParkWorks contracts with the City to recruit neighbors in cleaning up these blighted parcels. It has also undertaken a $20 million program to build eighty-two new school-yard parks. Twenty have been completed.

As in Portland, the Lila Wallace–Reader's Digest Fund's Urban Parks Initiative was

started in the 1990s to restore Cleveland parks, create new ones, and improve programming. The Trust for Public Land and Clean-Land Ohio received the funding to create four
park sites to bolster neighborhood revitalization. One of those projects was the first city
neighborhood greenway connection to Cleveland Metroparks' new Ohio & Erie Canal
Reservation. ParkWorks does not usually own land, but rather assists other organizations
in improving the public realm.

EcoCity Cleveland, led by Director David Beach, is an environmental policy think tank
that focuses on open-space and natural areas protection for the larger Cleveland region.
Its urban sustainability work "thinks big," advocating thinking, planning, and acting across
the entire urban region. Rather than implementing changes, EcoCity assists agencies to
generate resources and support and to clarify questions regarding open-space needs and
priorities. It also created a Web-based tour of the proposed Towpath Trail through
Cleveland to show vivid images of the landscape through which that 6-mile segment will
pass.[19] EcoCity Cleveland created a Citizen's Bioregional Plan for Northeast Ohio, including the notion of a second-generation greenbelt around the region, where the Metroparks
serve as the first generation.

Despite much progress, collaboration among separate state and local entities has proved
difficult, and EcoCity foresees that these agencies will not be able to create the kind of greenbelt the region needs. One study commissioned by EcoCity asked what type of organization
could get the various open-space plans implemented: "with all these organizations talking
about open space, what's missing? Three things stand out: a regional framework for all of the
organizations and activities to plug into, a coordination organization, and much greater public funding for land protection."[20] EcoCity claims that an organization is needed to plan for
open space at the regional scale, establish priorities, and coordinate the activities of the many
organizations involved. Chicago Wilderness is used as a model. "It's time to think big about
open space in Northeast Ohio. This is about our future quality of life and our legacy for
future generations. We only get one chance, and it's slipping away."[21]

The study compared a number of entities for their ability to manage green infrastructure implementation on a regional scale—conservancy districts, county park districts,
regional water and sewer districts, soil and water conservation districts, and county governments. It used a set of evaluative criteria to judge effectiveness: regional approach, simplicity, political accountability, financing options, park enabling authority, stormwater
authority, and maintenance capability. It also summarized the barriers to creating a
regional green infrastructure entity and, using those political and legal realities, recommended a combined effort whereby Cuyahoga County and Cleveland Metroparks would

collaborate on new park and trail initiatives, and the Northeast Ohio Regional Sewer District (NEORSD) would focus on stormwater management. However, this solution seems only partially promising, since both Cuyahoga County and Cleveland Metroparks operate within only one county. Perhaps NEORSD can be an important leader.

Although the Heritage Corridor is the most striking example of a green infrastructure conversion at a large scale, NEORSD, the wastewater authority for Cleveland and sixty surrounding communities, is becoming active in restoration, watershed planning, and greenways and trails. In 1999, a pilot effort to use natural channel design techniques to restore highly degraded urban streams began. NEORSD constructed three stream-restoration projects, covering about 1,250 feet of urban stream channel.[22] According to EcoCity Cleveland, new stormwater-management efforts present an opportunity to craft a regional approach from the ground up, integrating ecological systems and natural resource protection for green infrastructure objectives.[23]

In the last decade, watershed planning has proliferated in the Cleveland region, at least partly spurred by the Cuyahoga River Remedial Action Plan (RAP), in place for the past sixteen years. A dozen active watershed groups are in place for tributaries of the Cuyahoga River through Cleveland. Some were started by citizens and some by government agencies; still others are hybrids. For example, ten years ago the West Creek Preservation Committee mobilized when a parcel was proposed for golf course development. The residents wanted the land left natural and an interesting cross section of volunteers began working together toward that goal. The subsequent committee has acquired over 400 acres of land, and raised $7.5 million through two voter initiatives. The group has become articulate and knowledgeable about greenways and instrumental in establishing a riparian setback for the community.

West Creek is an interesting case of collaboration, again spurred by the notion of connecting to the Towpath. NEORSD, with state funding, is restoring the stream along a 1-mile stretch, including removing fish barriers, controlling erosion, and enhancing instream habitat. It was able to acquire highly competitive state funds for the project, partly because of organized grassroots support. In addition, the area was identified as a focus area in the Cuyahoga County open-space planning process, so the county planning role is also important. The West Creek Preservation Committee will hold conservation easements along the restored stream. The site on West Creek originally threatened by golf course development became one of the Cleveland Metroparks reservations in January 2006. Metroparks could be very important in filling other gaps for open-space connectivity along West Creek to the Cuyahoga River and the Towpath.

Cleveland does not lack creative initiatives for open space. Many exist, all sharing a common theme of connectivity—linkage through trails, bike paths, and scenic byways.[24] Various groups have led and followed—from park districts to watershed groups, to community development organizations to County Planning. A spine, the Ohio & Erie Heritage Corridor, is nearly complete. The Heritage Corridor was a strong beginning for regional efforts, but now the region needs a strong follow-up that is regionally focused and pulls the various green infrastructure pieces together.

According to some interviewees, connectivity is not well enough understood. For instance, in planning and management of city parks, connectivity has not been emphasized as a strong priority. There are many discrete holdings that serve small population areas. If they were linked with trail connections, it would be possible to eliminate redundant facilities, thereby avoiding site-specific handling of park needs that overlooks opportunities for systemwide thinking.

There is a good spirit of collaboration in Cleveland; interviewees report that trail initiatives have helped forge a collaborative attitude. The Board of Health, NEORSD, city, county, and Metroparks have all started operating with an increased focus on connectivity. The nonprofit sector is more collaborative than ever. A striking example is the Chagrin River Land Conservancy, merging with seven other land trusts in Northeastern Ohio in the largest land trust merger in the United States. The combined organization will become the Western Reserve Land Conservancy, serving fourteen counties over more than 4.2 million acres, an important illustration of the strengthening movement for regional open space.

Minneapolis–St. Paul: Diverse Green Infrastructure Experiments

In the decades since Horace Cleveland and Theodore Wirth, a strong sense of public priority over more decades has been more notable than the leadership of one individual or an expansive regional vision by any one organization. The Minneapolis Park and Recreation Board estimates that 99.4 percent of city residents live within six blocks of a park.[25] Alexander Garvin, Yale Professor of Urban Planning and a member of the New York City Planning Commission, has claimed that Minneapolis possesses "the best-located, best-financed, best-designed, best-maintained public open space in America."[26]

However, until quite recently there has been notable unwillingness to coordinate at a regional level across the 188 municipalities in the seven-county region. The metropolitan area is known for its reluctance to form partnerships within larger regional contexts; there is a strong history of opposition to regional authority, planning, and implementation.[27] Under these circumstances, regional government has been only partially effective.

According to interviewees, strong leadership could perhaps pull together a long history of open-space priority into a coherent regional system. That leadership is needed now more than ever, as the suburban and exurban communities proliferate in the Minneapolis–St. Paul region. The state Department of Natural Resources has recently begun filling that mandate. Before that, it was the responsibility of the Twin Cities regional government, the Metropolitan Council, to oversee any regional open-space work.

RIVER POWER: FEDERAL INFLUENCE ON THE
MISSISSIPPI, MINNESOTA, AND ST. CROIX

The Twin Cities, like Cleveland and many other cities, were built where rivers facilitate commerce and transportation. The three rivers that converge in the Twin Cities region create an important framework for green infrastructure thinking in the twenty-first century. The Mississippi, Minnesota, and St. Croix have different forms of protection, planning, and management, but all three contribute to the overall structure of connected open space for the region. They are cornerstones for green infrastructure patterns, particularly as trails, utilities, transportation, and housing line their banks. Each is protected and planned in a different way, but all three have federal designations that impact future use and development.

The St. Croix National Scenic Riverway, tracing the eastern edge of the metropolitan region and the border between Minnesota and Wisconsin, is the most removed from direct urban influences. Its strong north–south alignment has facilitated an ancient transportation corridor for people and materials, as well as an historic barrier to east–west travel. The river flows 165 miles from its source to the Mississippi River at Point Douglas, Minnesota. The upper St. Croix was designated a National Wild and Scenic River in 1968 and is one of the eight original rivers protected through the National Wild and Scenic Rivers Act. This designation ensures that the river is preserved in its free-flowing condition and that the character of the river and its immediate setting be protected.

In 1972, the Lower St. Croix National Scenic Riverway was created on the river's final 52 miles near the Twin Cities. Because there are over three thousand landholdings along this stretch and a couple of thousand watercraft in use on a typical summer weekend, the management of this Scenic Riverway is complex. The last 25 miles of the St. Croix form a wide, gentle river that provides excellent water quality for swimming and a host of other uses. Special land-use regulations are in effect for the riverway, and management is achieved jointly by the Lower St. Croix Management Commission, a partnership of the National Park Service and the Departments of Natural Resources for Wisconsin and

7.2 Saint Paul Riverfront Corporation

St. Paul and Minneapolis harbor a sibling rivalry extending back to the nineteenth century. St. Paul is known as a big small town and Minneapolis as a small big city. The
Minneapolis–St. Paul Magazine (*Mpls.St.Paul*) summarizes the relationship well: "Ever
since Minneapolis surpassed St. Paul in population and industrial muscle in the late 1800s,
St. Paul has been the grumpy, (slightly) older sibling, resentful of its ostentatious twin."
This tongue-in-cheek assessment helps explain the historic lack of coordination on river
planning between the two cities. That is starting to change.

The Mississippi River, flowing by 27 miles of St. Paul, has been somewhat isolated from
the city since the nineteenth century. It was a pragmatic industrial and transportation corridor. In contrast, "the recent retreat of the 'industrial glacier' has revealed a vast terrain
of opportunity in the river valley."[1] Many millions of dollars have been spent on improving water quality, clearing obsolete industrial remnants, and building new infrastructure.
The ultimate goal for the Saint Paul Riverfront Corporation, articulated in its *Saint Paul
on the Mississippi Development Framework,* is "a system of interconnected urban villages
nestled in the lush green of a reforested river valley."[2]

The framework, completed in 1997, recommends a number of changes to the
built environment of St. Paul and its relationship to the Mississippi River (Figure
7.13). It advocates investments in the public realm, a balanced network of movement,
and improved connectivity. Connectivity to the Mississippi in St. Paul is hindered by
dramatic topographic barriers. High bluffs separate the city and the river flats.
Railroad tracks, levees, wetlands, and highways serve to further isolate people. The
framework recommends creating links between the downtown and regional trails;
increasing access to the river by developing stairs, ramps, and elevators; improving
connections between parks; and preserving view corridors. It envisions a National
Great River Park will define the image of the city, providing a huge green corridor
stretching as a continuous spine through the city.

The Saint Paul Riverfront Corporation is a private nonprofit providing leadership for
implementing the framework. Its main partners are the City of St. Paul, Saint Paul Port

Authority, and Capital City Partnership, a collaborative of the city's largest corporations. The collaboration between the City of St. Paul and the Riverfront Corporation has led to over one hundred projects that relate to the city–river relationship.

---

[1] Saint Paul Riverfront Corporation, *Saint Paul on the Mississippi Development Framework*, 1997.
[2] Ibid., p. 5.

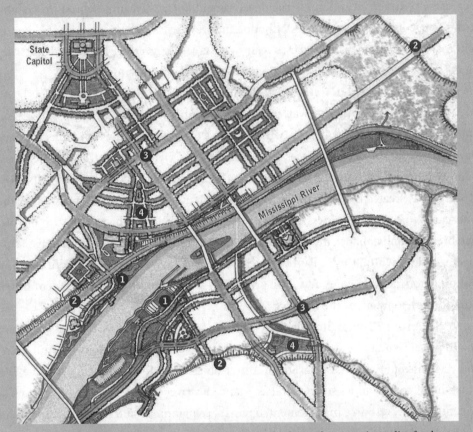

Fig. 7.13 Rendering that shows existing initiatives to establish an urban greening policy for downtown St. Paul and the riverfront: 1) green riverfront, 2) restored bluffs, 3) green streets, and 4) green parks/squares. (Courtesy of Saint Paul Riverfront Corporation, *Saint Paul on the Mississippi Development Framework*, June 1997.)

Minnesota. A new management plan was adopted in September 2000, following extensive participation by stakeholders in the region.

The Minnesota Valley National Wildlife Refuge is a 34-mile federally protected corridor starting at Fort Snelling State Park at the confluence of the Minnesota and Mississippi rivers and ending at Jordan, Minnesota, on the Minnesota River. It includes 14,000 acres of authorized land and is one of only four urban national wildlife refuges. Ironically, its visitor center is situated only a mile from the Mall of America. The refuge was established in 1976 to provide habitat for migratory waterfowl, fish, and other species threatened by increasing commercial and industrial development along the Minnesota River. Habitats in the refuge include hillside forest, floodplain forest, oak savanna, wet meadows, emergent marshes, fens, grasslands, lakes, streams, and creeks. The refuge has eight distinct segments, five of which have trails, interpretive signs, and other visitor facilities.

Finally, the Mississippi flows for 11.5 miles through Minneapolis and St. Paul, with St. Anthony Falls the only true waterfall along the entire length of the Mississippi. Much of the river is in public ownership, with a nearly continuous system of connected parkways, trails, and other open spaces (Figure 7.12). The river, part of the original Grand Rounds, is now designated the Mississippi National River and Recreation Area (MNRRA). MNRRA was created by Congress in 1988. The system includes over 350 parks and other landscapes for which Congress gave the National Park Service the mandate to (1) protect, preserve, and enhance the significant values of the waters and land of the Mississippi River Corridor within the St. Paul–Minneapolis Metropolitan area; (2) encourage cooperation among federal, state, and local programs; and (3) provide a management framework for development of the river corridor.

MNRRA runs 72 miles through five counties, encompassing over 53,000 acres of public and private land in the Twin Cities metropolitan area. The Minneapolis–St. Paul stretch of the Mississippi River is also part of an American Heritage River designation by the EPA, which helps communities seek federal assistance for river projects, ranging from navigation, public use, resource management, open-space planning, land use, and overall management and monitoring.

In 1994 and 1995, the Metropolitan Design Center at the University of Minnesota focused on the Mississippi River in a project called *Recreational Resource Planning in the Metro Mississippi Corridor*. Funded by the Minnesota legislature and other sources, the Design Center created a set of urban design principles for the river landscape and applied them along three reaches of the river. The project promoted design forms consisting of corridors, networks, and watersheds and aggregated those into the notion of "working

Fig. 7.12 A view looking over open land and the Mississippi River toward the St. Paul skyline. (Photo by Larry Deck.)

zones" on which to base interjurisdictional planning, funding, and implementation strategies. This project found that the physical connections to the Mississippi River could be powerful for integrating communities. It showed a set of thirty-four priority working zones where recreational and environmental connections to the Mississippi River could be made.

METROPOLITAN COUNCIL

Aside from Portland, Minneapolis–St. Paul is the only metropolitan region in the United States with a regional level of government.[28] The Metropolitan Council of Minneapolis and St. Paul, called Metro Council, was created in 1967 to coordinate development in a seven-county area (consisting of Anoka, Carver, Dakota, Hennepin, Ramsey, Scott, and Washington counties). In addition to planning functions, it operates a regional transit system, provides wastewater collection and treatment for 103 communities, and oversees a regional park system. This agency is not an elected government body and has not been as progressive in regulating the relationship between growth and open land as in Portland.

The regional parks system was established in 1974 in response to state legislation, designating about 31,000 acres of existing parks owned by the counties, cities, and special park districts as "regional recreational open space." During the late 1960s and early 1970s several legislative sessions tried to resolve the issue of how open-space needs in the Twin Cities region should be met. Metro Council, in 1971, created an Open Space Advisory Board, which developed a partnership concept that succeeded in the Minnesota legislature. It established a system for planning and funding responsibilities at the Metro Council level, with responsibility for ownership and operation at the county and municipal levels.

The regional park system now includes about 52,000 acres in forty-seven regional parks, six special recreation features (such as a zoo and a conservatory), and twenty-two regional trails along 170 miles. All of these properties are owned and operated by ten individual implementing agencies (seven counties and three municipalities). For instance, the Minneapolis Park and Recreation Board, the Grand Rounds manager, presides over 6,000 acres of parkland on 170 properties and maintains a strong sense of ownership and control over its own system.

The Metropolitan Council has not achieved the level of coordination necessary for the kind of regionwide open-space visioning achieved in Portland and elsewhere. Meanwhile, urban land has expanded 25 percent for every 10 percent increase in population in the Twin Cities.[29] In addition, population is expected to grow by a million people in the seven-county region by 2030.[30] Metro Council's new plan for 2030 proposes acquisition of new regional parks and trails. But the vision of connected open space for diverse modern needs is missing. According to Douglas Porter, who has written extensively on land use, "the vaunted inter-jurisdictional consensus that has supported the [Metro] council has eroded with changing central city demographics and growing fiscal and other disparities between suburban jurisdictions and the two central cities." Minnesota Governor Arne Carlson has called for the council to "become either relevant or extinct."[31]

METROPOLITAN DESIGN CENTER AT THE UNIVERSITY OF MINNESOTA

Through the 1990s, other organizations emerged to promote linear open spaces in the Twin Cities region, trying to cover gaps left by Metro Council. Again, the Trust for Public Land has actively promoted regional open-space planning in the Minneapolis region, through its Green Cities Initiative, projects along the Mississippi River Corridor, and other efforts. Similarly, the Metropolitan Design Center (formerly, Design Center for the American Urban Landscape) at the University of Minnesota has provided important data and analysis for integrated open-space planning. In the 1990s, the Design Center inherited Metro Council's role of coordinator, but without its budget, and the active discussion today regarding connected open space in Minneapolis is partly a result of the Design Center's work.

The Metropolitan Design Center, established in 1988 with a grant from the Hudson Foundation, is an endowed unit that investigates how design can be used to make the metropolitan landscape more livable. It focuses on four main areas—urban development, housing, active/healthy cities, and greenspace. Its work draws from the disciplines of architecture, landscape architecture, geography, planning, and landscape ecology. The Design Center seeks to help decision makers in the phases prior to deciding on a specific project. This is done by getting physical design onto the economic and social agenda and by highlighting the importance of the greenspace movement to the development community.

The Center works on projects that interpret, preserve, and design open spaces in urban and suburban areas. Open space and trails in the seven-county region were mapped by the Design Center, enabling those resources to be analyzed together for the first time. The resulting map illustrated the abundance of trails in the region and showed their potential linkages. The Design Center's unique inventory of Twin Cities parkways is a valuable reference, documenting the distinguishing characteristics of existing green streets. The Center shows how the parkways are greener than other roadways, how they provide critical public space, and how they connect important natural and cultural features.[32] Another project mapped the existing pattern of public and private greenspaces in the center city and related that to access by those with limited mobility—children, the elderly, the poor, and people without cars.[33] Other projects include a public service campaign to raise awareness about the need for protected open space in the Twin Cities, an urban forestry online image database, and a Mississippi River initiative to strengthen connections between the University of Minnesota and the river.[34]

MINNESOTA STATE DEPARTMENT OF NATURAL RESOURCES: METRO GREENPRINT

Building on the Design Center's work and other efforts, momentum grew in the late 1990s for a broader vision of regional open space in the Twin Cities region. The Department of Natural Resources' (DNR) Metro Greenways Program was first established in 1998, with $4.3 million in funding from the Minnesota legislature, championed by former representative Tom Osthoff.[35] According to Sharon Pfeifer at the DNR, "although christened a 'greenways program,' the Twin Cities' regional effort since its inception has focused on creating a green network from remaining or restored habitat hubs (or patches) and connectors, ranging from habitat corridors for fish and wildlife to trail ways for people."[36] Its goals include the following: identify and develop a network of significant natural areas, open spaces, and greenways across the seven-county area; protect and manage natural areas to sustain ecological functions; connect, buffer, and enhance these areas; provide opportunities for residents to understand and enjoy natural resources; build public and political support for a regional land network; and create and sustain funding to achieve the vision. Although the program is bounded by the same seven-county area as the Metro Council, there is some concern that a broader ring of "collar" counties around the Twin Cities should be included in these types of efforts.[37]

In 1997, DNR organized and facilitated a twenty-seven-member group of representatives from Twin Cities organizations and interested citizens. The Greenways and Natural Areas Collaborative published *Metro Greenprint: Planning for Nature in the Face of Urban Growth,* which outlined the building blocks for a green infrastructure plan and mapped potential green corridors for the metropolitan area.[38] Three types of open spaces were catalogued. *Natural areas* are sites untouched by human activity and providing the healthiest wildlife habitat. *Open spaces* are undeveloped sites affected by human activity, but providing food, buffering, or sense of community. Examples are golf courses, farmland, and high-use parks. Finally, *greenways* are defined as continuous areas of vegetation that allow the movement of humans and wildlife, providing linkages that increase connectivity and nonmotorized movement.

The program has a focused "bottom-up" approach, designed at its inception to work with local units of government and nonprofit groups. It relies on unprecedented partnerships with conservation organizations, agencies, institutions, private businesses, and landowners. The program has been developing a broad base of partner support for green infrastructure objectives across the seven-county region. The Greenways Program has several components—technical assistance, planning grants, land protection funds, and overall coordination. However, two main program components are critical: (1) funding for land acquisition and habitat restoration, and (2) funding for matching grants for land-cover inventories and greenway planning. The program's key criteria are ecological quality, willing donors/sellers, affordable cost, and strong levels of support from communities.[39]

From 1998 to 2004, $9.3 million was allocated to fund twenty-nine land protection and sixteen restoration projects in the Metro Greenways Program. This leveraged another $21 million for land protection and restoration from other sources, such as federal, state, regional, and local governments, foundations, corporations, nonprofit organizations, pollution mitigation settlements, and private citizens. These projects have protected about 2,500 acres and restored 606 acres, ranging from a 2-acre demonstration site to completion of a continuous 2,800-acre greenway on the St. Croix River. A number of land protection tools are used, but the most prevalent so far is land acquisition by a local entity, with the state holding a conservation easement on the property.

From 1999 to 2003, $900,000 in matching grants was awarded to local governments to conduct fifty-two natural-resources inventories, land-cover mapping projects, and natural resource management and greenway plans. Detailed land-cover mapping has been done for 75 percent of the region's land base.[40] Adequate funding from the legislature is a recent challenge and ongoing worry. The Metro Greenways program was not funded in 2005.

Despite recent funding shortages, the Metro Greenways Program has gained considerable momentum. One of its successes is, indeed, its regional scope. With the big landscape picture in mind, the agency can assure that smaller projects contribute to the regional green infrastructure system. In fact, work is under way to expand the spatial scope of the Metro Greenways Program by adding another four "collar" counties where growth is imminent and assessing growth impacts on natural resources for an even larger seventeen-county region.

Spin-off projects have also been important. In 2003, six nonprofit partners and the DNR (Metro Greenways and four other divisions) started the Metro Conservation Corridors program, receiving a $4.85 million allocation from the Minnesota legislature for habitat protection and restoration in twelve focus areas of the region. In this new approach, agencies or groups requesting funding for land protection need to work within the boundaries of these focus areas (Figure 7.14). The program has expanded into seven more counties around the Metro region and now works with a coalition of a dozen or more partners. In the designation process, two committees review applications for land-protection funds. One committee functions as a steering group to shape program elements and processes.[41] An additional layer of review continues the outreach to the community. The eleven-member Metro Greenways Community Advisory Committee consists of people concerned about land conservation, including a corporate executive, a developer, a lobbyist for hunting and fishing interests, and members of the Metro Council. Both groups review and evaluate each nomination for land-protection funding.

An important outcome of the Metro Greenways Program is that the Metropolitan Council has gradually accepted the importance of green infrastructure. For instance, the Metro Council used DNR's regional ecological assessment for locating park purchases in high-quality areas where population is increasing. Despite gains, both the Metro Council and DNR need to increase their outreach to local governments on green infrastructure initiatives. The benefits of green infrastructure planning need to be underscored: "Most local government staff and elected local officials need assistance if they are expected to plan and budget for green infrastructure to complement physical infrastructure development."[42] To

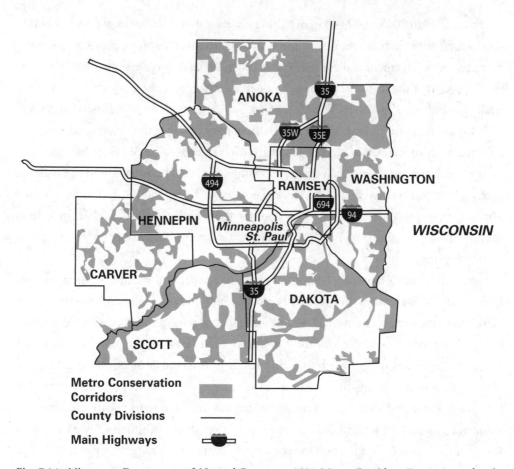

Fig. 7.14 Minnesota Department of Natural Resources 2005 Metro Corridors Focus Areas for the Minneapolis–St. Paul region. The corridors are part of a strategy for habitat protection, whereby limited funds are targeted toward twelve main high-priority focal areas. (Adapted from Minnesota Department of Natural Resources.)

that end, incentives must be used for interjurisdictional planning for green infrastructure.

HENNEPIN COMMUNITY WORKS

Green infrastructure is about linking natural systems with urban services and, further-more, about considering natural systems *as* urban services. Few other programs nationally have as broad a vision for this type of integration as Hennepin Community Works (HCW) west of Minneapolis. The county is sandwiched between the Mississippi River on the east and the Minnesota River to the south. A Parks and Public Works Commission created the inno-vative HCW program to coordinate investments in infrastructure, public works, parks, and the natural environment. By the 1990s Hennepin County was experiencing economic deterioration; in a series of summit meetings with elected officials, five problems were identified—crime, tax base, aesthetic environment, economic development, and housing quality. County officials decided to mitigate all five with one integrated program. HCW is based on the premise that "well designed and carefully integrated parks and public works projects maintain and enhance the long-term tax base of neighborhoods while improving their quality of life."[43] The commission proposed locating public amenities in urban and suburban communities that lack them, thereby improving the tax base, encouraging long-term investment, and providing durable employment opportunities with job training.

According to the Metropolitan Design Center, "the Hennepin Community Works program was, from the start, something of an anomaly ... But with one quarter of Minnesota's population, and a nearly $2 billion annual operating budget, Hennepin County can afford to behave differently ... The idea emerged that the County, through infrastructure investment, could help create 'greener' and more attractive urban sites, in preparation for investment and job growth."[44]

A Parks and Public Works Commission was formed late in 1993 with a remarkably wide mandate. It completed a study "to examine the feasibility of joint development of parks and public works activities with the goals of job creation, tax base enhancement, development of public works in high needs areas and removal of impediments to redevelopment, repair of ecological damage, and revitalization of cities and maintenance of urban infrastructure."[45] The commission's 1994 report, completed with assistance from the Metropolitan Design Center and other entities, recommended a new program and a series of pilot projects. Seven county, regional, and metropolitan partners cooperated to launch the program, with Hennepin County serving as the lead agency for coordination and development of HCW. According to the commission, "for projects to be most successful they must be part of a larger vision—an integrated system which crosses jurisdictional boundaries connecting each neighborhood to its ecological roots, to job opportunities which are sustainable, and to the community as a whole."[46] Specific principles of the HCW experiment are to (1) stimulate employment, (2) build bridges for effective planning and implementation, (3) enhance the tax base, (4) maintain and improve natural systems, and (5) strengthen communities through connections.

The last two principles are particularly apt for connected open-space work and its linkage to green infrastructure. The commission observed that some of the declining urban areas in Hennepin County tend to have isolated parks that are disconnected from parkway corridors or a trails network. The commission suggested increasing connectivity in order to "bring residents and parks into a larger system by building on- and off-street trails and expanding or establishing new parkway corridors."[47] Furthermore, the commission argued that, following the example of the Grand Rounds system, which has stimulated high property values for the Twin Cities, creek corridors in Hennepin County might offer similar settings and protect water quality and wildlife habitat, while also stimulating higher property values.

The "Works" in Hennepin Community Works harkens to the Works Progress Administration (WPA) projects, which tackled public infrastructure projects in the 1930s, while providing much-needed employment and job training. Similarly, one function of HCW is to train and hire unemployed and underemployed people in these large-scale public works projects, giving local residents work and training opportunities while at the same time supporting new construction projects.

The commission's final report identified three types of projects that HCW could take on—projects that (1) improve the physical quality of communities, (2) emphasize community linkages, and (3) promote, protect, and reclaim natural resources. Projects have focused on corridors where Hennepin County has responsibility for transportation infrastructure, with projects encompassing new roads, housing, bike paths, daylighting creeks, and other investments. Three initial projects were designed as infrastructure investments to anchor at-risk neighborhoods. The Humboldt Greenway, for instance, revitalized the Shingle Creek and Lind–Bohanon neighborhoods by creating a landscaped greenway, comparable to the Minneapolis parkway system, along Humboldt Avenue (Figure 7.15). HCW worked with neighborhood associations and

Fig. 7.15 The Humboldt Greenway at 50th Avenue, where a central green is created by dividing and curving traffic lanes. (Photo courtesy of Hennepin County.)

other public agencies along the eight-block corridor. About 210 residential and commercial properties were removed and replaced with 200 new homes in the $28.8 million project. The new parkway includes landscaped medians and boulevards, decorative lighting, wetlands, pedestrian mall, and new central green for passive recreation and community events. New residential units include senior housing, single-family homes, and townhouses along the parkway.

There are strong advocates for a green infrastructure approach in the Twin Cities region, but a paucity of regional leadership. On a positive note, the building blocks are in place for increasing connectivity and drawing awareness to the benefits of green infrastructure. State leadership has proven strong and reliable, although funding is unstable. Although a spirit of interjurisdictional collaboration for a regional open-space vision is just building in the Twin Cities, people recognize these collaborations are critical, not just discretionary. The region has an established regional government that includes open-space provision as part of its charge. What is needed now is follow-through. DNR planners are realizing that the modern chronicle of protected open space for Minneapolis and St. Paul is no longer the Grand Rounds, as wonderful as it is, but rather the rural–urban interface in the outer counties where growth pressure is squeezing natural resources and landscape integrity.

The federal protection mechanisms for the region's rivers are important pieces of the overall picture. Other corridors have also been rethought with green infrastructure ideas. Enlarging the model provided by Hennepin Community Works—where redevelopment includes parks, jobs, housing, ecology, and aesthetics—beyond that county's boundaries would be an enormous undertaking but could provide an amazing national model for metropolitan green infrastructure, and for the many benefits connected to it.

Green Infrastructure as Thrust for Connectivity

Glen Murray, mayor of Winnipeg, Manitoba, claimed that "what kills a city are people who want only low taxes, only want a good deal and only want cities to be about . . . pipes, pavement and policing." He was advocating municipal spending for the urban amenities that attract and retain the "creative class," which could be the redeemer of North American cities, according to Richard Florida.[48] If one accepts Florida's theories, cities will thrive economically where diverse populations flourish and where hip arts scenes and other cultural amenities are provided. Florida repeatedly cites success in places where parks, bike paths, trails, and other features are present, arguing that the new breed of entrepreneurs are attracted to these places. Indeed, one of his main economic arguments is that *place* matters.

Others counter that cities paying for these amenities, by raising their taxes, are not as economically stable.[49] Enter the green infrastructure idea for thinking about the built environment. Are there perhaps ways to lower the costs of gray infrastructure while providing enjoyable human-scaled environments? Take stormwater as an example. It is possible that the costs of treating urban runoff in natural swales and "green" infiltration systems would be less expensive than using hardened systems like storm sewers. And the physical space of these features—an urban greenway or other linear green zone—could provide enjoyable human experience in the outdoors.

The spatial structure and economic viability of green infrastructure is just beginning to be modeled, but connectivity is a glue that, as suggested in the first chapter of this book, binds landscape integrity. The greenways, parkways, greenbelts, and other forms that were designed and implemented long before the green infrastructure movement will be critical cornerstones, especially where they optimize environmental quality. Where these corridors combine with and enhance gray infrastructure corridors—sewers, roads, utilities, and canals—the green infrastructure notion will be advanced even further. Green infrastructure mitigates the need for and the cost of gray infrastructure.

The cities of Cleveland and Minneapolis–St. Paul reveal stories of accomplishment and also foretell vast potential. The Emerald Necklaces are cherished, but their circles need to be widened dramatically in both regions. Bridges over the Mississippi and Cuyahoga rivers are symbolic of artful, functional, historic infrastructure. Although human-made and not contributing to the environmental health of the city, these bridges are celebrated by the cities that made and use them. They provide stories about urban heritage and help people imagine where, when, and how the cities emerged. Perhaps for both cities the bridges will be critical pieces of green infrastructure systems, if not for environmental benefit, at least for highlighting the importance of the river landscape and providing access to it.

Both Cleveland and the Twin Cities have powerful stories to tell about industrial heritage at the river's edge. When these stories take physical form, as they do at Cleveland's Ohio & Erie Canal Reservation, the industrial landscape, past and present, is all the more relevant, clear, and meaningful. Cleveland's Heritage Corridor honestly celebrates what the city was—an infrastructure system of industry and work. As the Towpath Trail works its way up the Cuyahoga valley, the continued presence of functioning industry allows the perfect opportunity to reveal the transformation from gray to green infrastructure. Similar work along the Mississippi in Minneapolis and St. Paul documents the history of milling along its banks. The rivers are vital means of diffusing green infrastructure ideas throughout metropolitan regions.

Neighborhoods are an important spatial unit for building progressive connectivity projects across scales. Unfortunately, much of the talk about building neighborhoods is often whitewash for less altruistic motives. For example, homebuilders and developers are fond of saying they are not in the business of building houses, but of "creating neighborhoods" or "building communities." These not-so-subtle assertions play on our deep-seated desires to be part of a neighborhood. But what does neighborhood building really mean? What are the physical dimensions of new neighborhood design? Tangible features, many contend, include the sites where green infrastructure functions. In addition, rallying for open places galvanizes a sense of community.

In Cleveland, for instance, neighborhoods (in the form of watershed groups in some places) have mobilized around connecting to the Towpath. An incredible amount of neighborhood outreach was done before the Heritage Corridor was established. This outreach described the corridor vision and illustrated the potential connections between neighborhoods and the Towpath Trail, which in turn fueled extensive neighborhood-based planning. This neighborhood focus was astute: it showed that the Heritage Corridor was not just about the river, but about the creeks that feed into it. After all, almost nobody lived in the valley bottom, but people do live along the river's tributaries. In order to get the political support required for National Heritage Corridor designation, the Ohio Canal Corridor group needed letters from neighbors up and down the corridor. An enormous letter-writing campaign to Congress showed that people saw the potential value of the Heritage Corridor designation to their neighborhoods. As the broad vision took hold, each neighborhood took on the work of defining the specific vision for their community.

For the Twin Cities, the Hennepin Community Works example also illustrates the importance of neighborhood. Moreover, it demonstrates the history lessons of creative urban form. Over the past century economic development has paired with landscape preservation and beauty in the Grand Rounds. HCW is continuing to use parks, lakes, greenways, urban forests, and aesthetics to generate financial stability in neighborhoods.[50] The greenway development projects completed and being planned focus strongly on connections within and between neighborhoods. They concentrate commercial areas around transit nodes, providing mixed-income housing, and offering multimodal transportation options. Physical changes to neighborhood streets include on-street bicycle lanes, wider sidewalks, and landscaped boulevards, among other improvements.

Strong leadership and organizational capacity are needed to achieve the natural and human connections that are increasingly emphasized in urban areas. In the Twin Cities, that role has been filled, at least to some degree, by state government; Cleveland still struggles to find that leadership at a governmental level. However, EcoCity Cleveland has outlined work that needs to be done in several key areas and provides a leadership framework much needed in the community. This type of leadership—helping illustrate focused steps for going forward—is critically needed in many urban regions.

Part 3

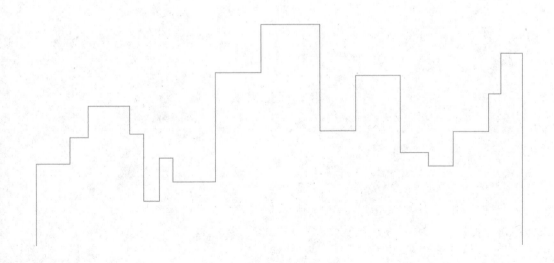

Synthesis: Key Ingredients, Challenges, and Strategic Trends

8

Lessons for Realizing Connected Open-Space Networks in North American Cities

Decisions about urban policy, or the allocation of resources, or
where to move, or how to build something, must use norms
about good and bad . . . Without some sense of better, any action
is perverse. When values lie unexamined, they are dangerous.

—*Kevin Lynch*[1]

The dozens of people who contributed their perspectives to this book relate to
open-space planning in diverse ways—as ecologists, planners, activists, bureaucrats,
designers, engineers, and geographers. They share the vision that a connected landscape
is better than a fragmented one: people and the environment benefit from linkages that
knit together neighborhoods, land uses, and natural features. Diverse opportunities and
constraints have arisen across North America as the connectivity norm is put to the application
test.

The linkage goal complicates efforts to protect and enhance urban open land. Even
accomplishing one linear corridor is daunting, often taking years of work by many different

individuals, agencies, and organizations. Connecting corridors to create a web of open space is vastly more difficult and demands several key elements to make headway. The oversight and leadership of one or more institutions or organizations are critical: collaboration among participants is essential. Projects in locales that have an historic open-space framework on which to build are at a distinct advantage but even they must consider a new range of contemporary objectives. In other places, the green infrastructure must be created from scratch. What are the patterns that emerge from both scenarios? What are the lessons that surface from the ten cities explored in this book? These lessons can be grouped by findings on institutional organization, key ingredients, challenges, and strategic approaches.

Institutional Structure

What agency or organization is most appropriate for accomplishing open-space networks and for providing a programmatic home? What levels and types of agencies have been most actively involved in similar projects in the past? Most cities where the network idea has emerged have at one time or another asked these questions and studied various models for organizational structure. Other questions also invariably arise, from "Who will own and manage the system?" to "How will various levels of government work together?"

Participants and Contributors

The combination of agencies and organizations active in open-space planning allows for results that outweigh the influence of any one group. Every level of government is involved in open-space work in the United States. In contrast, Canada, with negligible federal intervention, relies on the local, regional, and provincial governments that have jurisdiction over these issues. Private nonprofit groups, universities, private consultants, and the business sector are important participants in both nations but somewhat more so in the United States.

The U.S. federal government has had an active role, particularly along major American rivers, as shown in Cleveland and Minneapolis–St. Paul. The National Park Service Rivers, Trails, and Conservation Assistance program (RTCA) has served in many U.S. urban regions. It has been an important facilitator, broker, and networker for dozens of greenway projects. Although RTCA is not typically involved in implementing greenways, it provides research, planning expertise, and a process for public involvement. Despite diminishing federal budgets, RTCA funding and technical expertise for citizen participation have been critical. RTCA has focused on "working where invited" and supporting community-led projects, such as its participation with local organizations along the Chicago River and in Cleveland's Cuyahoga Valley. New strategic plans for RTCA place an even greater emphasis on physical networks of natural and outdoor recreation resources. The program has supported efforts in every American case study highlighted in this book.

State government agencies are almost always partners, if not leaders, in developing urban open-space systems, through either planning or funding. The role of the state in Minneapolis–St. Paul is particularly unique, where the Minnesota Department of Natural Resources is the regional home for the greenways program. In almost all cases, the Departments of Natural Resources, Environment, and Transportation play key roles. Several states, such as Maryland, Florida, and Georgia, administer comprehensive green-way programs at the state level, providing models for active state-level involvement in improving green infrastructure. Among the six states considered here, only Ohio has a statewide program and it relies heavily on nonprofit partners.

Canadian provinces exert considerable control over municipal governance relative to American states. However, they have largely been hands-off about metropolitan open-space issues. Ontario's involvement in open land is an exception; the province has been instrumental in protecting the Oak Ridges Moraine and Niagara Escarpment surrounding the Toronto region. Alberta's exceptional funding for urban river corridors is another example of the provincial government serving a prominent role.

At the regional scale, a number of distinctions are significant. Rarely are regional government levels in the United States directly responsible for open-space planning and protection. Portland and, to a lesser extent, Minneapolis–St. Paul are exceptions. Regional councils of government (COGs), advisory in nature, participate in developing and implementing green networks in Milwaukee, Chicago, Cleveland, and Denver. In Canada, the Greater Vancouver Regional District falls somewhere between the two American models: it has more power and responsibility than a COG, but somewhat less than Portland's elected Metro. In Ottawa and Toronto, metropolitan scales of government have essentially been created by the amalgamation of smaller municipalities into large cities. Despite variations, regional agencies are typically involved in some way in planning and implementing open-space systems, but rarely do they hold extensive implementation power.

In most cases, the local unit of government is the most influential level in the planning and implementation of open-space systems. (It is important to remember that the metropolitan region *is* the local level in some Canadian cities.) In cities the size of Chicago or Minneapolis–St. Paul, the regional open-space network may encompass dozens of local jurisdictions, each implementing short segments of the plan. For instance, the Chicago system is complicated by the complex nature of coordination among 269 municipalities and over 150 park districts. The Forest Preserves are separate government units whose mission is to preserve open space, maintain high-quality natural areas, and provide recreation. The Illinois home rule powers give virtually unlimited power to local towns, so cooperation and coordination are critical.

Canadian cities are increasingly creating public corporations for urban redevelopment. Special-purpose corporations have been established to take on particular development mandates, using both private and public capital. These corporations pursue public sector objectives with the capabilities of the private world, usually with some degree of independence from the local units of government that created them. Vancouver's waterfront projects, including open-space components, are one example. According to Matthew Kiernan, "the public corporations enjoy three critical resources historically denied to traditional planning departments: enormous capital budgets, a mandate actually to develop land rather than simply to plan and regulate it, and broad public and political support."[2]

The role of the private sector is becoming profoundly important. The cooperation of nonprofit groups and foundations helps give meaning and strength to community enhancement, environmental protection, and open-space planning. The private sector also provides access to funding, particularly through foundations that support open-space projects. Nonprofit groups are essential partners in the cases studied here, though more so in American than Canadian cities. In some cases these groups start within government and are privatized as independent nonprofit organizations in later stages; for example, Denver's Greenway Foundation started as a city entity and was later transformed into a private nonprofit organization. This highlights the diverse roles that government can have in both initiating and sustaining projects over time through cooperation with the private sector.

Nonprofit partners are of two main types: natural resource advocacy groups and land-acquisition groups. Each city has a long list of organizations dedicated to one specific type or location of open space. Many are special interest groups that advocate for one specific goal. Although these groups are proliferating, they do not always work well with one another and sometimes feel they are competing for scarce funding. Chicago Wilderness is a notable exception, since it specifically exists to pull organizations together around the biodiversity theme.

The primary land acquisition groups for greenways, at the national level, are the Trust for Public Land (TPL), The Nature Conservancy (TNC) and The Conservation Fund (TCF). Smaller, local land trusts also have a large impact. These groups are particularly important in implementation phases, because they are able to negotiate with private landowners and complete land deals quickly. Many interviewees mentioned that well-organized land conservation groups are crucial in the networking process with landowners, the business community, and the public. The Trust for Public Land is an important partner in all six American case studies in this book. With its urban focus, TPL has taken a leadership role in land protection for many open-space corridors, particularly in helping develop public funding opportunities and forming collaborations. The Conservation Fund buys both recreational and ecological lands, and then gives land to public agencies. Likewise, The Nature Conservancy is a major collaborator in some places, where it buys land with special ecological value and often retains ownership or easements. In Chicago, Corlands, a real estate affiliate of the Openlands Project, has acquired regionally significant open-space land, usually transferring ownership to local governments.

In Canada, the nonprofit sector for environmental planning is generally not as well developed as in the States and there is less private-sector involvement in regional issues. According to Andrew Sancton, "in Canada, regional issues remain the preserve of the developers, the land-use planners, and a small band of academics."[3] Vancouver is an apt example, where private funding has not been particularly important to greenway development. The city has found NGO collaborations to be thorny, as they sometimes raise hopes about a particular project that the city is not prepared to implement for some time.

The participation of the academic community is also important. The objectives at the Metropolitan Design Center at the University of Minnesota, for instance, have helped decision makers in early planning phases, particularly in inventories and analyses of landscapes and cultural factors in the Twin Cities. Researchers have helped place physical design on the economic and political agenda and have pulled the greenway movement out of the parochial realm and into the development community. In the Canadian context, the work of the Landscape Architecture Department at the University of British Columbia and the Center for Urban Ecology at Douglas College stands out.

The private sector is an increasingly important partner for open-space protection across the continent. The corporate sector helps to provide land, capital, expertise, and leadership: the corporations along the Cuyahoga River in Cleveland's Heritage Corridor are prime examples. Business partners are vital to the success of landscape-scale projects. In addition, a range of private consultants—landscape architects, planners, and engineers—often plays central roles in open-space planning and implementation. Physical design expertise is critical for making difficult connections across the landscape, and those talents are often sought in the private sector. This is especially true in the implementation phases, in which consultants can help a municipality go from the stage of planning and public involvement to building greenways on the ground. Trained professionals can relate to the Chambers of Commerce and corporate partners in pragmatic business terms about the financial, social, and management sides of open-space issues. Private firms, sometimes as "outsiders," can offer fresh, strategic advice that is difficult to generate from "inside" the project. While open-space issues can seem quite complex for local people who are immersed in them, a consultant can often summarize problems quickly and envision solutions creatively.

Models of Organizational Structure

Consider this scenario: a greenway network plan has been created for a metropolitan region. An institutional structure is needed—an organizing method or institutional arrangement for implementation. Local and regional agencies are the primary implementers of greenways and usually provide programmatic homes, although there are interesting exceptions. Table 8.1 helps explain relationships that might exist with three potential patterns differing in level of control, authority, and scope.

In the first model, a local level of government directly influences projects within a single jurisdiction. This model describes Calgary, Ottawa, and Milwaukee. Strong local control is both the main advantage and the primary drawback of Model 1. This model allows for a unified approach and direct local control, which are especially effective for smaller jurisdictions that are isolated from other urban areas, such as in Calgary and Ottawa. Grassroots efforts can take hold and projects can be accomplished at a manageable scale over a long period of time. Private groups have ample opportunities to put forth initiatives. Strong leadership, if available, can be effective and visible and citizens can often get involved in creating the broad vision.

There are disadvantages though, particularly in cities like Milwaukee that are part of far larger aggregations of urban communities. Without regional leadership for coordination, a shared, larger vision is lacking and regional connections are more difficult. In addition, there is less opportunity for funding possibilities to take root in a holistic way for the network. It is also difficult to connect to bordering jurisdictions or systems for broader open-space planning. Funding may be more difficult to obtain and leverage for interjurisdictional projects. Many of the cities working in this model are trying to evolve toward more regional coordination (Model 2 or 3).

Portland and Cleveland are examples for the second model, in which a senior level of government carries out a strong role with primary control over implementation. It serves as an umbrella group over multiple jurisdictions. For Cleveland, the federal government in the Ohio & Erie Canal Heritage Corridor provides a strong centralized focus that connects to county park districts and city programs, even though it has not provided a region-wide open-space vision.

Model	Example	Regional Coordination Body	Advantages	Disadvantages
1. Local government directly influences projects within a single jurisdiction.	Calgary	Large unicity concept; various city departments plan open space.	•Unified •Direct control •Effective for smaller jurisdictions within larger network •Strong leadership can be effective and visible •Good possibilities for citizen involvement in city-wide vision	•Potential difficulty in connecting to bordering jurisdictions •May not be able to leverage diverse sources of funding
	Ottawa	City itself encompasses large region, including rural lands.		
	Milwaukee	Council of government has some influence, but most open-space work done within individual cities and counties.		
2. Centralized entity serves as umbrella over multiple jurisdictions and has strong control over implementation.	Portland	Metro: regional government coordinates open-space planning and acquisition across region.	•Strong central leadership can coordinate multiple agency efforts; broader vision •Stronger funding base from wider geographic region •Coordination across wider geographic area •Allows more progressive jurisdictions to progress ahead of slower, more reluctant ones	•Plan may not be a priority within each local jurisdiction •Potentially less grassroots support and public participation
	Cleveland	Ohio & Erie Canal Heritage Corridor and Cuyahoga Valley National Park (federal) take strong leadership, but for corridor itself, not broader region.		
3. Regional or state agency empowers jurisdictions through initial stages and then partners for implementation.	Denver	Greenways Foundation and similar entities in other counties	•Encourages coordination among jurisdictions •Increased power at local levels •Leadership can develop in local jurisdictions •Regional or state funding can be prioritized across entire region	•Coordination may be optional between jurisdictions •Implementation may be slower with shared responsibility across many agencies
	Chicago	Northeastern Illinois Planning Commission, Openlands Project, Chicago Wilderness		
	Toronto	Waterfront Regeneration Trust		
	Vancouver	Greater Vancouver Regional District		
	Minneapolis–St. Paul	Minnesota Department of Natural Resources, Metropolitan Council		

○ Regional agency or organization   → Direction and strength of influence   ■ Dominant Role   ▨ Moderate role

☐ Local jurisdiction

Table 8.1 Three models of institutional structure for connected open-space planning, differing in level of government involvement, strength of control, and relationships across jurisdictions.

This institutional structure, too, has its advantages and disadvantages. A broad vision for the region can be coordinated across a diverse geographic area. Strong centralized leadership allows coordination of multiple agency efforts for land acquisition and development; more can be accomplished with a larger funding base from a wider geographic area. More progressive jurisdictions can proceed ahead of slower, more reluctant jurisdictions. On the other hand, coordination efforts may break down when implementing the open-space plan is not a priority for each local jurisdiction. When local units rely on regional, state, or federal agencies, there may be no connective element to create strong linkages between jurisdictions.

A third model shows a regional agency with moderate control that empowers local jurisdictions through the initial planning stages, partnering with them to implement and coordinate efforts between jurisdictions. Five of the ten cities examined in this book use some form of this collaborative model. Unlike in the first two models, neither the regional coordinator nor the local jurisdictions have primary control over funding. In fact, in Model 3 the organizational home may be a private organization, such as Toronto's Waterfront Regeneration Trust or Denver's Greenways Foundation. For other types of open-lands connections, both the water district and the council of government are important regional partners.

The state government assumes the coordination role in the Twin Cities, where its greenway and natural corridors programs are deliberately structured to foster coordination with and across local units of government. The Greater Vancouver Regional District works with local governments; again, the implementing power lies primarily at the local level, but regional government helps coordinate. Chicago's Northeastern Illinois Planning Commission partners with nonprofit organizations to facilitate greenway projects that are actually implemented by dozens of jurisdictions, forest preserves, and park districts. In addition, Chicago Wilderness assists in coordinating the big interjurisdictional vision.

Model 3 allows power at the local level, where leadership and cooperation can develop among local jurisdictions, facilitating intergovernmental agreements to lead and manage open-space programs. At the same time, the regional agency can prioritize funding from the state or federal level across the entire project, offer planning assistance, and act as a central hub for the program. This model also lends itself to public–private partnerships, where the nonprofit sector can provide the coordinating function. However, two main pitfalls may occur. Coordination between jurisdictions may be difficult, and implementation may be slower with shared responsibility across agencies. Even with their disadvantages, the second and third models are more robust for the regional oversight they provide.

Regionalism: Comparisons Between Canada and the United States

Regions are defined in many ways; an entire regional science is concerned with those diverse meanings. For this book, urban regions have been considered in two main ways—as landscapes that have unifying geographical features (for instance, those united by a river system or lakeshore), and as political areas that are controlled by multiple local and/or regional governments. The case studies have addressed physical connections across the former and cooperation between the latter. There is much discussion today about regionalism as an approach to solving urban problems, including the debate about the "old regionalism" that promoted regional levels of government (as in Portland) versus the "new regionalism" that seeks intermunicipal and public–private partnerships instead.[4] The amalgamation of local governments in Toronto and Ottawa is old regionalism in an extreme form.[5]

Richard Forman's advice about regional planning is particularly appropriate in the arena of open-space planning: "'Think globally, act locally' is a phrase much in vogue. Yet it has two problems. First, few people will ever give primacy to the globe in decision-making. Second, local considerations overwhelmingly determine actions. Indeed, these are two roots of environmental and societal problems etched widely in the land . . . we better 'think globally, plan regionally, and then act locally'."[6]

Whereas government institutions for regional decision making are relatively easy to create in Canada, they are difficult to accomplish in an American context. Canadian metropolitan areas generally have more well-developed regional governance and planning systems than U.S. cities do. However, the evidence from the ten case studies in this book argues for regionalism in accomplishing open-space goals, not necessarily as a level of government, but as a way of conceptualizing issues. The regional programs of Chicago Wilderness, Toronto and Region Conservation Authority, or the Minnesota Department of Natural Resources, for instance, illustrate that a wide range of organizations or agencies can do regional work. The most common way to meet regional needs in U.S. cities has been to implement special districts, most of which perform single functions (sewer, transit, housing, schools, etc.). Some claim that four levels of directly elected government is one too many.

Canada's public services have been positively reviewed around the world. In general, Canadian cities are more densely developed, and have fewer freeways, more public transit, and more public involvement in urban development.[7] In the 1990s Canada ranked first in the United Nations Human Development Index, a measure of quality of life. Some argue that these qualities arise from a high level of decentralization between the federal and provincial governments.[8] Canadian provinces exert far more influence on municipal services and settlement

patterns than American states. The political presence of provincial governments in local policy has caused more robust metropolitan-planning institutions. In contrast, the tendency in
the United States is toward increasing political fragmentation.[9] Home rule, with its built-in
protections of local government, does not exist in Canada. The political, legal, and fiscal stand-
ing of U.S. local governments allows them to be more powerful and autonomous.[10]

Provincial control has been credited with enhancing regional identity for Canadian
cities. One example is Vancouver, where most natural resource lands are under provincial jurisdiction, creating a greater sense of regional significance and identity. In contrast,
Frances Frisken asserts that there are "few if any institutions in the United States with
authority to make legally binding policies for the physical and social development of such
regions. It has been more successful in Canada . . . largely because Canadian provincial
governments have been more willing than American state governments to exercise their
authority over municipal affairs in matters of region-wide importance."[11]

For the spatial planning necessary to create and protect open space, Canadian metropolitan regions have both advantages and drawbacks. Unified city regions, such as Calgary,
Toronto, and Ottawa, create wonderful opportunities for coordinated open-space visions
across large urban landscapes. Some of those opportunities are yet to be realized. On the
other hand, the same provincial mandates that created these large city-regions have not
always supported progressive actions for open-space protection and planning.

Key Ingredients

Grassroots support is the hallmark of the open-space movement. Physical implementation is accomplished through a combination of assets that includes not only grassroots
activism but also committed leadership, expansive objectives, broad citizen involvement,
and collaborative partnerships. Historic urban patterns also have immense potential,
where they are at least partly intact.

The Power of Leadership

The most important elements of success might be commitment and leadership, not
money. Interviewers spoke at length about long-term commitments made by individuals
and organizations. Leadership for open-space systems takes various forms which are
needed in different stages. Two main phases need persuasive and effective leadership. First
is the critical conceptual phase, when leaders are needed to inspire people about a vision
of what could be achieved. Second is the implementation phase, which requires political
savvy, diplomacy, dogged determination, and innovative instincts for getting things done.

The evidence from these U.S. and Canadian cities supports Robert Searns's assertions that, nearly without exception, the success of open-space programs hinges on the committed leadership of an individual or group of individuals who champion a visionary plan. Leaders can be politicians, citizens, business leaders, or even entire organizations. Searns cites the example of Joe Shoemaker championing the $20 million Platte River Greenway in Denver, which had a string of other open-space leaders, including mayors Bill McNichols, Federico Pena, and Wellington Webb.

The determination and motivation of a political leader is critical; local organizers need to bring in prominent political figures who will demonstrate support throughout the life of a project. Elected officials must back the vision of connectivity for their regions or it is unlikely that collaborations will occur. Oregon's governors Tom McCall and Robert Straub were early promoters of the greenway concept, and Portland's project grew out of that foresight.

Several case studies show that a mayor's belief in a specific project increases its chance for survival and ultimate success. David Crombie, former mayor of Toronto, for instance, was the visionary behind the Royal Commission on the Future of the Toronto Waterfront project and was extremely influential in its success. Similarly, County Board Chairman Phil Elfstrom was crucial to the implementation of the Fox River Project, one of Chicago's greenway successes. He made the project his personal concern and campaigned for it vigorously. Chicago Mayor Richard M. Daley has also led remarkable efforts toward public open space for his city. Daley's recognition of the limitations of individual bureaucracies and the transformative power of bigger thinking illustrates his leadership on behalf of a more complete public realm.

In some cities, particular organizations are providing remarkable leadership—for instance, EcoCity Cleveland, Openlands Project in Chicago, and Waterfront Regeneration Trust in Toronto. The slogan for Chicago's Openlands Project is revealing: "Building Green Leaders, Supporting Green Spaces." Openlands has been a leader itself; more importantly, however, it aims to foster leadership for greenspaces within local areas that need them, and then back away. Similarly in Denver, the South Suburban Parks Foundation, working with former mayor Mary Carter from Littleton, led the effort for the Mary Carter Greenway, a part of the South Platte River greenway system.

Milwaukee and Ottawa have suffered from a paucity of influential leaders and advocates for connected greenway systems. In Milwaukee, former mayor John Norquist was a vocal supporter of the Hank Aaron State Trail, helping secure state funding appropriations. However, Milwaukee, unlike some other North American cities, currently has no powerful leader to advance the greenways vision. Some interviewees mentioned the local nonprofit sector's lack of maturity as a hindrance to a broader greenways vision in Milwaukee. Similarly, few influential greenway advocates and leaders in Ottawa are pushing a comprehensive regional vision. Although the greenbelt and parkways have their champions, any unified collaborative effort will need powerful leadership to pull together the disparate pieces as the new, larger city organizes.

Collaboration and Citizen Involvement

Rarely, if ever, is the initiator of an open-space project its sole implementer. In order to realize projects of metropolitan size and complexity, a number of partnerships are inevitable and necessary at subsequent stages. Nurturing these coalitions is sometimes difficult, but always imperative. Public–private partnerships are essential in many realms of civic life. Open-space planning is no exception. Especially as the positive economic impacts of open-space protection and development become clear, the private sector tends to cooperate and participate in greenway developments. A consistent theme among the professionals interviewed for this book was that the future is in working more closely with the development industry, with the corporate world, and with the private philanthropic community.

For each city examined in this book, the list of project cooperators is long and complex. It includes school boards, business groups, and birdwatchers. Some participants are active only in certain phases of the project; others are stable throughout a project's evolution. Participation also varies in its intensity and directness. A survey of participants from all member organizations of Chicago Wilderness showed that participation in collaborative activities, even if passive, leads to adoption of ecosystem management goals.[12]

Collaborations with scientists are increasing. The objective facts about open-space quality are compelling, but science alone is insufficient for accomplishing sound open-space systems: rather, subjective human needs, preferences, and perceptions are often decisive. Even scientists who promote connected corridors for their biological value realize this. Reed Noss has claimed that biologists often disregard the anthropocentric functions of open space in urban landscapes, ignoring the quality-of-life factors that help protect important resources. He observes that "scenery, recreation, pollution abatement, and land value enhancement are what usually motivate planners to draw corridors into their designs ... And many of these corridors are being drawn. It would be auspicious for biologists and planners to work together to develop corridor designs that can optimize the quality of both the human and the nonhuman environment."[13]

Partnerships across organizations and agencies are only part of the collaboration story. There is a difference between working with nonprofit advocacy groups and other organized citizens groups on the one hand and actively soliciting the public's opinions on the other. Involving individual citizens is critical. The ten cities studied here all have some level of citizen involvement for open-space planning, although the extent and nature of public participation vary. Ideally, these civic conversations lead to shared understanding about each other's political positions, environmental preferences, and economic constraints.[14] Many American metropolitan areas have benefited from the National Park Service's Rivers, Trails, and Conservation Assistance process for public involvement.

In some locales, no formal process for public participation exists at the regional level, such as in the Cleveland region. A loose grassroots network exists but is not focused on promoting a regionwide system. Portland's Metropolitan Greenspaces program has embraced organized citizen's involvement as part of its process from the beginning, as mandated by state law. Public involvement and education were particularly critical in the ultimate approval of the bond measure funding open-space acquisition.

Education generates public commitment and helps minimize reactionary opposition. Several of the cities we studied rely heavily on education as a means of getting people involved and ultimately getting projects accepted and funded. Education about biodiversity and urban ecology is a central focus for Chicago Wilderness. But education implies a one-way flow of information, whereas true collaboration with the public is much more. Vancouver's neighborhood greenways are wonderful examples, as are a number of greenway projects in the Denver region.

Building on Historic Frameworks

Many cities possess a legacy of open, public land that forms the foundation for contemporary visions. This historic element is visible for nearly all of the ten cases used here; capitalizing on it is one important key to success. The aesthetic principles of the City Beautiful movement laid formative patterns for one group of cities: Chicago, Denver, Milwaukee, and Vancouver. Several case study cities benefited from the park and parkway images imprinted by Frederick Law Olmsted, his students, and his heirs. That image was heavily weighted toward connected natural landscapes, particularly focusing on water resources. This was especially true for all of the U.S. cases studied here. In some cases, extant systems can be traced to those legacies—Metroparks in Cleveland and the Grand Rounds in Minneapolis. In others, the Olmsted vision is now being revived and completed—Portland's 40-Mile Loop and Denver's Platte River Greenway. Some cities are struggling to capitalize on those early frameworks. Milwaukee and Ottawa, for instance, have the out-lines for exceptional connected parkway networks, anchored by extensive river corridors in both cities. In addition, both cities have in place agencies and programs that value con-nected open space. However, a strong, coordinated regional open-space program has not emerged in either city. Both places are ripe for one.

Juggling Multiple Objectives

Systems are regularly interacting or interdependent groups of items that form a unified whole. In cities, interacting corridors of open land are bound to have diverse character-istics and functions. Corridors can emphasize a range of priorities—from recreation to transportation to community enrichment. Open land is expected to provide many other benefits, such as environmental education, neighborhood enhancement, or water qual-ity protection. The unifying purpose, overlaying a range of other objectives, should be eco-logical benefit. The new frontier for urban open-space planning lies in complex, multiob-jective projects that simultaneously deliver sound environmental benefits with other human needs.

In the cases we studied, integration was a prominent theme exhibited in two main ways—socially and ecologically. Many of the most exciting greenway efforts have a socially responsive purpose. Some provide disadvantaged populations with neighborhood revital-ization, employment opportunities, educational programs, and urban youth involvement. The efforts of Hennepin Community Works in the Minneapolis region are useful exam-ples of this approach. For most places, economic development has not been the central factor that motivates open-space planning at the outset. However, this is changing as the protection of public land creates predictable economic effects on surrounding private land. The multiple objectives of land-use planning and growth management are increasingly important stimuli for open-space protection.

Ecological thinking for open-space planning is often tied to water. Since most cities are situated on rivers or shorelines, the relationship of these resources to open-space planning has wide relevance. Water is the unifying force for open-lands protection across the conti-nent: abundant poll data show that citizens are concerned about water quality above most other environmental issues. Many open-space programs have focused closely on water-man-agement objectives, including the protection of stream corridors and planning for water-sheds. In Toronto, for instance, watersheds and bioregions have motivated the greenways vision. In the past decade, awareness of urban watersheds has grown (via stormwater man-agement plans), but this awareness is not often tied to smaller-scale greenway plans.

One strategy is to develop projects that create multiple public benefits. This goal has been pursued by Openlands Project in Chicago, where projects simultaneously feature water trails, land-based trails, and habitat corridors along streams, demonstrating compatibility objectives. A related strategy is to focus on the resource. Several case studies show that relational, rather than hierarchical, projects connected to a particular geographic feature (as opposed to hierarchical projects tied to political goals) often have more dynamic outcomes. They connect strongly to a particular geographical feature rather than to the political hierarchy that oversees it. Toronto's focus on the Lake Ontario waterfront or the Oak Ridges Moraine is an example. Working together for those physical places, with an emphasis on the myriad of human and environmental objectives, is more powerful than focusing on levels of bureaucracy.

Another important strategy for a multiobjective approach is to address complementary policies and incentives in the areas of transportation, neighborhood revitalization, and biodiversity protection, among others. For instance, one Chicago regional transportation plan focuses clearly on bicycle travel, with direct consequences for the development of nonmotorized greenway routes.

Finally, as communities address multiple objectives, whole new contexts, definitions, and meanings of open space are emerging. In Calgary, the exemplary path system is the nexus of open-space connectivity. In Vancouver, the redefinition of streets as important public open space connects directly to new objectives and broader thinking about infrastructure. Cleveland's focus is on a once-industrial river corridor, where beautiful and functional open-space land shadows not only the Cuyahoga River but also heavy industry and massive public utilities.

Challenges

It is useful to ponder why public ideas are so difficult to implement. From her experience with the Vancouver greenway project, landscape architect Moura Quayle summarized a number of roadblocks to getting things done. They include a culture of conformity and compliance, the political and bureaucratic fear of change and the unknown, a lack of a sustainable vision for the city, and visual, social, and ecological illiteracy.[15] These attitudinal barriers intertwine with pragmatic problems, including the need for funding, the difficulty of interjurisdictional cooperation, the unpredictability of policy and regulation, the puzzle of working at multiple scales, and the complexities of ownership and management. Even with these considerable challenges, hundreds of open-space advocates regularly achieve the impossible, sometimes because they just don't realize how impossible it is.

Funding: Critical, but Seldom the Main Obstacle

Funding is always a challenge, although not necessarily the primary one. Although every advocate yearns for money to accomplish more open-space work, more funding does not necessarily ensure a regional system's successful coordination. It is unwise to worry about funding too soon. Rather, it is better to make a plan, then step around the tougher, cost-lier areas and implement the easy parts first. Across the United States, communities are taxing themselves to protect open space. These measures consistently follow good plans that spell out the vision, principles, and criteria for open-lands protection. Open-space funding is more reliable where programs transcend partisan politics.

This study did not focus explicitly on means for funding open-space systems, but the research suggests that diverse funding sources are preferable to single sources and that money follows good ideas. There are many models for funding open-space projects, tied directly to the techniques used in open-lands protection. For instance, in the most val-ued districts, with rich combinations of natural, scenic, or historic resources, land acqui-sitions may make the most sense. In new developments, requiring open-space dedications through impact fees or other means may be useful. And in older, poorer suburbs open space may accompany redevelopment schemes. The funding needs and sources for fee-simple acquisition are different from those for obtaining conservation easements or imple-menting land trades. For each project, a comprehensive implementation plan should spell out those techniques and the types of funds that can support them.

Some sources have consistently funded U.S. projects, such as federal transportation monies for nonmotorized transportation. However, those funds are not necessarily *the* answer to successful implementation. In financing connected open space, all available financial partnerships need to be considered, and the more diverse the sources of funding, the better. This is especially true in light of the multiple objectives described earlier. As the goals being achieved broaden, so will the sources of both public and private funds. For instance, Seattle's new open-space plan will be implemented with funding from a variety of sources—rights-of-way already required of developers, the city's capital improvement budget, neighborhood matching funds, percent-for-art monies, and reapplication of budg-ets for standard street improvements.[16]

Canadian cities receive far less funding from the federal government and are subject to fewer federal regulations than their American counterparts, partly because of the political decentralization described earlier. Even so, the federal government can be a powerful shaper of urban form and can fund remarkable projects. The impact of the National Capital Commission in Ottawa is one example.

Most open-space programs use state / provincial and local funds. Two cities, Minneapolis and Portland, have regional government agencies that fund land acquisition. Foundations also play a critical role. Several foundations have supported greenway programs in these cities. In addition, other nongovernmental organizations play key roles in funding and real estate transactions, as when the Trust for Public Land or The Nature Conservancy facilitate land purchases.

Municipal budgeting approaches may be as important as funding sources. William Morrish, formerly at the Metropolitan Design Center, critiqued the way greenways are funded under cities' capital budgets. According to Morrish, greenways are capital improvements that should be funded as a row instead of a column, cutting across spatial and social issues in metropolitan financing, planning, and decision making—from neighborhood revitalization, to connectivity, security, development, or transportation. This method encourages a less provincial and more integrative approach, both in funding and in initial planning. It also creates the ability to address green infrastructure thinking in the context of roads, sewers, and other utilities. Another vital approach is to use limited local funding to leverage other public and private funding. Nearly every project uses such funding matches to piece together what is needed.

The Difficulty of Cooperation and Shifting Policy Environments

Regardless of the institutional structure or the size of the open-space vision, lack of coordination across agencies, cities, and organizations seems to be one of the biggest impediments to effective implementation. In many cases, simply getting different departments and personnel within the same city or county to work together is an enormous challenge. Unfortunately, coordination is hindered by separate agencies and departments dealing with their own fragment of the overall open-space system. The transportation department deals with road rights-of-way, the recreation department manages parks, and the housing authority plans vacant lots. An anecdote from one city helps illustrate this phenomenon: plans were being presented by two different departments at a city hearing on the same day, neither aware of the other. One plan was for stormwater retention and the other was for a greenway; both dealt with the same geographic area. Although these groups obviously had mutually beneficial concerns, they were not communicating or working in a unified way.

This phenomenon highlights two observations from the ten case studies. First, private sector involvement often helps cut through agency myopia. Nonprofit organizations or citizens groups can be the necessary liaison between agencies or municipalities. Second, the level of cooperation varies. Sometimes cooperation at the level of individual professionals is excellent but it is not matched by larger-scale collaboration in their respective agencies or organizations. Deliberate cooperation is obviously possible for individuals or small groups working together, but far more challenging at higher levels.

Interjurisdictional cooperation is even more challenging. Where there is lack of regional coordination, few incentives exist to plan across boundaries. In fact, there may be perverse incentives that create competitive rather than cooperative approaches across city or county lines. In many of the case studies examined here, a spirit of collaboration across jurisdictions seems to be increasing rapidly. The benefits of a more regional approach to many issues, including open space, are gaining speed. The Denver region is a good example, where suburban municipalities in several regions have collaborated for greenway corridors that link to the entire regional system.

Shifting policy and regulatory environments exacerbate coordination problems. For instance, in the Twin Cities region, state leadership has stimulated a regional vision for wildlife corridors and greenways, but diminished budget allocations from the state legislature have created ambiguity about the importance of the program. In addition, the political climate in individual jurisdictions can either help or hinder the adoption of a larger regional vision. For some metropolitan areas, the adoption of a greenway or open-space plan at local levels of government is an important step. In other cases the plan serves as a regional guideline or framework without any formal adoption. In Chicago, the Northeastern Illinois Planning Commission is an advisory planning agency, but when local jurisdictions adopt its plans, they are making policy decisions.

Working at Multiple, Interacting Scales

For maximum effectiveness, open-space networks need to be planned and created simultaneously at a range of scales, from the large metropolitan level down to individual towns and cities. At an even finer grain, work is done at the scale of particular features like a creek corridor. Important connections are sometimes only several yards long. The complexity of these multiple, interacting scales is an inherent challenge and seldom leads to a logical or orderly progression of work. The regional vision or plan is clearly advantageous. It can depict how open lands of different types fit together, especially as different types of corridors achieve different objectives. For instance, it can show how the network achieves water-quality goals through diverse types of landscapes. It gives credibility and a logical context to smaller projects that fit into it, showing step-by-step progress and where it will lead. This can help justify funding and other resources that might otherwise not be available in a more piecemeal approach.

In many places, the lack of a regional structure seems to be an enormous barrier. The large size of metropolitan open-space systems taxes public awareness and understanding. By and large, the general public has trouble visualizing an abstract land-use or geographic idea at a metropolitan scale without the deliberate outline that a regional plan can provide. Without it, greenway networks are more difficult and must rely on piecing together small projects without an overall roadmap. Breaking projects down into manageable and perceptible pieces helps. Defining specific corridors or local resources can help people commit themselves to a bigger vision. Several of the ten cities have done just that: Portland identified fourteen target natural areas and six trails and greenway projects in order to provide citizens an opportunity to see potential investments; Toronto planners divided the waterfront into fourteen landscape units. Identifying greenway priorities at the local level is a logical follow-up. For instance, some planners have found that helping local jurisdictions develop feeder trails is the key to getting them interested in regional trail systems.

The Rubber Meets the Road: Ownership and Management
Open-space systems usually traverse lands with diverse public and private owners. Creating a system across that mosaic is daunting, particularly where some lands are accessible to the public and others are not. When land converts to public ownership, long-term management must be worked out with the appropriate governmental, or even nongovernmental, entity. The devil is in these practical details, which range from public safety to facility maintenance to weed management. In Portland, for example, the twenty regional parks and trails acquired by Metro through Portland Greenspaces are not always managed by Metro, but by local jurisdictions or nongovernment organizations.

Open-space corridors do not always include trails, but when they do, controversy and resistance are likely. Apparently Robert Speer, the great visionary of Denver's parkway system, encountered vocal and bitter criticism for his trail proposals along the South Platte River.[17] Trails are particularly contentious. As one interviewee put it, trails represent "lines on a map that can cause people to freak out." Rural residents are often opposed to urban people using trails in their areas because they fear crime and other negative effects. A similar trend was seen across all cases: some level of opposition about public open-space acquisition, but remarkable acceptance once projects were in place and people could see positive results. Early public involvement and education are important for trails projects. Also critical are persistence and the ability to compromise.

In some cases, opposing factions are not necessarily against the idea of a greenway but they want money appropriated differently. There is often tension about public versus private ownership, which can lead to opposition. Concerns about taking land off the tax rolls are common, although they can sometimes be offset by increased property values near new public acquisitions. But increased taxes for those lands can be a burden for nearby landowners, so fiscal impacts need to be weighed and analyzed carefully.

Strategic Approaches

Creating a system of open-space land for a metropolitan region is never complete. The effort is constantly evolving as landscapes change, populations grow, and human needs vary. In fact, keeping important lands open and connected provides the flexibility for changing needs, whereas paved developed uses do not. By definition, open-space work is an adaptive process that, even with the best leadership, organizational structure, and appropriate goals, requires strategic approaches to assure evolutionary success.

Pursue Green Infrastructure

One billion dollars in infrastructure costs (water, sewer, roads) will be needed in Calgary over the next ten years to support the current rate of population growth.[18] This high cost may provide the catalyst for embracing green infrastructure, which considers energy, water, sewage, soil, habitat, food production, and biodiversity in new ways. Canada has the highest per capita energy use of any nation in the world, not only because of the cold climate but also because of the way development spreads across the landscape.[19] In Calgary and many other cities, green infrastructure needs to be on the agenda as a proven and practical public benefit.

On the scale of urban regions, green infrastructure is an abstract concept. Planners cannot afford to be vague about the benefits and costs of this new way of spatial thinking. With designers, they need to show the visible form that green infrastructure will take. In addition, new financial, technical, and management resources are needed. For successful green infrastructure approaches, far more expertise and exposure is required from the typical engineering firm. Educating engineers, particularly those doing various types of public work, is imperative for moving the green infrastructure idea from a niche solution to a mainstream one. Currently, much gets left to environmental advocacy groups rather than being institutionalized within executive boardrooms and decision-making teams.

Map What You Have; Show What You Want

The value of an overall vision, and its accompanying illustrations, cannot be overstated in open-space planning. Regional open-space plans are instrumental in Vancouver, Portland, and Chicago, for instance. They are spatially explicit in depicting protected hubs and connecting corridors. On the other hand, the overall metropolitan vision does not necessarily need to depict every small corridor: in Vancouver, neighborhood greenways are undefined since they are motivated by residents' interest and commitment. Flexible boundaries, rather than hard ones, can be valuable.[20]

Some cities have found that the inventory of existing open land not only reveals important information about landscape structure and change, but is also a persuasive tool that helps generate resources for open-space protection. This step was critical for the Portland region, where the entire region was flown with low-altitude color infrared photography in the late 1980s. The subsequent data were digitized and used in a geographic information system to show Metro the location of remaining greenspaces for the entire region. This mapping project created the first true image of the remaining natural areas and proved to be an incredibly important step that eventually led to Metro's Greenspaces Program.

The other aspect typically lacking in metropolitan open-space plans is a comprehensive categorization of the diverse types of open spaces remaining and proposed, showing not only remaining natural areas but also agricultural land, private open space, and other categories. As Chapter 1 showed, open space can be classified in a variety of ways. Too little attention has been paid to the classification of forms. Typologies can be used to match open-space types with diverse objectives.

One example is the way European greenspace planners are identifying layers according to their origins. The pre-urban layer focuses on natural features—woodlands, wetlands, streams, and floodplains that influence city development. The urban greenspace layer includes public parks, cemeteries, and playing fields. The third layer is the post-industrial layer of brownfield sites, landfills, and unused industrial lands. This typology is meant to fill a perceived gap in strategic approaches for coherent open spaces that provide ecological integrity. Stephen Pauleit recommends mapping the different layers of green structure and their functions, defining the city and regional programs that affect open space, and determining the urban development projects that could incorporate green structure planning.[21] One challenge for comprehensive assessments at the landscape scale is the awkward gap between the science of landscape ecology and spatial planning. Many theoretical ecological studies do not transfer results in the context of landscape patterns.[22]

This study did not ask how much open space is needed and how it should be configured for metropolitan areas. Any purportedly ideal shape, size, or pattern is suspect anyway, since each city region has unique circumstances. Nevertheless, some common requirements and guidelines are useful by way of comparison.

Few cities are deliberately designing the way farmland and urban land coincide. Christopher Alexander and his colleagues recommended urban fingers less than a mile wide and farmland more than a mile wide.[23] They also advocated that neighborhoods be separated by swaths of land at least 200 feet wide, with natural or human-made boundaries. A borderland open-space corridor could fit the bill quite nicely in many areas. At smaller scales, open-space corridors and their hubs are defined by building shape, density, height, and design. So it is difficult to design the negative (open) space in isolation from the design of the positive (built) space. Much has been written about the shaping of space at this level. Alexander et al. also advocate many small parks—or greens—scattered widely and profusely in the city, connected by accessible pedestrian routes and about five minutes from each resident. Vancouver has successfully implemented these mini-parks in its most densely populated neighborhoods. Again, plotting the pattern of these types of open-space amenities is instructive for evaluating the urban landscape.

Build on Small Successes

The "big bang" approach for implementing protected open space is seldom effective or even possible in most metropolitan areas. Rather, a number of cities have deliberately used the strategy of taking small steps, building support, demonstrating successes, and then tackling more. In Denver, planners have described a "virus" approach to greenway implementation. Basically, one thing led to another. One municipality tried a greenway corridor, the idea caught on, and then other municipalities completed projects and connected to their neighbors. Moura Quayle has described the Vancouver process as "the need for poking and prodding, nudging and needling until the ideas are implemented." One example is Vancouver's neighborhood greenway program, in which small demonstration projects can be completed in partnership with the community. In some cases, a neighborhood that completed one of these connections is then asked to advise other neighborhoods considering a similar project. In this organic fashion, ideas spread and successes multiply. This approach helps people feel more comfortable with new ideas and is perhaps the most authentic way to apply human ecology principles.

For this incremental approach to be successful, several factors must be in place. First, keeping the bigger picture in mind while undertaking small projects is important. Second, it is necessary to demonstrate accomplishments with solid facts. Accountability is crucial. Several of the ten cities have completed accessible report cards for their open-space programs, showing how monies are spent and comparing completed projects to the long-range vision. The status of corridor work can be a moving target, especially in large metropolitan regions, so periodic inventories are critical. This tracking takes time and money; some cities studied here were steadily completing open-space projects, but an overall accounting of acreages or mileage was hard to come by.

Finally, it is clear that some projects, due to their scope and complexity, need vast amounts of planning, capital investments, and specialized construction. The small demonstration project is sometimes infeasible. Vancouver's citywide greenways provide one example; Cleveland's Heritage Corridor is another. However, even for those, small segments can sometimes demonstrate the type of landscape that will eventually materialize. These smaller experiments, which help break down the overall project, can build support and even demand within the community.

Integrate Open Space with Growth Management

The planning of urban growth and open space has long been polarized. Open-space planners are concerned with pulling away from the bulldozer, whereas urban growth pushes toward it. The former is perceived as a reactive, passive activity, centered on negative, open space, while the latter is proactive, focused on positive, closed space. In tone and purpose, open-space planning leans toward the environment. Efforts to preserve open space provided a critical phase in the modern environmental movement, beginning after World War II with attempts to mitigate the problems of rampant development patterns.[24] For contemporary metropolitan areas, the link between open-space planning and new development is critical, as cities like Calgary, Denver, Minneapolis–St. Paul, Toronto, and Portland experience rapid and, in some cases, uncontrolled growth.

Open-space planning and growth-management strategies are linked in two primary ways—physical and fiscal. For instance, the recent smart growth movement is inherently interested in the relationship of spatial form and community investment. Smart growth demands careful attention to the location, pattern, and density of urban growth and the costs associated with those decisions.[25] Moreover, it asks deliberate questions about where *not* to build—questions characterizing the interface of smart growth and open-space planning. Open-space planning, in its many dimensions and definitions, concerns itself with the spatial layout of undeveloped land and the environmental, social, and economic impacts of that layout.

Even before the upsurge in activity around open-space protection over the last decade, the conceptual link between open space and growth management was strong. Long before the contemporary smart growth movement began, the planning literature advocated that open-space networks provide the organizing structure for development. William Whyte argued passionately for open-space protection but, unlike Ian McHarg, based his argument primarily on experiential rather than ecological grounds.[26] Lewis Mumford claimed that there are two ways to structure an urban area and to create connections within it: through its streets and other transportation, and through its open spaces—parks, plazas, and waterfronts.[27] Smart growth takes that idea and extends it out into the urban fringes, where transportation patterns have long shaped the suburbs and exurbs but open-space patterns typically have not.

Despite the promotion of open space as a structuring frame for development, open-space planning has often been a reactive activity at worst and a narrow one at best, focused on providing parks in sufficient acreages per capita. Rarely have vigorous open-space patterns been used in a holistic way to shape growth on a regional scale, despite planners' advocacy. For the exurban edges of cities, open space is still part of an underlying natural structure that changes slowly, and which could be tightly controlled relative to the more ephemeral layers overlain on it. According to the logic of this view, planning should intervene at this early stage, before other layers—buildings, roads—are added. Planning should also help control the form and rate of change of the basic open-space system. Instead, we often try to add open space as an object after the other phases.[28]

Few local governments are disciplined in preventing sprawl. While traditional approaches have restored and protected many stream valleys, open space is often considered a residual effect of development patterns. A Brookings Institution study found that the impact of open-space programs on shaping metropolitan growth is not well understood, even though many efforts to protect open space seek to save certain lands from development or redirect growth away from sensitive areas. It also found that open-space protection is usually not well coordinated with other policies that shape growth.[29]

Smart-growth advocates have outlined a broad set of goals for more efficient and humane growth, of which open-space preservation is one. The loss of open land—sometimes farmed, sometimes natural—has been one of the troubling effects of sprawl and uncontrolled growth. This appeal for open space stands beside, and sometimes overlaps with, other smart-growth objectives—for instance, farmland preservation, walkable neighborhoods, infrastructure efficiencies, natural area protection, brownfield redevelopment, and community cohesion.

The U.S. states have been particularly active in planning and funding both smart-growth and open-space programs. According to the American Planning Association, between 1999 and 2001 eight states issued task force reports on smart growth and twenty-seven governors made specific smart-growth proposals in 2001 alone. Part of the success of smart-growth programs is related to the link between planning reform and quality-of-life issues like open-space protection. Despite these efforts, or even because of them, a good deal of ambiguity and confusion still surrounds open-space planning as a distinct activity within the broader smart-growth agenda.

Strategies for connecting open space to growth management should consider several settings. Over the last twenty years open-space protection has motivated innovative development designs at the subdivision scale, primarily in conservation subdivisions and cluster developments. We have made good progress at this scale. But shaping intact metropolitan open-space systems on the larger scales at which smart-growth programs often operate is rare. In addition, we need connectivity in new settings, particularly between, not just within, new developments. The greenway movement has rightly been focused on river valleys. In some areas, though, it is now time to head uphill, to connect upland areas to the stellar corridors that have been created at the water's edge.

Perhaps the green infrastructure concept is one key to implementing the long-sought-after connection between open space and growth management. Maybe, like smart growth, it will catch the attention of the public, civic leaders, and open-space advocates. Although green infrastructure is a relatively new concept, it is surprising how closely its basic tenets have been espoused before, both in North America and elsewhere. As Ian McHarg wrote in 1970: "A structure for metropolitan growth can be combined with a network of open spaces that not only protects natural resources but also is of inestimable value for amenity and recreation."[30] Now, as then, we need a vision of a green network people can embrace as a smart, cost-effective approach for the metropolitan landscape.

Bibliography

Ahern, Jack. 1991. "Planning for an Extensive Open Space System: Linking Landscape Structure and Function." *Landscape and Urban Planning* 21(1–2): 131–145.

———. 1995. "Greenways as a Planning Strategy." *Landscape and Urban Planning* 33: 131–155.

———. 2002. *Greenways as Strategic Landscape Planning: Theory and Application.* Wageningen University, The Netherlands.

Alexander, Christopher, Sara Ishikawa, and Murray Silverstein. 1977. *A Pattern Language: Towns, Buildings, Construction.* Oxford, UK: Oxford University Press.

Arendt, Randall. 1999. *Growing Greener: Putting Conservation into Local Plans and Ordinances.* Washington, DC: Island Press.

Austin, Maureen, and Rachel Kaplan. 2003. "Resident Involvement in Natural Resource Management: Open Space Conservation Design in Practice." *Local Environment* 8(2): 141–153.

Bachrach, Julia Sniderman. 2001. *City in a Garden: A Photographic History of Chicago's Parks.* Staunton, VA: Center for American Places.

Bartholomew, Harland and Associates. 1928. *A Plan for the City of Vancouver, British Columbia, Including a General Plan of the Region.* St. Louis, MO: Harland Bartholomew and Associates.

Beatley, Timothy, and Kristy Manning. 1997. *The Ecology of Place: Planning for Environment, Economy, and Community.* Washington, DC: Island Press.

Beer, Anne R. 2000. "Aspects of the Link Between Urban Nature and City Planning in Northern European Countries." Paper presented at the Workshop on the Flemish Long-Term Vision of Nature in Urban and Suburban Areas. Brussels, Belgium.

Beer, Anne R., Tim Delshammar, and Peter Schildwacht. 2003. "A Changing Understanding of the Role of Greenspace in High-Density Housing: A European Perspective." *Built Environment* 29(2): 132–143.

Benedict, Mark, and Ed McMahon. 2002. "Green Infrastructure: Smart Conservation for the 21st Century." *Natural Resources Journal* 20(3): 12–17.

Botequilha Leitão, André, and Jack Ahern. 2002. "Applying Landscape Ecological Concepts and Metrics in Sustainable Landscape Planning." *Landscape and Urban Planning* 59(2): 65–93.

Bourne, Larry S. 1989. "Are New Urban Forms Emerging? Empirical Tests for Canadian Urban Areas?" *The Canadian Geographer* 33(4): 312–328.

Briffett, Clive. 2001. "Is Managed Recreational Use Compatible with Effective Habitat and Wildlife Occurrence in Urban Open Space Corridor Systems?" *Landscape Research* 26(2): 137–163.

Bryant, Rebecca. 1998. "Bigger Is Better." *Urban Land* 57(7): 60–62, 85–87.

Burch, William R., Jr. 1988. "Human Ecology and Environmental Management." In J. K. Agee and D. R. Johnson, eds., *Ecosystem Management for Parks and Wilderness*. Seattle: University of Washington Press.

Calthorpe, Peter, and William Fulton. 2001. *The Regional City: Planning for the End of Sprawl*. Washington, DC: Island Press.

Carr, Deborah S., and Daniel R. Williams. 1993. "Understanding the Role of Ethnicity in Outdoor Recreation Experience." *Journal of Leisure Research* 25(1): 22–38.

Catton, William R., Jr. 1994. "Foundations of Human Ecology." *Sociological Perspectives* 37(1): 75–95.

Chiesura, Anna. 2004. "The Role of Urban Parks in the Sustainable City." *Landscape and Urban Planning* 68(4): 129–138.

Cohn, Jeffrey P., and Jeffrey A. Lerner. 2003. "Integrating Land Use Planning and Biodiversity." Report, Defenders of Wildlife.

Cook, Edward A., and Hubert N. Van Lier, eds. 2000. *Landscape Planning and Ecological Networks*, Vol 6F in series *Developments in Landscape Management and Urban Planning*. Amsterdam: Elsevier.

Cook, Edward A. 2000. *Ecological Networks in Urban Landscapes*. Wageningen University, The Netherlands.

Cranz, Galen. 1989. *The Politics of Park Design: A History of Urban Parks in America*. Cambridge, MA: The MIT Press.

Cullingworth, J. B., and V. Nadin. 1997. *Town and Country Planning in the U.K.* New York: Routledge.

Cutler, Phoebe. 1985. *The Public Landscape of the New Deal*. New Haven: Yale University Press.

Davis, Timothy, Todd A. Croteau, and Christopher H. Marston. 1985. *America's National Park Roads and Parkways: Drawings from the Historic American Engineering Record*. Baltimore: Johns Hopkins University Press.

Diamond, Jared M., John Terborgh, Robert F. Whitcomb, James F. Lynch, Paul A. Opler, Chandler S. Robbins, Daniel S. Simberloff, and Lawrence G. Abele. 1976. "Island Biogeography and Conservation: Strategy and Limitations." *Science* 193: 1027–1032.

Dramstad, Wenche E., James D. Olson, and Richard T. T. Forman. 1996. *Landscape Ecology Principles in Landscape Architecture and Land-Use Planning.* Washington, DC: Island Press.

Eggleston, Wilfrid. 1961. *The Queen's Choice.* Ottawa: The National Capital Commission.

Enlow, Claire. 2002. "Streets as Parks: In Seattle, Open Space Is Where You Find It." *Planning* 68(5): 16–17.

Erickson, Donna. 2004. "Green Infrastructure: The Interplay of Historic City Form and Contemporary Greenway Implementation in Two North American Cities." *Landscape and Urban Planning* 68(2–3): 199–221.

———. 2004. "Connecting Lines Across the Landscape: Implementing Metropolitan Greenway Networks in North America." In Rob H. G. Jongman and Gloria Pungetti, eds., *Ecological Networks and Greenways: New Paradigms for Ecological Planning.* Cambridge, UK: Cambridge University Press.

Erickson, Donna, and Anneke Louisse. 1997. "Greenway implementation in metropolitan regions: A comparative case study of North American examples." National Park Service Rivers, Trails, and Conservation Assistance Program and Rails-to-Trails Conservancy.

Fabos, Julius G., and Jack Ahern. 1996. *Greenways: The Beginning of an International Movement.* Amsterdam: Elsevier.

Fleury, A. M., and R. D. Brown. 1997. "A Framework for the Design of Wildlife Conservation Corridors." *Landscape and Urban Planning* 37(3–4): 163–186.

Flink, Charles, and Robert M. Searns. 1993. *Greenways: A Guide to Planning, Design and Development.* Washington, DC: Island Press.

Flores, Alejandro, Steward T. A. Pickett, Wayne C. Zipperer, Richard V. Pouyat, and Robert Pirani. 1998. "Adopting a Modern Ecological View of the Metropolitan Landscape: The Case of a Greenspace System for the New York City Region." *Landscape and Urban Planning* 39(4): 295–308.

Florida, Richard. 2002. *The Rise of the Creative Class.* New York: Basic Books.

Forman, Richard T. T. 1995. *Land Mosaics: The Ecology of Landscapes and Regions.* Cambridge, England: Cambridge University Press.

———. 2003. *Road Ecology: Science and Solutions.* Washington, DC: Island Press.

Forman, Richard T. T., and Michel Godron. 1986. *Landscape Ecology.* New York: John Wiley & Sons.

Francis, Mark. 1998. "A Case Study Method for Landscape Architecture." Final report to the Landscape Architecture Foundation, Washington, DC.

Frisken, Frances, and Donald F. Norris. 2001. "Regionalism Reconsidered." *Journal of Urban Affairs* 23(5): 467–478.

Garber, Judith A., and David L. Imbroscio. 1996. "'The Myth of the American City' Reconsidered: Local Constitutional Regimes in Canada and the United States." *Urban Affairs Review* 31: 595–624.

Garvin, Alexander, and Gayle Berens. 1997. *Urban Parks and Open Space.* Washington, DC: Urban Land Institute.

Garvin, Alexander. 2002. *The American City: What Works, What Doesn't.* New York: McGraw-Hill.

Girling, Cynthia L., and Kenneth I. Helphand. 1994. *Yard–Street–Park: The Design of Suburban Open Space.* New York: John Wiley & Sons, Inc.

Gobster, Paul. 1995. "Perception and Use of a Metropolitan Greenway System for Recreation." *Landscape and Urban Planning* 33(1–3): 401–413.

———. 2001. "Neighborhood-Open Space Relationships in Metropolitan Planning: A Look Across Four Scales of Concern." *Local Environment* 33(2): 199–212.

Goode, D. A. 1989. "Urban Nature Conservation in Britain." *Journal of Applied Ecology* 26(3): 859–873.

Gurda, John. 1999. *The Making of Milwaukee.* Brookfield, WI: Burton & Mayer, Inc.

Gutzwiller, Kevin, ed. 2002. *Applying Landscape Ecology in Biological Conservation.* New York: Springer.

Harnik, Peter, and Jeff Simms. 2004. "Parks—How Far Is Too Far?" *Planning* 70(11): 8.

Harrison, Carolyn, and Jacquelin Burgess. 1988. "Qualitative Research and Open Space Policy," *The Planner* (November): 16–18.

Henry, A. C., Jr., D. A. Hosack, C. W. Johnson, D. Rol, and G. Bentrup. 1994. "Conservation Corridors in the United States: Benefits and Planning Guidelines." *Journal of Soil and Water Conservation* 54(4): 645–650.

Hill, Libby. 2000. *The Chicago River: A Natural and Unnatural History.* Chicago: Lake Claremont Press.

Hiss, Tony. 1990. *The Experience of Place.* New York: Alfred A. Knopf.

Hollis, Linda E., and William Fulton. 2002. "Open Space Protection: Conservation Meets Growth Management." Discussion paper for The Brookings Institution Center on Urban and Metropolitan Policy.

Homer-Dixon, Thomas. 2000. *The Ingenuity Gap: How Can We Solve the Problems of the Future?* New York: Alfred A. Knopf.

Hoover, Anne P., and Margaret A. Shannon. 1995. "Building Greenway Policies Within a Participatory Democracy Framework." *Landscape and Urban Planning* 33(1–3): 433–459.

Hough, Michael. 1995. *Cities and Natural Process.* London: Routledge.

———. 2001. "Looking Beneath the Surface: Teaching a Landscape Ethic." In Kristina Hill and Bart Johnson, eds., *Ecology and Design: Frameworks for Learning.* Washington, DC: Island Press.

Hudson, Wendy E., ed. 1991. *Landscape Linkages and Biodiversity.* Washington, DC: Island Press.

Hutchinson, Ray. 1987. "Ethnicity and Urban Recreation: Whites, Blacks, and Hispanics in Chicago's Public Parks." *Journal of Leisure Research* 19(3): 205–222.

Jacobs, Allan B. 1996. *Great Streets.* Cambridge, MA: The MIT Press.

Jacques Gréber. 1950. *Plan for the National Capital.* Ottawa: National Capital Planning Service.

Jim, C. Y., and Sophia S. Chen. 2003. "Comprehensive Greenspace Planning Based on Landscape Ecology Principles in Compact Nanjing City, China." *Landscape and Urban Planning* 65(3): 95–116.

Johnson, Mark. 1997. "Ecology and the Urban Aesthetic." In George F. Thompson and Frederick R. Steiner, eds., *Ecological Design and Planning.* New York: John Wiley & Sons.

Jongman, Rob H. G., and Gloria Pungetti, eds. 2004. *Ecological Networks and Greenways: New Paradigms for Ecological Planning.* Cambridge, England: Cambridge University Press.

Kay, Jane Holtz. 1997. *Asphalt Nation: How the Automobile Took Over America and How We Can Take It Back.* New York: Crown Publishers, Inc.

Keil, Roger, and Gene Desfor. 2003. "Ecological Modernization in Los Angeles and Toronto." *Local Environment* 8(1): 27–44.

Knack, Ruth Eckdish. 2004. "Chicago Metropolis 2020." *Planning* 70(4): 16–17.

Kostyack, John. 2003. "Protecting Green Infrastructure." *BioScience* 53(1): 5.

Labaree, Jonathan M. 1993. *How Greenways Work—A Handbook on Ecology.* National Park Service, Rivers, Trails, and Conservation Assistance Program.

Lecesse, Michael. 1998. "Statement: A Master Plan Repositions Ottawa's National Capital Greenbelt as a National Treasure and Redefines Its Economic Worth." *Landscape Architecture* 88(6): 35–39.

Lewis, Philip H., Jr. 1996. *Tomorrow by Design: A Regional Design Process for Sustainability.* New York: John Wiley & Sons.

Lindsey, G. 1999. "Use of Urban Greenways: Insights from Indianapolis." *Landscape and Urban Planning* 45(2–3): 145–157.

Little, Charles E. 1990. *Greenways for America.* Baltimore: Johns Hopkins University Press.

Lyle, John Tillman. 1999. *Design for Human Ecosystems: Landscape, Land Use, and Natural Resources.* Washington, DC: Island Press.

Lynch, Kevin. 1976. *Managing the Sense of a Region.* Cambridge, MA: The MIT Press.

———. 1984. *Good City Form.* Cambridge, MA: The MIT Press.

MacLellan, Duncan K. 1995. "Shifting from the Traditional to the New Political Agenda: The Changing Nature of Federal–Provincial Environmental Relations." *American Review of Canadian Studies* 25: 323–345.

Marcus, Clare Cooper, and Carolyn Frances, eds. 1998. *People Places: Design Guidelines for Urban Open Space.* New York: John Wiley & Sons, Inc.

McCann, Barbara. 2005. "Complete the Streets." *Planning* 71(5): 18–23.

McHarg, Ian L. 1970. "Open Space from Natural Processes." In D. A. Wallace, ed., *Metropolitan Open Space and Natural Process.* Philadelphia: University of Pennsylvania.

———. 1981. "Human Ecological Planning at Pennsylvania." *Landscape Planning* 8: 109–120.

Minnesota Chapter of the American Society of Landscape Architects. 2001. *Valued Places: Landscape Architecture in Minnesota.* Minneapolis: Minneapolis Chapter of the American Society of Landscape Architects.

Morrish, William, and Catherine Brown. 2000. *Planning to Stay: Learning to See the Physical Features of Your Neighborhood.* Minneapolis: Milkweed Editions.

Mumford, Lewis. 1968. *The City in History: Its Origins, Its Transformations, and Its Prospects.* New York: Harcourt, Brace & World.

National Park Service, Rivers, Trails, and Conservation Assistance Program. 1995. *Economic Impacts of Protecting Rivers, Trails and Greenway Corridors: A Resource Book,* 4th Edition. National Park Service.

Newton, Norman. 1971. *Design on the Land: The Development of Landscape Architecture.* Cambridge, MA: The Belknap Press of Harvard University Press.

Noel, Thomas, and Barbara Norgren. 1987. *Denver: The City Beautiful and Its Architects 1893–1941.* Denver: Historic Denver, Inc.

Noss, Reed F. 1987. "Corridors in Real Landscapes: A Reply to Simberloff and Cox." *Conservation Biology* 1(2): 159–164.

Noss, Reed F., and A. Cooperrider. 1994. *Saving Nature's Legacy: Protecting and Restoring Biodiversity.* Washington, DC: Island Press.

Odum, Eugene. 1997. *Ecology: A Bridge Between Science and Society.* Sunderland, MA: Sinauer.

Oldenburg, Ray. 1999. *The Great Good Place,* 3rd Edition. New York: Marlowe and Company.

Olson, Sherry. 2000. "Form and Energy in the Urban Built Environment." In Trudi Bunting and Pierre Filion, eds., *Canadian Cities in Transition: The Twenty-First Century,* 2nd edition. Oxford, UK: Oxford University Press.

Opdam, Paul, Ruud Foppen, and Claire Vos. 2002. "Bridging the Gap Between Ecology and Spatial Planning in Landscape Ecology." *Landscape Ecology* 16(2002): 767–779.

Orfield, Myron. 1997. *Metropolitics: A Regional Agenda for Community and Stability.* Washington, DC: The Brookings Institution Press; and Cambridge, MA: The Lincoln Institute of Land Policy.

Orr, David. 2002. *The Nature of Design: Ecology, Culture, and Human Intention.* New York: Oxford University Press.

Park, Robert E., and Ernest W. Burgess. 1921. *Introduction to the Science of Sociology.* Chicago: University of Chicago Press.

Pauleit, Stephan. 2006. "Ecological Approaches to Green Structure Planning in European Cities and Towns: Results from COST Action C11." In City of Helsinki and Urban Facts, eds., *Urban Research,* forthcoming.

Pickett, S. T. A., M. L. Cadensasso, J. M. Grove, C. H. Nilon, R. V. Pouyat, W. C. Zipperer, and R. Costanza. 2001. "Urban Ecological Systems: Linking Terrestrial, Ecological, Physical, and Socioeconomic Components of Metropolitan Areas." *Annual Review of Ecological Systems* 32: 127–157.

Pollock-Ellwand, Nancy. 2001. "Gréber's Plan and the 'Washington of the North.'" *Landscape Journal* 20(1): 48–61.

Porter, Douglas R. 1997. *Managing Growth in America's Communities.* Washington, DC: Island Press.

President's Commission on Americans Outdoors. 1987. *Americans Outdoors: The Legacy, the Challenge: The Report of the President's Commission with Case Studies.* Washington, DC: Island Press.

Punter, John. 2003. *Vancouver Achievement: Urban Planning and Design.* Vancouver: UBC Press.

———. 2002. "Urban Design as Public Policy: Evaluating the Design Dimension of Vancouver's Planning System." *International Planning Studies* 7(4): 265–282.

Putnam, Robert D. 2000. *Bowling Alone: The Collapse and Revival of American Community.* New York: Simon & Schuster.

Quayle, Moura, and Stan Hamilton. 1999. "Corridors of Green and Gold: Impact of Riparian Suburban Greenways on Property Values." Report for Fraser River Action Plan, Department of Fisheries and Oceans, Vancouver, BC.

Quayle, Moura. 1995. "Urban Greenways and Public Ways: Realizing Public Ideas in a Fragmented World." *Landscape and Urban Planning* 33(1–3): 461–475.

Quayle, Moura, and Tilo Driessen van der Lieck. 1997. "Growing Community: A Case for Hybrid Landscapes." *Landscape and Urban Planning* 39(2–3): 99–107.

Riger, Stephanie, and Paul J. Lavrakas. 1981. "Community Ties: Patterns of Attachment and Social Interaction in Urban Neighborhoods." *American Journal of Community Psychology* 9(1): 55–66.

Rishbeth, Claire. 2001. "Ethnic Minority Groups and the Design of Public Open Space: An Inclusive Landscape?" *Landscape Research* 26(4): 351–366.

Rome, Adam. 1998. "William Whyte, Open Space, and Environmental Activism." *Geographical Review* 88(2): 259–275.

Rosenberg, Daniel K., Barry R. Noon, and E. Charles Meslow. 1997. "Biological Corridors: Form, Function, and Efficacy." *BioScience* 47: 677–687.

Rothblatt, Donald N. 1994. "North American Metropolitan Planning: Canadian and U.S. Perspectives." *Journal of the American Planning Association* 60(4): 501–527.

Rottle, Nancy. 2006. "Factors in the Landscape-Based Greenway: A Mountains to Sound Case Study." *Landscape and Urban Planning* 76(1–4): 134–171.

Royal Commission on the Future of the Toronto Waterfront. 1992. "Regeneration: Toronto's Waterfront and the Sustainable City, Final Report." Toronto: City of Toronto.

Ruliffson, Jane A., Paul Gobster, Robert G. Haight, and Frances R. Homans. 2002. "Niches in the Urban Forest: Organizations and Their Role in Acquiring Metropolitan Open Space." *Journal of Forestry* 100(6): 16–23.

Sancton, Andrew. 2001. "Canadian Cities and the New Regionalism." *Journal of Urban Affairs* 23(5): 543–555.

Schaefer, Valentin, Hillary Rudd, and Jamie Vala. 2004. *Urban Biodiversity: Exploring Natural Habitat and Its Value in Cities.* Concord, Ontario: Captus Press.

Scheer, Brenda Case. 2001. "The Anatomy of Sprawl." *Places* 14(2): 28–37.

Searns, Robert M. 1995. "The Evolution of Greenways as an Adaptive Urban Landscape Form." *Landscape and Urban Planning* 33(1–3): 65–80.

———. 2003. "Happy Trails: Greenways Put Their Stamp on the Denver Area." *Planning* 69(1): 45–46.

Shomon, Joseph James. 1971. *Open Land for Urban America: Acquisition, Safekeeping, and Use.* Baltimore: Johns Hopkins University Press.

Smith, Daniel, and Paul Hellmund. 1993. *The Ecology of Greenways.* Minneapolis: University of Minnesota Press.

Smith, Daniel. 2004. "Impacts of Roads on Ecological Networks and Integration of Conservation and Transportation Planning: Florida as a Case Study." In Rob Jongman and Gloria Pungetti, eds., *Ecological Networks and Greenways: Concept, Design, Implementation.* Cambridge, England: Cambridge University Press.

Soule, Michael E., and John Terborgh. 1999. "Conserving Nature at Regional and Continental Scales—A Scientific Program for North America." *BioScience* 49: 809–817.

Spirn, Anne. 1985. "Urban Nature and Human Design: Renewing the Great Tradition." *Journal of Planning Education and Research* 5(1): 39–51.

———. 1985. *The Granite Garden.* New York: Basic Books.

———. 1998. *The Language of Landscape.* New Haven: Yale University Press.

Steiner, Frederick. 2000. *The Living Landscape: An Ecological Approach to Landscape Planning,* 2nd Edition. New York: McGraw-Hill, Inc.

———. 2002. *Human Ecology: Following Nature's Lead.* Washington, DC: Island Press.

Still, Bayrd. 1968. *Milwaukee: The History of a City.* Milwaukee: North American Press.

Sukopp, Herbert. 1998. "Urban Ecology—Scientific and Practical Aspects." In J. Breuste, H. Feldmann, and O. Uhlmann, eds., *Urban Ecology.* Berlin: Springer-Verlag.

Swanwick, Carys, Nigel Dunnett, and Helen Woolley. 2003. "Nature, Role and Value of Green Space in Towns and Cities: An Overview." *Built Environment* 29(1): 94–106.

Szulczewska, Barbara, and Ewa Kaliszuk. 2003. "Challenges in the Planning and Management of 'Greenstructure' in Warsaw, Poland." *Built Environment* 29: 144–156.

Tankel, Stanley B. 1963. "The Importance of Open Space in the Urban Pattern." In L. J. Wingo, ed., *Cities and Space: The Future Use of Urban Land.* Baltimore: Johns Hopkins University Press.

Tansley, Arthur G. 1935. "The Use and Abuse of Vegetational Concepts and Terms." *Ecology* 16: 284–307.

Taylor, James, Cecelia Paine, and John FitzGibbon, 1995. "From Greenbelt to Greenways: Four Canadian Case Studies." *Landscape and Urban Planning* 33(1–3): 47–64.

Thompson, Catharine Ward. 2002. "Urban Open Space in the 21st Century." *Landscape and Urban Planning* 60(2): 59–72.

Thompson, George F., and Frederick R. Steiner, eds. 1997. *Ecological Design and Planning.* New York: John Wiley & Sons, Inc.

Tittle, Diana. 2002. *A Walk in the Park: Greater Cleveland's New and Reclaimed Green Spaces.* Athens, OH: Ohio University Press.

Tjallingii, Sybrand. 2003. "Green and Red: Enemies or Allies? The Utrecht Experience with Green Structure Planning." *Built Environment* 29(2): 107–116.

Todhunter, Rodger. 1983. "Vancouver and the City Beautiful Movement." *Habitat* 26(3): 8–13.

Tomalty, Ray, Robert B. Gibson, Donald H. M. Alexander, and John Fisher. 1994. "Ecosystem Planning for Canadian Urban Regions." Report, ICURR Publications, Toronto.

Tyler, Mary Ellen. 2000. "The Ecological Restructuring of Urban Form." In Trudy Bunting and Pierre Filion, eds., *Canadian Cities in Transition: The Twenty-First Century,* 2nd edition. Oxford, UK: Oxford University Press.

Vengroff, Richard, and Zaira Reveron. 1997. "Decentralization and Local Government Efficiency in Canadian Provinces: A Comparative Perspective." *International Journal of Canadian Studies* 16: 195–214.

Walzer, M. "Public Space: Pleasures and Costs of Urbanity." *Dissent* 33(4): 470–475.

Wheeler, Stephen M. 2002. "The New Regionalism: Key Characteristics of an Emerging Movement." *Journal of the American Planning Association* 68(3): 267–278.

———. "The Evolution of Urban Form in Portland and Toronto: Implications for Sustainability Planning." *Local Environment* 8(3): 317–336.

Whyte, William H. 1968. "Securing Open Space for Urban America: Conservation Easements." Technical Bulletin No. 36, Urban Land Institute, Washington, DC.

———. 1968. *The Last Landscape.* New York: Doubleday & Co.

———. 1980. *The Social Life of Small Urban Spaces.* Washington, DC: The Conservation Foundation.

Wondolleck, Julia M., and Steven L. Yaffee. 2000. *Making Collaboration Work: Lessons from Innovation in Natural Resource Management.* Washington, DC: Island Press.

Woolley, Helen. 2003. *Urban Open Spaces.* London: Spon Press.

Wornell, Heather. 2001. "Laying Down Routes: An Evaluation of the Greater Vancouver Regional District's Regional Recreation Greenway Program." Master's Thesis, Simon Fraser University, Vancouver, BC.

Young, Gerald. 1974. "Human Ecology as an Interdisciplinary Concept: A Critical Inquiry." *Advances in Ecological Research* 8: 1–105.

Notes

Preface and Acknowledgments

1. Donna Erickson and Anneke Louisse, "Greenway Implementation in Metropolitan Regions: A Comparative Case Study of North American Examples," Monograph published by the National Park Service Rivers, Trails, and Conservation Assistance Program and Rails-to-Trails Conservancy, 1997.

2. Donna Erickson, "Green Infrastructure: The Interplay of Historic City Form and Contemporary Greenway Implementation in Two North American Cities," *Landscape and Urban Planning,* 68 (Numbers 2–3, 2004):199–221.

3. Donna Erickson, "Connecting Lines Across the Landscape: Implementing Metropolitan Greenway Networks in North America," in Rob H. G. Jongman and Gloria Pungetti, eds., *Ecological Networks and Greenways: New Paradigms for Ecological Planning* (Cambridge, UK: Cambridge University Press, 2004), p. 200–221.

Chapter 1

1. Quoted in Dan Shine, "Ann Arbor Plan Seeks Greenbelt Around City," *Detroit Free Press,* August 8, 2003.

2. Quoted in R. J. King, "Ann Arbor Greenbelt Sets Off Land Rush," *Detroit News,* December 7, 2003.

3. Linda E. Hollis and William Fulton, "Open Space Protection: Conservation Meets Growth Management." Discussion paper for The Brookings Institution Center on Urban and Metropolitan Policy, April 2002.

4. Michael P. Johnson, "Environmental Impacts of Urban Sprawl: A Survey of the Literature and Proposed Research Agenda," *Environment and Planning A,* 33 (2001):717–735.

5. Carys Swanwick, Nigel Dunnett, and Helen Woolley, "Nature, Role and Value of Green Space in Towns and Cities: An Overview," *Built Environment,* 29 (Number 1, 2003):94–106.

6. Land Trust Alliance, "Land Vote 2002," Report from The Trust for Public Land and the Land Trust Alliance, January 2003.

7. Anne R. Beer, Tim Delshammar, and Peter Schildwacht, "A Changing Understanding of the Role of Greenspace in High-Density Housing: A European Perspective," *Built Environment,* 29 (Number 2, 2003):132–143.

8. Beer, Delshammar, and Schildwacht, 2003, p. 134.

9. See for instance R. C. Ready, M. C. Berger, and G. C. Blomquist, "Measuring Amenity Benefits from Farmland: A Comparison of Hedonic Pricing and Contingent Valuation Techniques," *Growth and Change,* 28 (1997):428–459; and V. Kerry Smith, Christine Poulos, and Hyun Kim, "Treating Open Space as an Urban Amenity," *Resource and Energy Economics,* 24 (2002):107–129.

10. National Park Service, Rivers, Trails, and Conservation Assistance Program, *Economic Impacts of Protecting Rivers, Trails and Greenway Corridors: A Resource Book,* 4th Edition (National Park Service, 1995).

11. Randall Arendt, *Growing Greener: Putting Conservation into Local Plans and Ordinances* (Washington, DC: Island Press, 1999).

12. Peter Calthorpe and William Fulton, *The Regional City: Planning for the End of Sprawl* (Washington, DC: Island Press, 2001).

13. Chicago Metropolis 2020, "The Metropolis Plan: Choices for the Chicago Region," Report of Commercial Club of Chicago, March 2003.

14. Frederick Steiner and Kent Butler, "The Green Heart of Texas," Paper delivered at the 5th International Workshop on Sustainable Land-Use Planning, Wageningen, The Netherlands, 2004.

15. C. Y. Jim and Sophia S. Chen, "Comprehensive Greenspace Planning Based on Landscape Ecology Principles in Compact Nanjing City, China," *Landscape and Urban Planning,* 65 (Number 3, 2003):95–116; Barbara Szulczewska and Ewa Kaliszuk, "Challenges in the Planning and Management of 'Greenstructure' in Warsaw, Poland," *Built Environment,* 29 (2003):144–156; D. A. Goode, "Urban Nature Conservation in Britain," *Journal of Applied Ecology,* 26 (Number 3, 1989):859–873; Edward A. Cook and Hubert N. Van Lier, eds., *Landscape Planning and Ecological Networks,* Vol. 6F in series *Developments in Landscape Management and Urban Planning* (Amsterdam: Elsevier, 2000); Alejandro Flores, T. A. Pickett Steward, Wayne C. Zipperer, Richard V. Pouyat, and Robert Pirani, "Adopting a Modern Ecological View of the Metropolitan Landscape: The Case of a Greenspace System for the New York City Region," *Landscape and Urban Planning,* 39 (Number 4, 1998):295–308.

16. Paul Goldberger, *Up From Zero: Politics, Architecture, and the Rebuilding of New York* (New York: Random House, 2005).

17. Lower Manhattan Development Corporation, "Principles and Revised Preliminary Blueprint for the Future of Lower Manhattan," 2002, p. 11. For a good overview of the benefits—social, environmental, and economic—of urban open space, see Helen Woolley, *Urban Open Spaces* (London: Spon Press, 2003).

18. Karen Payne, "Graph Theory and Open-Space Network Design," *Landscape Research,* 27 (2002):167–179, p. 167.

19. Anne Beer, "Aspects of the Link Between Urban Nature and City Planning in Northern European Countries," Paper presented at the Workshop on the Flemish Long-Term Vision of Nature in Urban and Suburban Areas, Brussels, Belgium, November 2000, p. 3.

20. National Wildlife Federation, "Green Infrastructure: A Framework for Smart Growth," 2003, http://www.nwf.org/smartgrowth/infrastructure.html.

21. Hollis and Fulton, "Open Space Protection," 2002.

22. Beer, Delschammar, and Schildwacht, "A Changing Understanding of the Role of Greenspace," 2003, p. 132.

23. Jane Holtz-Kay, "Closing Down 'Open Space,'" *Landscape Architecture,* 59 (Number 1, 2001):120.

24. Lisa S. Nelson and Andrew Kalmar, "Building a Constituency Base for Open Space Protection in the Metro-Rural Interface: A Case Study," *Journal of Soil and Water Conservation,* 50 (1995):34.

25. Catharine Ward Thompson, "Urban Open Space in the 21st Century," *Landscape and Urban Planning,* 60 (Number 2, 2002):59–72.

26. Moura Quayle and Tilo Driessen van der Lieck, "Growing Community: A Case for Hybrid Landscapes," *Landscape and Urban Planning,* 39 (Numbers 2–3, 1997):99–107.

27. Mark Johnson, "Ecology and the Urban Aesthetic," in G. F. Thompson and F. R. Steiner, eds., *Ecological Design and Planning* (New York: John Wiley and Sons, 1997), p. 176.

28. Thompson, "Urban Open Space," 2002, p. 60. M. Walzer also builds these ideas into a definition of open space: "Public space is space where we share with strangers, people who aren't our relatives, friends or work associates. It is space for politics, religion, commerce, sport; space for peaceful coexistence and impersonal encounter. Its character expresses and also conditions our public life, civic culture, everyday discourse." M. Walzer, "Public Space: Pleasures and Costs of Urbanity," *Dissent,* 33 (Number 4, 1986):470–475.

29. Paul Gobster, "Neighborhood–Open Space Relationships in Metropolitan Planning: A Look Across Four Scales of Concern," *Local Environment,* 33 (Number 2, 2001):199–212; Maureen Austin and Rachel Kaplan, "Resident Involvement in Natural Resource Management: Open Space Conservation Design in Practice," *Local Environment,* 8 (Number 2, 2003):141–153; Anna Chiesura, "The Role of Urban Parks in the Sustainable City," *Landscape and Urban Planning,* 68 (Number 4, 2004):129–138.

30. Claire Rishbeth, "Ethnic Minority Groups and the Design of Public Open Space: An Inclusive Landscape?" *Landscape Research,* 26 (Number 4, 2001):351–366; Ray Hutchinson, "Ethnicity and Urban Recreation: Whites, Blacks, and Hispanics in Chicago's Public Parks," *Journal of Leisure Research,* 19 (Number 3, 1987):205–222; Deborah S. Carr and Daniel R. Williams,

"Understanding the Role of Ethnicity in Outdoor Recreation Experience," *Journal of Leisure Research*, 25 (Number 1, 1993):22–38; R. Hutchinson, "A Critique of Race, Ethnicity, and Social Class in Recent Leisure–Recreation Research," *Journal of Leisure Research*, 20 (1988):10–27.

31. R. G. Lee quoted in Carr, "Understanding the Role of Ethnicity," 1993, p. 24.
32. Thomas Homer-Dixon, *The Ingenuity Gap: How Can We Solve the Problems of the Future?* (New York: Alfred A. Knopf, 2000).
33. Calthorpe and Fulton, *The Regional City*, 2001, p. 55.
34. Edward A. Williams and the firm of Dean, Eckbo, Austin & Williams, *Open Space: Choices Before California: The Urban Metropolitan Open Space Study* (San Francisco: Diablo Press, 1969); Joseph James Shomon, *Open Land for Urban America: Acquisition, Safekeeping, and Use* (Baltimore: Johns Hopkins University Press, 1971).
35. Anne Spirn, *The Language of Landscape* (New Haven: Yale University Press, 1998).
36. Stanley B. Tankel, "The Importance of Open Space in the Urban Pattern," in L. J. Wingo, ed., *Cities and Space: The Future Use of Urban Land* (Baltimore: Johns Hopkins University Press, 1963) p. 57–71.
37. Ibid., p. 59.
38. Woolley, "Urban Open Spaces," 2003.
39. Anne Beer, "Aspects of the Link Between Urban Nature and City Planning," 2000, p. 3.
40. Swanwick, Dunnett, and Woolley, "Nature, Role, and Value of Green Space," 2003.
41. Ibid., p. 100.
42. Beth Curda, "Open Space Land Prioritized," *The Davis Enterprise*, November 3, 2003.
43. Pierce County, Washington, www.co.pierce.wa.us/text/abtus/ourorg/at/open_space.htm.
44. Randall Arendt, *Growing Greener*, 1999.
45. Wenche E. Dramstad, James D. Olson, and Richard T. T. Forman, *Landscape Ecology Principles in Landscape Architecture and Land-Use Planning* (Washington, DC: Island Press, 1996); Richard Forman and Michel Godron, *Landscape Ecology* (New York: John Wiley, 1986).
46. Goode, "Urban Nature Conservation," 1989, p. 864.
47. Joshua Olsen, "Open Space May Not Be All It's Cracked Up to Be," American Planning Association Web site, accessed July 9, 2004. www.planning.org/viewpoints/openspace.htm.
48. Ibid.
49. If this distinction is, in fact, needed; see Frederick Steiner, *Human Ecology: Following Nature's Lead* (Washington, DC: Island Press, 2002). Theoretical roots for connectivity lie largely in the landscape ecology literature: see Richard T. T. Forman, *Land Mosaics: The Ecology of Landscapes and Regions* (Cambridge, England: Cambridge University Press, 1995); Michael E. Soule and John Terborgh, "Conserving Nature at Regional and Continental Scales—A Scientific Program for North America," *BioScience*, 49 (1999):809–817; and André Botequilha Leitão and Jack Ahern, "Applying Landscape Ecological Concepts and Metrics in Sustainable Landscape Planning," *Landscape and Urban Planning*, 59 (Number 2, 2002):65–93.
50. Reed F. Noss and Allen Y. Cooperrider, *Saving Nature's Legacy: Protecting and Restoring Biodiversity* (Washington, DC: Island Press, 1994).

51. Michael E. Soule and John Terborgh, "Conserving Nature at Regional and Continental Scales—A Scientific Program for North America," *BioScience,* 49 (1999):809–817.

52. Daniel K. Rosenberg, Barry R. Noon, and E. Charles Meslow, "Biological Corridors: Form, Function, and Efficacy," *BioScience,* 47 (1997):677–687; Jeffrey P. Cohn and Jeffrey A. Lerner, "Integrating Land Use Planning and Biodiversity," Report published by Defenders of Wildlife, 2003.

53. Reed Noss, "Corridors in Real Landscapes: A Reply to Siberloff and Cox," *Conservation Biology,* 1 (Number 2, 1987):159–164, p. 159.

54. Daniel Smith and Paul Hellmund, *The Ecology of Greenways* (Minneapolis: University of Minnesota Press, 1993).

55. Jared M. Diamond, John Terborgh, Robert F. Whitcomb, James F. Lynch, Paul A. Opler, Chandler S. Robbins, Daniel S. Simberloff, and Lawrence G. Abele, "Island Biogeography and Conservation: Strategy and Limitations," *Science,* 193 (1976):1027–1032. See also Kevin Gutzwiller, ed., *Applying Landscape Ecology in Biological Conservation* (New York: Springer, 2002).

56. Rosenberg, Noon, and Meslow, "Biological Corridors," 1997, p. 685.

57. A. C. Henry Jr., D. A. Hosack, C. W. Johnson, D. Rol, and G. Bentrup, "Conservation Corridors in the United States: Benefits and Planning Guidelines," *Journal of Soil and Water Conservation,* 54 (Number 4, 1999):645–650.

58. Noss, "Corridors," 1987.

59. Ibid., p. 159.

60. Henry, Hosack, Johnson, Rol, and Bentrup, "Conservation Corridors," 1999.

61. A. M. Fleury and R. D. Brown, "A Framework for the Design of Wildlife Conservation Corridors," *Landscape and Urban Planning,* 37 (Numbers 3–4, 1997):163–186.

62. Rosenberg, Noon, and Meslow, "Biological Corridors," 1997, p. 685.

63. Frederick Steiner, *Human Ecology: Following Nature's Lead* (Washington, DC: Island Press, 2002), p. 107.

64. Ibid.

65. Gerald Young, "Human Ecology as an Interdisciplinary Concept: A Critical Inquiry," *Advances in Ecological Research,* 8 (1974):1–105, p. 54.

66. Peter Harnik and Jeff Simms, "Parks—How Far Is Too Far?" *Planning,* December 2004.

67. S. T. A. Pickett, M. L. Cadenasso, J. M. Grove, C. H. Nilon, R. V. Pouyat, W. C. Zipperer, and R. Costanza, "Urban Ecological Systems: Linking Terrestrial, Ecological, Physical, and Socioeconomic Components of Metropolitan Areas," *Annual Review of Ecological Systems,* 32 (2001):127–157.

68. William R. Burch, Jr., "Human Ecology and Environmental Management," in J. K. Agee and D. R. Johnson, eds., *Ecosystem Management for Parks and Wilderness* (Seattle: University of Washington Press, 1988) p. 151.

69. Commonwealth of Pennsylvania, "Greenways: An Action Plan for Creating Connections," http://www.pagreenways.org/greenways101-story.htm.

70. Claire Enlow, "Streets as Parks: In Seattle, Open Space Is Where You Find It," *Planning,* May 2002.

71. Pickett, Cadenasso, Grove, Nilon, Pouyat, Zipperer, and Costanza, "Urban Ecological Systems," 2001.

72. Fred Siegel, "The Sunny Side of Sprawl," *The New Democrat,* 11 (Number 2, 1999).

73. Kevin Lynch, *Managing the Sense of a Region* (Cambridge, MA: The MIT Press, 1976), p. 4.

74. Steiner, "Human Ecology," 2002.

75. A. G. Tansley, "The Use and Abuse of Vegetational Concepts and Terms," *Ecology,* 16 (1935): 284–307. Tansley defined ecosystems, showing that they can be of any size as long as the focus is on the interaction of organisms and their environment. Ecosystems are spatial units that cover all organisms in a given area as well as their relationship to the physical environment. Further interpreted by Pickett, Cadenasso, Grove, Nilon, Pouyat, Zipperer, and Costanza (2001, p. 148), "the boundaries of an ecosystem are drawn to answer a particular question. Thus, there is no set scale or way to bound an ecosystem. Rather the choice of scale and boundary for defining any ecosystem depends upon the question asked and is the choice of the investigator."

76. Timothy Davis, Todd A. Croteau, and Christopher H. Marston, *America's National Park Roads and Parkways: Drawings from the Historic American Engineering Record* (Baltimore: Johns Hopkins University Press, 2004). See also Phoebe Cutler, *The Public Landscape of the New Deal* (New Haven: Yale University Press, 1985).

77. Norman Newton, *Design on the Land: The Development of Landscape Architecture* (Cambridge, MA: The Belknap Press of Harvard University Press, 1971), p. 596.

78. Ibid.

79. Ibid., p. 597.

80. Cynthia L. Girling and Kenneth I. Helphand. 1994. *Yard–Street–Park: The Design of Suburban Open Space.* New York: John Wiley & Sons, Inc., p. 223.

81. J. B. Cullingworth and V. Nadin, *Town and Country Planning in the U.K.* (New York: Routledge, 1997).

82. Tankel, "The Importance of Open Space," 1963; William H. Whyte, *The Last Landscape* (Garden City, NY: Doubleday & Co., 1968); Michael Hough, *Cities and Natural Process* (London: Routledge, 1995).

83. William H. Whyte, *The Last Landscape* (Garden City, NY: Doubleday & Co., 1968), p. 162.

84. Larry Orman, "Strategies for Metropolitan Open Space," in D. R. Porter, ed., *Managing Growth in America's Communities* (Washington, DC: Island Press, 1997).

85. Whyte, *The Last Landscape,* 1968.

86. Royal Commission on the Future of the Toronto Waterfront, "Regeneration: Toronto's Waterfront and the Sustainable City, Final Report," 1992.

87. Charles E. Little, *Greenways for America* (Baltimore: Johns Hopkins University Press, 1990); William Whyte, "Securing Open Space for Urban America: Conservation Easements," Technical Bulletin No. 36, Urban Land Institute, Washington, DC, September 1968.

88. Robert Searns, "The Evolution of Greenways as an Adaptive Urban Landscape Form," *Landscape and Urban Planning,* 33 (Numbers 1–3, 1995):65–80, p. 65.

89. President's Commission on Americans Outdoors, *Americans Outdoors: The Legacy, the Challenge: The Report of the President's Commission with Case Studies* (Washington, DC: Island Press, 1987).

90. Smith and Hellmund, *Ecology of Greenways*, 1993; Hough, *Cities and Natural Process*, 1995.

91. Donna Erickson, "Green Infrastructure: The Interplay of Historic City Form and Contemporary Greenway Implementation in Two North American Cities," *Landscape and Urban Planning*, 68 (Numbers 2–3, 2004):199–221.

92. Anne P. Hoover and Margaret A. Shannon, "Building Greenway Policies Within a Participatory Democracy Framework," *Landscape and Urban Planning*, 33 (Numbers 1–3, 1995), p. 435.

93. Little, *Greenways for America*, 1990.

94. Charles Flink and Robert M. Searns, *Greenways: A Guide to Planning, Design and Development* (Washington, DC: Island Press, 1993).

95. National Park Service, "Economic Impacts," 1995. For Canadian research on this topic, see also Moura Quayle and Stan Hamilton, "Corridors of Green and Gold: Impact of Riparian Suburban Greenways on Property Values," Report for Fraser River Action Plan, Department of Fisheries and Oceans, Vancouver, BC, April 1999.

96. G. Lindsey, "Use of Urban Greenways: Insights from Indianapolis," *Landscape and Urban Planning*, 45 (Numbers 2–3, 1999):145–157.

97. Paul Gobster, "Perception and Use of a Metropolitan Greenway System for Recreation," *Landscape and Urban Planning*, 33 (Numbers 1–3, 1995):401–413.

98. Jonathan M. Labaree, *How Greenways Work—A Handbook on Ecology* (National Park Service, Rivers, Trails, and Conservation Assistance Program, 1993); Edward A. Cook and Hubert N. Van Lier, eds., *Landscape Planning and Ecological Networks*, Vol. 6F in series *Developments in Landscape Management and Urban Planning* (Amsterdam: Elsevier, 2000); Rob H. G. Jongman and Gloria Pungetti, eds., *Ecological Networks and Greenways: New Paradigms for Ecological Planning* (Cambridge, England: Cambridge University Press, 2004).

99. Donna Erickson and Anneke Louisse, "Greenway Implementation in Metropolitan Regions: A Comparative Case Study of North American Examples." Monograph published by the National Park Service Rivers, Trails, and Conservation Assistance Program, 1997; Erickson, "Green Infrastructure," 2004.

100. Jack Ahern, "Planning for an Extensive Open Space System: Linking Landscape Structure and Function," *Landscape and Urban Planning*, 21 (Numbers 1–2, 1991):131–145; Jack Ahern, "Greenways as a Planning Strategy," *Landscape and Urban Planning*, 33 (1995):131–155; Jack Ahern, *Greenways as Strategic Landscape Planning: Theory and Application* (Wageningen University, The Netherlands, 2002).

101. Searns, "The Evolution of Greenways," 1995.

102. Ibid., p. 79.

103. Heather Wornell, "Laying Down Routes: An Evaluation of the Greater Vancouver Regional District's Regional Recreation Greenway Program," Unpublished Master's Thesis, Resource and Environmental Management Program, Simon Fraser University, Vancouver, BC, 2001.

104. Beer, Delshammar, and Schildwacht, "A Changing Understanding," 2003, p. 132.

105. Ibid., p. 133.

106. J. H. A. Meeus, "Geneentelijk Groenbeleid" (Municipal Green Area Policy). Groene Reeks 13. Report published by The Netherlands Ministry of Agriculture, Nature and Fisheries and Ministry of Housing, Spatial Planning and the Environment, Wageningen, The Netherlands, 1989.

107. Sybrand Tjallingii, "Green and Red: Enemies or Allies? The Utrecht Experience with Green Structure Planning," *Built Environment,* 29 (Number 2, 2003):107–116.

108. Edward McMahon, "Words Matter," *Common Ground,* newsletter of The Conservation Fund, January–March 2003.

109. Mark A. Benedict and Edward T. McMahon, "Green Infrastructure for the 21st Century," *Renewable Resources Journal,* 20 (Number 3, 2002), p. 12.

110. John Kostyack, "Protecting Green Infrastructure," *BioScience,* 53 (Number 1, 2003):5.

111. Ibid., p. 5.

112. Clive Briffett, "Is Managed Recreational Use Compatible with Effective Habitat and Wildlife Occurrence in Urban Open Space Corridor Systems?" *Landscape Research,* 26 (Number 2, 2001):137–163.

114. Holtz-Kay, "Closing Down 'Open Space,'" 2001, p. 120.

Chapter 2

1. Lewis Mumford, *The Culture of Cities* (New York: Harcourt, Brace & Co., 1938), p. 5.

2. Anne Spirn, "Urban Nature and Human Design: Renewing the Great Tradition," *Journal of Planning Education and Research,* 5 (Number 1, 1985):39–51, p. 42.

3. Frederick Steiner, *Human Ecology: Following Nature's Lead* (Washington, DC: Island Press, 2002), p. 102.

4. Roger Keil and Gene Desfor, "Ecological Modernization in Los Angeles and Toronto," *Local Environment,* 8 (Number 1, 2003):27–44.

5. Mark Francis, "A Case Study Method for Landscape Architecture." Final report to the Landscape Architecture Foundation, Washington, DC, 1998, p. 6.

6. Robert Yin, *Case Study Research: Design and Methods* (Beverly Hills, CA: Sage Publications, 1994), p. 13.

7. Francis, "A Case Study Method," 1998.

8. Ibid., p. 6.

9. See, for example, Barney G. Glaser and Anselm L. Strauss, *The Discovery of Grounded Theory: Strategies for Qualitative Research* (New York: Aldine Publishing Company, 1967); Michael Q. Patton, *Qualitative Research and Evaluation Methods* (Thousand Oaks, CA: Sage Publications, 2002); Kenneth G. Shipley and Julie McNulty Wood, *The Elements of Interviewing* (San Diego, CA: Singular Publishing Group, Inc., 1995); Robert Yin, *Case Study Research,* 1994.

10. Helen Woolley, *Urban Open Spaces* (London: Spon Press, 2003), p. 79.

11. Mary-Ellen Tyler and William T. Perks, "A Normative Model for Urban Ecology Practice:

Establishing Performance Propositions for Ecological Planning and Design," in J. Breuste, H. Feldmann, and O. Uhlmann, eds., *Urban Ecology* (Berlin: Springer-Verlag, 1998), p. 229.

12. Spirn, "Urban Nature and Human Design".

13. Mark Benedict and Ed McMahon, "Green Infrastructure: Smart Conservation for the 21st Century," *Natural Resources Journal*, 20 (Number 3, 2002):12–17.

Chapter 3

1. David Orr, *The Nature of Design: Ecology, Culture, and Human Intention* (New York: Oxford University Press, 2002), p. 20.

2. Metropolitan Toronto and Region Conservation Authority, "Lake Ontario Waterfront Regeneration Project 1995–1999," Report to the Municipality of Metropolitan Toronto, April 1994.

3. Marti Bjornson, "Chicago Greening Puts Nature in the City," *Conscious Choice*, May 1998.

4. Chicago Region Biodiversity Council, "A Summary of the Biodiversity Recovery Plan," Report to Chicago Wilderness, September 1999.

5. Chicago Rivers Demonstration Project, "Chicago's Living Rivers," Report published by the National Park Service, no date given.

6. Chicago Region Biodiversity Council, "Biodiversity Recovery," 1999.

7. Office of Technology Assessment, "The Technological Reshaping of Metropolitan America," OTA-ETI-643, September 1995.

8. Stephen M. Wheeler, "The Evolution of Urban Form in Portland and Toronto: Implications for Sustainability Planning," *Local Environment*, 8 (Number 3, 2003):317–336.

9. City of Toronto Parks and Recreation Department, "Strategic Plan 2004: Our Common Grounds," 2004.

10. Suzanne Barrett, *A Decade of Regeneration* (Toronto: Waterfront Regeneration Trust, 2000).

11. Royal Commission on the Future of the Toronto Waterfront, "Regeneration: Toronto's Waterfront and the Sustainable City, Final Report," 1992.

12. Ray Tomalty, Robert B. Gibson, Donald H. M. Alexander, and John Fisher, "Ecosystem Planning for Canadian Urban Regions," Report, ICURR Publications, Toronto, November 1994, p. 4.

13. Ibid., p. 4.

14. Royal Commission on the Future of the Toronto Waterfront, "Access and Movement," Report of the Access and Movement Work Group to the Royal Commission on the Future of the Toronto Waterfront, 1989.

15. James Taylor, Cecelia Paine, and John FitzGibbon, "From Greenbelt to Greenways: Four Canadian Case Studies," *Landscape and Urban Planning*, 33 (Numbers 1–3, 1995):47–64.

16. Waterfront Regeneration Trust, www.waterfronttrail.org.

17. Waterfront Regeneration Trust, "Lake Ontario Greenway Strategy," Report, May 1995.

18. Ibid.

19. Waterfront Regeneration Trust, www.waterfronttrail.org.

20. Toronto and Region Conservation Authority, "Terrestrial Natural Heritage System Strategy," 2004, p. 7.

21. Toronto Waterfront Revitalization Task Force, "Our Toronto Waterfront: Gateway to the New Canada," Report to the Prime Minister of Canada, Premier of Ontario, and Mayor of Toronto, March 2000.

22. Jane A. Ruliffson, Paul Gobster, Robert G. Haight, and Frances R. Homans, "Niches in the Urban Forest, Organizations and Their Role in Acquiring Metropolitan Open Space," *Journal of Forestry,* September 2002.

23. Quoted from 1913 state enabling legislation in Rullifson, Gobster, Haight, and Homans, "Niches," 2002.

24. Rullifson, Gobster, Haight, and Homans, "Niches," 2002.

25. Northeastern Illinois Planning Commission and Openlands Project, "Northeastern Illinois Regional Greenways Plan," September 1992.

26. Openlands Project, www.openlands.org.

27. Northeastern Illinois Planning Commission and Openlands Project, "State of the Greenways Report: A Report on Implementation of the Northeastern Illinois Regional Greenways Plan," July 1994.

28. Northeastern Illinois Planning Commission and Openlands Project, "Regional Greenways and Trails Implementation Program: An Update of the Northeastern Illinois Regional Greenways Plan," June 1997.

29. Mary Kate Hogan, "Chicago Wilderness Catches Fire," *Conscious Choice,* May 1996, p. 2.

30. Debra Shore, "What is Chicago Wilderness?" *Chicago Wilderness,* Fall 1997.

31. Elmer W. Johnson, "Chicago Metropolis 2020: Preparing Metropolitan Chicago for the 21st Century," Report to the Commercial Club of Chicago, January 1999. See also Chicago Metropolis 2020, "The Metropolis Plan: Choices for the Chicago Region," Report of Commercial Club of Chicago, March 2003.

32. Ruth Eckdish Knack, "In Another State, a Regional Plan Might Not Be Such a Big Deal," *Planning,* April 2004.

33. Chicago Area Transportation Study, www.catsmpo.com.

34. Julia Sniderman Bachrach, *City in a Garden: A Photographic History of Chicago's Parks* (Staunton, VA: Center for American Places, 2001).

35. Michael Hough, "Toronto Parkland Naturalization Update," Report to City of Toronto, 1999, p. 4.

36. Ruliffson, Gobster, Haight, and Homans, "Niches," 2002, p. 21.

37. Ibid., p. 21.

Chapter 4

1. William H. Whyte, *The Last Landscape* (New York: Doubleday & Co., 1968), p. 162.

2. Anne Spirn, *The Granite Garden* (New York: Basic Books, 1985), p. 41.

3. U.S. Census, 2000.

4. Statistics Canada, 2002.

5. Bayrd Still, *Milwaukee the History of a City* (Milwaukee: North American Press, 1948).

6. A. L. Kurtz, "The Value of Comprehensive Plans for Sewer Systems," *American City*, 1926, p. 394–395.

7. Southeastern Wisconsin Regional Planning Commission, "A Regional Natural Areas and Critical Species Habitat Protection and Management Plan for Southeastern Wisconsin," Planning Report no. 42, 1997.

8. William Clausen, "Early Planning for Land Use and Community Parks in the City of Milwaukee." Fifth Annual Professional Improvement Conference. Historical perspectives. University of Wisconsin–Extension, Stevens Point, WI, 1980, p. 18.

9. Ibid.

10. Ibid.

11. Southeastern Wisconsin Regional Planning Commission, "A Park and Open Space Plan for Milwaukee County," Community Assistance Planning Report no. 132, 1991.

12. John Gurda, *The Making of Milwaukee* (Brookfield, Wisconsin: Burton & Mayer, Inc., 1999), p. 269.

13. Ibid., p. 270–271.

14. Clausen, "Early Planning," 1980, p. 10.

15. Gurda, *The Making of Milwaukee*, 1999.

16. Federal Plan Commission of Ottawa and Hull, "Report of the Federal Plan Commission on a General Plan for the Cities of Ottawa and Hull," 1915, p. 14.

17. Jacques Gréber, *Plan for the National Capital* (Ottawa: National Capital Planning Service, Ottawa, 1950), p. 119.

18. Nancy Pollock-Ellwand, "Gréber's Plan and the 'Washington of the North,'" *Landscape Journal*, 20 (Number 1, 2001):48–61.

19. Federal Plan Commission of Ottawa and Hull, "Report of the Federal Plan Commission," 1915, p. 14–15.

20. David L. Gordon, "Frederick G. Todd and the Origins of the Park System in Canada's Capital," *Journal of Planning History*, 1 (Number 1, 2002): 29-57.

21. Federal Plan Commission of Ottawa and Hull, "Report of the Federal Plan Commission," 1915, p. 14–15.

22. Ibid., p. 105.

23. National Capital Commission, www.canadascapital.gc.ca/corporate/index_e.asp.

24. Gréber, *Plan for the National Capital*, 1950.

25. Wilfrid Eggleston, *The Queen's Choice* (Ottawa: The National Capital Commission, Ottawa, 1961).

26. Pollack-Ellwand, "Gréber's Plan," 2001, p. 54–55.

27. Eggleston, *The Queen's Choice*, 1961.

28. Ibid.

29. Douglas L. McDonald and John W. P. Cole, "Urban Greenbelts," Report to the National Capital Commission, 1973.

30. Ibid.

31. Michael Hough, "Toronto Parkland Naturalization Update," Report to City of Toronto, 1999, p. 3.

32. Milwaukee County Park Commission, "Guide for Growth: Milwaukee County Park System," 1972.

33. Southeastern Wisconsin Regional Planning Commission, "Park and Open Space Plan," 1991.

34. Ibid.; Southeastern Wisconsin Regional Planning Commission, "An Inventory of Vacant or Underutilized Lands in the Riverine Areas of Central Milwaukee County," Memorandum Report no. 40, 1989.

35. Southeastern Wisconsin Regional Planning Commission, "Alternative Futures for Southeastern Wisconsin," Technical Report no. 25, 1980.

36. Phil Lewis, *Tomorrow by Design: A Regional Design Process for Sustainability* (New York: John Wiley & Sons, 1996).

37. Southeastern Wisconsin Regional Planning Commission, "Regional Natural Areas," 1997.

38. National Capital Commission, www.canadascapital.gc.ca/corporate/index_e.asp.

39. Ibid.

40. Michael Lecesse, "Statement: A Master Plan Repositions Ottawa's National Capital Greenbelt as a National Treasure and Redefines Its Economic Worth," *Landscape Architecture,* 88 (Number 6, 1998):35–39, p. 38.

41. Ibid.

42. Daniel Nixey, "The Future Greenbelt, Economic Analysis," National Capital Commission, Ottawa, 1991.

43. Lecesse, "Master Plan," 1998.

44. See Michael Hough, *Cities and Natural Process* (London: Routledge, 1995) and Hough Stanbury Woodland Limited, "Ecological Analysis of the Greenbelt," National Capital Commission, Ottawa, 1991.

45. National Capital Commission, "Greenbelt Master Plan," 1996.

46. James Taylor, Cecelia Paine, and John FitzGibbon, "From Greenbelt to Greenways: Four Canadian Case Studies," *Landscape and Urban Planning,* 33 (Numbers 1–3, 1995):47–64.

47. National Capital Commission, "Greenbelt Master Plan," 1996.

48. National Capital Commission, www.canadascapital.gc.ca/corporate/index_e.asp.

49. City of Ottawa, "Official Plan," 2003.

50. City of Ottawa, Dept. of Engineering Works, "Land and Water Background Report: State of the Environment Reporting Program," 1993.

51. City of Ottawa, "Official Plan," 1991.

52. City of Ottawa, www.ottawa.ca/index_en.html.

53. City of Ottawa, "Natural and Open Space Study," October, 1998.

54. City of Ottawa, "Downtown Ottawa Urban Design Strategy 20/20," March, 2004.

55. City of Ottawa, "Official Plan," 2001.

56. Tony Hiss, *The Experience of Place* (New York: Alfred A. Knopf, Inc., 1990).

Chapter 5

1. Rainer Maria Rilke (1875–1926), German poet. repr. in *Rodin and Other Prose Pieces* (1954), Worpswede (1903).

2. Denver Regional Council of Governments, "Metro Vision 2020 Plan," July 2000.

3. Thomas J. Noel, "Denver History," 2004, http://www.denvergov.org/AboutDenver/history.asp.

4. City of Calgary, "Wetland Conservation Plan," May 2004.

5. James Michener, *Centennial* (New York: Random House Publishing, 1974).

6. Robert Searns, "Greenways: Where From, Where To," Presentation notes for Platte River Greenway Tour, October 3, 2004; Thomas Noel and Barbara Norgren, *Denver: The City Beautiful and Its Architects 1893–1941* (Denver: Historic Denver, Inc., 1987).

7. Horace Cleveland, quoted in Searns, "Greenways," 2004.

8. Searns, "Greenways," 2004.

9. Noel, "Denver History," 2004.

10. Colorado Department of Transportation, Bike–Pedestrian Study, 1999. www.dot.state.co.us/Bikeped/Study.

11. City of Calgary, "Calgary Municipal Development Plan," 1998.

12. Alberta Recreation and Parks, "Alberta's Urban Parks," 1989, p. 5.

13. City of Calgary, "Calgary Urban Park Master Plan: A Plan for the Future of Our River Valley Parks," 1994, p. 12.

14. City of Calgary, "Calgary Pathway and Bikeway Plan Report," May 2000.

15. City of Calgary, "Calgary Pathways and Bikeways Implementation Plan (Map)," 2001.

16. City of Calgary, www.calgary.ca.

17. City of Calgary, "Open Space Plan," July 2002.

18. Ibid.

19. Denver Water has decided, for water conservation purposes, to cease water delivery in the lower 22 miles of the canal in 2010. High Line Canal Partners was subsequently formed to preserve the open-space resource of this lower third of the canal. The group received funding from Great Outdoors Colorado, completed a High Line Canal Future Management Study, and formed an intergovernmental agreement for maintenance and preservation. The management study recommended that the future canal be permanently dedicated to open space, that multijurisdictional oversight be combined with significant local control, and that sufficient water be made available to maintain trees. For more information, see Wenk Associates, "High Line Canal Future Management Study, 2002."

20. Project for Public Spaces, "Greenway Vision Saves River and Generates Investment," 2004, www.pps.org/buildings/info/how_to/benefits_bb/success_Denver.

21. Ibid.

22. South Platte River Commission, "Long Range Management Framework: South Platte River Corridor," 2000.

23. See Robert Searns' summary of Denver's greenway story: Robert Searns, "Happy Trails: Greenways Put Their Stamp on the Denver Area," *Planning,* January 2003.

24. Project for Public Spaces, "Why Open Space Promotes Urban Development," 2004, www.pps.org/buildings/info/how_to/benefits_bb/whyopenspace.

25. Searns, "Greenways," 2004, p. 36.

26. Noel, "Denver History," 2004.
27. City of Denver Parks and Recreation Department, "Game Plan," 2003.
28. Peter Harnik and Jeff Simms, "Parks—How Far Is Too Far?" *Planning*, December 2004.
29. City of Denver Parks and Recreation Department, "Game Plan," 2003.
30. Denver Regional Council of Governments, "Open Space Element of the Metro Vision 2020 Plan: Resources and Opportunities," July 1999.
31. Denver Regional Council of Governments, "Metro Vision," 2000.
32. Congress enacted the six-year Intermodal Surface Transportation Efficiency Act (ISTEA) in 1991. It authorized a broad set of federal transportation programs, including funding for non-motorized transportation. In 1998 the act was reauthorized as TEA-21—Transportation Equity Act for the Twenty-First Century, for another six years. ISTEA contributed over a billion dollars for multiuse trail development during its six-year run. Transportation enhancement monies have helped fund bicycle and pedestrian trails, sidewalks, scenic beautification, and historic preservation. Since the expiration of TEA-21, the program has been funded by short-term extensions.
33. Richard T. T. Forman, *Road Ecology: Science and Solutions* (Washington, DC: Island Press, 2003); Daniel Smith, "Impacts of Roads on Ecological Networks and Integration of Conservation and Transportation Planning: Florida as a Case Study," in Rob Jongman and Gloria Pungetti, eds., *Ecological Networks and Greenways: Concept, Design, Implementation* (Cambridge, England: Cambridge University Press, 2004).
34. Claire Enlow, "Streets as Parks: In Seattle, Open Space Is Where You Find It," *Planning*, May 2002.
35. Barbara McCann, "Complete the Streets," *Planning*, 71 (Number 5, 2005):18–23.

Chapter 6
1. Aldo Leopold, *A Sand County Almanac* (New York: Oxford University Press, 1949).
2. For Portland, this figure is for the Metropolitan Statistical Area, which encompasses seven counties, not the three-county Metro regional government boundary.
3. Quote from Toronto Saturday Night, referenced in Stuart MacDonald, *Distant Neighbors: A Comparative History of Seattle and Vancouver* (Lincoln, NE: University of Nebraska Press, 1987).
4. John Punter, "Urban Design as Public Policy: Evaluating the Design Dimension of Vancouver's Planning System," *International Planning Studies*, 7 (Number 4, 2002):265–282.
5. Judy Oberlander, "History of Planning in Greater Vancouver," in Chuck Davis, ed., *The Greater Vancouver Book: An Urban Encyclopedia* (Vancouver: Linkman Press, 1997), p. 247.
6. Harland Bartholomew and Associates, *A Plan for the City of Vancouver, British Columbia, Including a General Plan of the Region* (St. Louis, MO: Harland Bartholomew and Associates, 1928), p. 10.
7. Ibid., p. 25.
8. Rodger Todhunter, "Vancouver and the City Beautiful Movement," *Habitat*, 26 (Number 3, 1983):8–13.
9. Ibid.

10. Ibid., p. 183.

11. Todhunter, "Vancouver," 1983, p. 13.

12. Harland Bartholomew and Associates, *A Plan for the City of Vancouver*, 1928, p. 237.

13. William Toll, "The Oregon History Project," 2003, www.ohs.org.

14. Ibid.

15. City of Portland, "Portland Parks and Recreation Historic Timeline, 1852–2000," www.parks.ci.portland.or.us/History.

16. Ibid.

17. Ann McAffee, "City Plan," in Chuck Davis, ed., *The Greater Vancouver Book: An Urban Encyclopedia* (Vancouver: Linkman Press, 1997).

18. John Punter, *The Vancouver Achievement: Urban Planning and Design* (Vancouver: UBC Press, 2003).

19. City of Vancouver, Urban Landscape Task Force, "Greenways–Public Ways," May 1999.

20. Some of the waterfronts are formally managed in the city's Engineering Department, but perceptually they are part of the parks system. The Parks Department maintains the "green" part; Engineering, the hardscape portions. In addition, the waterfront is highly complex; ownership often changes at the high water mark, and some parks are on land grants from the provincial or federal governments. Fisheries and Oceans at the federal level is also involved as are the First Nations (for instance, four different First Nations have land claims on Stanley Park alone).

21. City of Vancouver, Greenways program Web site, www.city.vancouver.bc.ca/engsvcs/streets/greenways/2003.

22. Ibid.

23. Corner bulges round the sidewalk out into the street intersection, thereby enlarging the pedestrian corner and narrowing the driving lanes. They are one form of traffic calming.

24. Jenyfer Neumann, "Urban, Community-Based Habitat Restoration Case Studies." Paper presented at 16th International Conference, Society for Ecological Restoration, Victoria, BC, August 2004.

25. Greater Vancouver Regional District, "Livable Region Strategic Plan," 1996.

26. Ray Tomalty, "Growth Management in the Vancouver Region." The Assessment and Planning Project, BC Case Report No. 4, Department of Environment and Resources Studies, University of Waterloo, March 2002.

27. Greater Vancouver Regional District, "Greater Vancouver Regional Greenway Vision," July 1999.

28. Heather Wornell, "Laying Down Routes: An Evaluation of the Greater Vancouver Regional District's Regional Recreation Greenway Program," Unpublished Master's Thesis, Resource and Environmental Management Program, Simon Fraser University, Vancouver, BC, 2001, p. iii.

29. Valentin Schaefer, "Green Links and Urban Connectivity: An Experiment," *Urban Nature Magazine*, Winter 1998.

30. Douglas R. Porter, *Managing Growth in America's Communities* (Washington, DC: Island Press, 1997).

31. City of Portland, "Parks 2020 Vision," 2001, p. 16.

32. Davis & Hibbitts, Inc., "Portland Survey," 2001.

33. City of Portland, "2020 Vision," p. 27.

34. Metro Planning Department, "2004 Performance Measures Report: An Evaluation of 2040 Growth Management Policies and Implementation," December 2004.

35. Metro, www.metro-region.org.

36. Metro, "The Nature of 2040: The Region's 50-Year Plan for Managing Growth," 1995.

37. Metro, "Metropolitan Greenspaces Master Plan," 1992.

38. Metro, "Metro's Open Spaces Land Acquisition Report to Citizens," May 1999.

39. Beaver Creek Canyon Greenway, Clackamas River Greenway, Fanno Creek Greenway, OMSI to Springwater Corridor, Peninsula Crossing Trail, and Burlington Northern Rails-to-Trails.

40. Metro, "Regional Trails & Greenways: Connecting Neighborhoods to Nature," June 2003.

41. Metro Planning Department, "2004 Performance Measures Report: An Evaluation of 2040 Growth Management Policies and Implementation," December 2004.

42. Suzanne Snowdon, "Sense of Community: Definition and Characteristics," Unpublished manuscript, 2001.

43. Stephanie Riger and Paul J. Lavrakas, "Community Ties: Patterns of Attachment and Social Interaction in Urban Neighborhoods," *American Journal of Community Psychology,* 9 (Number 1, 1981):55–66.

44. Robert D. Putnam, *Bowling Alone: The Collapse and Revival of American Community* (New York: Simon & Schuster, 2000).

45. Ray Oldenburg, *The Great Good Place,* 3rd Edition (New York: Marlowe and Company, 1999).

46. Carolyn Harrison and Jacquelin Burgess, "Qualitative Research and Open Space Policy," *The Planner* (November, 1988):16–18.

47. Allan B. Jacobs, *Great Streets.* (Cambridge, MA: The MIT Press, 1996), p. 4.

48. City of Vancouver, "Vancouver Greenways Plan," 1995.

Chapter 7

1. Michael Hough, *Cities and Natural Process* (London: Routledge, 1995), p. 6.

2. *USA Today,* "10 Great Places to Take a Hike in the Big City," September 19, 2003, p. 3D. The other cities cited are San Francisco, New York, Boston, Philadelphia, Portland, OR, Washington, DC, Seattle, Denver, and Chicago.

3. Sam Tamburro, "Ohio & Erie Canal in Cleveland," Cuyahoga Valley National Park, March 2002.

4. For a good summary of Cleveland's open-space history, see Diana Tittle, *A Walk in the Park: Greater Cleveland's New and Reclaimed Green Spaces* (Athens, OH: Ohio University Press, 2002).

5. Ibid., p. 4.

6. Sharon Pfeifer, "Focusing actions to protect and restore natural habitats in the Twin Cities Region." Proceedings: 16th International Conference of Society for Ecological Restoration, August 2004, Victoria, BC, Canada.

7. U.S. Census, 2000.

8. H. W. S. Cleveland, 1888 lecture, "The Aesthetic Development of the United Cities of Saint Paul and Minneapolis." Quoted in *Valued Places: Landscape Architecture in Minnesota.*

9. Minnesota Chapter of the American Society of Landscape Architects, *Valued Places: Landscape Architecture in Minnesota* (Minneapolis: Minneapolis Chapter of the American Society of Landscape Architects, 2001), p. 8.

10. Ibid.

11. Linda Mack, "Landscape Architects Blaze Trails," *Minneapolis Star Tribune*, April 24, 2005.

12. Ohio & Erie Canal Association, "Ohio & Erie Canal National Heritage Corridor Management Plan," June 2000.

13. Diana Tittle, *A Walk in the Park: Greater Cleveland's New and Reclaimed Green Spaces* (Athens, OH: Ohio University Press, 2002), p. 10.

14. See Tittle, *A Walk in the Park,* 2002; and Bobbi Reichtell, "Park Partnerships," *Urban Land,* November 1998.

15. Steven Litt, "The Forgotten Valley." A five-part series originally published by the *Cleveland Plain Dealer,* November 19–23, 2000.

16. Ibid.

17. Only Portage County in the eight-county region lacks a parks district.

18. Cuyahoga County, "The Cuyahoga County Greenprint," 2002.

19. http://www.ecocitycleveland.org/transportation/towpath_tour/towpath_intro.html.

20. EcoCity Cleveland, www.ecocitycleveland.org.

21. Ibid.

22. Mark A. Link, "Restoring Streams on the Edge of Destruction: An Urban Case Study." Proceedings: 16th International Conference of Society for Ecological Restoration, August 2004, Victoria, BC, Canada.

23. Ken Silliman, "A Green Infrastructure Development Authority for Greater Cleveland." Study Commissioned for EcoCity Cleveland, December 2003.

24. Ibid.

25. The six-block standard dates back more than fifty years in policy. Minneapolis blocks are very long, however. Six of them can total a half mile in length. See Peter Harnik and Jeff Simms, "Parks—How Far Is Too Far?" *Planning,* December 2004.

26. Alexander Garvin, *The American City: What Works, What Doesn't* (New York: McGraw-Hill, 2002).

27. Myron Orfield, *Metropolitics: A Regional Agenda for Community and Stability* (Washington, DC: The Brookings Institution Press, and Cambridge, MA: The Lincoln Institute of Land Policy, 1997).

28. The Twin Cities region is also one of the only metropolitan regions with tax-base sharing. It was implemented in the seven-county region in 1971. Communities contribute 40 percent of the tax income from rising commercial and industrial property taxes. These funds are then redistributed based on each jurisdiction's population and fiscal capacity. The system has reduced tax-base disparities dramatically, although not completely.

29. Orfield, *Metropolitics,* 1997.

30. Metropolitan Council, "2030 Regional Parks Policy Plan," 2005.

31. Douglas R. Porter, "A 50-Year Plan for Metropolitan Portland," *Urban Land,* July 1995, p. 40.

32. Design Center for American Urban Landscape, "Community Parkways: An Urban Design Survey of Green Streets in the Twin Cities," Design Center for American Urban Landscape, University of Minnesota, 2003.

33. Jason Zimmerman, "Mapping Green Spaces in the Center of the Twin Cities Region," Design Center for the American Urban Landscape. Design Brief, Number 6, November 2003.

34. See "A Case Study Integrating Urban Design and Ecology," Design Center for the American Urban Landscape, University of Minnesota, College of Architecture and Landscape Architecture publications, Volume 2, Numbers 1–6, 1994–1995.

35. An additional $1.5 million was allocated from the state legislature in 2000 and $2.73 million in 2001 from the state's Environmental Trust Fund. The program received no additional funding in 2002, but received just $1 million in 2003.

36. Sharon Pfeifer, "A Comparative Examination of Selected Regional Green Infrastructure Programs in the United States and Northern Europe," Unpublished report, 2005.

37. Ibid.

38. Minnesota Department of Natural Resources, "Metro Greenprint: Planning for Nature in the Face of Urban Growth," December 1997.

39. Ibid.

40. Sharon Pfeifer, Margaret Booth, Kate Drewry, Joy Drohan, and Mark Benedict, "Metro Greenways, MN: Linking Partners and Programs for Resource Conservation and Restoration," Online article published by The Conservation Fund and USDA Forest Service, www.greeninfrastructure.net/?article=2015&back=true.

41. Ibid.

42. Pfeifer, "A Comparative Examination," 2005.

43. Hennepin County Parks and Public Works Commission, "Hennepin Community Works: An Employment, Public Works and Tax Base Development Program," June 1994, p. 1.1.

44. Metropolitan Design Center, www.designcenter.umn.edu.

45. Hennepin County Parks and Public Works Commission, "Hennepin Community Works," 1994.

46. Ibid.

47. Ibid., p. 2.5.

48. Richard Florida, *The Rise of the Creative Class* (New York: Basic Books, 2002).

49. See the following rebuttal of Florida's creative class arguments: Steven Malanga, "The Curse of the Creative Class," *City Journal,* Winter 2004.

50. Rebecca Bryant, "Bigger Is Better," *Urban Land,* 57 (Number 7, 1998):60–62, 85–87, p. 61.

Chapter 8

1. Kevin Lynch, *Good City Form* (Boston: The MIT Press, 1984).

2. Matthew J. Kiernan, "Land-Use Planning," in Richard A. Loreto and Trevor Price, eds., *Urban Policy Issues: Canadian Perspectives* (Toronto: McClelland & Stewart, Inc., 1990).

3. Andrew Sancton, "Canadian Cities and the New Regionalism," *Journal of Urban Affairs,* 23 (Number 5, 2001):543–555, p. 553.

4. Stephen M. Wheeler, "The New Regionalism: Key Characteristics of an Emerging Movement," *Journal of the American Planning Association,* 68 (Number 3, 2002):267–278.

5. Sancton, "Canadian Cities," 2001.

6. Richard Forman, *Landscape Mosaics: The Ecology of Landscapes and Regions* (Cambridge, UK: Cambridge University Press, 1995), p. 435.

7. Larry S. Bourne, "Are New Urban Forms Emerging? Empirical Tests for Canadian Urban Areas," *The Canadian Geographer,* 33 (Number 4, 1989):312–328.

8. Canada has been a model of decentralization for both industrial and developing nations, and few other federations are as decentralized. Decentralization is the transfer of responsibility from the central government to subordinate levels of government, semi-autonomous public authorities or corporations, or nongovernmental organizations. See Richard Vengroff and Zaira Reveron, "Decentralization and Local Government Efficiency in Canadian Provinces: A Comparative Perspective," *International Journal of Canadian Studies,* 16 (1997):195–214.

9. Donald N. Rothblatt, "North American Metropolitan Planning: Canadian and U.S. Perspectives," *Journal of the American Planning Association,* 60 (Number 4, 1994):501–527; Duncan K. MacLellan, "Shifting from the Traditional to the New Political Agenda: The Changing Nature of Federal–Provincial Environmental Relations," *American Review of Canadian Studies,* 25 (1995):323–345.

10. Judith A. Garber and David L. Imbroscio, "'The Myth of the American City' Reconsidered: Local Constitutional Regimes in Canada and the United States," *Urban Affairs Review,* 31 (May, 1996):595–624.

11. Frances Frisken and Donald F. Norris, "Regionalism Reconsidered," *Journal of Urban Affairs,* 23 (Number 5, 2001):467–478.

12. Elizabeth McCance, "Chicago Wilderness: A Case Study of Learning About Ecosystem Management," Unpublished PhD dissertation, University of Michigan, 2003.

13. Reed F. Noss, "Corridors in Real Landscapes: A Reply to Simberloff and Cox," *Conservation Biology,* 1 (Number 2, 1987):159–164, p. 162.

14. Anne P. Hoover and Margaret A. Shannon, "Building Greenway Policies Within a Participatory Democracy Framework," *Landscape and Urban Planning,* 33 (Numbers 1–3, 1995), p. 433–459.

15. Moura Quayle, "Urban Greenways and Public Ways: Realizing Public Ideas in a Fragmented World," *Landscape and Urban Planning,* 33 (Numbers 1–3, 1995):461–475.

16. Claire Enlow, "In Seattle, Open Space Is Where You Find It," *Planning,* 68 (Number 5, 2002):16–17.

17. Robert M. Searns, "Greenways: Where From, Where To," Presentation notes, Platte River Greenway Tour, October 3, 2004.

18. Mary Ellen Tyler, "The Ecological Restructuring of Urban Form," in Trudy Bunting and Pierre Filion, eds., *Canadian Cities in Transition: The Twenty-First Century*, 2nd edition (Oxford, UK: Oxford University Press, 2000), p. 481–501.

19. Sherry Olson, "Form and Energy in the Urban Built Environment," in Trudi Bunting and Pierre Filion, eds., *Canadian Cities in Transition: The Twenty-First Century*, 2nd edition (Oxford, UK: Oxford University Press, 2000), p. 224–243.

20. Nancy Rottle, "Factors in the Landscape-Based Greenway: A Mountains to Sound Case Study," *Landscape and Urban Planning*, 76 (numbers 1–4, 2006) : 134–171.

21. Stephan Pauleit, "Ecological Approaches to Green Structure Planning in European Cities and Towns: Results from COST Action C11," in City of Helsinki and Urban Facts, eds., *Urban Research*, forthcoming, 2006.

22. For an exploration of this gap, see Paul Opdam, Ruud Foppen, and Claire Vos, "Bridging the Gap Between Ecology and Spatial Planning in Landscape Ecology," *Landscape Ecology*, 16 (2002):767–779.

23. Christopher Alexander, Sara Ishikawa, and Murray Silverstein, *A Pattern Language: Towns, Buildings, Construction* (Oxford, UK: Oxford University Press, 1977).

24. Adam Rome, "William Whyte, Open Space, and Environmental Activism," *Geographical Review*, 88 (Number 2, 1998):259–275.

25. The American Planning Association defines smart growth as "the planning, design, development and revitalization of cities, towns, suburbs and rural areas in order to create and promote social equity, a sense of place and community, and to preserve natural as well as cultural resources. Smart growth enhances ecological integrity over both the short- and long-term, and improves quality of life for all by expanding, in a fiscally responsible manner, the range of transportation, employment and housing choices available to a region."

26. William Whyte, *The Last Landscape* (Philadelphia: University of Pennsylvania Press, 1968).

27. Lewis Mumford, *The City in History: Its Origins, Its Transformations, and Its Prospects* (New York: Harcourt, Brace & World, 1968).

28. For an excellent argument about this approach to urban morphology, see Brenda Case Scheer, "The Anatomy of Sprawl," *Places*, 14 (Number 2, 2001):28–37.

29. Linda E. Hollis and William Fulton, "Open Space Protection: Conservation Meets Growth Management." Discussion paper prepared for The Brookings Institution Center on Urban and Metropolitan Policy, Washington, DC. April 2002.

30. Ian L. McHarg, "Open Space From Natural Processes," in D. A. Wallace, ed., *Metropolitan Open Space and Natural Process* (Philadelphia: University of Pennsylvania, 1970), p. 10–52.

Index

Italicized page numbers refer to boxes, figures, and tables.

Northeastern Illinois Planning Commission
(NIPC), *50, 53*, 88–90, 100
Northeastern Illinois Regional Greenways Plan,
50, 88, *89*, 91, 100, 103
Northeast Greenway Corridor (Denver), *50*,
175
Northeast Ohio Regional Sewer District
(NEORSD), 249–50
Noss, Reed, 22–23

Oak Leaf Trail (Milwaukee), 122, *123, 125*
Oak Ridges Moraine, 64, *65*, 66, *75–77, 81*, 82,
84, *85–86*, 103
Ohio & Erie Canal Heritage Corridor, 230,
237–44, *239, 240, 242–43*, 250, 264–65, 273
Ohio & Erie Canal Reservation, 240, *242–43*,
244, 248
Ohio Canal Corridor, 238, *242*
Oldenburg, Ray, 222
Olmsted, Frederick Law, *26*, 48, *50*, 56, 67, 106,
111, 226, 235
Olmsted Brothers, 147, 188, 190–91, *212–13,
220*, 232
Openlands Project (Chicago), *50*, 88–91, 96,
98
Open space, 7–19, *8*, 29–36, 309n28
Open-space plans, *48, 50*; for Calgary region,
151–65, *161*; for Chicago region, 71,
88–102; for Cleveland region, 237–50;
for Denver region, 165–78; for Milwaukee
region, 122–27; for Minneapolis–St. Paul
region, 237, 250–63; for Ottawa region,
122, 128–36; for Portland region, 192,
207–22, *218*; for Seattle region, 179; for
Toronto region, 71–88; for Vancouver
region, 179, 192–207, *193, 203. See also
names of plans*
Oregon Trout, 217
Orfield, Myron, 100
Osthoff, Tom, 257
Ottawa (Ont.), *31*, 42, *42*, 44, *45, 50, 52*; and
greenbelts, *116*, 120–21, 128–31, *129, 131*;
and greenways, 132–35, *133*; and historic
precedents, 106–7, 113–22, *114, 116,
117–18, 119, 121*; population of, *45*, 107,
134; and recreation, 56, 106–7, 113–22,
117–18, 128–36

Pacific Spirit Regional Park (Vancouver), 186,
197
Parks, 7, 25, 56, 105; in Calgary region, 152–53,
154–55, 155–65, *162–63*; in Chicago region,
68, 90–91, *94, 98*, 100–102; in Cleveland
region, 43, 226–27, 230–32, *231*, 240,
242–43, 244–46, 248, 250; in Denver
region, 140, 147–49, 166–69, *166*, 171–72,
176; in Milwaukee region, 110–11, *112*, 113,
122, *123*, 124, *125–26*; in Minneapolis–St.
Paul region, 43, 226, 235, *236*, 250, 254–56,
261, 323n25; in Ottawa region, 119, 122,
133; in Portland region, 182, 188, 190–91,
207–22, *208, 212–13*; in Toronto region,
72–73, *77*, 78, 84, 87; in Vancouver region,
186–87, 192, 194–95, *197*, 202–3, *203*, 206,
321n20
Parks Vision (Portland), 209, 211, *213*, 214
Parkways, 29–31, *30, 31*, 36, 106; in Cleveland
region, 230, 232; in Denver region, 140,
147–48, *148*, 166, 172; in Milwaukee region,
110–11, 113, *123*, 124; in Minneapolis–St.
Paul region, 226, *234*, 235, 254, 257, 262–63;
in Ottawa region, 120, 128, 131–32; in
Portland region, 190, *220*; in Vancouver
region, 187
ParkWorks (Cleveland), 247–48
Partnerships, 51; in Chicago region, 69, 88,
94–95, 100; in Cleveland region, *242–43*; in
Denver region, 168, 170, 174, *176*; in
Minneapolis–St. Paul region, 250, 256, 258;
in Portland region, 210–11, 216; in
Vancouver region, 196. *See also*
Multijurisdictional scope
Pathways. *See* Trails
Payne, Karen, 7
Perry, Kim, *197*
Pfeifer, Sharon, 257
Pollack-Ellwand, Nancy, 119
Pollution. *See* Environmental degradation
Porter, Douglas, 256
Portland (Ore.), 42, *42, 45, 50, 53*; and
community, 58, 182–83, 188–91, 207–22;
and historic precedents, 182–83, 188–92,
189, 190; and parks, 182, 188, 190–91,
207–22, *208, 212–13*; population of, *45*,